IDENTITY WORK IN SOCIAL MOVEMENTS

Social Movements, Protest, and Contention

Series Editor: Bert Klandermans, Free University, Amsterdam

Associate Editors: Ron R. Aminzade, University of Minnesota
David S. Meyer, University of California, Irvine
Verta A. Taylor, University of California, Santa Barbara

For more books in the series, see page 306.

IDENTITY WORK IN SOCIAL MOVEMENTS

Jo Reger, Daniel J. Myers, and Rachel L. Einwohner, Editors

Social Movements, Protest, and Contention
Volume 30

University of Minnesota Press
Minneapolis • London

Published by the University of Minnesota Press
111 Third Avenue South, Suite 290
Minneapolis, MN 55401-2520
http://www.upress.umn.edu

Library of Congress Cataloging-in-Publication Data

Identity work in social movements / Jo Reger... [et al.], editors.
    p. cm. — (Social movements, protest, and contention series ; v. 30)
    Includes bibliographical references and index.
    ISBN 978-0-8166-5139-9 (hc : alk. paper) — ISBN 978-0-8166-5140-5
(pb : alk. paper)
    1. Social movements. 2. Identity (Philosophical concept). 3. Feminism.
4. Gays — Identity. 5. Lesbians — Identity. I. Reger, Jo.
    HM881.I44 2008
    303.48′4—dc22   2008005219

Printed in the United States of America on acid-free paper

The University of Minnesota is an equal-opportunity educator and employer.

15 14 13 12 11 10 09 08   10 9 8 7 6 5 4 3 2 1

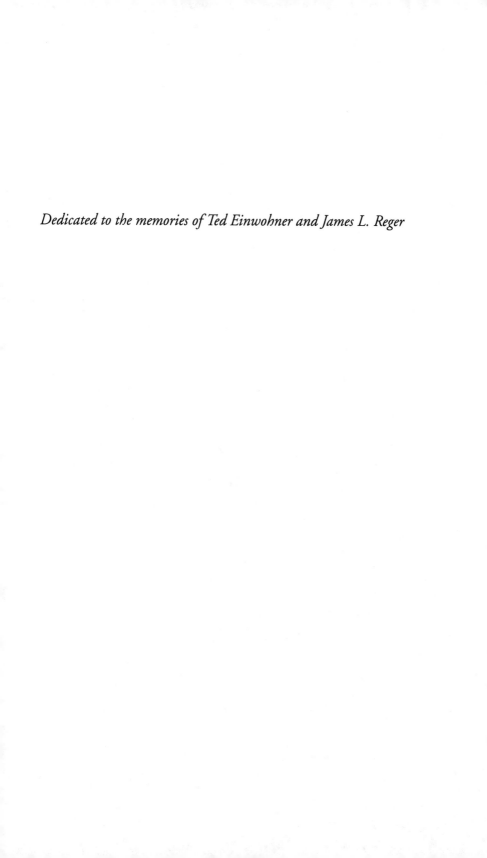

Dedicated to the memories of Ted Einwohner and James L. Reger

Contents

Part II. Working through Identities

Acknowledgments

We are grateful to a number of people for their help in this project, in particular the participants and audience at the Identity and Social Movements session at the 2003 Midwest Sociological Society meetings in Chicago. Their scholarship and intellectual enthusiasm helped bring this work to fruition.

We also thank Jason Weidemann; Social Movements, Protest, and Contention series editors Bert Klandermans, Verta Taylor, Ron R. Aminzade, and David S. Meyer; and an anonymous reviewer for comments and assistance with the manuscript.

Finally, we thank the contributors to this volume, who are vital in shaping a dynamic dialogue on social movements and identity.

Introduction

Identity Work, Sameness, and Difference in Social Movements

Rachel L. Einwohner, Jo Reger, and Daniel J. Myers

Enmeshed in a fight against a local antigay ballot proposal in Cincinnati, Ohio, gays, lesbians, bisexuals, and transgendered coalition members find their unity undercut by internal debates over strategies of assimilation versus more radical direct action. Using organizational and ideological strategies, the Coalition of Labor Union Women (CLUW) finds ways to create a central identity, overcoming the racial, ethnic, and class issues that fragment other U.S. women's groups. In Brazil, poor women carefully negotiate gender identity in their efforts to provide for themselves and their families and avoid repression for their activism. Drag queens performing in a club in Key West, Florida, use their performances to "trouble" binary assumptions about gender and sexuality and create commonalities among the diverse audiences that attend their shows.

What do all these cases have in common? Each illustrates the complexities of identity processes within collective efforts for social change. As scholars have long understood, social movements and the people and ideas within them are oppositional in nature. Yet it is *how* movement participants arrive at their oppositional stance—whether oriented toward achieving change or preventing change from occurring—that has become one of the central concerns in the field of social movements. Part of that process involves activists' development of a sense of themselves as a collectivity united in their beliefs, goals, and actions and in opposition to some other group, body, or force. One of the keys to creating this collectivity is the construction of a collective identity.

The importance of identity—what David A. Snow and Doug McAdam (2000) refer to as a "pivotal concept" in the study of social movements—is evident in the well-established literature devoted to the topic (see Polletta and Jasper 2001; and Snow 2001 for reviews). The concept of identity is prominent in several recent edited volumes on social movements, including David S. Meyer, Nancy Whittier, and Belinda Robnett's *Social Movements: Identity, Culture, and the State* (2002) and Sheldon Stryker, Timothy J. Owens, and Robert W. White's *Self, Identity, and Social Movements* (2000). Even more telling, an electronic search of Sociological Abstracts using the phrase "identity and social movements" yields over nine hundred entries. Scholars interested in identity and social movements—or those who "look at movements from the inside out" (Meyer 2002, 12)—have explored how activists' sense of identity shapes a variety of movement dynamics, including emergence (Melucci 1989; Pfaff 1996); initial participation (Calhoun 1994; Friedman and McAdam 1992; W. Gamson 1992; Neuhouser 1998; Polletta 1998); commitment and sustained participation over time (Futrell, Simi, and Gottschalk 2006; Futrell and Simi 2004; Hirsch 1990; Nepstad 2004; Taylor 1989); framing activities (Hunt, Benford, and Snow 1994); strategic choices (Bernstein 1997; Clemens 1996; Gotham 1999); organizational form (Clemens 1996); and success (Einwohner 1999). Others have reversed the direction of inquiry by examining the various factors that shape activists' identity, including the historical context in which a distinct generation of activists joins a movement (Whittier 1995), organizational characteristics of activist groups and events (J. Gamson 1996; Reger 2002a, 2002b), and the views of targets and other external audiences (Adair 1996; Einwohner 2002; Haines 2006). In sum, identity is seen as a factor implicated in all aspects of movement activity, from emergence to outcomes (Polletta and Jasper 2001).

Nonetheless, the contributors to this volume argue that there are still some gaps in our understanding of identity and its role in social movements. More specifically, they suggest that although identity is central to collective action, it is problematic at the same time. That is, the identities that are relevant to social movements are not necessarily arrived at easily, nor is it always clear that the "we" in social movements always exists in direct opposition to some "they." Instead, identity processes in social movements can be fraught with contradiction and controversy. Constructing and maintaining identity therefore requires a great deal of identity *work*.

This book explores the work involved in the construction, maintenance, and renegotiation of collective identity in social movements. Its impetus came from a panel at the 2003 Midwest Sociological Society meetings in Chicago. Each of the papers at that session—some of which appear, in revised forms, as chapters in this volume—addressed the broad topic of identity and social movements. Their authors—Kim Dugan, Rachel Einwohner, Todd Schroer, and Cihan Tugal—presented analyses of four very different cases of collective action, yet they arrived at similar conclusions. The papers noted the complex ways in which activists constructed their collective identity and made decisions about how to present themselves to others. More specifically, these papers described the struggles that activists face as they arrive at and present their sense of selves—internal struggles between movement factions as well as externally oriented battles over how activists appear to the outside world. The panelists concluded that these struggles often center on topics related to sameness and difference. Furthermore, what was particularly exciting about that panel was the fact that these papers examined identity processes in four very different settings: Islamist politics in contemporary Turkey; battles between gay and lesbian activists and Christian conservatives in Cincinnati; Internet activism among white racialists; and Jewish resistance in Nazi-occupied Poland. This volume builds upon that initial dialogue to more fully detail issues of sameness and difference in identity construction during collective action.

In this introductory chapter, we outline the two central themes of this book, which are elaborated further in the chapters. The first theme addresses the kinds of activities involved in the construction and strategic use of identities in social movements. Building on Snow and his colleagues' (Snow and McAdam 2000; Snow and Anderson 1987) concept of "identity work," we describe how movement participants actively work to create their sense of who and what they are. Key to these constructions are the notions of "sameness" and "difference," referring to activists' similarities to and differences from targets, opponents, and even each other. A second, related theme centers on the challenges and struggles involved in identity work. Activists are often faced with the task of building solidarity among a diverse membership, which can require very careful, deliberate identity work. Disagreements about who "we" are—or should be—can become quite costly, taking time and resources away from other activist tasks and even alienating participants or fragmenting the movement.

Crosscutting these two themes is a focus on the broader environment in which activists operate. Movement participants construct their collective identity, but this work is not just an internally focused process. Activists construct and present themselves with an eye toward the potential reactions of external audiences and also respond to the demands of the broader institutional environment and structure of political opportunities. Identity work is, therefore, strategic; activists must grapple with both the "inside" and the "outside," to use David Meyer's terms, in creating an identity that serves their needs in a given setting. Here, we discuss these themes in more detail and provide a brief summary of the chapters that follow.

Identity Work in Social Movements

What do we mean when we say that identity takes "work"? As a number of scholars have demonstrated, the identities that are relevant to collective action are not static entities but instead are dynamic forces shaped by participants' interaction. Identity is described as an "emergent" property of collective action and as an "interactional accomplishment" that is "negotiated" by members of the collective (Fantasia 1988; W. Gamson 1992; Hunt, Benford, and Snow 1994; Melucci 1989; Snow 2001; Snow and Anderson 1987; Taylor and Whittier 1992). This approach is what Snow and McAdam refer to as a "constructionist perspective" on identity and social movements, or one that focuses on "construction and maintenance [of identities] through joint action, negotiation, and interpretive work" (2000, 46). "Identity work," then, refers to all the activities involved in creating and sustaining identity. While Snow and Leon Anderson originally used this concept to refer to the work of individuals—in their case, homeless people—to "create, present, and sustain personal identities that are congruent with and supportive of the self-concept" (1987, 1348), Snow's later work extends the concept to refer to a broader variety of identity-related activities, including the construction as well as maintenance of collective identity in social movements (Snow and McAdam 2000; see also Hunt and Benford 1994; and Lichterman 1999 on "identity talk," a form of "identity work").

Although the concept of "identity work" is well established, the exact nature of this work, especially in relation to social movements, deserves further inquiry. In particular, we call attention to the role of "sameness" and "difference" in activist identity work. Current scholarship posits that, through collective action, movement participants construct a shared sense of identity by emphasizing their similarities to each other as well as their (shared) differences from those whom they oppose. Verta Taylor and Nancy Whittier provide one of the more elaborate discussions of this point by outlining three distinct, yet overlapping, components of collective identity: "boundaries," or markers of difference between movement participants and dominant groups; "consciousness," defined as "the interpretive frameworks that emerge from a group's struggle to define and realize members' common interests in opposition to the dominant order" (1992, 114); and "negotiation," which refers to the various actions through which movement participants oppose the status quo. Bernstein's (1997) influential work on identity "deployment" in the gay and lesbian movement goes a step further, noting that movements are not always entirely oppositional but sometimes emphasize their members' similarities to the mainstream, especially if doing so makes sense for strategic reasons. As she shows, gay and lesbian activists seeking policy change in New York in the early 1970s chose strategies that emphasized their differences from heterosexual society, whereas activists working in Oregon during the same time period, who enjoyed more of an "insider" status due to strong ties with state and local authorities, adopted more conservative tactics that emphasized gays' similarities to the mainstream. Referring to this same phenomenon among feminist activists, Francesca Polletta and James M. Jasper write,

> Activists seeking legal change on behalf of women and minorities often struggle to decide whether to play up or down the differences on which their disadvantages rest. Discrimination cases brought by women have been limited by the implicitly male standard to which they must analogize their own situation. "Difference," whether it is the biological capacity to get pregnant or a dislike for high-pressure sales jobs, is seen as "deviance," and activists must decide between the equally unacceptable alternatives of trying to be "like" men or to justify "special" treatment with its implications of inferiority. (2001, 295)

According to current research, therefore, activist identity work draws on both sameness and difference; activists understand themselves in opposition to the mainstream yet make strategic decisions about whether to "celebrate" or "suppress" (Bernstein 1997) those differences when presenting themselves to others. We argue, however, that sameness and difference can be reflected in activists' identity work in even more complex and nuanced ways. While we agree that movement identities are oppositional, we caution that the line between "us" and "them" is not as clear as most scholarship would suggest. Furthermore, whereas much of the current research treats sameness and difference as distinct options from which activists choose when constructing collective identity, we argue instead that activists' identity work addresses both sameness and difference simultaneously. Following Bystydzienski and Schacht (2001) and the broader literature on the "intersectionalities" approach—which posits that identities such as gender cannot be understood separately from other identities with which they are intertwined, such as those based on race, class, and sexual orientation (see Collins 2000)—we acknowledge the multiple, intersectional identities that activists bring with them to their work. These multiple identities necessitate recognition of both sameness and difference in activist identity work.

In addition, we suggest that there are burdens associated with the competing demands of sameness and difference in identity work. This means that while a collective identity can solidify a movement, participants often must negotiate this identity, both with the dominant society and with each other. In doing so, social movement participants negotiate issues of sameness, either through creating solidarity within a movement or by attempting affiliation with some aspect of the dominant society. At the same time, movement actors also negotiate issues of difference by working to define the boundaries between themselves and their opposition, as well as divisions among activists, who may share little in common except values and beliefs. These activities are central to social movements and therefore deserve further inquiry.

Identity "Workloads"

An explicit recognition of the burdens associated with identity work leads us to our second theme, which focuses on identity "workloads." That is, we suggest that at some times, in some contexts, and for some people, the "work" of identity construction can be more difficult than others. At times, those who come together in support of a common cause can feel an instant connection with one another. For instance, activists often report feelings such as relief and joy upon joining a movement and finding other people "just like them." Furthermore, participation in a social movement community and in the activities that sustain its collective identity, such as music festivals and Internet chat rooms (Futrell, Simi, and Gottschalk 2006; Futrell and Simi 2004; Taylor and Whittier 1995), can be a very enjoyable experience. In such situations, identity work is hardly work at all. In others, however, the activities involved in creating and sustaining collective identity can be considerably more taxing and even painful.

The "hard work" of identity creation and maintenance comes into play, for instance, when movements speak for diverse populations and when different factions within movements struggle to have their voices heard. Moreover, as Bystydzienski and Schacht note, the divisions between "us" and "them" can exist within a movement, such that "even seemingly progressive individuals . . . still typically view those individuals having the 'other' identity with trepidation, as bothersome, or irrelevant at best (e.g., men trying to join feminist women's groups)" (2001, 5). Internal disagreements over goals and strategies, which are in themselves statements about identity (Polletta and Jasper 2001), constitute examples of this hard work as well. This point is illustrated by Haines' (2006) discussion of Amnesty International's contentious internal disagreements about whether or not to take a stand against the death penalty as part of the organization's broader focus on human rights. As Haines shows, the debate centered on the organization's public identity and how it might suffer if it were seen as supporting "unsavory" individuals such as death row inmates. We therefore see a need for more research on identity work in social movements and especially research that explores the conditions under which identity work is "easy" or "hard."

An Intersectional Approach to the Study of Identity Work

Current work on identity and social movements recognizes that activists draw on notions of sameness and difference when constructing identity internally and strategically deploying identity externally yet treats sameness and difference as discrete choices (see Figure I.1). Thus, activists are thought to stress either their difference from or sameness to some "other" but not to do both at the same time. These discrete choices are represented in Figure I.1 by a table with separate cells. In contrast, we propose that the boundaries between sameness and difference are blurred rather than distinct, and that there is potential for overlap between the two (see Figure I.2). While Figure I.2 allows for discrete choices—represented by those areas of the diagram with no overlap between the spheres—it emphasizes that sameness and difference need not be mutually exclusive but can, in fact, be featured in activist identity work simultaneously. Each figure draws on two central dimensions or concerns in identity work: the focus taken when identity is constructed (i.e., whether the focus is on sameness or difference) and the intended audience for those constructions (i.e., the movement itself or some external audience, such as opponents or policy makers).

Figure I.2 also illustrates the potential for variable identity workloads. An area of no overlap between the spheres represents a relatively "easy" workload, or a situation in which activists target a single audience (either internal or external) and focus solely on their similarities to or differences from that audience. With these relatively clear-cut foci, identity work is hypothesized to proceed rather smoothly and consensually. In contrast, those areas of

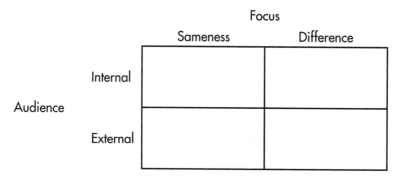

Figure I.1. Discrete choices in identity work.

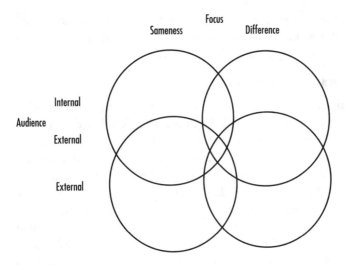

Figure I.2. Intersectional constructions in identity work.

overlap between any of the four spheres suggest more difficult identity work, characteristic of situations when the negotiations of sameness and difference become more complex. As this volume illustrates, such complexities arise, for example, when activists work to create solidarity among diverse constituencies or struggle with having to publicly present themselves as similar to those whom they oppose in private. Moreover, the greater the overlap between the four spheres, the heavier the workload. That is, as activists find that they need to negotiate both sameness and difference while constructing their public and private identities, there is greater potential for disagreement and controversy and the identity work becomes more difficult. We therefore hypothesize that, as the studies in the volume exemplify, the region in the center of the diagram would feature the most difficult identity work of all.

Activist Environments: Micro, Meso, and Macro

Of course, activists' identity work does not occur in a vacuum. The importance of the environment in which activists operate and the ways in which environmental factors shape identity work is, therefore, another theme addressed by the chapters in this volume.

By "activist environment" we mean the entire set of social, cultural, and historical factors surrounding and shaping social movement activity. Social movement scholars have already developed a number of concepts that are useful for describing the various environmental factors that affect movement activity; these include "political opportunity" (McAdam 1982; Meyer and Staggenborg 1996; Tarrow 1994; Tilly 1978), "cultural opportunity" (Johnston and Klandermans 1995), "micromobilization context" (McAdam 1988), and "political generation" (Whittier 1995). Drawing on this broad body of work, we conceptualize activist environments at the macro, meso, and micro levels. At the macro level, cultural, historical, and political patterns shape activists' identity work. Here again, Bernstein's (1997) work is instructive. She locates activists' decisions to emphasize similarity or difference not in internal discussions about gay and lesbian identity but in features of the broader political opportunity structure, such as activists' access to the polity. Robnett's (1997) analysis of African American women in the civil rights movement also shows how the broader environment shapes activists' identity. Because their activism took place in a cultural and historical setting shaped by Jim Crow laws and practices, African American women activists felt a strong sense of solidarity with African American men who suffered from white oppression. Women activists therefore identified themselves more in terms of race and culture, as shaped by the larger societal environment, than in terms of gender. As a result they ended up with a very different understanding of women's roles in the movement than did northern white women participants who, as members of the dominant racial group, focused on sexism within the movement.

Environmental factors at the meso level affect activists' identity work as well. Scholars conceptualize the meso level through such terms as "social movement community" (Buechler 1990; Staggenborg 1998), "multi-organizational field" (Curtis and Zurcher 1973; Klandermans 1992), and local "political field" (Ray 1999). Meso-level settings serve as the contexts for groups to construct a collective identity. However, the meso level not only provides only a place for articulating a collective identity, but it also is the site of various dynamics that shape the formation of identity. Some scholars have studied meso-level effects on identity by examining organizational contexts. As Joshua Gamson argues, "Collective identities, although they are not organizational inventions, are continually filtered and reproduced through organizational bodies" (1996, 235.) In his account of gay and lesbian film festivals in New York, he illustrates how the film festivals' institutional constraints—for instance, meeting high artistic standards for the films—shaped organizational decisions, which in turn shaped the festivals (described as an "identity home" for the gay and lesbian movement). Similarly, Reger's (2002a, 2002b) analyses of different chapters of the National Organization for Women (NOW) also show how, at the meso level, distinct cultural and geographical profiles of each organization affected the feminist identity that was constructed by each chapter. She argues that this process is a reciprocal one with identity processes shaping organizational structure and vice versa.

Finally, at the micro level, individuals do the work of face-to-face interaction. As Taylor and Whittier (1992) show in their analysis of lesbian feminist communities, constructing an activist identity shared by a group is ongoing work, work that can sometimes be contentious. Disagreements among activists therefore constitute and can also create a need for identity work. For instance, Gamson (1995) outlines internal disagreements, some of which became quite heated, within the gay and lesbian community in San Francisco over the appropriateness of the term "queer." It is at the micro level that individuals must continually make decisions about who they are as a group, shaping the content and form of the collective identity. Micro-level analyses also illustrate how identity work is shaped not by static features of activist environments but by activists' *perceptions* of what is going on in the world around them. For instance, Montini's (1996) research on breast cancer activism shows that activists seeking concessions from particular targets (in her study, policy makers) had to present themselves strategically in order to counter their targets' perceptions of them as overly emotional women. Thus, it was not simply that these activists worked in a setting shaped by broad social and cultural meanings that cast the activists as emotional (and, therefore, without credibility); it was also the activists' assessment of how, in that setting, their targets would react to them that determined the identity work they performed during legislative hearings. (See also Einwohner 1999; Groves 1997; and Whittier 2001 for additional examples of what Hochschild [1979, 1983] calls the "emotion work" required of activists in different settings.) Such perceptions, which are themselves shaped by interpretive work among activists (Hunt, Benford, and Snow 1994), therefore add to the complex nature of identity construction in social movements as well.

Identity Work in Different Activist Environments

The ideas outlined previously—the concept of identity work, the simultaneity of sameness and difference, and the role of multiple levels of the broader environment in shaping each—are central to the chapters in this book. In what follows, social movement scholars explore how movement participants work through issues of sameness and difference to define themselves in relation to the environments around them. These authors address questions such as the following: What kinds of strategies do activists use to manage sameness and difference in identity work? How do issues of sameness and difference affect mobilization and goal attainment? What factors or issues facilitate the construction of collective identity among diverse activists, and what precludes it? These questions are answered with analyses of a wide variety of cases, including American social movements on both the left and the right of the political spectrum as well as collective action in Europe and Latin America.

The chapters are organized in two parts. Part I examines the various identity strategies used by activists and illustrates the use of sameness and difference in identity work. The chapters in this part focus on the construction of boundaries between movement participants and various "others" but go beyond simple distinctions between "us" and "them" to explore more subtle, overlapping lines of sameness and difference and their effect on activists' abilities to forge alliances and recruit new members. Kimberly B. Dugan's analysis of actions taken by the Christian Right and gay, lesbian, bisexual, and transgender activists contesting an antigay ballot initiative in Cincinnati demonstrates how activist strategy reflects both sameness and difference from the dominant society. She draws on a variety of qualitative data to show both sides fought to portray themselves in a particular light to the voting public. As she concludes, what mattered in this contest was not movement members' "real" sense of identity but the believability of their public image in the media. The chapter written by Elizabeth Kaminski and Verta Taylor takes a different empirical approach to the work involved in identity construction by examining musical performances as a strategy for attracting external support. Using the case of drag queen performances at a club in Key West, they suggest that the use of music helps draw boundaries between participants at the same time that it helps construct solidarity among the diverse members of the audiences.

Todd Schroer's chapter on the white racialist movement also examines the work done by activists to shape their public identity. By focusing on these activists' use of the Internet, he identifies a number of framing practices used to destigmatize their collective identity and to change the way they are seen by external audiences. However, he concludes that the success of these efforts is limited because relatively few members of the general public ever view these materials. Jo Reger's analysis of young women's activism in two different communities highlights how activists' perceptions of their environment shape the activist networks that individuals join, along with their sense of collective identity. In the case of a community hostile to feminism, young women formed a community based on their experiences with sexism; in the other case, which was located in an environment more open to feminism, young women joined a broader collective based on racial, ethnic, transgender, and queer identities. Thus, Reger shows that features of the activist environment help determine the relevant lines of sameness and difference for each community.

This section ends with two empirical examinations of identity work in non-U.S. settings. Rachel L. Einwohner's chapter offers a look at the crucial role of "passing" among Jewish resistance fighters in the Warsaw Ghetto. She shows how activists working on the Aryan side of the ghetto walls had to hide their identity as Jews in order to carry out important resistance tasks, such as smuggling arms and transporting forged identity papers. To succeed in this type of identity work, activists therefore had to first recognize Jews' difference from others and then work actively to mask those differences by appearing as similar as possible to non-Jewish Poles. The concluding chapter of Part I is by Kevin Neuhouser and offers another look at activists' use of sameness and difference to present themselves to various audiences. His discussion of gender identity among women who participated in an episode of collective action in an impoverished area of Recife, Brazil demonstrates that the participants—whose actions involved resisting the police—were acting "like men," yet successfully avoided repression by emphasizing to the police that they were "still women." Within the community, however, the women downplayed their feminine gender identity in order to gain support of their husbands and brothers who may have been otherwise hesitant to join a "women's" movement.

Part II of this volume continues the book's overall theme of identity work in different movement settings, yet focuses on cases that illustrate the hard work of identity construction. Daniel J. Myers's chapter on the gay and lesbian movement explores this topic by examining identity processes among movement allies. His inquiry focuses on the "politically gay," or heterosexual members of the gay and lesbian movement. Drawing on the social psychological literature on altruism, he addresses recruitment patterns among these activists as well as the impact of their involvement on the collective identity of the movement as a whole. He notes the difficulties associated with the ally identity, such as burdens of providing proof of commitment and sincerity and the potential for introducing internal tensions. Susan Munkres's chapter also examines movement allies by offering an analysis of a Midwest solidarity organization whose members support a village in El Salvador. The relationship between the American activists and their Salvadoran counterparts—described as "sistering"—helps blur boundaries by allowing the American activists to identify with the Salvadoran community. However, Munkres also shows that there is a limit to this solidarity: these blurred boundaries prevent American activists from understanding their own privileges, one result of which is that they fail to recognize the behind-the-scenes work done by Salvadoran activists to maintain the "sisterly" community.

The final three chapters address the challenges associated with diversity within social movements. In particular, these chapters develop an understanding of how social movement participants construct their collective identity while negotiating differences in race, ethnicity, gender, class, religion, and sexuality. The chapter by Silke Roth draws on qualitative and quantitative data in its analysis of race, class, and gender identity among members of CLUW, an organization whose founding members stressed the inclusion of women of color. Roth examines the characteristics that have allowed this diverse organization to continue into its thirtieth year; these include leaders' insistence that officers be representative of all union members and the allowance for the formation of new group structures. Jane Ward's chapter examines another case of activists struggling to construct the collective identity of a diverse group. Her analysis of two lesbian and gay organizations in Los Angeles describes various organizational strategies for maintaining unity, such as the explicit promotion of sameness through statements implying that race, class, and gender differences are inconsequential to movement structure. However, her analysis also illustrates the disadvantages of such identity work, especially when different segments of the collective feel ignored or unwelcome. Finally, Benita Roth draws on themes of sameness and difference in identity construction to explain the emergence of the "second wave" white women's liberation movement in the 1960s. Her analysis highlights the importance of a shift in white women's identity from one that emphasized sameness with leftist men to one that stressed difference from them. More importantly, she suggests that the identity constructions that facilitate movement emergence reflect activists' assessment of other groups, and especially the potential of those groups to be similar to movement members. An afterword by Mary Bernstein, whose work conceptualizes many of the ideas of sameness and difference built upon by the authors, concludes the volume.

The following chapters present a dialogue of scholars—each focusing on a particular group, setting, and time period—who all address the importance of understanding identity work and its role in social movements. Their insights both document and clarify the complexities of the identity processes that are crucial to collective action.

References

Adair, Stephen. 1996. "Overcoming a Collective Action Frame in the Remaking of an Antinuclear Opposition." *Sociological Forum* 11: 347–75.

Bernstein, Mary. 1997. "Celebration and Suppression: The Strategic Uses of Identity by the Lesbian and Gay Movement." *American Journal of Sociology* 103: 531–65.

Buechler, Steven M. 1990. *Women's Movements in the United States.* New Brunswick, N.J.: Rutgers University Press.

Bystydzienski, Jill M., and Steven P. Schacht, ed. 2001. *Forging Radical Alliances Across Difference.* Lanham, M.D.: Rowman & Littlefield.

Calhoun, Craig. 1994. *Neither Gods nor Emperors.* Berkeley: University of California Press.

Clemens, Elisabeth S. 1996. "Organizational Form as Frame: Collective Identity and Political Strategy in the American Labor Movement, 1880–1920." In *Comparative Perspectives on Social Movements,* ed. D. McAdam, J. D. McCarthy, and M. N. Zald, 205–26. Cambridge: Cambridge University Press.

Collins, Patricia Hill. 1991. *Black Feminist Thought: Knowledge, Consciousness, and the Politics of Empowerment.* New York: Routledge.

Curtis, Russell L., and Louis A. Zurcher, Jr. 1973. "Stable Resources of Protest Movements: The Multi-organizational Field." *Social Forces* 52: 53–61.

Einwohner, Rachel L. 2002. "Bringing the Outsiders In: Opponents' Claims and the Construction of Animal Rights Activists' Identity." *Mobilization* 7: 253–68.

———. 1999. "Gender, Class, and Social Movement Outcomes: Identity and Effectiveness in Two Animal Rights Campaigns." *Gender & Society* 13: 56–76.

Fantasia, Rick. 1988. *Cultures of Solidarity.* Berkeley: University of California Press.

Friedman, Debra, and Doug McAdam. 1992. "Collective Identity and Activism: Networks, Choices and the Life of a Social Movement." In *Frontiers in Social Movement Theory,* ed. A. D. Morris and C. M. Mueller, 156–73. New Haven, Conn.: Yale University Press.

Futrell, Robert, Pete Simi, and Simon Gottschalk. 2006. "Understanding Music in Movements: The White Power Scene." *The Sociological Quarterly* 47: 275–304.

Futrell, Robert, and Pete Simi. 2004. "Free Spaces, Collective Identity, and the Persistence of U.S. White Power Activism." *Social Problems* 51: 16–42.

Gamson, Joshua. 1996. "The Organizational Shaping of Collective Identity: The Case of Lesbian and Gay Film Festivals in New York." *Sociological Forum* 11: 231–61.

———. 1995. "Must Identity Movements Self-destruct? A Queer Dilemma." *Social Problems* 42: 390–407.

Gamson, William A. 1992. *Talking Politics.* New York: Cambridge University Press.

Gotham, Kevin Fox. 1999. "Political Opportunity, Community Identity, and the Emergence of a Local Anti-expressway Movement." *Social Problems* 46: 332–54.

Groves, Julian McAllister. 1997. *Hearts and Minds: The Controversy Over Laboratory Animals.* Philadelphia: Temple University Press.

Haines, Herbert H. 2006. "Dangerous Issues and Public Identities: The Negotiation of Controversy in Two Movement Organizations." *Sociological Inquiry* 76: 231–63.

Hirsch, Eric L. 1990. "Sacrifice for the Cause: The Impact of Group Processes on Recruitment and Commitment in Protest Movements." *American Sociological Review* 55: 243–54.

Hochschild, Arlie Russell. 1983. *The Managed Heart.* Berkeley: University of California Press.

———. 1979. "Emotion Work, Feeling Rules, and Social Structure." *American Journal of Sociology* 85: 551–75.

Hunt, Scott A., and Robert D. Benford. 1994. "Identity Talk in the Peace and Justice Movement." *Journal of Contemporary Ethnography* 22: 488–517.

Hunt, Scott A., Robert D. Benford, and David A. Snow. 1994. "Identity Fields: Framing Processes and the Social Construction of Movement Identities." In *New Social Movements: From Ideology to Identity*, ed. E. Laraña, H. Johnston, and J. R. Gusfield, 185–208. Philadelphia: Temple University Press.

Johnston, Hank, and Bert Klandermans. 1995. "The Cultural Analysis of Social Movements." In *Social Movements and Culture*, ed. H. Johnston and B. Klandermans, 3–24. Minneapolis: University of Minnesota Press.

Klandermans, Bert. 1992. "The Social Construction of Protest and Multi-Organizational Fields." In *Frontiers in Social Movement Theory*, ed. A. D. Morris and C. M. Mueller, 77–103. New Haven, Conn.: Yale University Press.

Lichterman, Paul. 1999. "Talking Identity in the Public Sphere: Broad Visions and Small Spaces in Sexual Identity Politics." *Theory and Society* 28: 101–41.

McAdam, Doug. 1988. "Micromobilization Contexts and Recruitment to Activism." *International Social Movement Research* 1: 125–54.

———. 1982. *Political Process and the Development of Black Insurgency.* Chicago: University of Chicago Press.

Melucci, Alberto. 1989. *Nomads of the Present.* Philadelphia: Temple University Press.

Meyer, David S. 2002. "Opportunities and Identities: Bridge-building in the Study of Social Movements." In *Social Movements: Identity, Culture and the State*, ed. D. S. Meyer, N. Whittier, and B. Robnett, 3–21. New York: Oxford University Press.

Meyer, David S., and Suzanne Staggenborg. 1996. "Movements, Countermovements, and the Structure of Political Opportunity." *American Journal of Sociology* 101: 1628–60.

Meyer, David S., Nancy Whittier, and Belinda Robnett, ed. 2002. *Social Movements: Identity, Culture and the State*. New York: Oxford University Press.

Montini, Theresa. 1996. "Gender and Emotion in the Advocacy for Breast Cancer Informed Legislation." *Gender & Society* 10: 9–23.

Nepstad, Sharon Erickson. 2004. "Persistent Resistance: Commitment and Community in the Plowshares Movement." *Social Problems* 51: 43–60.

Neuhouser, Kevin. 1998. "'If I had Abandoned My Children': Community Mobilization and Commitment to the Identity of Mother in Northeast Brazil." *Social Forces* 77: 331–58.

Pfaff, Steven. 1996. "Collective Identity and Informal Groups in Revolutionary Mobilization: East Germany in 1989." *Social Forces* 75: 91–118.

Polletta, Francesca. 1998. "'It was Like a Fever . . .': Narrative and Identity in Social Protest." *Social Problems* 45: 137–59.

Polletta, Francesca, and James M. Jasper. 2001. "Collective Identity and Social Movements." *Annual Review of Sociology* 27: 283–305.

Ray, Raka. 1999. *Fields of Protest: Women's Movements in India*. Minneapolis: University of Minnesota Press.

Reger, Jo. 2002a. "Organizational Dynamics and the Construction of Multiple Feminist Identities in the National Organization for Women." *Gender & Society* 16: 710–27.

———. 2002b. "More Than One Feminism: Organizational Structure, Ideology and the Construction of Collective Identity." In *Social Movements: Identity, Culture and the State*, ed. D. S. Meyer, N. Whittier, and B. Robnett, 171–84. New York: Oxford University Press.

Robnett, Belinda. 1997. *How Long? How Long? African American Women in the Struggle for Civil Rights*. Oxford: Oxford University Press.

Snow, David A. 2001. "Collective Identity and Expressive Forms." In *International Encyclopedia of the Social and Behavioral Sciences*, ed. Neil J. Smelser and Paul B. Baltes, 2212–19. Oxford: Pergamon Press.

Snow, David A., and Leon Anderson. 1987. "Identity Work among the Homeless: The Verbal Construction and Avowal of Personal Identities." *American Journal of Sociology* 92: 1336–71.

Snow, David A., and Doug McAdam. 2000. "Identity Work Processes in the Context of Social Movements: Clarifying the Identity/Movement Nexus." In *Self, Identity, and Social Movements*, ed. S. Stryker, T. J. Owens, and R. W. White, 41–67. Minneapolis: University of Minnesota Press.

Staggenborg, Suzanne. 1998. "Social Movement Communities and Cycles of Protest: The Emergence and Maintenance of a Local Women's Movement Organization." *Social Problems* 45: 180–204.

Stryker, Sheldon, Timothy J. Owens, and Robert W. White, ed. 2000. *Self, Identity, and Social Movements*. Minneapolis: University of Minnesota Press.

Tarrow, Sidney. 1994. *Power in Movement*. Cambridge: Cambridge University Press.

Taylor, Verta. 1989. "Social Movement Continuity: The Women's Movement in Abeyance." *American Sociological Review* 54: 761–75.

Taylor, Verta, and Nancy Whittier. 1995. "Analytical Approaches to Social Movement Culture: The Culture of the Women's Movement." In *Social Movements and Culture*, ed. H. Johnston and B. Klandermans, 163–87. Minneapolis: University of Minnesota Press.

———. 1992. "Collective Identity in Social Movement Communities: Lesbian Feminist Mobilization." In *Frontiers in Social Movement Theory*, ed. Aldon D. Morris and Carol McClurg Mueller, 104–29. New Haven, Conn.: Yale University Press.

Tilly, Charles. 1978. *From Mobilization to Revolution*. New York: McGraw-Hill.

Whittier, Nancy. 2001. "Emotional Strategies: The Collective Reconstruction and Display of Oppositional Emotions in the Movement against Child Sexual Abuse." In *Passionate Politics*, ed. J. Goodwin, J. M. Jasper, and F. Polletta, 223–50. Chicago: University of Chicago Press.

———. 1995. *Feminist Generations: The Persistence of the Radical Women's Movement*. Philadelphia: Temple University Press.

Part I
Doing Identity Work

1

Just Like You: The Dimensions of Identity Presentations in an Antigay Contested Context

Kimberly B. Dugan

The Christian Right has long made it its business to fight against gay rights. Because of that reality, the gay, lesbian, and bisexual movement and the Christian Right lock into conflict with one another (Zald and Useem 1987; Meyer and Staggenborg 1996) in an "opposing movement" contest (Bernstein 1995, 1; see also 1997). When one side pursues an issue or cause, the other commonly follows by either countering or initiating a separate but derivative offensive move (see also Dugan 2004; Dugan 2005). Campaigns for social change that require the public's support are fertile ground for opposing movements that compete over the definition of the situation (Thomas 1923). As such, the control of the public's perceptions of each movement's collective identity is hotly contested.

Collective identities are articulated, manipulated, packaged, and deployed by movement actors to maximize resources and support from constituents. This "identity work" is used strategically by movements to reach and relate to different segments of the population. Movement actors create and promote identity messages that can depict the movement to be the same as the majority of the general public or as different and even critical of them (Bernstein 1997). Thus, themes of "sameness" and "difference" appear at various stages, including movement mobilization and recruitment of popular support. Such collective identity construction and presentation efforts are critical in "opposing movements" (Bernstein 1995; Meyer and Staggenborg 1996) where movement actors vie for public support. In addition to constructing and articulating particular versions of a movement's collective identity for mass appeal, movement actors attempt to create and deploy identities of the opposing movement.

My focus here is on the strategic presentation of collective identity in a case where two opposing social movements—the Christian Right and the gay, lesbian, and bisexual movement—struggled over an antigay ballot initiative in Cincinnati, Ohio. Both movements in the contest attempted to deploy messages about themselves and the "other" against whom they struggled. A key part of the clash between opposing movements is the conflict over the believability of the collective identity depictions offered through media and other venues. What matters in such a contest, in which the general public is expected to take a position, is not members' "real" or lived identities but rather the *discourse about identity* that the public believes. Through the analysis of the media and other discourse, I examine collective identity presentation as a strategic tool to be manipulated and deployed by opposing movement actors. I explore whether or not, and to what extent, each of the movements deployed an identity of themselves as well as their opponent in terms of its sameness or difference from the majority or managed a "mixed model of identity deployment" (Bernstein 1997, 557)—doing both simultaneously. This chapter therefore illustrates identity work in social movements and also raises questions about the importance of the opposing movements in identity deployment processes.

Theoretical Considerations

Defined as "the shared definition of a group that derives from its members' common interests, experiences, and solidarity" (Taylor and Whittier 1992, 105; see also Melucci 1989), collective identities are crafted to recruit and sustain members and to maintain movements in hostile climates (Rupp and Taylor 1987). As Steven Epstein argues, "collective identities are rarely stable and that shows how they may be as much the product as the prerequisite of movement activism" (1999, 77). Scholars note that identities are situational (Dugan 2004; Bernstein 1997; see also Gitlin 1995; Seidman 1993) and utilitarian in the sense that the ways in which identities are *framed* (Goffman 1974) dictate the support that movements garner from potential recruits and supporters and from the public in general (Benford and Snow 2000; Snow and Benford 1988; Gamson 1992; see also Polletta and Jasper 2001).

Collective identity *presentations* are articulations or frames presented to audiences that are designed to convey messages about the lived identities of movement participants. The job of movement actors is to "*produce meaningful realities*" for the targeted audience (Holstein and Miller 1990, 105, emphasis in original). Collective identity presentations follow the same compositional structure as "real" collective identities and thus include the three interconnected components of collective identity identified by Verta Taylor and Nancy Whittier (1992): boundaries, consciousness, and negotiation. First, boundaries refer to the ways that a social movement or "challenging group" separates itself from the "dominant group." Though conceived as operative for challenging groups, this concept can be extended to include opposing movements who engage the state as well as other social movements. As Taylor and Whittier define it, "boundaries mark the social territories of group relations by highlighting differences between activists and the web of others in the contested social world" (1992,111). Social movement actors strive to separate themselves (i.e.,"us") from both the opposing movement and the dominant group. Collective identity presentations would also then articulate this same line between "us" and "them."

Second, consciousness represents "the interpretive frameworks that emerge from a group's struggle to define and realize members' common interests in opposition to the dominant order" (Taylor and Whittier 1992, 114). These are the processes in operation within social movements as members identify the issues and attribute the causes of their discontent. Clearly defined causes are essential components of the rhetoric deployed by movements. Third, negotiation is that aspect whereby movements adopt symbols of their culture, exhibit resistance against the opposition, and work to change the systems that they oppose and view as dominant. Negotiation is also conveyed in the collective identity presentations or frames.

Identities can be classified as playing differing roles, including empowerment as a goal and as a strategy (Bernstein 1997). Particularly useful here is Mary Bernstein's (1997) notion of "identity as strategy" or "identity deployment" (see also Taylor and Raeburn 1995) that can take one of two forms—"identity as critique" or "identity for education." As Bernstein argues, "Identities may be deployed strategically to criticize dominant categories, values, and practices (for critique) or to put forth a view of the minority that challenge dominant perceptions (for education)" (2002, 539). One option for movements is to deploy identities in such a way that similarities with the majority population are emphasized, which is a strategy that serves the purpose of educating the masses (or target population). A second option is where movements deploy identities that highlight their differences from the majority and in so doing act as a mechanism for "cultural critique" (Bernstein 2002, 539).

In her examination of gay and lesbian campaigns for antidiscrimination statutes, Bernstein (1997) found that the movement deployed strategies of "identity for critique," where they "castigated the homophobic practices of mainstream society" (quoted in Polleta and Jasper 2001, 294). It is argued that movements who have different access or stronger support might utilize the "identities for education" strategy where similarities with the majority are emphasized (Polleta and Jasper 2001, 294).

Increasingly, scholars are recognizing the role of movement outsiders, including opposing movements, in a social movement's identity processes (Einwohner 2002; Bernstein 1997) and framing activities (Fetner 2001; McCaffrey and Keys 2000; Stein 1998; Zuo and Benford 1995). Social movement actors "package" and "sell" messages and images to particular audiences who maintain at least some control over the desired policy outcome (see Snow and Benford 1998). Collective identity portrayals are part of the framing process (see Gamson 1992). However, little work exists that examines the ways in which opposing movements compete with each other over identity portrayal, and especially their conflicts over defining the more publicly palatable collective identity presentations depicting each side (see Dugan 2005; 2004). The work of movements is to have specific audiences "buy" the presentations of the movement as well as the adversary against whom they organize. In this process, social movement actors face competition for attention, recognition, and support from leaders and the general public (see McCarthy, Smith, and Zald 1996). Opposing social movements are therefore in direct competition over collective identity presentations.

Building on scholarship of collective identity (Taylor and Whittier 1992), identity as strategy (Bernstein 1997), and identity framing (Gamson 1990; Snow and Benford 1992, 1986; see also Hunt, Benford, and Snow 1994), I draw attention to how movements not only vie for believable and palatable movement or self-collective identities but also for the control over the definition and perception of the opponent's collective identity. Opposing movements are actively struggling to control, interrupt, disrupt, and define the collective identity of the opponent. Further, collective identity presentation and deployment is a rhetorical strategy used to "persuade others to adopt and act on preferred understandings" of the movements (Holstein and Miller 1990, 105; see also Burke 1950).

What is also clear from previous research on the lesbian and gay movement (see Bernstein 1997) is that the type of identity deployment can change over the course of time depending on a host of factors. In this chapter, I focus on collective identity presentation as a strategy of the Christian Right and the gay, lesbian, and bisexual movement as they struggled against one another in a short time period. The intensity of the campaign lasted about three months—from the time the issue was placed on the ballot (late summer) until the November election. I examine the strategies that two opposing movements took against each other. In doing so, I not only expose the ways in which two opposing movements manipulate identity discourse but also show how one side successfully deployed simultaneous identity presentations of other as the same and as different from the majority (and, at times, as mixed). Rather than selecting one strategy or even one strategy that shifts in time, I show how the Christian Right was able to simultaneously deploy this mixed identity presentation in a single campaign in a short period. That the gay rights movement neglected to apply this mixed strategy may provide some insight into the defeat of the movement's goal of stopping the antigay ballot initiative. More broadly, this chapter illustrates the simultaneous role of sameness and difference in activists' identity work.

The Issue 3 Campaign Context

Cincinnati's antigay initiative was one of the first of its kind at the city level. In November 1993 voters in Cincinnati, Ohio passed Issue 3, an amendment to the city charter eliminating gay, lesbian, and bisexual persons' legal protection against discrimination and prohibiting their recognition as a group or class. This Christian Right initiative emerged largely in response to the inclusion of "sexual orientation" in the city's newly enacted Human Rights Ordinance. Just one year prior to the Issue 3 ballot measure, Cincinnati's City Council passed the Human Rights Ordinance 7–2. The Cincinnati initiative fell immediately on the heels of two widely publicized statewide antigay initiatives—Colorado and Oregon.

The Test Cases in Colorado and Oregon

In the fall of 1992, voters in both the State of Oregon and Colorado were faced with ballot decisions on the fate of legislation designed to eliminate legal protection against discrimination for gays, lesbians, and bisexuals. Oregon's Measure 9 was the Christian Right's failed attempt to not only repeal several cities' existing ordinances granting legal protection to gay, lesbian, and bisexual residents but also draft law explicitly equating homosexuality with pedophilia, sadism, and masochism (Herman 1997, 145).

The other "test" case was in Colorado (Bull and Gallagher 1995, 40). Colorado's 1992 Initiative, Amendment 2, was narrowly passed by voters 53 percent to 47 percent (see Herman 1997; *Gaybeat* 1995, 5; People For the American Way 1993). Amendment 2 was a statewide voter initiative passed in 1992 prohibiting legal protection to gay men, lesbians, and bisexual persons. The Colorado Christian Right stuck to a more legalistic strategy rather than one that included such highly charged things as pedophilia (see Herman 1997). The Colorado victory was only temporary. In 1996, the United States

Supreme Court ruled to overturn the discriminatory Amendment 2 (Lowe 1996; Greenhouse 1996; Mauro 1996; Barrett 1996; see also Epstein 1999).

The Oregon and Colorado cases preceded Cincinnati's Issue 3 by just one year. They were among the first states to have citizens vote on antigay initiatives. While the right wing lost its fight in Oregon, it won Colorado and, at the citywide level, with a ballot measure in Tampa, Florida that same year (People For the American Way 1993, 1). The People for the American Way (PFAW) argued that the right was "encouraged by their success in Colorado and Tampa, the antigay rights movement has expanded their efforts, launching antigay initiatives in nine states and nine localities in the 1993–1994 election cycle" (PFAW 1993, 1). Among the first of those localities was Cincinnati, Ohio with the Issue 3 Charter Amendment.

Cincinnati's Battleground

Many of the battles between the gay, lesbian, and bisexual movement and the Christian Right in and around the 1990s took place at either the state or local level (Button, Rienzo, and Wald 1997; see also Bull and Gallagher 1996). While there were national level social movement organizations (SMOs), such as the Christian Right's Christian Coalition and the gay rights movement's National Gay and Lesbian Task Force, it was local social movement organizations that led on the Cincinnati battlefield. Cincinnati SMOs received guidance and information as well as some other resource support (see McCarthy and Zald 1977; Freeman 1983) from movement organizations outside of Cincinnati including those from both sides of the Colorado campaign.

Cincinnati has a unique and interesting history where at different times one side mobilized in response to their opponent's activities. Long known for its conservatism, this polite and comparably diverse[1] city has had a unique blend of Christian anti-obscenity and pro-family or Christian Right successes mixed with a few progay and lesbian gains in the form of policies. In the 1980s the right organized to eliminate the sale of pornographic materials and the business of strip clubs. In 1990 conservatives successfully fought to close down the display of the famous Mapplethorpe homoerotic photographs at the city's art museum. Despite this conservative track record, in 1991 a new policy took effect allowing gay and lesbian city employees protection against discrimination in the workplace. The following year, city council enacted a human rights ordinance (HRO) that, along with other protected classes,[2] included protection on the basis of sexual orientation. However, just months before its official enactment, Christian Right opponents began forming a counterattack (Sturmon 1992).

As the plan became a reality, the Christian Right movement culled support from established local conservative and national antigay networks, coalesced existing organizations, and formed new movement organizations that culminated in an effective petition drive and a highly successful issue campaign. Issue 3 originated with Take Back Cincinnati (TBC), the group that gathered the signatures to get on the ballot. Once on, the organization became Equal Rights Not Special Rights (ERNSR)[3] and drew its leaders primarily from the top of a local "pro-family" organization, Citizens for Community Values (CCV). They also recruited assistance from the Black Baptist Ministers Association by hiring a spokesman from that organization who then encouraged support from its members. The campaign was managed by a small group of leaders. Roles were clearly defined so that each leader was responsible for tasks that were within their area of professional expertise. One local conservative SMO leader headed the new campaign organization. Members were drawn from established networks of conservative Christians throughout the greater Cincinnati area. At the onset of the antigay campaign, the opposing gay, lesbian, and bisexual movement quickly coalesced and created a campaign organization, Equality Cincinnati, to engage in the conflict. With the exception of the campaign director, a straight white woman recruited for her campaign experience, the leadership drew heavily from Cincinnati's gay rights organization, Stonewall Cincinnati. In addition to the manager, a few local gay rights leaders ran the campaign. Given the salience of discrimination to gay, lesbian, and bisexual people (see Reger and Dugan 2000; Dugan 2005; see also Dugan and Reger 2006), supporters came from varied backgrounds and through various means. Issue 3 opponents were drawn from Stonewall Cincinnati, local direct action activist groups such as AIDS Coalition To Unleash Power (ACT UP)/Gay and Lesbian March Coalition[4] and from nonactivist community members. Furthermore, it was these local and newly emergent campaign organizations—ERNSR and Equality Cincinnati—that made decisions and executed plans for the Issue 3 campaign. ERNSR activists succeeded in passing the measure that amended the city's charter, preventing it from "[e]nacting, adopting, enforcing or administering any ordinance, regulation, rule or policy which provides that homosexual, lesbian, or bisexual orientation, status, conduct, or relationship constitutes, entitles, or otherwise provides a person with the basis to have any claim of minority or protected status, quota preference or other preferential treatment" (Junior League of Cincinnati 1993).

Methods and Data Analysis

The data for this study are qualitative. There are three main sources for the study: (1) in-depth interviews with twenty-four key informants consisting of movement leaders, activists, supporters, political and civic officials, and professionals associated with the Issue campaign or movements; (2) print and other media including a comprehensive collection of articles from the two leading Cincinnati papers, all paid television advertisements for the campaign, documentary video, and national magazine and movement organization articles and reports; and (3) organizational documents from the two campaign organizations, as well as institutionalized conservative and gay and queer organizations.

During the period of June 1996 through July 1997, I conducted intensive interviews with twenty-four movement proponents and opponents, political and civic leaders, and other community members. Using newspaper reports and snowball sampling, I identified key informants (Tremblay 1957) who represented campaign leaders, all the main social movement organizations involved in gay rights issues, as well as less publicized community leaders, activists not part of the campaign organizations, and supporters. Most interviews were conducted in-person and lasted between sixty and ninety minutes.

The second data source involved print and other media, including a comprehensive collection of articles from the two leading city papers, *The Cincinnati Enquirer* and *The Cincinnati Post*, all campaign television advertisements, documentary video, and national magazine and movement organization articles and reports. Visual media were converted to text and content analyzed along with the paper sources.

The third source was documents from all local SMOs, including the two organizations formed specifically for the campaign, Equal Rights Not Special Rights and Equality Cincinnati, and from Citizens for Community Values, GLMA/ACT UP, and Stonewall Cincinnati. The different collections included a range of material, including public speaking packets, talking points, political action committee finance report(s), solicitation letters, postcards, and other mailers, newsletters, meeting minutes and other internal correspondence, event flyers and information, and other documentation.

Data were coded to address the primary objectives of the study (Blee and Taylor 2002), including a breakdown of various identities deployed. The different sources allow for the triangulation of data, which strengthens the reliability of the findings (see Snow and Trom 2002; Lofland 1996; Babbie 2004). I turn here to an analysis of the collective identity presentations deployed in the Issue 3 campaign.

Collective Identity Portrayals Deployed

During the course of the campaign, both the Christian Right and the gay, lesbian, and bisexual movements deployed messages about themselves and their opponents. The Christian Right managed to deploy a "self" collective identity presentation that was designed to educate and align with as well as separate from the majority. Interestingly, they did the very same thing in their construction and presentation of the collective identity of the opposing gay rights movement. The basic discourse in the Issue 3 campaign was centered on notions of equality and special rights. The Christian Right actually controlled the debate (Dugan 2004; Dugan 2005) and through an elaborate media campaign promoted the message that gays and lesbians were not a minority and did not deserve any recognition as such. In contrast, the gay rights movement was the defensive player in the campaign. They focused on a simple but abstract antidiscrimination theme that set themselves up as defenders of equality and characterized Issue 3 proponents as villains attempting to legislate discrimination. I now discuss the Christian Right identity presentation or framing process including the deployment of an identity of self and other I follow with a description of the Gay, Lesbian and Bisexual movement collective identity portrayals.

The Christian Right's Deployments

Promoters of Equality vs. Special Rights Seekers

From the onset of the campaign, the Christian Right portrayed itself as a movement of "the people," or the majority of Cincinnatians from whom the gay rights movement greedily sought to take more than their fair share of rights. To deploy this "majority" identity presentation, the Christian Right not only cast themselves as part of the majority, but also built a case against the gay, lesbian, and bisexual movement opposition by depicting them as critically different than everyone, even as "fringe." In their promotional mailings for instance, the social movement organization charged with gathering the required signatures for the issue to get on the ballot, Take Back Cincinnati, had as its stated mission—"To *promote debate* for the purpose of *educating and motivating voters* for the November election so '*We, the People*,' can voice our opinion at the ballot box"[5] (emphasis in original). Here the Christian Right movement organization explicitly stated its desire to educate the voters and identify themselves with the majority.

The Christian Right also portrayed themselves as equality promoters. Throughout the campaign they promoted the message distinguishing between "true" minorities and homosexuals. In the process of separating the two constructs, they effectively made the case that homosexuals were seeking "special rights" that were well above the equal rights that the U.S. Constitution affords everyone. To further that end, the leadership named its primary campaign organization "Equal Rights Not Special Rights." In so doing they painted themselves as patriotic Americans promoting equality and offering protection against those wanting more than their fair share. As one leader in the campaign stated, "Everyone has Constitutional rights, and they're pretty much stated right in there. I think that's why 'Equal Rights Not Special Rights' was a very good title for the campaign . . . because we do believe in equal rights."[6] They made it clear that their sole purpose was to uphold the strong American value of equality. Furthermore, in one of their television advertisement, the narrator reported, "The U.S. Constitution gives homosexuals equal rights. Now they're demanding special rights. And, that's not right. What makes them so special? Shouldn't we stop this in Cincinnati? Yessiree, vote yes on Issue 3."[7]

Another voice for the campaign explained that the movement's goal was "to show [that] these people [are] radical, extremists, [who are] pushing a special rights agenda, which is very unpopular."[8] Not only was this unpopular but it would not be fair, and it certainly would not fall in line with "equal rights for all." The Christian Right cultivated and deployed their own "equality" identity presentation in large part by portraying their opponent as wanting and taking more than their fair share. Thus, the Christian Right deployed a collective identity presentation "celebrating" (Bernstein 1997) its similarities with the voters.

Racial and Cultural Representatives vs. White Economic Privilege and Power

The Christian Right also deployed an image of themselves as diverse and of their opponent as representative of the dominant/powerful group. This traditionally white movement (Herman 1997) actively worked on the local level to incorporate a black community leader in to the leadership core. One campaign leader shared that they were "looking for high-profile people on our side . . . [in the] Black community. . . . We felt we had to [have to] . . . to win the election" (Interview with Author, 1996a). Getting such support facilitated, at least, the visual representation of the Christian Right as racially diverse. Further, media images were constructed and deployed showing the movement promoting Issue 3 to be inclusive of black and white citizens and, therefore, characteristic of Cincinnati.[9] Television advertisements and numerous speaking engagements were narrated or led by a person or persons of color. In one of the local television advertisements, for instance, an African American spokeswoman was shown taking a stand against the comparison between *being* African American with homosexual behavior. The woman said, "Some people say that homosexual behavior is the same as being black. Does anyone really believe that? This makes no sense to me. We need to stop this in Cincinnati. I am voting yes on Issue 3."[10] The incorporation of blacks in a full third of the television advertisements, on all the billboards, in several newspaper editorials, and in local Christian organizational newsletters was striking. These data support the argument that the Christian Right deployed a collective identity presentation of themselves as similar to the general public.

All at the same time, the Christian Right attempted to construct and deploy an identity of gays and lesbians as a group of white, economically and politically privileged people. Images were borrowed from the widely distributed documentary *Gay Rights/Special Rights: Inside the Homosexual Agenda*[11] and focused narrowly on white gays and lesbians. In doing so, they promoted the message that gays are not like the diverse "rest of us"; rather they fit into the elite. The film segments used also showed survey statistics that highlighted disparities in income between homosexuals and the "average" American, and homosexuals and blacks (again, the contrast implying that gays are only white) in income level, education, numbers of persons in managerial position, and more. For instance, in one television advertisement homosexual income was presented at $55,430 compared to the average American income reported at $32,144. In some of the print literature, the income figures of homosexuals ($55,430) were compared to "disadvantaged" African Americans, also referred to as "blacks with 1–3 years of high school," who reportedly earned just over twelve thousand a year ($12,166).[12] Gays and lesbians were therefore portrayed as different from both blacks and whites; although gays and lesbians were seen as "white," like the majority, they were seen as distinct from other whites who recognize that historically disadvantaged groups deserve "special" rights that level the playing field. Rather, gays and lesbians were portrayed as undeservedly trying to pawn themselves off as exceptions requiring disadvantaged status.

The political strength of the gay rights movement was highlighted as well. Using segments from the *Gay Rights/Special Rights* video, one television advertisement asked the question, "Are homosexuals really powerless?," while showing footage of the U.S. Supreme courthouse and of thousands of people marching in the 1993 Gay and Lesbian March on Washington.[13] The narrator then detailed gay and lesbian power by documenting gay people's claims to have donated 3.4 million dollars to Bill Clinton's presidential election campaign, showing footage of scores of people at the 1993 March, displaying cover stories and news articles about gays and lesbians, and citing the appointment of openly lesbian Roberta Achtenberg to the U.S. Department of Housing and Urban Development. To further the political strength identity depiction, at many public events Equal Rights Not Special Rights spokespeople exclaimed that "for the first time in Cincinnati history, City Council is controlled by those who have a pro-homosexual agenda."[14] According to the Christian Right's construction, gay and lesbian people have substantially higher incomes than others and wield considerably more power than their fair share. Thus, they were seeking "special rights" above and beyond what is equal.

Rational and Unemotional vs. Irrational and Emotional

The Christian Right movement also portrayed itself as comprised of rational and unemotional people. They were strict about maintaining a "rights prag-matist" discourse (Herman 1997) in their messages and claims rather than an alternate and historically used strategy that depicts gays as sinners and sick. Although there was some of that in this campaign (see Dugan 2005; Dugan 2004), for the most part the Christian Right set out to show themselves to be level-headed and rational, much like the mainstream society's self percep-tion. The Christian Right adhered to the conviction that the campaign needs to be about rights rather than an attack on individuals. To that end, Issue proponents were adamant that they would not use terms that they found offensive in characterizing their homosexual movement opponent. "Queer" was among those terms. For instance, a media expert for the Christian Right campaign shared the following:

> We [or] I would not allow the "buzz word" to be used. Buzzwords on our side would be the word "queer" or "fag." I would not allow anybody who said that over the air, or if they call[ed] in on a talk show, I'd say, "No, we're not going to use that word. That's a buzzword. It's an offensive word." On the other side, if they called us a "bigot" or a "homophobe," I would say, "no, that's a buzz word, I'm not a bigot." And we'd go through the defini-tion of what a bigot was and why we were not . . . bigot[s] and that kind of helped. I think buzzwords just bring out the emotion and not the content of the issue.[15]

To this activist, the words "queer" and "fag" were as offensive as the terms "bigot" or "homophobe" despite the fact that many in the gay, lesbian, and bisexual community themselves embraced some of these terms as self-descrip-tors and as appropriate labels for the community as a whole.

The campaign leaders also refused to associate or debate in a queer con-text. As one leader in the Issue 3 initiative explained, "I refused to speak at . . . [the conference called] 'Queer Nation,' or something like that. I said, 'I'd like talking to you, the homosexuals.' They call themselves Queers, you know. I said, 'I'm not going top be a part of this.' I don't even want to be around somebody that calls them Queers. . . . Well, count me out. I don't like that . . . I think to call a person a homosexual is degrading because you're identifying them strictly on how they have sex. I'd rather call them homo-sexual activists rather than homosexuals."[16] This commitment to staying with the rational and avoiding any "emotional" encounter lends support to the claim that the Christian Right attempted to deploy a collective identity presentation that cast them as being the same as the majority. Much like the majority, the Christian Right wanted to be "politically correct," nonconfron-tational, and nonemotive. They were very careful not to set themselves apart from the majority in this regard. The Christian Right did not want to be characterized as bigots or extremists, thus limiting their use of terms to those that, on the surface, appear devoid of emotionally charged politics.

Though not explicit, the implication then is that the gay and lesbian opponent was emotional and even potentially explosive. The fact that gays and lesbians referred to themselves as queer, for instance, was used as evi-dence of the emotionality and confrontational (i.e., irrational and illogi-cal) nature of gays and lesbians who defy principles of fairness. To further explicate this emotionality and confrontational identity portrayal, the widely used film *Gay Rights/Special Rights* showed footage of diverse and out of the mainstream gays and lesbians at a parade, including BDSM and leather com-munity members. This focus on nonconformists facilitates paints a picture of gays and lesbians as "freaks" and clearly attempts to differentiate them from the mainstream.

Religious Christians First: Self-identity as Difference vs. the Secular Gays and Majority

At the same time that they cast themselves as similar to the mainstream, the Christian Right also deployed an identity presentation of difference in this campaign. Namely, they portrayed themselves as religious Christians moti-vated by belief and biblical scripture to oppose homosexuality. While we know that the majority of Americans identify as Christian (NORC 1999), this particular set of religious fundamentalism and political involvement separates the Christian Right from the rest of the population.

This identity of difference was subtle compared to the strategies of sameness previously documented. Perhaps the subtlety was intended to gar-ner targeted support from likeminded Christian fundamentalists, while simul-taneously not alienating the majority. From the beginning of the campaign, the Christian Right associated themselves with well-known pro-family movement organizations and political fundamentalist Christians. The originator of the ballot initiative and the man who led the charge to get the Issue on the ballot was also a well-known Christian minister and political figure. He even wrote and published a book where the conservative politics and religion came together.[17] The lead spokesman for the campaign was also a prominent local minister. While his status as minister was not stated publicly, it was known to most people in the area.

The Christian Right's speaking engagement material also reveals many fundamentalist religious and pro-family movement associations. Among these materials were pamphlets from the Pure Life Ministries on "Breaking Free from the Bondages of Sexual Sin," as well as pamphlets from Focus on the Family and a report and newsletter from The Family Research Council.[18] In addition, on the back page of one campaign organizational newsletter books were advertised, including "Sodom's Second Coming: What You Need To Know about The Deadly Homosexual Assault."

Financial reports reveal that Equal Rights Not Special Rights paid its membership to the Christian Coalition during the campaign and that on at least one occasion they purchased three hundred brochures from the Family Research Institute. As part of their repertoire for public speaking engagements was the video *Gay Rights/Special Rights* produced and distributed by the ultra conservative Christian organization, Traditional Values Coalition. The Christian Right also helped to sell and, later, widely distribute this video free of charge.

Moreover, the main organization from which Equal Rights Not Special Rights campaign organization emerged is a not-for-profit organization called Citizens for Community Values. Similar organizations exist elsewhere in the country, including Colorado for Family Values, which is the organization at the helm of the statewide antigay amendment that passed and was later overturned by the U.S. Supreme Court. Locally, Cincinnati's CCV is well known as a faith-based organization that fights obscenity and pornography as well as issues such as gay rights. One example of CCV's notoriety was in 1990 when the Robert Mapplethorpe photography exhibit was on display at the Cincinnati Contemporary Arts Center. This showing set off a swell of protest and arrests over six of the photographs that were explicitly homoerotic in nature.[19] It was widely known that CCV was the organization fighting this "obscenity."

In addition, one leader identified his religious beliefs as the primary motivation for his involvement. Not only was his personal identity intricately bound up with his Christian beliefs, but also his sense was that his campaign peers identified similarly. He shared this belief in a common identity by stating that "we're Christians and . . . we're going to stand for the Lord."[20] His congregation as well as many religious members of the black community joined him in the fight for Issue 3. He was not the only leader who said religion motivated his participation. Another shared that personal, religious identity was an impetus. He explained, "And of course I'm a Christian, so I don't believe God creates people in that lifestyle. And I think that's basically why I took part in the campaign, is to try to put the genie back in the bottle, and to help people—how can I say?—make a testimony to the fact that there is absolutes. There are absolutes."[21]

These few examples help to illustrate the collective identity presentation strategy of difference utilized by the Christian Right. While a direct and clearly articulated cultural critique is absent, what is present is a critique through association. Fundamentalist Christians and the pro-family movement have long been dissatisfied with mainstream society and have expressed this in various formats (e.g., television programs such as the *700 Club* and other religious broadcasts, as well as countless articles in magazines and newspapers and presentations at public speaking engagements). The identity that Cincinnati's Christian Right movement deployed was one that aligned itself to this oppositional group and thereby deployed difference from the majority.

By default, the implication of these religious themes in collective identity presentation deployment was that the gay rights movement, along with the mainstream society, was too secular. That the Christian Right was acting out of biblical motivation and strong belief allowed for the alignment of gays with the majority. By the same token, a message here is that if God does not create people as homosexuals, then homosexuals are acting out against God's plan. This mixed strategy simultaneously paints gays as secular and in line with the majority on the one hand, and quite different than the mainstream that may be secular but does not act against God.

It is clear that there were at least two self-identity portrayals deployed in this campaign—one that "celebrated" and one that "suppressed" difference from the majority (Bernstein 1997). While the sameness "self" identity presentation was primary in the campaign, the difference identity of religious Christian was ever-present. Both existed together in this opposing movement struggle. The gay rights movement was distinctly depicted as different from and the same as the majority. There was also a mixed deployment where they were simultaneously portrayed as both. The collective identity presentation of "other" was primarily deployed as different. Gay rights movement members were characterized as breeching the balance of equality and in some ways going against God. Concurrently, gay and lesbian people were linked to the average citizen who deserves and receives his or her fair share of rights—equal rights. They were also characterized as a group unmoved to do God's work or heed God's word, a clear alignment with the mainstream secular society.

The Gay, Lesbian, and Bisexual Movement's Deployment

Like the Christian Right, gay, lesbian, and bisexual activists on the other side of Issue 3 engaged in identity work by strategically deploying self-portrayals during the campaign. The gay, lesbian, and bisexual movement portrayed itself primarily as "defenders against discrimination," do-gooders against "evil," and even equality promoters, all in line with what the majority values. This portrayal was largely implied by the contrast set up against the imagery of the "other" as demonic. The gay, lesbian, and bisexual movement spent the larger part of its energy and resources constructing and deploying an identity portrait of their opponent as being quite different than the majority. To truly capture the essence of the gay rights self-identity presentation, it is essential to get a picture of the media images used by the gay rights campaign that strictly characterized the Christian Right as evil.

Another Voice For Equality (Defenders Against Discrimination) vs. Evil

The gay rights movement painted an identity picture of the proponents of the antigay issue as clearly different from the general public by making direct comparisons to Adolf Hitler, the Ku Klux Klan (KKK), and the homophobic and anticommunist Senator Joseph McCarthy. Images of these "three faces of evil" (see Dugan 2005; Dugan 2004) were presented in nearly all the campaign media, including the television advertisement, billboards, T-shirts, and mailers.

The single television advertisement produced and aired included familiar film footage of Hitler speaking before a crowd, a group of Klansmen walking with one of their own children who was also dressed in a robe, and Senator Joseph McCarthy speaking at what appears to be a court proceeding. The short slogan associated with the campaign was "Vote No, Never Again, On Issue 3." Narrated by what sounds like an average, white, professional man, the script printed on the screen reads: "There is a large group of fervent Cincinnati citizens drawn together by a common belief they know what is best for the rest of us. They promote a kind of discrimination that comes from another time and another place. We must not let their hate and prejudice start again. We must stand up to them and preserve rights that belong to all of us. Vote No, Never Again, On Issue 3."[22]

In addition, much of the print literature referred to the issue proponents as "extremists," "extremist right," and as a "hate group."[23] By portraying the Christian Right opponents as comparable to Hitler, the KKK, and Joe McCarthy, the gay, lesbian, and bisexual movement effectively constructed the other's identity presentation as demonic or at least as extremely different from the majority and portrayed their own collective identity as proponents of equality. Again, equality promoters and defenders fit in with the majority view. Just as the Christian Right did, the gay rights movement depicted their own collective identity presentation as the same as the general public, who value equality.

Print media also contributed to the gay, lesbian, and bisexual movement's identity portrayal as the defender of equality. For instance, one pamphlet read, "Issue 3 is discrimination. Discrimination is wrong. We will not tolerate discrimination in our city. And we are voting No, Never again on Issue 3." Voting "no" meant protecting equality and fighting discrimination. Another piece of print literature mailed to homes further played up this theme: "Approving Issue 3 would prohibit the City from enforcing the law of equal opportunity for all of its citizens. It will permanently prevent the City from passing laws to provide equality for all." [24] Other print pieces included letters mailed to residents, which stated that "[t]he issue proposes making a permanent change to our City's charter—our constitution. Approving Issue 3 would prohibit the City from enforcing the law of equal opportunity for all of its citizens. It will permanently prevent the City from passing laws to provide equality for all." [25] Thus, the gay rights movement made considerable efforts to set up the us/them dynamic of other as vastly different from the majority and self as aligned with the masses promoting equality.

We Are Just Like You: Diverse

Equality Cincinnati[26] also characterized itself along with the masses as "a diverse coalition (including) every religious denomination . . . and every ethnic background . . . men and women, gay and straight, people of all colors." Print material such as a postcard[27] mailed to voters illustrated this diversity by listing endorsements from about seventy-five leading local and regional organizations representing various categories of people. In addition to community organizations, the list included the Archdiocese of Cincinnati, Greater Cincinnati Region of the National Conference of Christian and Jews, Black Lawyers Association of Cincinnati, and the Greater Cincinnati Appalachian PAC. The depiction of self as diverse only went as far as the coalitions built, however. In everyday life, Equality Cincinnati's leadership was all white (though both straight and gay people were represented), and the visible membership was also largely white. With a few exceptions, speaking engagements displayed a white leadership.

Some gay rights activists took issue with the depiction of the local movement and movement organizations as diverse. One African American activist articulated her discontent with the movement's diversity presentation: "They say about what they would like to have in diversity [but] they [i.e. Equality Cincinnati] don't have it and it was not their true agenda. They don't have a plan [for diversity], they don't care. They were trying to scramble and find just the right people—which was their problem from the start."

She continued on to say, "All of them have a statement about diversity, but I know that every time something like this comes up they're looking for a spokesperson. And that's because those people are not part of their organizations anyway" (Interview with Author 1997). Another community activist articulated that diversity or "race is our Achilles heel." He went on to discuss the difficulty he encountered as a white man reaching out to the black community and that it could be perceived as "tokenism." He referred to race as a "problem." He stated that "there is a lot of homophobia in the Black community, everyone knows that. And, there is an awful lot of racism in the [gay] community, too, which shouldn't come as a surprise to anyone" (Interview with Author 1996b). Despite his and the other activists' voices who articulated discontent and concern over the real connections between blacks and whites and the involvement of blacks in the campaign and its organizations, Equality Cincinnati pursued and promoted an image of itself as representing a broad range of racial and ethnic individual and community support.

We Could Be Victims, But Let's Not Talk about That

At the same time that gay rights activists portrayed themselves as "just like you" to the voting public, however, the data also indicate that the gay, lesbian, and bisexual movement deployed an identity presentation of itself as different from the majority. What I call a "we could be victims" theme ran through the campaign. The message was that if indeed the Issue passed, gay and lesbians would be at the losing end of the equality stick. While this point was barely addressed in the campaign, mentions of a gay and lesbian "victim" did come through. For instance, in a letter written to *the Cincinnati Enquirer*, one anti-Issue 3 activist discussed the "three faces of evil" identity deployment frame strategy and at the same time revealed the potential consequences for gay and lesbian people:

> Those of us who belong to that segment of the population know about the Ku Klux Klan's recent pledges to terrorize queers. We remember Sen. Joseph McCarthy's witch hunts, in which hundreds of "perverts" lost their

livelihoods, and we recall that Hitler sent tens of thousands of homosexuals to the gas chambers. The KKK chiefly targets African Americans; McCarthy was notorious for hunting Communists; most of Hitler's victims were Jews. But if you examine any of these monsters' laundry lists of people to be purged, you always find queers, too. We just don't see a big step between eliminating our rights and eliminating us.[28]

This message was also deployed through the campaign's print literature. In one piece, Equality Cincinnati made clear that lesbians and gays were different from the majority because if Issue 3 passed they could be fired from their jobs or evicted from their homes simply because of their sexual orientation.[29] While the difference theme in the collective identity presentation—in this case "the potential victim"—was downplayed by the gay, lesbian, and bisexual movement's campaign, it was present nonetheless.

The gay, lesbian, and bisexual movement deployed messages about their own identity and that of their opponent. To some extent they used a mixed strategy to depict themselves both celebrating and suppressing (Bernstein 1997) their differences from the majority. Their characterizations of the Christian Right's collective identity was narrowly focused as the evil other. By portraying the Christian Right in this way, the gay rights movement attempted to set their opponent as extreme and vastly different from the norm.

Discussion and Conclusion

In this chapter, I show how social movements actively create and deploy collective identity in an attempt to shape the public's perceptions. The Christian Right and the gay rights movement also competed for control of the opponent's identity portrayal. Using scholarship of collective identity, identity strategy, and framing as a guide, I explore the movement deployments in terms of "sameness" and "difference" with the general public. I found that these opposing movement's identity portrayals are not summarized easily by the language of either "sameness" or "difference"; in fact, both movements emphasized their similarities and their differences from the mainstream.

The Christian Right painted itself as both similar to and separate from the general public. Three themes run through the analysis of the self-deployed Christian Right collective identity presentation as the same as the majority. First, they portrayed themselves as promoters of equality. Second, the Christian Right strategically deployed messages and images characterizing themselves as racially and culturally diverse. Third, they offered themselves as rational and thinking community members promoting Issue 3.

Counter-positioned against these self-depictions were the identity portraits deployed by the Christian Right about their gay, lesbian, and bisexual movement opponent. The presentation of gays and lesbians was largely different than the majority. Gay, lesbian, and bisexuals were shown to be special rights seekers, white, economically and politically privileged persons, who were irrational, emotional, and confrontational. At the same time, gays and lesbians were strategically characterized as equal, just like everyone else. The Christian Right effectively used both a strategy of difference from and similarity to the majority. This mixed strategy may have been critical to the success of the Christian Right.

The gay rights movement took a more limited approach to identity deployment. They deployed a collective identity presentation of themselves as similar to the majority who embrace equality and loathe discrimination. Like their Christian Right counterparts, they promoted images and messages about themselves as defenders of equality. In a minor way, they also depicted themselves as different from the public; namely, by characterizing themselves as potential victims of discrimination. Despite the reality of this message, this theme was not granted much attention.

Cincinnati's Christian Right movement was a force with which to contend. They used mixed deployment strategies for themselves and the gay, lesbian, and bisexual movement. The gay rights movement on the other hand, focused on narrow identity presentations and stayed away from multithemed identities. While to some extent they did deploy a simultaneous self-identity, their characterization of the other was singular and limited. Elsewhere I argue (Dugan 2004; see also 2005) that the gay rights movement's failure in the Issue 3 campaign was due in part to their lack of response to the opposing movement messages. Here, I extend that argument to include the possibility that these activists' failure to achieve their goal was due in part to the limited characterization of their opponent. The only collective identity portrait of the Christian Right offered by the gay rights movement was as evil. This demonic presentation was not palatable to those who had neighbors and colleagues who identified as Christian Right or pro-Issue 3 (see also Dugan 2004, 2005).

Further investigation could explore the extent to which such narrow depictions of the opposing movement (e.g., as only different than the majority) impact a movement's ability to garner public support. Future inquiry could also ask if an opposing movement is required to deploy simultaneous presentation strategies to alter movement outcomes. That is, must depictions of the opposing movement be mixed strategies of sameness and difference? Part of the gay rights movement's failure here with Issue 3 may have been that the deployment ignored other dimensions of the opposing movement to which the public could relate. These data show that the "side" with the mixed strategy was also the one who succeeded. However, the relationship described here between specific collective identity presentation strategy and movement outcome may be simply context specific. Fuller understanding may come from examining the identity presentations of additional sites of opposing movement conflict. For instance, it would be informative to include in these data locations that battled over similar issues, such as in the case of Colorado or Oregon in the early 1990s or Maine in 2005 (where voters rejected a measure that would have overturned existing gay rights protections). It might also be theoretically instructive to explore different policy battles between the gay rights movement and the Christian Right as well as opposing movement conflict that occurs over other issues such as those dealing with the rights of (illegal or undocumented) immigrants.

The current study also raises the question of whether or not it is possible for a movement to influence a voting public by deploying a broader and more diverse solitary strategy of either sameness or difference and which type of deployment is more fruitful. For movement participants, seeing oneself as similar to other participants and distinct from the opponent, or opposing movement as I would argue, is the crux of collective identity boundary setting (Taylor and Whittier 1992). If we apply the concept of boundaries to the discursive arena, it logically follows that creating an image of the opposing movement as distinct from the majority would allow the public to distance themselves from this difference by aligning with the movement. In the competition over public support, I suspect that movements are better off if they deploy collective identity presentations of themselves as like the majority and their opponent as different rather than the reverse.

While other studies of identity deployment focus on more progressive movements like the gay rights movement, this study focuses on the ultraconservative Christian Right and the gay rights movement as equal players constructing, deploying, and contesting collective identity presentations. This study foregrounds the role of the opposing movement in the fundamental process of establishing understandings about the collective identity presentation of its contender.

References

Anonymous. 1996. "Colorado Argues for Its Bias Law." *Gaybeat*. April 28: 5.

Babbie, Earl. 2004. *Practice of Social Research*. 10th ed. Belmont, Calif.: Wadsworth.

Barrett, Paul. 1996. "Court Rejects Ban on Laws Protecting Gays." *Wall Street Journal*, Eastern Edition, May 21, Vol. 227:B1.

Benford, Robert D., and David Snow. 2000. "Clarifying the Relationship Between Framing and Ideology." *Mobilization* 5: 55–60.

Bernstein, Mary. 2002. "Identities and Politics: Toward a Historical Understanding of the Lesbian and Gay Movement." *Social Science History* 26: 531–81.

———. 1997."Celebration and Suppression: The Strategic Uses of Identity by the Lesbian and Gay Movement." *American Journal of Sociology* 103: 531–65.

———. 1995. "Strategies, Goals, and Lesbian/Gay Policy Outcomes in the Face of Organized Opposition." Paper Presented at the Annual Meeting of the American Sociological Association, Washington, D.C., August.

Blee, Kathleen, and Verta Taylor. 2002. "Semi-Structured Interviewing in Social Movement Research." In *Methods of Social Movement Research*, ed. Bert Klandermans and Suzanne Staggenborg, 92–117. Minneapolis: University of Minnesota Press.

Bull, Chris, and John Gallagher. 1996. *Perfect Enemies: The Religious Right, the Gay Movement, and the Politics of the 1990s*. New York: Crown Publishers, Inc.

Burke, Kenneth. 1950. *A Rhetoric of Motives*. Englewood Cliffs, N.J.: Prentice Hall.

Button, James W., Barbara A. Rienzo, and Kenneth D. Wald. 1997. *PrivateLives, Public Conflicts: Battles Over Gay Rights in American Communities*. Washington, D.C.: Congressional Quarterly Press.

Dugan, Kimberly B. 2005. *The Struggle Over Gay, Lesbian, and Bisexual Rights: Facing Off in Cincinnati*. New York: Routledge.

———. 2004. "Strategy and 'Spin': Opposing Movement Frames in an Anti-gay Voter Initiative." *Sociological Focus* 37: 213–35.

Dugan, Kimberly, and Jo Reger. 2006. "Voice and Agency in Social Movement Outcomes." *Qualitative Sociology* 29: (Winter) 4: 467–84.

Einwohner, Rachel 2002. "Bringing the Outsiders In: Opponents' Claims and the Construction of Animal Rights Activists' Identity." *Mobilization*, 7: 253–68.

Epstein, Steven. 1999. "Gay and Lesbian Movements in the United States: Dilemmas of Identity, Diversity, and Political Strategy." In *The Global Emergence of Gay and Lesbian Politics: National Imprints of a Worldwide Movement*, ed. Barry D. Adam, Jan Willem Duyvendak, and André Krouwel, 30–90. Philadelphia: Temple University Press.

Fetner, Tina. 2001. "Working Anita Bryant: The Impact of Christian Anti-gay Activism on Lesbian and Gay Movement Claims." *Social Problems* 48: 411–28.

Freeman, Jo. 1999. [1983.] "On the Origins of Social Movements." In *Waves of Protest: Social Movements Since the Sixties and Seventies*, 7–24. Lanham, Md.: Rowman and Littlefield.

Gamson, William A. 1992. *Talking Politics*. New York: Cambridge University Press.

Gitlin, Todd. 1995. *The Twilight of Common Dreams: Why America Is Wracked by Culture Wars*. New York: Metropolitan Books.

Goffman, Erving. 1974. *Frame Analysis*. New York: Harper Colophon Books.

Greenhouse, Linda. 1996. "Court Voids Colorado's Anti-gay Amendment." *The Plain Dealer*, May 21: 1A, 6A.

Herman, Didi. 1997. *The Antigay Agenda: Orthodox Vision and the Christian Right*. Chicago, Ill.: University of Chicago Press.

Holstein, James A., and Gale Miller. 1990. "Rethinking Victimization: An Interactional Approach to Victimology." *Symbolic Interactionism*: 103–22.

Hunt, Scott A., Robert D. Benford, and David A. Snow. 1994. "Identity Fields: Framing Processes and Movement Identities." In *New Social Movements*, ed. Enrique Laraña, Hank Johnston, and Joseph R. Gusfield, 185–208, Philadelphia: Temple University Press.

Interview with Author. 1996a. August 5. Cincinnati, Ohio.

Interview with Author. 1996b. August 5. Cincinnati, Ohio.

Interview with Author. 1997. July 24. Cincinnati, Ohio.

Junior League of Cincinnati. 1993. "Issue 3: Human Rights Ordinance: The City of Cincinnati Ordinance 490–1992." Board of Elections, Cincinnati, Ohio.

Lofland, John. 1996. *Social Movement Organizations: Guide to Research on Insurgent Realities*. New York: Aldine De Gruyter.

Lowe, Roger K. 1996. "Anti-gay Rights Law Overruled." *The Columbus Dispatch*, May 21: 1A, 2A.

Mauro, Tony. 1996. "Colorado Ruling Called Historic." *USA Today*, May 21: 1.

McCaffrey, Dawn, and Jennifer Keys. 2000. "Competitive Framing Processes in the Abortion Debate: Polarization-vilification, Frame Saving, and Frame Debunking." *The Sociological Quarterly* 41: 41–61.

McCarthy, John D., Jackie Smith, and Mayer Zald. 1996. "Accessing Public, Media, Electoral, and Governmental Agendas." In *Comparative Perspectives on Social Movements: Political Opportunities, Mobilizing Structures, and Cultural Framings*, ed. Doug McAdam, John D. McCarthy, and Mayer N. Zald, 291–311. New York: Cambridge University Press.

McCarthy, John D., and Mayer N. Zald. 1977. "Resource Mobilization and Social Movements: A Partial Theory." *American Journal of Sociology* 82: 1212–41.

Melucci, Alberto. 1989. *Nomads of the Present*. Philadelphia: Temple University Press.

Meyer, David S., and Suzanne Staggenborg. 1996. Movements, Countermovements, and the Structure of Political Opportunity." *American Journal of Sociology* 101: 1628–60.

NORC. 1999. General Social Surveys, 1972–1998: *Cumulative Codebook*. Chicago: National Opinion Research Center, 1999.

People for the American Way. 1993. *Hostile Climate: A State by State Report on Antigay Activity*. Washington, D.C.: People for the American Way.

Polletta, Francesca, and James Jasper. 2001. "Collective Identity and Social Movements." *Annual Review of Sociology* 27: 283–305.

Reger, Jo, and Kimberly Dugan. 2000. "Constructing a Salient Identity: Outcomes and Continuity in Two Social Movement Contexts." Paper presented at the American Sociological Association annual meeting, Hilton Washington and Towers and the Marriott Wardman Park, Washington, D.C., August 12–16.

Rupp, Leila, and Verta Taylor. 1987. *Survival in the Doldrums: The American Women's Rights Movement, 1945 to the 1960s.* New York: Oxford University

Seidman, Steven. 1993. "Identity and Politics in a 'Postmodern' Gay Culture: Some Historical and Conceptual Notes." In *Fear of a Queer Planet: Queer Politics and Social Theory*, ed. Michael Warner, 105–42. Minneapolis: University of Minnnesota Press.

Snow, David A., E. Burke Rochford, Steven K. Worden, and Robert D. Benford. 1986. "Frame Alignment Processes, Micromobilization, and Movement Participation. *American Sociological Review* 51: 464–81.

Snow, David A., and Robert D. Benford. 1988. "Ideology, Frame Resonance, and Participant Mobilization." In *From Structure to Action: Comparing Social Movement Research Across Cultures (International Social Movement Research*, vol. 1), ed. Bert Klandermans, Hanspeter Kriesi, and Sidney Tarrow, 197–217. Greenwich, Conn.: JAI Press.

Snow, David, and Danny Trom. 2002. "The Case Study and the Study of Social Movements." In *Methods of Social Movement Research*, ed. Bert Klandermans and Suzanne Staggenborg, 146–72. Minneapolis: University of Minnesota Press.

Stein, Arlene. 1998. "Whose Memories? Whose Victimhood? Contests for the Holocaust Frame in Recent Movement Discourse." *Sociological Perspectives* 41: 519–40.

Sturmon, Sarah. 1992. "Group Opposes Legal Protection for Gays." *The Cincinnati Post*, May 20, 1992, p. 10A.

Taylor, Verta, and Nicole Raeburn. 1995. "Identity Politics as High-Risk Activism: Career Consequences for Lesbian, Gay, and Bisexual Sociologists." *Social Problems*, 42: 252–73.

Taylor, Verta, and Nancy Whittier. 1992. "Collective Identity in Social Movement Communities: Lesbian Feminist Mobilization." In *Frontiers in Social Movement Theory.* ed. Aldon D. Morris and Carol McClurg Mueller, 104–32. New Haven, Conn.: Yale University Press.

Thomas, W. I. 1923. *The Unadjusted Girl.* Boston: Little, Brown, and Co.

Tremblay, Marc-Adélard. 1957. "The Key Informant Technique: A Non-Ethnographic Application." *American Anthropologist* 59: 688–701.

Zald, Mayer N., and Bert Useem. 1987. "Movement and Countermovement Interaction: Mobilization, Tactics, and State Involvement." In *Social Movements in
an Organizational Society*, ed. Mayer N. Zald and John D. McCarthy, 247–72.
New Brunswick, N.J.: Transaction.

Zuo, Jiping, and Robert Benford. 1995. "Mobilization Processes and the 1989 Chinese Democracy Movement." *Sociological Quarterly* 36: 131–56.

Notes

1. While the state of Ohio's population is 85 percent white and 11.5 percent
black, the city of Cincinnati along with Cleveland and Columbus boasts larger numbers of African Americans (http://www.state.ohio.us). Around the time of the Issue
campaign, nearly half (44.7 percent) of the blacks in the state of Ohio lived in cities
of Cincinnati, Cleveland, and Columbus (U.S. Bureau of Census 1990). In addition, sources assert that more than one third (38 percent) of the city of Cincinnati
was comprised of black people compared to figures of 58–60 percent white (http://
www3.akron.edu; U.S. Bureau of Census 1990).

2. Categories covered included race, gender, age, color, religion, disability status, marital status, ethnic, national or Appalachian origin, and sexual orientation.

3. Note that this same organizational name was used in the Colorado antigay
campaign.

4. Gay and Lesbian March Association was formed to aid in the organizing of the
National March on Washington in 1993. They remained active by combining with ACT
UP, a well-known organization whose activism revolved primarily around AIDS.

5. Equal Rights Not Special Rights/Take Back Cincinnati Document Collection. 1993. Binder no. 2, emphasis in original.

6. Interview no. 22.

7. Equal Rights Not Special Rights/Take Back Cincinnati Document Collection. 1993. "Equal Rights," Equal Rights Not Special Rights Television Advertisement no. 3. October 9.

8. Interview no. 12.

9. While the state of Ohio's population is 85 percent white and 11.5 percent
black, the city of Cincinnati along with Cleveland and Columbus boasts larger numbers of African Americans (http://www.state.ohio.us). Various statistics are available.
One reliable source claims that more than one third (38 percent) of the city is comprised of black people compared to 58 percent whites (http://www3.akron.edu).

10. Equal Rights Not Special Rights/Take Back Cincinnati Document Collection. 1993. "Some People Say" Equal Rights Not Special Rights Television Advertisement no. 1. October 9.

11. Traditional Values Coalition. 1993. *Gay Rights/Special Rights: Inside the Homosexual Agenda*. Jeremiah Films, Inc. TVC: Anaheim, California.

12. Equal Rights Not Special Rights/Take Back Cincinnati Document Collection. 1993. "Income," Equal Rights Not Special Rights Television Advertisement no. 6. October 9.; Traditional Values Coalition. 1993. *Gay Rights/Special Rights: Inside the Homosexual Agenda*. Jeremiah Films, Inc. Traditional Values Coalition: Anaheim, California.; Equal Rights Not Special Rights/Take Back Cincinnati Document Collection. 1993. Take Back Cincinnati "Solicitation Letter," June, Binder no. 2. Interestingly, in the videotape the same figure was reported as the average for African Americans in general without the "1–3 years of high school" qualifier.

13. Equal Rights Not Special Rights/Take Back Cincinnati Document Collection. 1993. "Politically Powerless," Equal Rights Not Special Rights Television Advertisement no. 5. October 9.

14. Equal Rights Not Special Rights/Take Back Cincinnati Document Collection. 1993. Binder no. 1:p4.

15. Interview no. 8.

16. Interview no. 6.

17. *Ruling and Reigning in the '90s* by Charles Winburn. 1989. Ridgeacres Christian.

18. Equal Rights Not Special Rights/Take Back Cincinnati Document Collection. 1993. Binder no. 1, no. 2.

19. Interview no. 6 and Interview no. 20.

20. Ibid.

21. Interview no. 23.

22. Equality Cincinnati Document Collection/Equality Cincinnati PAC. 1993. Campaign Television Advertisement—"Vote No On Issue 3." Cincinnati, Ohio.

23. Equality Cincinnati Document Collection/Equality Cincinnati PAC. 1993. File no. 1 and no. 2.

24. Equality Cincinnati Document Collection/Equality Cincinnati PAC. 1993. File no.1.

25. Ibid.

26. Ibid.

27. Ibid.

28. MacLarty, Scott. 1993. "READERS' VIEWS Issue 3 will deprive gays of equal rights" The Cincinnati Enquirer, October 23: A07.

29. Equality Cincinnati Document Collection/Equality Cincinnati PAC. 1993. File no. 1.

2

"We're Not Just Lip-synching Up Here": Music and Collective Identity in Drag Performances

Elizabeth Kaminski and Verta Taylor

Social movement scholars have demonstrated that the construction of a collective identity among participants is essential to the mobilization and success of such social movements as feminism (Roth 2000; Rupp and Taylor 1999), peace activism (Hunt and Benford 1994), and gay and lesbian movements (Taylor and Whittier 1992; Valocchi 1999). Taylor and Whittier define collective identity as a "shared definition of a group" or a "sense of 'we'" (1992, 105, 110) and suggest that it entails an ongoing process of negotiating boundaries between insiders and outsiders. Numerous scholars have documented the ways in which movement participants establish such boundaries (e.g., Morris and Braine 2001; Stein 2001; Waite 2001) and merge their personal identities with the collective identity of a social movement community (Snow and McAdam 2000; Klandermans and deWeerd 2000; Taylor and Rupp 1993).

Despite the well-established importance of collective identity to social movements, the boundaries of political communities are neither clear nor immutable. Social movement researchers have identified a variety of internal movement and external contextual processes associated with boundary demarcation. Scholars such as Gamson (1996), Esterberg (1997), Stein (1997), Reger (2002), and Gilmore and Kaminski (2007) have shown that the collective identities of gay, lesbian, and feminist communities are fluid in part because of the boundary contestation that occurs when particular subgroups battle to gain legitimate standing within a movement. Bernstein (1997) and Whittier (1995) have found that social movement boundaries shift because collective identity is negotiated over the life course of a movement in response to changes in the political context. Social movement actors also reach across identity boundaries to enlist allies and attract new participants and sympathizers, and this complicates a movement's collective identity. For example, Broad (2002) shows how members of the group Parents, Families, & Friends of Lesbians & Gays organize around the identity of ally, simultaneously positioning themselves as outsiders and participants of the gay and lesbian movement. The research reported thus far supports the general contention that collective identity construction in social movements is a complicated process that involves both articulating and transcending boundaries between social movement actors and their targets.

Although there is general agreement that the construction of collective identity is one of the most central tasks of any movement (W. Gamson 1991), much remains to be learned about the causal mechanisms at work in the alignment of personal and collective identities. Kemper (2001) suggests that this process depends not only on a movement's ability to invoke solidarity among participants but also on the emotional response of bystanders sympathetic to the group's plight. In her research on the animal rights movement, Einwohner (2002) found support for the view that emotion is bound up in identity construction. Attacks by opponents who accused animal activists of being overly emotional and irrational were critical to the activist identity negotiated by the movement. As these studies suggest, social movements are engaged in a complex process of negotiation to create solidarity and collective agency among participants while simultaneously reaching out to potential allies.

Researchers can learn a great deal about collective identity formation by studying the toolkit (Swidler 1986) of specific tactics used by a set of collective actors. The tactical repertoires used by social movements have an *internal* movement-building function and are directed at *external* targets. Protest events serve as sites for negotiating the relationship and boundaries between a set of political actors, their opponents, and the authorities to which they direct their claims (McAdam, Tarrow, and Tilly 2001; Taylor and Van Dyke 2004). In this chapter we are interested in the role of music and song in shaping identity and consciousness. Music and songs are commonly used tactical repertoires of social movements, and music can evoke the kind of strong emotional response that Melucci (1995) and others (Eyerman and Jamison 1998; Whitter 2001; Taylor and Rupp 2002; Roscigno and Danaher 2004; Futrell, Simi, and Gottschalk 2006) have found to be fundamental to identity negotiation. Here, we suggest that musical performances facilitate identity work by building a sense of solidarity among diverse constituencies.

We present an analysis of drag queen performances—that is, shows in which biological men dress and perform songs as women—to understand the ways in which music and song contribute to the formation of collective identities. We begin by describing how drag performances have been an important gay and lesbian movement tactical repertoire that melds politics and entertainment to challenge conventional understandings of gender and sexuality and to illuminate gay life for mainstream heterosexual audiences. Then we present an analysis of drag performances to illustrate how music and song are used both to build solidarity and collective agency among gays and lesbians and to forge connections with heterosexuals. Analyzing the lyrics and the performances, we identify four ways in which music and song denote identity and create community. Our analysis extends the literature on the use of music by social movements (e.g., Roscigno and Danaher 2001; Eyerman and Jamison 1998; Flacks 1999) and provides a general framework for understanding music as a commonly used tactical repertoire of social movements that creates solidarity among participants at the same time that it blurs the divisions between "us" and "them."

Drag Shows as Oppositional Culture

An important component of collective identity is the creation and sustenance of an oppositional consciousness. Collective identity not only defines who "us" is but also acknowledges some injustice done to "us" and attributes it to structural causes (Taylor and Whittier 1992; W. Gamson 1992; Morris and Braine 2001). Francesca Polletta and James M. Jasper emphasize that "collective identities are expressed in a group's cultural materials—names, narratives, symbols, verbal styles, rituals, clothing, and so on" (2001, 284). When these rituals, symbols, and patterns of interaction foment a sense of injustice and critique the dominant social order, they constitute an oppositional culture. Social movements emerge from and are sustained by these oppositional cultures (Mansbridge and Morris 2001). Morris (1984), for example, describes how racial segregation facilitated the creation of separate, oppositional institutions, such as black churches, among African Americans. These institutions were beds of oppositional culture that fostered the sense of solidarity and injustice necessary to sustain the civil rights movement.

Here we consider drag shows as sites where a gay oppositional culture is created, although the performances also depend on some degree of participation by outsiders or heterosexuals who represent dominant groups. Scholars have documented the existence of drag shows as vibrant elements of gay culture not only in large, urban areas of the United States, such as New York, Chicago (Newton 1979), and San Francisco (Boyd 2003), but also in smaller towns, such as Key West, Florida (Rupp and Taylor 2003), Louisville, Kentucky (Gagné and Tewksbury 1996), Kansas City, Missouri (Newton 1979), and Spokane, Washington (Schacht 2000). In addition to drag queen shows, drag king performances are gaining in popularity across the United States and in Canada (Halberstam 1998; Troika, Lebesco, and Noble 2002).

Leila Rupp and Verta Taylor's (2003) research on drag performances, from which the data for this chapter come, suggests that drag queen performances constitute an important part of the lesbian and gay movement's collective action repertoire that is used strategically for the purpose of disrupting hegemonic gender and sexual categories and hierarchies. Historical evidence (e.g., Boyd 2003; Chauncey 1994; Garber 1989; Katz 1976; Mumford 1997) supports this argument by showing that throughout the twentieth century, drag performances have been not only large social gatherings but also precursors of community organizing and overt political action on behalf of gays and lesbians. Drag performers have often played important roles in such acts of resistance as the 1969 Stonewall riots (Duberman 1994; Kaiser 1997)—in which patrons and employees of a gay bar fought back against police harassment—and in conjunction with public rallies, marches, demonstrations, and other performative tactics used by the modern gay movement (J. Gamson 1989). Because of their willingness to identify themselves as gay in public, drag queens have been central to affirming gay collective identity and creating the kind of cognitive, affective, and moral attachments among gay individuals that lead to investments in social movement activity.

While drag shows have built solidarity and political consciousness among gays and lesbians, since the late nineteenth century, drag shows also have been popular forms of entertainment for heterosexual audiences. Drawing from newspaper evidence, Chauncey shows that drag balls in 1930s New York attracted several thousand gay and heterosexual onlookers, contributing to what he terms "a pansy craze" (1994). In Harlem in particular, drag balls attracted crowds that were diverse not only with respect to sexuality but also along lines of class and race (Garber 1989). During World War II, drag found a surprising home when soldier drag queens, both black and white, put on elaborate shows to entertain their buddies, and the army provided scripts, music, lyrics, set designs, and dress patterns (Bérubé 1990). More recently, Hollywood films that center on drag queens, such as *The Birdcage*; *To Wong Foo, Thanks for Everything, Julie Newmar*; and *Connie and Carla*, suggest that drag shows continue to appeal to a diverse audience. The mainstream popularity of drag queens is also apparent in a 2005 *New York Times Magazine* (February 13, 2005) article on professional matchmakers, which included a photograph of drag queen Dame Edna dressed in a cupid-style costume, complete with bow and arrow, wings, and a purple wig.

Music and song are vital to understanding how drag shows serve as vehicles for the expression of gay identity and culture (Kaminski 2003). Up until the 1960s, drag queens actually sang, accompanied by live music. However, the repression of gay culture following World War II led some areas to ban female impersonation in cafés, restaurants, and other establishments, and female impersonators in some cities had to carry cabaret cards to prove they were performers (Drexel 1997). The legal restrictions against crossdressing entertainers channeled drag performances into more disreputable commercial establishments that catered more exclusively to gay crowds. These gay clubs employed younger, more marginal, and confrontational "street impersonators" who would lip-synch to recorded music (Newton 1979). Throughout the 1960s, both in gay clubs and in tourist-oriented nightclubs, such as Finnochio's in San Francisco or the Jewel Box Review in Miami, drag performers began to appropriate a fairly standard repertoire of songs made up of mainstream popular music, show tunes, and songs with explicitly gay lyrics. As the gay and lesbian movement gained momentum beginning in the 1970s, drag shows in various parts of the country began to take on a ritualized quality, drawing heavily on camp, which is a gay cultural practice that uses humor and dialogue to parody the social conventions that exclude gay men and lesbians (Sontag 2002). Contemporary drag shows are made up of a relatively standard repertoire of songs, dialogue, humor, and routines that make them a central part of the oppositional culture of the gay community. In some contemporary drag shows, performers sing in their own voices. Most commonly, however, drag queens lip-synch to recordings of songs by female artists to emphasize the disjuncture between their biological sex and their performance of femininity.

The role that drag shows play in gay cultural life cannot be fully understood without attention to the music and song in the performances. To understand how contemporary drag shows function as vehicles for political expression, our analysis builds on the social movement literature that finds that music is a useful resource in social protest because it enhances solidarity (Roscigno and Danaher 2001). We focus on the integral role that music and song play both in forging a sense of solidarity and common fate among gays and lesbians and in appealing to sympathizers and potential heterosexual allies.

Data and Methods

We base our analysis on a field study of drag queen performances at the 801 Bourbon Bar & Cabaret in Key West, Florida, over a three-year period from

1998 to 2001 (Rupp and Taylor 2003). Key West has a thriving drag entertainment industry, and the 801 Cabaret hosts a two-hour show that begins at eleven o'clock every night of the year. The 801 Cabaret provides an apt case to examine complex identity negotiations because of the diversity of its audiences. Located in a popular tourist destination, the cabaret attracts audience members—gay and heterosexual, men and women—from around the world.

One reason why the 801 Cabaret attracts a diverse audience is that the performers stand on the sidewalk on Duval Street, the main street in Key West, in full drag in order to recruit passersby to the show. The drag queens remind people on the street that the performances are free, which is an incentive to come to the show because entertainment can be expensive in Key West. As a result, the 801 draws in audience members who have never before seen a drag show, and the drag queens work particularly hard to recruit newcomers and heterosexuals because they consider their presence crucial to the performance. The audiences typically include both men and women from all points on the sexual spectrum, as well as people from various religious, racial, and class backgrounds.

Our analysis is based on multiple data sources. First, we observed, recorded, and transcribed over fifty drag performances, paying attention to the costumes, dialogue, music, and audience interactions. Second, we conducted content analyses of seventy-four songs that were used repeatedly in the shows we observed and were identified by the performers as part of their standard repertoire. We examined the lyrics of each song, the talk used to introduce it, and the audience interaction typically associated with it. Our third source of data are interviews with nine drag queens—Milla, Sushi, Gugi, RV, Kylie, Margo, Scabola Feces, Inga, and Desiray—who performed regularly at the 801 Cabaret. For purposes of this analysis, we are interested in the performers' descriptions of why they chose particular songs and the songs' impact on the audience. Finally, unlike earlier studies of drag that concentrate mainly on the performers (e.g., Newton 1979; Schacht 2000), we conducted twelve focus groups with members of the audience in order to understand the role of music and song in shaping the identity and consciousness of participants. The focus groups consisted of forty people: nineteen women, twenty men, and one person who identified as intersexed. More than two-thirds of the focus group participants identified as gay, lesbian, bisexual, or transsexual. Tables 2.1 and 2.2 summarize these characteristics of the focus group participants. Those willing to come to the focus groups were more likely to have liked or been affected by the show and to be gay. To overcome this bias, we conducted informal conversations and short interviews with an additional 55 audience members, three-fourths of whom identified as heterosexual.

Table 2.1. Characteristics of focus group participants

Race			Education			Class Identification			Religion			Age	
	n	%		n	%		n	%		n	%		
White	36	90	Some High School	4	10	Working Class	8	20	Catholic	10	25	Median	35
Latino/a	2	5	High School Degree	5	12.5	Lower-Middle Class	0	0	Jewish	9	22.5	Low	19
Mixed Race	2	5	Some College	9	22.5	Middle Class	10	25	Protestant	7	17.5	High	62
			College Degree	12	30	Upper-Middle Class	18	45	Other	4	10		
			Graduate or Professional Degree	10	25	Upper Class	4	10	None	10	25		
Totals	40	100		40	100		40	100		40	100		

Table 2.2. Additional characteristics of focus group participants

	Sex		Sexual Identification			Residence		
	n	%		n	%		n	%
Female	19	47.5	Gay or Lesbian	23	57.5	Full-time Key West Locals	11	27.5
Male	20	50	Bisexual	2	5	Outside of Key West	24	60
Intersexed	1	2.5	Heterosexual	12	30	Dual Residence		
			Did not mark /			(Key West and Elsewhere)	5	12.5
			Other[a]	3	7.5			
Totals	40	100		40	100		40	100

[a]Other Comments included "queer" and "trysexual"

Using Music to Affirm and Cross Identity Boundaries

Music and song in drag performances are integral to the boundary work that constitutes a central dynamic in collective identity construction. Drag shows bring gays and heterosexuals together in an environment that melds entertainment and politics. Many of the songs that drag queens perform articulate grievances and opportunities that relate to the oppression experienced by gays and lesbians and promote the construction of a collective self and other, an "us" and "them," between gay/lesbian/bisexual and heterosexual audience members. At the same time, the shows at the 801 simultaneously create a second level of collective identity and sense of unity across identity categories. The drag queens' repertoire of numbers includes widely known popular songs and show tunes that tap into the experiences of heterosexual audience members and build bridges between gay and heterosexual members of the audience.

In our focus group interviews, gay, lesbian, bisexual, and heterosexual audience members described feeling a sense of solidarity during the performances. This sense of community was emphasized especially by people who live in Key West and attend the shows regularly. For example, a local heterosexual woman described the 801 crowd as a "family." Similarly, a local gay man described the show as being "about community. It's about all of us. We're all here for the same reason. Like we all love each other but we're all here because we love the great show." The drag queens themselves also talk about the close-knit networks organized around the shows. Describing the performers and audience members at the 801, for example, performer Milla explained, "We are a group. We are a community."

Other focus group participants who were tourists spoke less of the specific, intimate networks created at the 801 but nonetheless described a general sense of "gay" culture and solidarity that emerges during the drag performances. When asked why they attended the show, two young lesbians from Orlando, Florida, replied in unison "for the community." A twenty-three-year-old lesbian health teacher from New Jersey explained why she and her partner came to the show, stating: "I think the reason we came here . . . was because we knew we would be in an atmosphere where we could be ourselves and not have a problem. Yes, we came to see the show, but we also came because we knew it would be okay for us to be here and be ourselves since it is what you would call a gay event." Likewise, a thirty-six-year-old lesbian who had attended other drag shows in New York, New Orleans, and San Francisco explained that she attends the shows because drag is "a form of gay entertainment."

While many gay men and lesbians in the audience explained that they came to the drag shows in order to experience being part of a gay community, heterosexuals also described a sense of belonging associated with being in the audience. For example, a forty-six-year-old heterosexual woman from Boca Raton expressed her delight in the show, explaining that she enjoyed it because even as a member of the audience, "we were part of the entertainment." A heterosexual woman from New York who had attended the same show commented on how the drag queens "got everybody engaged and kept everybody engaged and not too focused on one group or another. . . . I like the fact that the audience was so diverse and it's not just one type." A college student from Columbus, Ohio explained that as she walked into the show, she initially felt that she might not belong there because she was heterosexual. Over the course of the evening, however, her feelings changed: "I think my initial thought when we were going to go in was I am entering into someone else's territory—like this isn't my space. . . . But then I think that the show really loosens people up, and it doesn't matter." Gays and lesbians in the audience echoed this theme of inclusion. One gay man explained "It's men, women, we're all here together, we're all straight, gay, it's ok." A young gay man who vacations in Key West every year and attends the shows every night he is in town described what the show signifies to him: "We have these differences but we are all together within this small space, communing, interacting, being entertained, having a good time. . . . And I think the idea of being able to make some sort of utopia, or this is the way it could be. Once we leave this bar if we can all see four different people that are different and commune together or at least respect each other, then wouldn't the world be a little bit better place?"

Drag performers are able to construct a sense of solidarity among such a diverse audience in part because of their strategic use of music (for a discussion of other identity construction processes in drag shows, see Taylor, Rupp, and Gamson 2007). Drag queens utilize songs that accomplish four identity-related processes. First, drag queens work to build solidarity among gays and lesbians by repetitiously performing widely known songs associated with gay culture; these songs serve a *ritual* function in drag performances. Second, drag queens include in their repertoire songs that *educate* heterosexual members of the audience about the experiences and grievances of gay men, lesbians, and transgendered individuals. Third, drag queens perform songs that mock, critique, and *disidentify* with heterosexuality, creating a space that challenges heteronormativity.[1] Finally, drag shows include songs that facilitate *interaction* between gay and nongay members of the audience so that heterosexuals are integrated into the performances, even as they are made aware of their presence, criticized, and held accountable for the oppression of gays and lesbians. Table 2.3 classifies the seventy-four typical drag songs

Table 2.3. Typical drag songs used at the 801 (n = 74)

Song Title	Ritual	Education	Disidentification	Interaction
"All that Jazz"				X
"Automatic" / "I'm So Excited"		X		
"Barbie Girl"			X	
"Bitch"			X	X
"Bohemian Rhapsody"		X		
"Boogie, Woogie, Bugle Boy"	X			
"Brass in Pocket"			X	X
"Break it to Me Gently"			X	
"Cabaret"	X			X
"Carpenter's Medley"			X	
"Cell Block Tango"			X	X
"Chicago, Illinois"				X
"Crazy World"	X	X	X	
"Cruela De Vil"			X	
"Dream Girls"			X	
"Erotica"	X			X
"Free Your Mind"		X		
"From a Distance"	X			
"Hanky Panky"	X		X	X
"Heaven's What I Feel"				X
"Hey Big Spender"				X
"I am the Body Beautiful"				X
"I Am What I Am"	X			
"I Kissed a Girl"		X	X	X
"I Love the Nightlife"		X		
"I Think He's Gay"	X	X		
"I Will Survive"	X		X	
"If You Could Read my Mind"		X	X	
"I'm a Woman"			X	X
"I'm Beautiful Dammit"	X			

Table 2.3. Typical drag songs used at the 801 (n = 74) (continued)

Song Title	Ritual	Education	Disidentification	Interaction
"I'm Not a Fucking Drag Queen"			X	
"I'm the Only One"			X	X
"It's Not Right, But It's Okay"			X	X
"Jefferson's Theme Song"			X	X
"Justify My Love"	X			X
"Kiss Me"			X	X
"Lady Marmalade"	X	X	X	X
"Le Jazz Hot"				X
"Look at Me"	X		X	X
"Mountain's O' Things"			X	
"My Discarded Men"	X			
"My Heart Will Go On"				X
"No One Else on Earth"				X
"The Oldest Profession"		X	X	
"One Man's Trash is Another Man's Treasure"		X	X	
"Oye"				X
"Passionate Kisses"			X	X
"Pour Me a Man"			X	X
"The Pussycat Song"		X	X	
"Queen of the Night"			X	X
"Saved"	X		X	
"The Shady Dame from Seville"	X			
"Special"			X	X
Spice Girls' Medley			X	
"Strut"				X
"Stuff Like That There"	X			
"Take Me or Leave Me"	X	X		X
"Tell Me"			X	X
"There Are Worse Things I Could Do"			X	
"This Kiss"				X
"Torn"			X	X
"Tyrone"		X	X	X
"We are What We Are"	X	X		
"Wedding Bell Blues"			X	X
"What Makes a Man a Man"	X	X		
"What's Up"		X		X
"When a Man Loves a Woman"	X		X	X
"When You're Good to Mamma"			X	
"Where Is My Man"	X		X	X
"Why Don't You Do Right"				X
"You Don't Own Me"			X	X
"We Are Family"	X			
"You Oughta Know"		X	X	X
"You've Got to See Mamma, Every Night"				X
Totals	23	18	39	44

according to these categories, with some songs coded as serving multiple identity functions. We turn now to an analysis of the music and song in the show, making clear how music contributes to the audience members' feelings of belonging to a collectivity and to political consciousness.

Ritual

In drag shows, we find that particular songs associated with gay culture are used repeatedly, not only at the 801 Cabaret but also in drag bars across the United States and in other countries (Kaminski 2003). Performers and audience members alike sometimes referred to these songs as "gay anthems." These songs enhance a feeling of solidarity among gays and lesbians through their familiarity and appeal to common experiences. Of the seventy-four typical drag songs analyzed here, we coded twenty-three (31 percent) as gay anthems.

One song that was frequently described as a "gay anthem" was Gloria Gaynor's 1970s hit song "I Will Survive." A participant in one of the focus groups explained how this song appeals to him by reminding him of his experiences coming out as a gay man: "The songs like 'I Will Survive' or any of the disco anthems, they're always about relationships and love and sex and having a good time and things like that and usually I associate them with when I was younger and single and going out to the bars and having a good time and having fun. . . . Those songs remind me of those times."

Other songs that were considered gay anthems—or "classic fag," as one drag queen remarked—include Patti LaBelle's "Lady Marmalade" and songs by Bette Midler, Cher, Madonna, Tina Turner, Eartha Kitt, and several artists from the 1970s disco genre. The continued popularity of disco in gay culture is likely due to an historical association: the emergence of disco coincided with the elaboration of gay institutions across the United States in the 1970s. These songs enhance gay solidarity by reinforcing a sense of common history. Ronald Eyerman and Andrew Jamison (1998) suggest that references to shared history are a typical way in which musical lyrics build collective identity. Moreover, as Judy Kutalas (2003) notes, female disco artists—including the heroine who survives a lost love affair in the Gloria Gaynor song—often project images of sexual liberation, assertiveness, and pride. These images resonate with the cultural ideals of gay communities, which focus on transforming shame over a stigmatized sexual identity into gay pride (Britt and Heise 2000; Gould 2001).

Another song that was sometimes introduced during the shows as the "gay national anthem" is "I Am What I Am" from the musical *La Cage Aux*

Folles (*The Bird Cage*). At the 801, this song is performed by Margo, the oldest performer at the cabaret—or as she refers to herself, "the oldest living drag queen in captivity." Like the disco anthems, the lyrics of this song articulate a sense of pride and assertiveness. The lyrics also use the familiar "closet" metaphor specifically to address the coming out process among gays and lesbians: "It's one life and there's no return and no deposits. / One life so it's time to open up your closets." In drag shows, this song becomes a ritual not only because of the frequency of its inclusion but also because the manner in which it is performed is highly predictable. During each performance of the song, Margo removes her wig at the end of the number, breaking the illusion of femininity by exposing her underlying short and thinning hair. This performance was expected for audiences who attended the 801 on a regular basis, but it was also familiar to audience members who had attended drag shows elsewhere. Removing the wig at the end of this song is a common technique institutionalized by drag performers across the country. Members of our focus groups described seeing the same performance in such locations as Provincetown, Massachusetts and Columbus, Ohio. This style of performing "I Am What I Am" is so common that Sushi, the house queen at the 801, referred to it as "old-school drag" and wondered why audiences never tire of it.

Despite the repetitive style of performance, gay audience members identified this song as a favorite. Describing her feelings the first time she saw a drag queen perform "I Am What I Am" during a show in Provincetown, Massachusetts, one focus group participant stated: "He ended up taking off the makeup and singing 'I Am what I Am,' and I always get choked up now when I hear that song because there was a thing of acceptance, and I was really struggling with accepting being gay and I just felt a connection. And I think that's what made me want to keep coming back is feeling that connection." This quotation describes the transformation of shame into pride that is central to the political mobilization of such marginalized groups as gays and lesbians (Britt and Heise 2000; Gould 2001; Taylor 2000). It also illustrates how music and ritualized performances facilitate the emotional transformation necessary to construct a sense of solidarity and belonging. Other scholars of social movements, including Eyerman (2002) and Vincent Roscigno and William Danaher (2001), have noted that such ritualistic behaviors as dancing and shouting surround musical performances and foster a sense of commonality. Here we suggest that ritualized performances in drag shows contribute in a similar way to a sense of solidarity among gays and lesbians in the audience.

Education

Of the seventy-four drag songs that typically make up the shows at the 801 Cabaret, the lyrics of eighteen (24 percent) focus on the experiences, sexual practices, and problems that gays and lesbians face. Drag queens perform these numbers to educate heterosexual audience members about gay life. One of the most common drag show songs identified by name in the focus groups is French singer-songwriter Charles Aznouvar's "What Makes a Man a Man." The song provides a first-person account of the life of a drag queen, and the lyrics describe a drag performance from the eyes of a performer. RV, who performs the song regularly at the 801 Cabaret, explained that he first heard it at "Wigstock," a "dragstravaganza" held annually between 1983 and 2002 in New York City that attracted drag performers, gay men, lesbians, and transgendered individuals. RV performs the song by coming onto the stage in "full drag," wearing makeup, a wig, and a sequined dress. As the song progresses, RV removes his makeup with a towel, takes off his wig and falsies, and finally exchanges his dress for a pair of sweatpants and a T-shirt, eventually emerging as his male persona.

Although the song emphasizes the social and performative aspects of gender, it also addresses the homophobia that drag queens confront as gay men. The lyrics depict an individual being taunted for not conforming to conventions of masculinity and heterosexuality; they state, "So many times we have to pay / For having fun and being gay." This verse of the song revealingly begins with the pronoun "we," rather than "I," which was used in the first verse. In this way, the lyrics address not only the individual experiences of a drag queen but also the homophobia gay men and lesbians encounter collectively.

Several focus group participants emphasized how this song educates heterosexuals about the difficulties faced by gays and lesbians. A twenty-three-year-old lesbian from New Jersey stated: "If they [heterosexuals] look into those songs and really try to listen to the words, especially 'What Makes a Man a Man,' then maybe they would start thinking about what it means to be gay. . . . You know, especially for people who aren't really sure about what it is, and I think they could—if they're looking for a message or if they really pay attention—I think that they could get it." RV similarly explains the response he receives from members of the audience after performing the song: "With 'What Makes a Man a Man,' mothers come up to me on that one. And they say, 'you just put it all into a nutshell, what my son goes through. Now, I can understand what my son's going through.' It makes me shiver just thinking about it." A heterosexual local Key West woman commented, "I mean it just makes you cry. . . . [I]t really touched me."

In addition to describing homophobia, the song also presents the singer asserting a positive self-identity and refusing to internalize the negative images of gays and lesbians: "I know my life is not a crime / I'm just a victim of my time." The lyrics therefore empower the gay listener at the same time that they educate the heterosexual audience about the hatred and oppression directed at gays and lesbians.

Interviews with performers suggest that the choice of such songs is deliberate. Sushi is self-conscious that drag shows provide an opportunity for him to educate audience members about gay life. In an article in the local Key West newspaper, Sushi emphasized, "We're not just lip-synching up here, we're changing people's lives by showing people what we're all about" (*Key West Citizen*, June 2, 2001). In another context, she explains that her drag shows aim to promote tolerance: "I have a platform now to teach the world. We have so many people from everywhere in the world. . . . Even in less than five minutes of talking to somebody—just that little moment I share with somebody from New Zealand or Africa or your college professor or whoever—they go back to their hometowns. They remember that five-minute conversation, and they realize, 'I'm not gonna call this person a fag.' You know what I mean? It's just a little part that I am a real person."

Some songs used in the shows are not directly about gay life, but in the context of the drag show, the lyrics take on new meaning and can be interpreted as describing issues faced by the gay community. One popular example is the song "Bohemian Rhapsody," originally performed by Freddie Mercury and the band Queen in the early 1980s and rerecorded by the pop duo The Braids. The song was originally written to describe the pain and suffering that result from gang violence.[2] When Milla introduces the number at the 801 show, however, she explains that it is dedicated to friends she has lost to AIDS: "This song goes out to a lot of friends, some very dear friends of mine. I just want to say that we're here, baby, we're not going anywhere. And this is for all my dearest, and for the rest of you." Milla also suggests that the performance is a collective experience, and that she, as the performer, needs the support of the crowd: "Please at this time give it up for Milla. Come on, I need you tonight." The lyrics of the song are strangely applicable to the agony of dying from AIDS:

Sends shivers down my spine,
Body's aching all the time.
Goodbye, everybody, I've got to go,
Gotta leave you all behind and face the truth.

Margo explains the emotional impact that the song has on her and other drag queens who are watching back stage: "It's very funny when you hear somebody doing it and you know they're lip-synching but it's as if they're doing it. She put so much of her anger into it. You could see it on stage. And we all sat back sobbing every time that she did that." By alluding to the pain and suffering encountered all too often by members of the gay and lesbian community, the song evokes anger and sorrow, emotionally appealing to the listener.

Not all songs about gay life evoke such serious emotions. Some rely on humor and make use of popular stereotypes of gay men. For example, RV performs "The Oldest Profession," a song from *The Life*. In the musical, the song is performed by a prostitute who laments, "I'm getting too old for the half hour session / I'm getting too old for a pro." In the context of a drag show, however, the song's references to promiscuity and numerous male sexual partners describe the stereotypical image of the hypersexualized gay man. (For a discussion of the hypermasculine and hypersexual gay male identity, see Levine 1998.) Likewise, the song "I Think He's Gay" conjures up stereotypical and recognizable images of gay men. The singer, whose voice sounds like a woman (though the song was actually recorded by a drag queen) laments that her male love interest is likely gay because "He speaks of Jane Russell / And how he loves the hustle / Talks like Liberace/ Walks like Wilma Flintstone."

Both of these songs appeal to the audience through humor. The use of stereotypical images may seem self-deprecating on the surface. However, the dialogue between songs contradicts this interpretation through positive affirmations of gay life. For example, as Margo frequently states on stage, "We are faggots in dresses . . . and we are proud of what we do." Rather than degrade, the humor asserts gay identity and images—even those deemed negative in the dominant culture—in the face of heterosexuals in audience. Therefore, both the humorous and the serious songs educate heterosexuals about gay life. A thirty-two-year-old gay man from Vermont explains in a focus group that the major point of drag shows is to educate heterosexuals about gays: "I think they show, more or less, to the straight people that we're not as bad as the media make us out to be. . . . It [the gay community] is just a variety of different people who just do something different that they're not used to, and they [heterosexuals] leave here thinking, 'well, okay, to each their own.'" Kylie explains why oppositional lyrics are so important in the shows, describing how she performs Mary Chapin Carpenter's "Passionate Kisses" to communicate that gay people deserve the same kind of dignity and worth that others have: "What I'm trying to convey is the emotion of the song, which is standing up for what you want and saying do I deserve this and shouldn't I also have this to other people. And everyone needs to do that."

The music and songs in drag shows, to some extent, serve a similar function as rap music. Black urban youth created rap and hip-hop culture in the 1970s in order to express their struggles for respect and equality (Rose 1994). Rap uses oppositional lyrics to describe racism, poverty, police brutality, and urban crime and brings these issues into the public consciousness (Rose 1994; Keyes 2004). Similarly, drag shows provide a ritualized context in which gay people use music and song not only as an act of identity expression and community acknowledgement but also to express grievances to heterosexuals in order to make them conscious of the plight of gay, lesbian, and transgendered people.

Disidentification

Because of the oppositional nature of the performances, drag queens select songs that parody traditional codes of femininity and masculinity. These songs critique heterosexuality and draw clear boundaries between a collective self composed of gays and lesbians and a collective other made up of heterosexuals who are keenly aware that they are in a gay space. Disidentification is a strategy of transforming culture from within by taking dominant cultural symbols and working against them to critique hegemonic roles and identities and create new identities (Muñoz 1999, 11–12). For example, in drag shows, performers commonly use songs that evoke images of marriage and heterosexuality only to disidentify with those institutions. Of the drag songs analyzed here, thirty-nine (53 percent) use disidentification in which the performers appropriate dominant gender and sexual practices and symbols but use the fact that femininity and heterosexuality are being performed by gay men to convey a hybrid and more fluid model of gender and sexuality.

One example of a performance that implements disidentification is Scabola Feces's rendition of the 1970s Laura Nyro hit, "Wedding Bell Blues." The lyrics of the song portray a woman begging her boyfriend to marry her; her angst over the matter is her "wedding bell blues." Scabby's performance mocks the image of femininity and dependency that is implicit in the song's words. Scabby appears on stage in a torn wedding dress, phony rotten teeth, a teased wig, and garishly excessive makeup. In the middle of the song, she often pulls a young handsome heterosexual man out of the audience, embraces him, and refuses to let him return to his seat for the duration of the number. The result is a performance that encourages the audience to laugh and look critically at dominant constructions of sexuality, femininity, and marriage. Scabby's performance scrutinizes these cultural ideals, and the political message affirms a gay identity in opposition to mainstream heterosexuality. One gay male focus group participant explained that he loved it when the drag queens "hassle the straight men." A second focus group participant chimed in, "That's one of the best things. We love that."

In addition to "hassling straight men" and disidentifying with heterosexuality, the drag performers also formulate serious critiques of masculinity. Kylie explains how she performs Sheena Easton's "Strut," which is a song about how men want women as sex objects: "I try to convey that message. This is what you want from women. You know I try to be very aggressive and mean and I'll slap a man in the audience with the whip." One of Milla's standard performances at the 801 show is of the song "When a Man Loves a Woman." As in "Wedding Bell Blues," the lyrics of the song initially appear to paint a romanticized picture of heterosexual romance. The words describe how a man who has fallen in love, "Can't keep his mind on nothing else / He'll trade the world for the good thing he found." Milla's performance of the song and his strategic choice of the recording by gay icon Bette Midler, however, cast the lyrics in a new light. Near the end of the song, a key change signals both the musical climax of the piece and a sudden transformation of the meaning of the lyrics. Through Midler's rendition, Milla questions the romanticized portrayal of masculinity and heterosexuality, saying "Well, you told me you love me, baby" but "this is a man's world." With this last line, the song exposes the patriarchy that underlies chivalry and dominant sex and gender relations, suggesting that the romanticism described earlier cannot be trusted "in a man's world." Milla's gestures during the performance underscore this interpretation. At the beginning of the song, she holds her hands close to her face and chest, enacting demure femininity. Throughout the number, her gestures grow angrier and she clenches her fists and raises them in the air as she finishes the number. At the end of the song, she typically turns away from the audience and walks off stage in an apparent display of disgust. A gay man in one of our focus groups recognized the contestation inherent in the performance and described Milla as "attack[ing] the audience not necessarily in a mean way, but just kind of like forcing you to stop and think."

In an interview, Milla reveals that the disidentification with masculinity in her performances is intentional. She also explains how music enables this critique: "All my songs are similar. They're about being victimized by men, and pain, and anger." By utilizing songs by such "powerful women" as Bette Midler, Eryka Badu, or Alanis Morrisette, Milla replaces hegemonic definitions of gender with new definitions of femininity: "All the women that I have chosen are women who are strong and they believe in themselves. I wouldn't sing about it if they didn't believe in themselves." Expressing the view of the majority of the gays and lesbians in our focus groups, one gay man thought that the show "really pushes gender identity and gender role and homophobia issues with straight people."

In their performances the drag queens also take dominant depictions of masculinity and femininity and combine them in ways that create new gender possibilities. During his performance of the Melissa Etheridge song "I'm the Only One," Kylie grabs the ceiling rafters and swings from the stage into the audience. Describing this performance, a gay man in a focus group stated, "I think it's neat to see a woman expressing all sides of her. . . . It's a man but I mean . . . no, I mean it's a woman who can explore her masculine side. Can jump through the rafters." His boyfriend, with whom he attended the show, elaborated: "It's like a different persona all together than male/female. I look at them as a woman because that's what you see. But I mean when you see it and the performance and everything else it's way more than being a woman; and it's definitely not being a man." Most other audience members had similar difficulty categorizing the drag queens as men or women. By juxtaposing women's voices, feminine clothing, and makeup with men's bodies and masculine gestures, drag queens blur these distinctions and force the audience to think beyond binary categorization.

Through their strategic use of song and skillful performance, drag queens disidentify with dominant conceptions of gender and sexuality. Drag performers select songs that invoke romanticized portrayals of heterosexuality and hegemonic definitions of masculinity and femininity. Yet they raise these images only to critique, parody, or otherwise reject them. In their place, the performers construct positive images of powerful femininity and identities that defy simple categorization as male or female or gay or straight.

Interaction

Although the critiques of hegemonic gender and sexuality often target or "hassle" heterosexuals, drag performances nonetheless appeal to straight audience members. Heterosexuals not only enjoy the performances but also describe a sense of belonging during the show, and three-fourths of our focus group participants described the shows as creating a sense of equality and unity between different genders and sexualities. Drag performers are able to maintain this sense of solidarity by using popular songs to facilitate interaction between audience members. Of the seventy-four songs performed in the show, forty-four (59 percent) involve interaction between the drag queens and audience members, and much of that interaction is explicitly sexual. In her discussion of "music in everyday life," DeNora (2000) notes that music can elicit social behaviors and can therefore be considered a cultural script for interactions. When drag performers bring popular songs into the shows, audience members often respond to the familiar music by dancing and singing along, sometimes even jumping on to the stage to perform, thereby becoming part of the act themselves.

At the 801 Cabaret, the drag queens do not simply wait for the audience to be aroused to participate, but they frequently call people up to the stage and use them as props for their songs. An example of a song that serves multiple identity functions is Alanis Morrisette's "You Oughta Know," a popular drag song performed by Milla and Gugi. The lyrics portray a woman's fantasy of telling her ex-lover how much he disrupted her life by leaving her for another woman, declaring, "I'm here / To remind you / Of the mess you made when you went away." Milla, whose legal name is Dean, explained that this song allows her to convey the anger he feels as Dean toward men, such as ex-boyfriends as well as his own father, who abused him. The song therefore educates the audience about the ways in which gay men can feel abused by other men. It is also an example of disidentifying with hegemonic masculinity, and Milla's rendition almost always involves interaction with a male member of the audience. The first time Milla performed the song he portrayed his anger by pulling a man out of the audience onto the stage and pushing him around, physically challenging him:

> I could feel I was talking to my father. . . . I was talking to every mother fucking man that ever hurt me, and to every man that ever hurt anybody. At one point in the song I was so angry, I was almost crying. I was so angry, releasing it. I take this guy—I don't know where the energy came from—where the strength for me came from, especially in those heels and everything, and this is when I was still teetering on those heels. And I took him and I pulled him onto the stage, and there was no struggle. It was just like a flop, like a bird plucking a fish out of the ocean. And I just yanked him and threw him on that fucking chair, and I beat the hell out of him. I don't mean literally—he didn't walk away bleeding. And the audience went crazy. And that's when I realized I was going to get success with this.

The crowd's enthusiastic response to this number suggests that members of the audience understand the sentiment that Milla conveys and feel a sense of solidarity with the performer.

In addition, drag performers frequently use songs with sexualized lyrics to arouse audience members—often in ways that contradict their own sexual identifications. For example, a popular number at the 801 is "Hanky Panky," recorded by Madonna and performed by Sushi and Desiray. In the lyrics, the singer makes clear the sexual attention she wants from her lover:

Treat me like I'm a bad girl
Even when I'm being good to you.
I don't want you to thank me
You can just spank me.

When Desiray lip-synchs the words at the 801, she directs the performance toward members of the audience. Moments into the song, a man in the audience gets onto the stage and literally acts out the lyrics by spanking Desiray, much to the delight of Desiray and the cheering audience. When Sushi performs the number, she invites an audience member to spank her, then she sits him down in a chair, pulls his head back, and straddles his face in imitation of oral sex.

One focus group participant described the way that such songs facilitated not only sexualized interaction but also sexual arousal. A fifty-year-old, self-identified heterosexual man stated: "I'm sitting there and there's a little bit of me saying, 'this is sexually exciting,' and there's another part of me saying 'wait, you're not supposed to be sexually excited. This is a man. . . . '" That's why, I think, when they were not in synch with the music, as they were in a couple of cases, we were taken aback a bit." This audience member clearly describes the way that music creates a sexualized script that draws in members of the audience. When drag performers are in synch with the music, audience members follow the script and feel sexually excited by the performance. However, when the performers are out of synch with the music, the script is broken and audience members feel self-conscious about their sexual arousal. Still, it is clear that the performer–audience interaction causes some to question preconceived sexual identities.

Scabola's humorous rendition of Jill Sobule's "I Kissed a Girl" makes an important point about the fluidity of sexuality without generating homophobic reactions from the audience. A gay man dressed as a woman with garish makeup and false eyelashes, Scabby skips around the bar kissing women and acting embarrassed, lip-synching a song about two presumably heterosexual women who are complaining about their boyfriends and end up making out with each other: "I kissed a girl, her lips were sweet / She was just like kissing me."

The sexualized interaction and arousal between audience members and drag performers bridges divides based on gender and sexuality categories. Another heterosexual male focus group member explained, "I think that one of the beauties of attending a show like this is that you realize what you didn't know when you walked in. You know, you shouldn't walk out and say, 'I only like men,' and you shouldn't say, 'I only like women.' It all just kind of blends together a lot more." The interactions between the drag queens and the audience thus blur sexual identity categories, and the performers intentionally perform songs designed to elicit strong emotion, even visceral reactions, from the audience. In an interview, Gugi explains that their routines undermine rigid identity categories: "Lesbians in the audience always approach me after the show to tell me they are in love with me." Milla similarly explains that "we have created something that we are attractive to everybody. We have taken gender and thrown it out of the way, and we've crossed a bridge here. And when we are all up there, there is no gay, straight, or anything."

The songs performed in drag shows provide a script for interaction between performers and audience members. Drag queens select numbers that depict real-life experiences of gay men and lesbians and play upon the audience's emotions so that the music facilitates the forging of community. In this way, music and song play a critical part in blurring the boundaries between performers and audience members, as well as between gays and heterosexuals in the audience.

Conclusion

Scholars have argued that music is a powerful resource for social movements, such as the civil rights (Morris 1984), labor (Flacks 1999; Roscigno and Danaher 2001, 2004), feminist (Schippers 2002; Staggenborg, Eder, Sudderth 1994), and white power (Eyerman 2002; Futrell, Simi, and Gottschalk 2006) movements. In this paper, we have argued that music and song have also played a central role in the history and protest tradition of the gay and lesbian movement. Drag performances have a long tradition in same-sex communities as vehicles for expressing gay identity, creating and maintaining solidarity, and staging political resistance. The performances at the 801 Cabaret demonstrate how music is a resource for building identity and solidarity among a wide range of people—the identity work necessary to social movement mobilization.

Drag shows as we know them today draw on cultural resources and practices lodged in the oppositional tendencies of camp that, while built upon a perception of injustice, did not highlight it in the same way that contemporary drag does. Although scholars have debated an exact definition of "camp" (for a review see Cleto 2002), most view it as a unique aspect of gay culture, a "homosexual taste" (Newton 1979) or "gay sensibility" (Babuscio 2002). Sontag defines camp as "the love of the exaggerated, the 'off,' of things-being-what-they-are-not" (2002, 56). Some social theorists advance structural explanations of camp. Dyer (2002) suggests that camp is a defense mechanism through which gay men have responded to homophobia. "[T]he fact that gay men could so sharply and brightly make fun of themselves meant that the real awfulness of their situation could be kept at bay" (Dyer 2002, 110). Camp is therefore a strategy of resistance and survival used by those not accepted into the mainstream (Barbuscio 2002).

Because of their roots in the camp sensibility of the gay world, it is remarkable that drag performances have moved into mainstream culture. For some heterosexual men and women, a drag show is their first encounter with gay life. If drag shows are often commercial entertainment, we have argued here that they are also a form of political expression that elicits strong emotions and even sexual responses, and such visceral moments have a powerful impact on participants. We have concentrated here on the role that music and song play in creating meaning and identity in drag. Drawing from our research on the performances at the 801 Cabaret, we have identified four causal mechanisms—ritual, education, disidentification, and interaction—that allow us to understand how music and song build solidarity, critique dominant culture, express grievances, and supply alternatives; these are the very cultural resources that give meaning to social movement protest. Music enables drag performers to highlight the differences among audience members while creating a space for the coexistence of disparate collective identities. By utilizing popular songs—frequently, songs that depict romanticized portrayals of heterosexuality—drag performances invoke hegemonic sexual scripts and symbols to draw in audience members. However, these dominant cultural codes are simultaneously criticized, resisted, and undermined. Heterosexuals in the audience become "outsiders within" (Collins 1991); they are integrated into the show but confronted with critiques of heterosexuality that remind them that they are in a gay space. In this space, the audience members—gay, straight, bisexual, and as one focus group member identified, "trysexual"—are all part of an oppositional community that challenges heteronormativity.

Commenting on the role of identity in political protest, Josh Gamson argues that "fixed identity categories are both the basis for oppression and the basis for political power" (1996, 396). As a result, social movements face a dilemma of trying to build solidarity while also trying to deconstruct the identity categories that are the basis for hierarchy. Our analysis demonstrates that drag performances are one setting in which group identity is simultaneously solidified and confused. Through the strategic use of music, drag performers are able to integrate heterosexual audience members into a distinctive, gay oppositional culture. Drag shows thus crystallize gay identity while also blurring the division between gays and straights. Music is central to this process because music enters into what Eyerman and Jamison (1998) refer to as the "collective memory." Songs conjure up memories of the past, awaken emotions that ordinarily lurk far beneath the surface, and create feelings of common purpose even among individuals with no previous connection to each other. Over and over, audience members at the 801 Cabaret described the shows as "just entertaining," but then moved quickly into discussions of gender disturbance, the acceptance of sexual and gender diversity, and the way that the shows forge collective identity and solidarity between different groups.

Although drag shows may be a practice unique to gay and lesbian organizing, we suggest that musical performances are an effective strategy used by various movements to accomplish the boundary work involved in maintaining difference while creating feelings of belonging to a collectivity among sympathizers and potential allies. Although the four dimensions we have used to explain how music contributes to the construction of collective identity relate specifically to drag shows, we present this as a framework that might be extended and adapted to understand how music contributes to identity work in other social movements. Finally, we offer this research as a contribution to the literature in social movements on repertoires of contention and social movement tactics. Scholars such as Rupp and Taylor (2003), and Roscigno and Danaher (2004) have argued that cultural performances constitute an important but understudied tactical repertoire of social movements. This chapter extends the research on social movement tactics by examining the way music and song are used strategically in social protest to construct collective identity and to align personal and collective identities.

References

Babuscio, Jack. 2002. "The Cinema of Camp (*aka* Camp and the Gay Sensibility)." In *Camp: Queer Aesthetics and the Performing Subject*, ed. F. Cleto, 117–35. Ann Arbor: University of Michigan Press.

Bernstein, Mary. 1997. "Celebration and Suppression: Strategic Uses of Identity by the Lesbian and Gay Movement." *American Journal of Sociology* 103: 531–65.

Bérubé, Allan. 1990. *Coming Out Under Fire: The History of Gay Men and Women in World War Two*. New York: Plume.

Boyd, Nan Alamilla. 2003. *Wide Open Town: A History of Queer San Francisco to 1965*. Berkeley: University of California Press.

Broad, Kendal. 2002. "Social Movement Selves." *Sociological Perspectives* 45: 317–36.

Britt, Lory, and David Heise. 2000. "From Shame to Pride in Identity Politics." In *Self, Identity, and Social Movements*, ed. S. Stryker, T. J. Owens, and R. W. White, 252–68. Minneapolis: University of Minnesota Press.

Chauncey, George. 1994. *Gay New York: Gender, Urban Culture, and the Makings of the Gay Male World, 1890–1940*. New York: Basic Books.

Cleto, Fabio, ed. 2002. *Camp: Queer Aesthetics and the Performing Subject*. Ann Arbor: University of Michigan Press.

Collins, Patricia Hill. 1991. *Black Feminist Thought: Knowledge, Consciousness, and the Politics of Empowerment*. New York: Routledge.

D'Emilio, John. 1983. *Sexual Politics, Sexual Communities: The Making of a Homosexual Minority in the United States, 1940–1970*. Chicago: University of Chicago Press.

DeNora, Tia. 2000. *Music in Everyday Life*. Cambridge: Cambridge University Press.

Drexel, Allen. 1997. "Before Paris Burned: Race, Class, and Male Homosexuality on the Chicago South Side, 1935–1960." In *Creating a Place for Ourselves: Lesbian, Gay, and Bisexual Community Histories*, ed. B. Beemyn, 119–44. New York: Routledge.

Duberman, Martin. 1994. *Stonewall*. New York: Plume.

Dyer, Richard. 2002. "It's Being So Camp as Keeps Us Going." In *Camp: Queer Aesthetics and the Performing Subject*, ed. F. Cleto, 110–16. Ann Arbor: University of Michigan Press.

Einwohner, Rachel L. 2002. "Motivational Framing and Efficacy Maintenance: Animal Rights Activists' Use of Four Fortifying Strategies." *The Sociological Quarterly* 43: 509–26.

Esterberg, Kristin. 1997. *Lesbian and Bisexual Identities: Constructing Communities, Constructing Selves*. Philadelphia: Temple University Press.

Eyerman, Ronald. 2002. "Music in Movement: Cultural Politics and Old and New Social Movements." *Qualitative Sociology* 25: 443–58.

Eyerman, Ronald, and Andrew Jamison. 1998. *Music and Social Movements: Mobilizing Traditions in the Twentieth Century*. Cambridge: Cambridge University Press.

Flacks, Richard. 1999. "Culture and Social Movements: Exploring the Power of Song." Paper presented at the Annual Meeting of the American Sociological Association. Chicago, Ill.

Futrell, Robert; Pete Simi; and Simon Gottschalk. 2006. "Understanding Music in Movements: The White Power Music Scene." *Sociological Quarterly* 47: 275–304.

Gamson, Joshua. 1996. "Must Identity Movements Self-Destruct? A Queer Dilemma." In *Queer Theory / Sociology*, ed. S. Seidman, 395–420. Oxford: Blackwell Publishers.

———. 1989. "Silence, Death, and the Invisible Enemy: AIDS Activism and Social Movement 'Newness.'" *Social Problems* 36: 351–67.

Gamson, William A. 1992. *Talking Politics*. Cambridge: Cambridge University Press.

————. 1991. "Commitment and Agency in Social Movements." *Sociological Forum* 6: 27–50.

Garber, Eric. 1989. "A Spectacle in Color: The Lesbian and Gay Subculture of Jazz Age Harlem." In *Hidden From History: Reclaiming the Gay and Lesbian Past*, ed. M. Duberman, M. Vicinus, and G. Chauncey, 318–31. New York: New American Library.

Gilmore, Stephanie and Elizabeth Kaminski. 2007. "A Part and Apart: Lesbian and Straight Feminist Activists Negotiate Identity in a Second-wave Organization." *Journal of the History of Sexuality* 16: 95–113.

Gould, Deborah. 2001. "Rock the Boat, Don't Rock the Boat, Baby: Ambivalence and the Emergence of Militant AIDS Activism." In *Passionate Politics: Emotions and Social Movements*, ed. J. Goodwin, J. M. Jasper, and F. Polletta, 135–57. Chicago: University of Chicago Press.

Halberstam, Judith. 1998. *Female Masculinity*. Durham, N. Car: Duke University Press.

Hunt, Scott A., and Robert D. Benford. 1994. "Identity Talk in the Peace and Justice Movement." *Journal of Contemporary Ethnography* 22: 488–517.

Kaiser, Charles. 1997. *The Gay Metropolis, 1940–1996*. Boston: Houghton Mifflin.

Kaminski, Elizabeth. 2003. "Listening to Drag: Music, Performance, and the Construction of Oppositional Culture." Dissertation completed at Ohio State University

Katz, Jonathan Ned. 1976. *Gay American History: Lesbians & Gay Men in the U.S.A.* New York: Meridian.

Kemper, Theodore D. 2001. "A Structural Approach to Social Movement Emotions." In *Passionate Politics: Emotions and Social Movements*, ed. J. Goodwin, J. M. Jasper, and F. Polletta, 58–73. Chicago: University of Chicago Press.

Keyes, Cheryl L. 2004. *Rap Music and Street Consciousness*. Urbana: University of Illinois Press.

Klandermans, Bert, and Marga De Weerd. 2000. "Group Identification and Political Protest." In *Self, Identity, and Social Movements*, ed. S. Stryker, T. J. Owens, and R. W. White, 68–90. Minneapolis: University of Minnesota Press.

Kutulas, Judy. 2003. "'You Probably Think This Song Is About You': 1970s Women's Music from Carole King to the Disco Divas." In *Disco Divas: Women and Popular Culture in the 1970s*, ed. S. A. Inness, 172–93. Philadelphia: University of Pennsylvania Press.

Levine, Martin P. 1998. *Gay Macho: The Life and Death of the Homosexual Clone*. New York: New York University Press.

Mansbridge, Jane, and Aldon Morris, ed. 2001. *Oppositional Consciousness: The Subjective Roots of Social Protest*. Chicago: University of Chicago Press.

McAdam, Doug; Sidney Tarrow; and Charles Tilly. 2001. *Dynamics of Contention.* Cambridge: Cambridge University Press.

Melucci, Alberto. 1995. "The Process of Collective Identity." In *Social Movements and Culture,* ed. H. Johnston and B. Klandermans, 41–63. Minneapolis: University of Minnesota Press.

Morris, Aldon. 1984. *The Origins of the Civil Rights Movement: Black Communities Organizing for Change.* New York: The Free Press.

Morris, Aldon, and Naomi Braine. 2001. "Social Movements and Oppositional Consciousness." In *Oppositional Consciousness: The Subjective Roots of Social Protest,* ed. J. Mansbridge and A. Morris, 20–37. Chicago: University of Chicago Press.

Mumford, Kevin J. 1997. *Interzones: Black/White Sex Districts in Chicago and New York in the Early Twentieth Century.* New York: Columbia University Press.

Muñoz, José Esteban. 1999. *Disidentifications: Queers of Color and the Performance of Politics.* Minneapolis: University of Minnesota Press.

Newton, Esther. 1979. *Mother Camp: Female Impersonators in America.* Chicago: University of Chicago Press.

Polletta, Francesca, and James M. Jasper. 2001. "Collective Identity in Social Movements." *Annual Review of Sociology* 27: 283–305.

Reger, Jo. 2002. "Organizational Dynamics and Construction of Multiple Feminist Identities in the National Organization for Women." *Gender & Society* 16: 710–27.

Roscigno, Vincent J., and William F. Danaher. 2004. *The Voice of Southern Labor: Radio, Music, and Textile Strikes, 1929–1934.* Minneapolis: University of Minnesota Press.

———. 2001. "Media and Mobilization: The Case of Radio and Southern Textile Worker Insurgency, 1929–1934." *American Sociological Review* 66: 21–48.

Rose, Tricia. 1994. *Black Noise: Rap Music and Black Culture in Contemporary America.* Hanover: University Press of New England.

Roth, Silke. 2000. "Developing Working-Class Feminism: A Biographical Approach to Social Movement Participation." In *Self, Identity, and Social Movements,* ed. S. Stryker, T. J. Owens, and R. W. White, 300–323. Minneapolis: University of Minnesota Press.

Rupp, Leila J., and Verta Taylor. 2003. *Drag Queens at the 801 Cabaret.* Chicago: University of Chicago Press.

Rupp, Leila, and Verta Taylor. 1999. "Forging Feminist Identity in an International Movement: A Collective Identity Approach to Twentieth-Century Feminism." *Signs: Journal of Women in Culture and Society* 24: 363–86.

Schacht, Steven P. 2000. "Four Renditions of Doing Female Drag: Feminine Appearing Conceptual Variations of a Masculine Theme." Paper presented at the annual American Sociological Association meetings, August, Washington, D.C.

Schippers, Mimi. 2002. *Rockin' out of the Box: Gender Maneuvering in Alternative Hard Rock.* New Brunswick, N.J.: Rutgers University Press.

Snow, David A., and Doug McAdam. 2000. "Identity Work Processes in the Context of Social Movements: Clarifying the Identity/Movement Nexus." In *Self, Identity, and Social Movements*, ed. S. Stryker, T. J. Owens, and R. W. White, 41–67. Minneapolis: University of Minnesota Press.

Sontag, Susan. 2002. "Notes on 'Camp'" In *Camp: Queer Aesthetics and the Performing Subject*, ed. F. Cleto, 53–65. Ann Arbor: University of Michigan Press.

Staggenborg, Suzanne; Donna Eder, and Lori Sudderth. 1994. "Women's Culture and Social Change: Evidence from the National Women's Music Festival." *Berkeley Journal of Sociology* 38: 31–56.

Stein, Arlene. 2001. "Revenge of the Shamed: The Christian Right's Emotional Culture War." In *Passionate Politics: Emotions and Social Movements*, ed. J. Goodwin, J. M. Jasper, and F. Polletta, 115–31. Chicago: University of Chicago Press.

———. 1997. *Sex and Sensibility: Stories of a Lesbian Generation*, Berkeley: University of California Press.

Swidler, Ann. 1986. "Culture in Action: Symbols and Strategies." *American Sociological Review* 51: 273–86.

Taylor, Verta. 2000. "Emotions and Identity in Women's Self-help Movements." In *Self, Identity, and Social Movements*, ed. S. Stryker, T. J. Owens, and R. W. White, 271–99. Minneapolis: University of Minnesota Press.

Taylor, Verta, and Leila J. Rupp. 2002. "Loving Internationalism: The Emotion Culture of Transnational Women's Organizations, 1888–1945." *Mobilization* 7: 141–58.

———. 1993. "Women's Culture and Lesbian Feminist Activism: A Reconsideration of Cultural Feminism." *Signs: Journal of Women in Culture and Society* 19: 32–61.

Taylor, Verta; Leila J. Rupp; and Joshua Gamson. 2007. "Performing Protest: Drag Shows as Tactical Repertoires of the Gay and Lesbian Movement." In *Authority in Contention (Research in Social Movements, Conflict and Change*, Vol. 25), ed. D. J. Myers and D. M. Cress, 105–38. Oxford, UK: Elsevier Ltd.

Taylor, Verta, and Nancy Whittier. 1992. "Collective Identity in Social Movement Communities: Lesbian Feminist Mobilization." In *Frontiers in Social Movement Theory*, ed. A. Morris and C. M. Mueller, 104–30. New Haven, Conn.: Yale University Press.

Troika, Donna Jean; Kathleen Lebesco; and Jean Bobby Noble, ed. 2002. *The Drag King Anthology*. New York: Harrington Park Press.

Valocchi, Steve. 1999. "The Class-inflected Nature of Gay Identity." *Social Problems* 46: 207–24.

Waite, Lori G. 2001. "Divided Consciousness: The Impact of Black Elite Consciousness on the 1966 Chicago Freedom Movement." In *Oppositional Consciousness: The Subjective Roots of Social Protest*, ed. J. and A. Morris, 170–203. Chicago: University of Chicago Press.

Whittier, Nancy. 2001. "Emotional Strategies: Oppositional Emotions in the Movement Against Child Sexual Abuse." In *Passionate Politics: Emotions and Social Movements*, ed. J. Goodwin, J. M. Jasper, and F. Polletta, 233–50. Chicago: University of Chicago Press.

———. 1995. *Feminist Generations: The Persistence of the Radical Women's Movement*. Philadelphia: Temple University Press.

Notes

1. In her analysis of the identity deployment strategies used by the gay and lesbian movement, Mary Bernstein (1997, 538) distinguishes between identity for education where activists' goals are to gain legitimacy by challenging self-conceptions used by dominant groups to justify their minority status and identity for critique where activists engage in identity work to oppose the values, practices, and identity categories of the dominant culture. Our analysis of the way drag queens use their performances to educate audiences about gay, lesbian, and transgender lives and simultaneously critique hegemonic sex and gender categories provides further empirical evidence for Bernstein's framework. In the afterword to this book, Bernstein draws more explicitly on this conceptual distinction, tying it back to the analysis we present here.

2. While there is debate about Freddie Mercury's intended meaning of the song, the interpretation that it is about inner city violence is underscored in the Braids' video, which begins with a young woman in an alley with blood on her hands. The video documents her attempts to evade the police, only to be caught, thrown to the ground, and handcuffed at the end.

3

Technical Advances in Communication: The Example of White Racialist "Love Groups" and "White Civil Rights Organizations"

Todd Schroer

One of the hardest and most necessary tasks for any social movement is image control. The public's perception of movement organizations and their members is vital to any movement's ability to attract new members, raise funds, and achieve movement goals, among other things. In general, the more positive an image that a movement and its members have in the public's view, the easier it is for organizations within the movement to succeed. With a negative public image, the ability of movement organizations to do even the most mundane of tasks becomes increasingly difficult. Thus, trying to control or influence how the public perceives a movement is one of the most essential tasks.

The mass media is usually the major source of information about any social movement for the public. Because of this, social movement actors often use a variety of tactics to try to gain access to the media to reach the largest audiences possible with their messages. However, for most organizations, the ability to gain publicity for their causes through the mass media is severely limited in two main ways. First, members of the media act as gatekeepers in the sense that they control whether a movement's members and issues ever get presented to the public. Obviously, it is more difficult for movement members to achieve their goals if they cannot disseminate their messages to the bulk of society. Second, even if a movement does manage to gain access to the mass media, members of the media control the ways in which the movements' members and organizations are presented. Negative media portrayals can severely damage a movement's image and strongly influence the public's view of the acceptability of movement organizations and members (Friedman and McAdam 1992; Gamson 1992; Gitlin 1980; Jensen 1995; Melucci 1995).

Virtually all movements are concerned with their public image, but for some movements this concern is critical. One movement for which identity issues are especially significant is the white racialist movement.[1] The widely held negative images of racialists severely complicates their ability to achieve movement goals, whether to create an all-white nation or the more mundane goal of gaining access to public property to hold meetings. The members of this movement feel their negative image is due to the concerted efforts of the "Jewish controlled" mass media. Racialists would agree with the view of the Knights of the Ku Klux Klan's (KKKK) National Director Thom Robb[2] that members of "the media as a whole [are] usually quite liberal in their own personal beliefs so they will quite often tailor the stories [presented] to fit their own agenda" (1997 interview). This results in the media giving what KKK Grand Wizard Troy Murphy described as a "negative portrayal of [racialists based on] . . . misinformation, false information, actual lies, you know or myths" (1997 interview). Racialists in general feel that due to the efforts of the media and other social institutions to denigrate them, the average American views racialists as *racists*, who are criminal, violence-prone terrorists and uneducated, ignorant haters.

How, then, does the racialist movement attempt to overcome the negative view much of society has of its members? In what ways does it go about trying to positively change the image of its members, especially given racialists' inability to access mainstream media in a meaningful way? This chapter explores these questions, focusing on white racialists' efforts to counteract their negative public image by engaging in identity work. I will examine the main ways in which racialists are attempting to modify their image and how they are attempting to disseminate a more positive collective identity. After a brief discussion of my data, racialists' five main strategic self-framing efforts will be examined along with their reliance on the Internet as a conduit through which to spread these new identity messages. I end with a discussion of the effectiveness of these measures.

This chapter builds on previous work on collective identity and social movements. As the other chapters in this volume demonstrate, the creation of a collective identity, a feeling of "we-ness," or an understanding of an "us" versus "them" or "the other" is crucial for the way social movement organizations (SMOs) and others create images of movement members. How collective identities are framed is important to micromobilization efforts, and it influences the ability of SMOs to attract new recruits and achieve movement goals (Jensen 1995; Taylor and Whittier 1992). In relation to movement actors, as Friedman and McAdam point out, "from the view of the leaders of the SMO, the kind of collective identity they shape for consumption will, in large part, determine both the number and the kind of people who are likely to be attracted" (1992, 164).

However, activists often have problems disseminating their interpretations of the collective identity of movement members. These problems arise when the characteristics imputed to a movement's collective identities are contested internally within the movement (Benford 1993), but they arise more often when the characteristics are challenged by movement antagonists or the media (Gamson 1992, 1995; Gitlin 1980; Friedman and McAdam 1992; Jensen 1995; Melucci 1995). Because of these problems, many activists feel that the public image of members of their movement is misunderstood or completely incorrect (Gamson 1995; Gitlin 1980; Turner and Killian 1987) thus affecting their ability to achieve movement goals. Therefore white racialist groups have begun to engage in identity work to recast the public's perception of themselves through new technologies, such as the Internet, which are not controlled by others as are the more traditional forms of the media.

The data in this paper were gathered as part of my ongoing research relating to the white racialist movement. By gaining information from as many sources as possible, my understanding of the movement and its members is more complete than it would be if only a subset of these were used (Denzin 1970). Starting in the early 1990s, I began acquiring information on racialists in a variety of ways. Among the more traditional methods used, I have written to and received by mail information from hundreds of movement organizations and have attended movement events and conducted phone and correspondence interviews with more than thirty racialists; many of them are the more prominent leaders within the movement. These interviews focused on issues related to identity, the Internet, and white power music. Along the less traditional paths, at least when I began my research over a decade ago, I started to acquire data from racialists' Usenet newsgroups and dial-up bulletin boards in 1992. Then, very shortly after former Klan member Don Black's Stormfront Web site went online in 1995, I began to focus on racialist Web sites and since that time have analyzed more than seven hundred of them. Today, I still monitor many Web sites, subscribe to dozens of e-mail newsgroups, and visit numerous chat rooms and discussion boards. Overall, this has produced tens of thousands of pages of data on the movement.

Although I have acquired data from numerous sources, throughout I have tried to get information that covers the diversity of the movement. The racialist movement is comprised of various types of organizations, from membership organizations to churches and businesses. Some of the more common categories of membership organizations I have focused on would include the KKK, neo-Nazis, World Church of the Creator (WCOTC), and skinhead organizations. The most common types of racialist churches I have concentrated on would be Christian Identity and Odinist/Asatru, the former believing that Aryans are the true Israelites and that Jews are the spawn of Satan, while the latter focuses on the Viking and Norse mythos for their main beliefs. I have also studied a variety of racialist businesses selling clothes, books, music, and other types of racialist paraphernalia. Despite their diversity, these organizations share a similar ideology, creating a movement centered on the belief in the inherent superiority of whites over all other races and the inferiority of all nonwhites to whites. The groups also usually hold anti-Semitic views and blame Jews for the current problems faced by whites throughout the world. For this chapter, I have sorted the data into themes, such as organizational identity and identity perception, tactics and strategies, and conceptions of deviance.

Reframing the Deviant Identity

Efforts made by racialists to recreate their collective identity can best be understood by using two theoretical approaches: labeling and framing perspectives. Although both have roots in the interactionist school and are similar in a number of ways, they usually are not used in conjunction when analyzing social movements. Within the social movement literature, the framing approach has become a major framework through which the activities of social movements are analyzed, while the labeling perspective has been used primarily to study identity issues within the fields of deviance and social problems. Beginning with the framing perspective, the main points of each that are relevant to the identity work of racialists will be discussed in this section.

According to Goffman, frames are "schemata of interpretation" (1974, 21) that give meanings to events, experiences, and issues in everyday life. Frames not only help individuals make sense of the world but also influence the actions that they take; thus, frames and framing are especially relevant to the study of collective action. Movement actors actively engage in framing issues, events, and collective identities to achieve organizational goals (Snow and Benford 1988). These "strategic framings" usually articulate grievances (Snow et al. 1986) and attribute blame for current conditions (Gamson 1995; Klandermans 1992; Snow and Benford 1988, 1992; Tarrow 1992). These framing efforts do not take place in a vacuum, however, and their effectiveness in achieving movement goals is mediated by a number of concerns.

First, how well movement frames resonate with the culture, beliefs, and experiences of audiences and bystander publics is critical to movement success (Gamson and Modigliani 1989; Snow and Benford 1988, 1992; Snow et al 1986; Taylor and Whittier 1992). Because of this, movement actors attempt to better align their frames with those of their audiences by engaging in a number of tactics (Snow et al 1986). One form of frame alignment relevant to the white racialist movement is "frame transformation," which involves transforming the values and interpretations of individuals, replacing old ones with new values and new framings of beliefs to gain support and new recruits. This is an absolute necessity when "the programs, causes, and values that some SMOs promote . . . [do] not resonate with, and on occasion may even appear antithetical to, conventional lifestyles or rituals and extant interpretive frames" (Snow et al 1986, 473). Examples of this process would include the consciousness raising actions of the second wave of the U.S. women's movement, which attempted to reframe traditional gender roles and expectations to attract more support and recruits. For many movements whose members are seen as deviant by the wider society, much organizational activity is focused on doing the identity work of convincing others that they are nondeviant. This is often attempted through frame transformation efforts aimed at reframing current deviant identities as nondeviant or by framing those who have labeled them as deviant as incorrect and as having ulterior motives for the application of the label.

Second, since movement framings allow movement actors to place their own spin on issues, events, and symbols, framings are points of struggle; that is, they are contests over meanings (Gamson 1992; Jensen 1995; Snow and Benford 1988; Swidler 1995; Tarrow 1992). As Snow and Benford (1992, 136) point out, framing "denotes an active, process-derived phenomenon that implies agency and contention at the level of reality construction." These struggles over meanings, such as how topics should be strategically framed or what is the "true" framing of an issue, take place within the movement, between movement actors and SMOs, and, in the larger societal context, between SMOs and their antagonists (Benford 1993). Who wins these "battles" influences SMOs' mobilization efforts and their ability to manage an otherwise hostile environment (McAdam 1996). Moreover, successful framings can, on a larger scale, change public opinions and common sense understandings of issues, actors, and events (Billig 1995). Whatever the effectiveness of other types of framings by movement actors, one of the main issues with which movement actors must concern themselves is the portrayal of members of their movement.

Among labeling theorists, much of the focus is either on the social processes by which behaviors and people are defined as deviant, or on the way societal reactions influence the self-image and subsequent behaviors of individuals labeled as deviant, or on the way being labeled deviant has negative repercussions. A less prevalent focus has been on the labors of individuals and groups to refute the deviant nature of their social identities. This is the approach taken by John Kitsuse (1980), who focuses on attempts to neutralize and refute the social audiences who view and label a group as deviant. Kitsuse notes that members of various minority groups, such as gays, the blind, and paraplegics, try to "*counter and neutralize* those who define them as deviants" (italics in original, 1980, 11). He uses the term *tertiary deviance* "to refer to the deviant's confrontations, assessment, and rejection of the negative identity [imposed by society] . . . and the transformation of that identity into a positive and viable self-conception" (1980, 9). Tertiary deviance, then, is a form of identity work and is being done through the strategic framing efforts of movement actors due to the negative repercussions of being labeled as deviant.

Deviance and the Racialist Movement

Historically in the United States, racialist organizations did not need to concern themselves with their public image being damaged by their beliefs in white supremacy. The United States was a nation founded by whites for whites, a fact that was affirmed in the original U.S. Constitution and in state and local laws and customs. Although there have always been some who viewed racialist organizations in a negative manner, generally until the 1930s (and until much more recently in the South), the overall views held of these organizations were primarily positive for the bulk of white Americans. Today this is less likely to be the case. Racialists interviewed confirm this view of themselves. As Doug, a member of the white power band Straightlaced Nightmare puts it, racialists are often seen as "white trash" (2002 interview). Or more generally, as an Exalted Cyclops of the American Knights of the Klu Klux Klan[3] (AKKKK) said, racialists are seen as an "a bunch of rednecks, . . . a bunch of hatemongers . . . [who] all start trouble" (1997 interview).

These negative views are one of the main problems described by racialists today who feel that such opinions keep the movement from achieving its goals. According to them, the deviant label *racist* or *supremacist* and the negative auxiliary traits associated with it (such as being hate-filled criminals) hurts the movement in several ways. First and foremost, it decreases their ability to gain new recruits. As KKKK member Pastor Thom Robb stated, "I don't think the average American wants, wants to hate Black people you know.

And as long as they project, or perceive that they have to hate Black people to join the Klan, well, that's a big stumbling block" (1997 interview).

A similar point was made by Lawrence Malstab on the Newdawn Web site in regards to the violent image most people have of the movement warding "off the more intelligent, idealistic, evolved whites," while "swelling the ranks . . . with hypersensitive freaks, sociopaths, outcasts, losers, common thugs and others attracted to the negative, violent" image (1996).

Racialists also remark on their negative image hurting their ability to disseminate information and hold events. As Victor Gerhard, the racialist author and entrepreneur who is currently the vice-chairman of White Revolution, stated,

> We have to deal with that kind of atmosphere where pretty much the entire establishment, and by that I mean academia, I mean television media, print media, local, state, federal government, almost every power institution in the country is against us, fervently against us. And you're trying to have a get together and even if it's on private property, these people will attempt to stop you from doing it. Like I said, we don't live in a free country. We can't even get together on our own property, to say what we want and think what we want and do what we want. (2002 interview)

Other racialists have made similar comments, such as Byron, the Web master of Tightrope.cc, who stated that racialist concerts he helped arrange were shut down in Buffalo and Minneapolis due to the actions of "the cops or Leftists. . . . I mean we have opposition obviously, and they're gonna, you know, interfere with us anyway they can" (2002 interview).

At the personal level, there are many repercussions to being known as a racialist, ranging from minor annoyances to those that are life-threatening. Among the more minor negative effects are that racialist Web sites and accounts may be terminated. As one individual said—who only wanted to be known as a "person who espouses the concept of 'Leaderless Resistance'"—he had been "censored from two so-called free page companies: geocities. com and tripod.com" because of his political views (1997 interview). On the other end of the spectrum, some racialists fear for the safety of themselves and their families if their beliefs are known. As an Exalted Cyclops of the American KKKK described, "it's just a fact of life that if you belong to the Klan, your family could die" (1997 interview).

Besides physical threats, among the more severe problems faced are those that influence a racialist's livelihood. Gerhard said he had faced difficulty "trying to put a business together online [with] all the people that wouldn't do business with you; that went out of their way to cause you trouble; that wouldn't design sties; that wouldn't do the simplest economic transactions" because of the racialist products he was attempting to sell (2002 interview). Others, such as Byron comment on the risks faced by racialists at their jobs if their views are found out by their fellow workers: "you're gonna offend somebody at work and get fired" (2002 interview). A very common example given by racialists of the risks they face related to their economic livelihoods is that of the World Church of the Creator's Matt Hale being denied his license to practice law after passing the Illinois bar due to his beliefs.

The negative reactions from others are also emotionally draining. Gerhard said, "You can't have every single person around you having a negative reaction to you and get through the day, it's a bit difficult in that sense" (2002 interview). Because of the negative consequences and the emotional strain associated with defending themselves and their views, many racialists engage in a variety of stigma management techniques (Goffman 1963), such as limiting the amount of information they share about their views with others or by engaging in identity work that attempts to redefine their identities as being nondeviant, which is the focus of the following section.

Identity and the Internet

The ability of racialists to present their arguments about the "true" nature of their identity and motivations is severely hampered due to their inability to access the mass media. However, with the Internet, racialists gained a new medium in which to disseminate their information while controlling the image of racialists presented, and many within the movement have gone online with new messages about who racialists *really* are. This can be seen throughout the movement within all categories of organizations. For example, Pastor Pete Peters' Christian Identity Web site (http://www .scripturesforamerica.org) has sections specifically refuting negative media reports about his and his followers' beliefs. Many Klan Web sites are similar, such as Pastor Robb's Web site (http://www.kkk.bz). Even some segments of the movement that traditionally eschewed these reframing efforts in the past are now attempting to create a more positive image. For instance, the Nationalist Movement's Richard Barrett, a long-time activist who branched out into trying to attract more young people into the movement, is currently attempting to change the image of skinheads with his new Web site (http:// www.skinheadz.com). For example, this Web site, while still having rather traditional, and in some cases violent, pictures of skinheads, presents the common activities of group members as very benign, ranging from being an "Internet guru—managing e-mails and directing chat-rooms—to becoming a spokesman—doing radio, TV and talk-shows" for the cause (2005a).

Many racialists share the hope David Duke expressed in an article posted to his Web site entitled "The Coming White Revolution" that "the same race that created the brilliant technology of the Internet, will—through this powerful tool—be awakened from its long sleep." The Internet is seen as vital in this process since, as the National Socialist White People's Party Winston Smith stated in his NSNet e-mail newsletter, it "enables White people to COMMUNICATE with one another, to exchange ideas and information laterally, directly, without filtering communication through the System news media and allowing the System to monitor the formation of their thoughts and ideas" (Smith 1997a). In other words, the Internet allows racialists to deploy a positive identity to mass audiences of Whites for the first time, without the traditional media controlling the content and presentation. In fact the Internet and computers now provide racialists with multiple outlets for disseminating unfiltered racialist messages and depictions of who they are and what they stand for (Back, Keith, and Solomos 1998).

Many racialists hope that their use of the Internet will be so effective that there "will begin a chain reaction of racial enlightenment that will shake the world by the speed of its intellectual conquest" (Duke 2000). Once again this effort is seen as possible since "no single or small group of plutocrats can totally block access of politically incorrect information [through the Internet, so] . . . White Nationalists can portray themselves in their own light, unhindered by media editing and smear jobs" (John Calvin Society for Racial Theology 1996). A member of the National Socialist organization New Dawn similarly stressed that there is "no more hearing about us from *60 Minutes*, now the propaganda comes straight from the horses' mouth" (1997 interview). This control over their messages allows racialists a new freedom to engage in identity work, presenting the "true" characteristics of their identities in any way in which they see fit.

When presenting themselves and their organizations, they are often trying to transform what they see as the inaccurate picture of racialists held by many Americans. In particular, racialists try to change the fact that most people "when they hear the words 'White Power', automatically think 'Racist-Bigot-Redneck-Klansman-Skinhead-Nazi-Beer Drinker-Hatemonger'" (New Kastle Kounty Knightriders 1996). Toward this aim, racialists present five overlapping frames as to why they should best be seen as legitimate, nondeviant members of society: the redefinition of the racialist identity; the reframing of movement opponents; the normalization of racialist identities; the professionalizing of their organizations; and the reframing of their motives.

Redefinition of Identity

First, members of the movement feel that the most common terms used to define them in public are very negative or have negative connotations. As Alex Curtis, the editor of the *Nationalist Observer* and an outspoken racial activist on the Web before being sentenced to three year in federal prison for civil rights violations, stated that racist "is a smear word by the media and it also falls in with these words like hate or bigot," which are often used to describe activists (1997 interview). Most racialists feel these terms have primarily been created and used by their enemies to stigmatize them (Malstab 1996), and this has influenced how racialists have attempted to label themselves. As Director Rick Cooper of the National Socialist Vanguard summarizes,

> there is a connotation with the word racist, which is a negative connotation . . . some people try to shake that negative connotation because they feel that as soon as they identify themselves as a racist that a lot of people will really not pay too much attention to what they have to say. So, in order to be more easily received and get people to listen to them for what they have to say a little bit better, they try to use a more acceptable term, such as patriotic white American or racialist or some other term than racist (1997 interview).

Similarly, Pastor Robb stated when asked about what term he uses to describe movement members, he felt the terms "white nationalists" or "racialists" were acceptable, but that "the term that would not be correct, that is used only by the media, is white supremacist. [Since] very, very few people in the white racialist movement are white supremacist" (1997 interview). Another prime example of this comes from the Skinheadz Web site (2005b), which actually lists words for organizational members to avoid when describing themselves, such as separatists, survivalists, and supremacists, and suggests instead to talk of themselves as Americans, rightists, or patriots.

Reframing Opponents

Second, racialists often try to vilify or denounce those who are judging or defining them as deviant. They do this by attempting to reframe their opponents as the true haters and deviant criminals, suggesting that it is enemies of the movement who are the ones acting in negative ways, such as by using violence. In this vein, Tommy Voelker, the creator of *M.R.M.E.T.A.L.* (Metal Racial Music Empowering the Aryan Legions) newsletter, argued that it is the antiracist groups like "the ARA [Anti-Racist Action] and the globalist groups who are the ones who act like [violent] animals, not racialists" (2002 interview). Chris Evans, then marketing director for Resistance Records, also talked about being attacked by countermovement members for his beliefs, such as when he recounted in a 2003 *Creativity* newsletter his encounter with antiracialist "punks" with "baseball bats" who assaulted him. Many racialists share Gerhard's assessment that the ARA and other opposition groups "are practically free of any constraints of the law. They're pretty free to beat up, if they catch someone alone, whether it's a (racialist) girl or some young kid, they can beat the shit out of them and they're not gonna face any police problems whatsoever" (2002 interview).

However, the most common arguments made are that racialists' opponents are trying to deny their constitutional rights to express their opinions and assemble, and that those who oppose them are acting as censors, infringing on racialists' free speech rights. This argument can be found on almost all racialist Web sites and throughout much movement literature covering almost all mediums and types of venues racialists have tried to use to disseminate their information. In regards to the Internet, racialist bookstore owner Dennis Nix argues that "the Anti-Defamation League, the Simon Wiesenthal Center, and similar Jewish organizations are coordinating their efforts to censor the Internet in ALL countries" (1997 interview). Racialists have also talked of being denied access to public meeting places, such as when the World Church of the Creator was denied access to a library meeting room by the library's executive director due to his belief that minority members of his staff were at risk of being attacked during the speeches (WCOTC 2001). Racialists make similar arguments about the media limiting their access to the public and deny their requests to buy advertising space on radio, television, or in newspapers (1997 interview with Imperial Klaliff Johnson).

The media also is lambasted by racialists not only for denying them access but also for its biased reporting and negative presentations of racialists. Racialists, it is argued, are always portrayed in the media as "having brawls all the time" (1997 interview with Matt Hale) and "acting in a really ignorant profane violent manner" (1997 interview with Pastor Robb). Racialists feel that this occurs through the media's focus upon fringe elements of the movement or by setting up the interactions on talk shows, for example, "in a fashion that attempts to make racial people look like morons" (1997 interview Tom Metzger). Although most feel this occurs because of the control of the media by their enemies (i.e., Jews), some also argue that the media slanders them for profit, and that their negative image is perpetuated because it benefits the media economically. Imperial Klaliff Johnson said, "The media always try to portray us in the worst possible light. Again because articulate, educated, well-reasoned thought from a Klansman don't sell ratings.

But what does sell is venomous diatribe, and hatred and, you know, fiery speeches, you know, the black helicopter crap. And that stuff sells, and when the media choose [*sic*] to cover one of our rallies, you know the first guy who says nigger is going to be the one on TV" (1997 interview).

"Normalizing" Identity

A third type of identity work is illustrated by statements that show that racialists are similar to "normal" people or groups. In this regard racialists discuss how they are average citizens or, as Klaliff Johnson put it, "work-a-day-Joes" (1997 interview). Many racialists argue that they are similar to others in that their beliefs are not extreme and are actually shared by most whites. Gerhard argues that the bulk of whites are "afraid to complain" about issues such as nonwhite immigration and white victimization because of the possible repercussions of being seen as racist (2002 interview).

In their attempts to normalize their identities, some racialists state that although their views may be seen as deviant today, they were actually held by the mainstream only a few decades ago and for much of this country's history, as Don Black argued during a 1998 appearance on ABC's *Nightline*. One way in which they try to persuade people of this is by showing that their views on racial matters were shared by many admired historical figures. Articles such as "What world famous men said about the Jews" (http://www.stormfront.org, nd) present anti-Semitic quotes from many great figures ranging from Thomas Jefferson and Charles Lindburgh to Mark Twain in efforts to convince the audience of the acceptability of racialist views. Among the more extreme ways racialists try to show the similarity of their beliefs to those of famous historical figures can be seen on Gerhard Lauck's NSDAP/AO Web site. This neo-Nazi leader, made famous for serving time for distributing racist literature from his headquarters in the United States to Germany, has cartoons on his Web site, such as a disembodied Abraham Lincoln head floating with eyes spinning while a computerized voice reads quotes from Lincoln arguing against blacks being in any way the equals of whites (2005).

Professionalizing Organizations

Racialists attempt to show the nondeviant nature of their organizations in a number of ways. To this end, they often deploy identities as members of professional, legitimate organizations, not as members of violent, fringe hate groups that terrorize nonwhites. As Grand Wizard Troy Murphy described the aim of his efforts:

I just want to make it clear that we're not a bunch of, you know, slack jawed illiterate white trash that run around fields in the middle of the night setting crosses on fire. We are the Knights of the Ku Klux Klan. . . . You know it is not our mission to terrorize negroes or make any one feel uncomfortable, but it's our mission to educate white people and to let them know that there is an organization that is concerned for the future of their children and that special rights for some negate the rights of others. (1997 interview)

A similar message declaring the legitimate nature of his organization can be found on Pastor Robb's Web site, with its front page declaring "Welcome to The Knights Party. America's Largest, Oldest, and Most Professional White Rights Organization—We Love you!" (KKKK 2005). Racialist Rachel Pendergraft reiterates the professional nature of the KKKK, describing it as "an organization built on professionalism . . . honor and integrity [with] the support of thousands of God fearing, hard working, good Christian men and women" (2005a).

These attempts to reframe themselves as professional organizations, however, go beyond just words and slogans and include personal presentations of self. As the National Socialist White People's Party's Winston Smith (aka Harold Covington) described in his newsletter (1997b), "the National Socialist uniform of today is the business suit, the coat and tie." Similarly, Pastor Robb's Klan does not wear Klan robes at any public functions. As he described, "we don't wear our robes at a rally because we want to project again something that people can identify with. It's salesmanship I suppose" (1997 interview). In other words, members of these organizations are "dressing for success" by trying to professionalize their image through the clothes they wear.

Surprisingly, racialists, who are members of a movement that is almost the quintessential example of one based on notions of a collective identity of *difference* from others (Jews, blacks, etc.), also try to legitimate their groups by arguing their *similarity* to mainstream racial and ethnic organizations that are seen by the bulk of American's as nondeviant. This is a tactic that Berbrier (1998) has discussed in great depth in which racialists are "presenting themselves in ethnic ways, and framing their proclamations to evoke American ethnic group membership" by "offering a series of equivalences between an entity called 'whites' and a number of other entities though of collectively as 'racial' and or 'ethnic' groups" (438–40).

Many racialists are clear that they view their organizations as similar to other ethnic organizations. As Imperial Klaliff Johnson stated, "we're a civil rights organization. . . . Mexicans have their civil rights groups, . . . [Blacks] the NAACP . . . and that's what we're shooting for, to become a political and accepted organization" (1997 interview). An Exalted Cyclops made a similar point while extending this analogy to racialists' tactics when he described that they "do not suggest for [their] members to do anything illegal. . . . [W]e want to make change the way the civil rights movement made change. . . . [W]e consider ourselves basically a white civil rights movement" (1997 interview). Probably the best example of this framing strategy was when David Duke named one of his organizations the National Association for the Advancement of White People, a direct effort to show the similarity of his group to the NAACP.

Further, in an effort to reframe their collective identity as similar to those of members of other ethnic organizations, many racialists ironically make use of the same civil rights master frame used by the NAACP and others in which "blame is externalized in that unjust differences in life circumstances are attributed to encrusted, discriminatory structural arrangements rather than to the victims' imperfections" (Snow and Benford 1992, 139). In their use of the civil rights master frame, racialists' framing efforts often try to present the notion of whites, especially men, as being the victims of reverse discrimination and as the only truly disadvantaged group due to societal organization. Racialists often state that the denigration of their identities plays a large role in this and occurs so that certain groups, usually those doing the defining, benefit at the expense of whites in society.

This "reversal" (Berbrier 1998) of racial-ethnic victimization is illustrated by David Dukes' assessment on his Web site that "European-Americans now face the most extensive racial discrimination in American History. . . . Today, the Federal Government is forcing an across-the-board racial discrimination against European-Americans in employment, promotions, scholarships, and in college and union admittance. This racial bias is pervading all sectors of our national life, including civil service, education and business" (2000). Further, they feel that one reason racialists are misrepresented in the media is to ensure that white activists cannot achieve political power. Shaun Walker, Chairman and CEO of the National Alliance (a group made infamous by the belief that the novel *The Turner Diaries*, written by its founder Dr. William Pierce, was a blueprint for the Oklahoma City federal building bombing), made this clear in one of his 2005 American Dissident Voices shortwave radio broadcasts, where he argued that "[a]nybody trying to stand for elected office, who does not adhere to the lies of multiracialism, or who is opposed to Jewish Supremacist, or who is pro-White, faces either a news blackout, or, even worse, staggering smears, lies and half truths about them being fed to the voting public by the Jewish controlled media." To summarize, these professionalizing efforts are attempting to gain racialist organizations a nondeviant standing in society that is equal to those of more mainstream ethnic organizations, while still preserving the notion of a threatened white race that is at a disadvantage in today's multicultural society, to help mobilize whites to take action.

Reframing Motives

Finally, racialists are attempting to counter the common perception that movement members have deviant motives for their actions. They are presenting themselves as not motivated by hate, with desires to dominate or victimize others. As Dixie, a member of the Southern Cross Militant Knights, stressed, "I would like to emphasize it is not a matter of hate" (1997 interview). Instead, in describing what motivates their activities, racialists state that their activities and views are "based on love for our nation, love for our people, love for our culture . . . [and] not based upon hatred" (1997 interview with Pastor Robb). This theme of love of the white race is also carried on Robb's Web site, where Rachael Pendergraft writes,

> We are not Klansmen and Klanswomen because we hate anyone. We belong to The Knights because we dream of a better world for our children—a safe and secure world. It is not hatred but rather the glimmer of hope in the eyes of our children that motivates us. . . . The Knights of the Ku Klux Klan is a love group not a hate group. We love America and the Christian foundation of our nation. We love our white brothers and sisters world wide [*sic*] and we recognize the contributions they have made to civilization. (2005b)

Similarly the goals of these groups are framed in a very nondeviant manner. Most argue that one of their major goals is to help educate whites about their history and culture (1997 interview Matt Hale). Others have described being motivated by wanting to act as civil rights spokespeople "on the behalf of Whites" (Johnson 1997 interview). Additionally, members of many groups express a goal of raising consciousness among whites. As Dixie argued, "white people need to understand that it is alright to be white and proud of who you are." This is something she felt is necessary, since, "this society has for years made white people and white children in schools feel like they need to feel sorry for these races and minorities and even to the point where they owe the other races something just because they are white. Whites today need to be taught to take pride in who they are and where they came from" (1997 interview). Thus, it can be seen that, although racialists are keeping the core of their beliefs intact, such as a persecuted white race that is controlled by the media manipulating Jews and their allies, they are repackaging their issues in a much more positive manner.

The overall goals of these identity deployment efforts are twofold: first, to reduce existing racialists' stigmatization due to the public's negative perception of them, and second, to attract new recruits by making being a racialist more palatable. Obviously, the stigma attached to being a racialist would be decreased if most whites could see racialists as members of legitimate civil rights organizations motivated by love. Likewise, more whites would probably be willing to become racialists if their identities would not suffer due to their movement membership. Although many racialists view the Internet positively, the effectiveness of their efforts to rework their identities needs to be evaluated.

Conclusion

Racialists can be seen as suffering much harm both personally and organizationally due to the commonly held perception of them as deviant. To decrease this, racialists have made strategic decisions about how best to transform the public's view. Their identity work actions are very similar to those engaged in by many other movements that are deemed deviant by society. For example, the efforts made to take control over the term used to describe movement members trying to change from the negative terms "racist" or "supremacist" to the less stigmatized "racialist" are similar to the attempts made by homosexuals to rename themselves as gay (Kitsuse 1980) or by lepers to rename themselves as suffers of Hansen's Disease (Gussow and Tracy 1968). Likewise, in terms of reframing their opponents as the true deviants with ulterior motives for their seemingly benign actions, their efforts are very similar to groups within the Gay Liberation and Black Power movements, which have attempted to tie the stigma associated with their identities to the oppressive designs of those doing the defining (Anspach 1979). This approach can also be seen in the identity work activities of others, such as people with AIDS and the obese, who have tried to show that the negative traits associated with their identities are due to the ignorance and prejudice of those creating the definition (Martin 2000; Weitz 1990; see also Chapter 1).

The ability of racialists to better control their image and present positive views of their character has been facilitated by their widespread use of the Internet. This medium has allowed some organizations to frame themselves in a more positive manner and attract new recruits and funding (Schroer 2001). Most groups that have accomplished this feat have completely eschewed any ties to the movement; for instance, they use no common racialist symbols, terms, or organizational names, and thus would not really be engaging in tertiary deviance. They have entered the mainstream by, in many ways, cutting off all ties to the movement and denying that they are *racialists*, let alone *racists*. Examples include Jared Taylor and his *American Renaissance* magazine and Web site and many of the "Southern Heritage" organizations that hold similar beliefs to more overt racialists but distance themselves from aspects of the movement. Overall, the effectiveness of some racialists' efforts in changing the traits associated with that identity and the stigma attached to them by social audiences have been severely hampered in many ways.

First, some segments of the movement revel in the "bad-boy," violent, deviant image of racialists and make every effort to propagate it. Usually, this is done by organizations that target today's youth, and examples of this can be found widely within skinhead organizations and the white power music scene. These segments often rely on the outsider, dangerous image to attract rebellious youth to the movement. These efforts to entrench the identity of racialists as deviant can obviously hamper the identity work of others to reframe their collective identity and send mixed messages to bystander publics about "true" racialists and their motivations.

Second, there is an ongoing debate within the movement over which is the best path to take to achieve movement goals of gaining power. On one side are those attempting to reframe racialists collective image in an attempt to gain power through more traditional and legitimate means. On the other side, many within the movement feel that a more effective approach to bring about change is to use the strategy of leaderless resistance in which racialists have no ties to traditional organizations but instead engage in terrorist actions to achieve their goals. They argue for military type training and strive for the formation of small cells of racialists (to avoid infiltration by governmental agents) who will use violence against the enemies of the white race.

Most who advocate leaderless resistance hold attempts to soften the image of the reframing movement. A prime example of this would be Tom Metzger, the head of White Aryan Resistance. He said, he has a lack of respect for "racists, even people who are very active racists [who] have this problem with backing down when confronted with straight questions and do everything they can to try to make whomever's talking to them, or who they are talking to, like them by saying that a, well, they are not really racists, they just love their race and this and that" (1997 interview). They also feel that by attempting to soften up their image to gain mainstream respectability, racialists are being co-opted by the system. As Voelker declared, "most people that I have come in contact with resent the mainstream and look at it as a place for sell-outs" (2002 interview).

This debate over tactics within the movement decreases the effectiveness of the Internet presentations in that viewers once again are getting conflicting messages about the characteristics of *true* racialists. It could be argued that it undermines the efforts of one wing of the movement to present themselves as members of nonviolent civil rights organizations when other racialists are advocating violent, noninstitutional means for change.

Third, in order for the racialists' redefinitions to affect the public, the masses have to come in contact with their messages. The public, however, is unlikely to come in contact with these messages randomly. The people who usually find racialist Web sites are specifically looking for them and already share many of their views. They are often curious and feel that the anonymous nature of the Internet allows them to find out more about these groups without risking being seen as racialist themselves (Schroer 2001). In other words, those most often coming in contact with the messages already are sympathetic to their views and are not people who hold a negative view of racialists

More important, the efforts of racialists to destigmatize their image are paltry compared to the power of the media and other institutions, such as schools, to spread the view of racialists as deviants. This holds true even in terms of the Internet, where a vastly larger audience is going to be exposed to an article framing racialists as deviants on a mainstream news Web site like MSNBC.com than to a racialists' presentation of nondeviant identities. Because of this, many racialists feel they are waging an uphill battle. As an Exalted Cyclops opined, even with the Internet "it's a never ending task because the [mainstream media] has so much more power" (1997 interview). Similarly, as Byron of Tightrope.cc put it, "if you stand up and say that you're white and you like being white and you appreciate your heritage, the majority of people in America are gonna thing you're a fucking jack-ass. I don't give a fuck if you're wearing a suit, or if you're wearing boots and braces" (2002 interview).

In sum, although the Internet is a useful tool for racialists in these identity work efforts, since it provides them with a forum in which to present these positive reframings of their collective identities, their efforts are severely curtailed due in large part to the small amount of people who ever hear the racialists' messages. Even on the Internet, the racialists' positive framing efforts are like a drop of water in the sea compared to the overwhelmingly negative presentations that exist there of racialists as deviant. Thus, in combination with the huge hurdle of trying to overcome the predominant existing view of racialists as deviant and the continual negative presentation of racialists in the media, racialists' identity work activities to change societal views can be seen as having largely failed overall to produce widely held positive views of racialists.

These findings suggest numerous paths for further future study. The most valuable studies would focus more specifically on the gendered nature of racialist identities. Many researchers feel that the movement is primarily "a men's movement" (Ezekial 2002, 54), with women playing auxiliary roles (Bushart et al. 1998; Coates 1987). Others argue that women have played significant roles in the movement in the past (Berlet & Lyons 2000), and in some cases do today (Blee 2002). However, most agree that the portrayal of women in racialist rhetoric is usually limited to images of women in traditional roles, often focusing on their importance as mothers who perpetuate the white race and as needing the protection of men or as overly sexualized supermodel beings.

The idea that men are the majority of the members of the movement seems to be supported when looking at who is producing much of the discourse presented on the Internet and who are the stated leaders and spokespeople of most racialist organizations. However, with more women entering into the racialist discourse in chat rooms, discussion boards, and through their creation of Web sites, as well as through the attempts of existing organizations to attract larger numbers of female recruits, the importance of the gendered identity work by these individuals is increasing. What changes, if any, will be made by males in the movement to make the collective identity of racialist women more attractive to potential recruits? What characteristic movement will women be incorporating into a new female racialist identity? How will the efforts of women to take control of their own identity be received by the existing racialist establishment? These and many other important questions remain to be analyzed.

References

Anspach, Renee R. 1979. "From Stigma to Identity Politics: Political Activism Among the Physically Disabled and Former Mental Patients." *Social Science and Medicine* 13 (A): 765–73.

Back, Les, Michael Keith, and John Solomos. 1998. "Racism on the Internet: Mapping Neo-Fascist Subcultures in Cyberspace." In *Nation and Race*, ed. J. Kaplan and T. Bjørgo, 73–101. York, Pa.: Northeastern University Press.

Becker, Howard S. 1963. *Outsiders: Studies in the Sociology of Deviance.* New York: Free Press.

Benford, Robert D. 1993. "Frame Disputes Within the Nuclear Disarmament Movement." *Social Forces* 71: 677–701.

Berbrier, Mitch. 1998. "'Half the Battle': Cultural Resonance, Framing Processes, and Ethnic Affectations in Contemporary White Separatist Rhetoric." *Social Problems* 45: 431–50.

Berlet, Chip, and Matthew N. Lyons. 2000. *Right-wing Populism in America: Too Close for Comfort.* New York: Guilford.

Billig, Micahel. 1995. "Rhetorical Psychology, Ideological Thinking, and Imagining Nationhood. In *Social Movements and Culture*, ed. Hank Johnston and Bert Klandermans, 64–81. Minneapolis: University of Minnesota Press.

Black, Don. 1998. "Hate and the Internet: Hate Web Sites and the Issue of Free Speech." *Nightline.* January 13.

Blee, Kathleen M. 2002. *Inside Organized Racism: Women in the Hate Movement.* Berkeley: University of California Press.

Bushart, Howard L., John R. Craig, and Myra Barnes. 1998. *Soldiers of God: White Supremacists and Their Holy War for America.* New York: Pinnacle Books.

Byron. 2002. Webmaster of Tightrope.cc, interviewed September, 2002.

Coates, James. 1987. *Armed and Dangerous: The Rise of the Survivalist Right.* New York: Hill and Wang.

Cooper, Rick. 1997. Director of the National Socialist Vanguard, interviewed February, 1997.

Curtis, Alex. 1997. Editor of the John Calvin Society for Racial Theology's Nationalist Observer, interviewed March, 1997.

Denzin, Norman. 1970. *The Research Act in Sociology.* Chicago: Aldine.

Dixie. 1997. Anonymous Klan Member, interviewed April, 1997.

Doug. 2002. Straightlaced Nightmare band member, interviewed October, 2002.

Duke, David. 2001. "End Racial Discrimination against European Americans." http://www.whitecivilrights.com/end_discrimination.shtml (accessed August 14, 2003).

———.2000. "The Coming White Revolution." http://www.duke.org/writings/Internet.html (accessed November 21, 2000).

E. C. 1997. Exalted Cyclops of the Realm of Delaware, American Knights of the Ku Klux Klan, interviewed May, 1997.

Evans, Chris. 2003. "A Rebuttal of Claims Made againt [sic] Gliebe and the NA." *Creativity* e-mail newsletter, August 21.

Ezekiel, Rapheal S. 2002. "An Ethnographer Looks at neo-Nazi and Klan Groups: The Racist Mind revisited. *American Behavioral Scientist* 46: 51–71.

Friedman, Debra, and Doug McAdam. 1992. "Collective Identity and Activism: Networks, Choices, and the Life of a Social Movement." In *Frontiers in Social Movement Theory*, ed. Aldon D. Morris and Carol McClung Mueller, 156–73. New Haven, Conn.: Yale University Press.

Gamson, William A. 1995. "Constructing Social Protest." In *Social Movements and Culture*, ed. Hank Johnston and Bert Klandermans, 85–106. Minneapolis: University of Minnesota Press.

———.1992. "The Social Psychology of Collective Action." In *Frontiers in Social Movement Theory*, ed. Aldon D. Morris and Carol McClung Mueller, 53–76. New Haven, Conn.: Yale University Press.

Gamson, William A., and Andre Modigliani. 1989. "Media Discourse and Public Opinion on Nuclear Power: A Constructionist Approach." *American Journal of Sociology*, 95: 1–37.

Gitlin, Todd. 1980. *The Whole World Is Watching: Mass Media in the Making and Unmaking of the New Left*. Berkeley: University of California Press.

Gerhard, Victor. 2002. Head of White Power Records, interviewed November 2002.

Goffman, Erving.1974. *Frame Analysis*. New York: Harper Colophon Books.

———.1963. *Stigma*. Englewood Cliffs, N.J.: Prentice-Hall.

Gusrow, Z., and G. S. Tracy. 1968. "Status, Ideology, and Adaptation to Stigmatized Illness: A Study of Leprosy. *Human Organization* 27: 316–25.

Hale, Matt. 1997. Pontifix Maximus of the World Church of the Creator, interviewed February, 1997.

Jensen, Jane. 1995. "What's in a Name? Nationalist Movements and Public Discourse." In *Social Movements and Culture*, ed. Hank Johnston and Bert Klandermans, 107–26. Minneapolis: University of Minnesota Press.

John Calvin Society for Racial Theology. 1996. "Racialist Advocacy on the Web." http://members.tripod.com/~Calvinism/web (accessed October 4, 1996).

Johnson, Cristopher. 1997. Imperial Klaliff, and Grand Dragon of California, Knights of the Ku Klux Klan (HQ North Salem, IN), interviewed May, 1997.

Kitsuse, John. 1980. "Coming Out All Over: Deviants and the Politics of Social Problems." *Social Problems* 28: 1–13.

Klandermans, Bert. 1992. "The Social Construction of Protest and Multiorganizational Fields." In *Frontiers in Social Movement Theory*, ed. Aldon D. Morris and Carol McClung Mueller, 77–103. New Haven, Conn.: Yale University Press.

KKKK. 2005. "Homepage." http://www.kkk.bz/index1.htm (accessed June 6, 2005).

Lauck, Gerhard. 2005. "Negro Equaltiy [*sic*]? Fudge!" http://www.nsdap.biz/anxlincoln001/anxlincoln001.html (accessed June 5, 2005).

Lemert, Edwin. 1967. *Human Deviance, Social Problems, and Social Control*. New York: Prentice-Hall.

L. R. 1997. Interviewed May 1997.

Malstab, L. 1996. "KILL ALL THE (fill in the blank) OR Why the One World Government Loves Uptight Skinheads and How You Can Make it Otherwise." http://diamond.nb.net/~newdawn/act.htm (accessed September 16, 1996).

Martin, Daniel D. 2000. "Organizational Approaches to Shame: Avowal, Management, and Contestation." *The Sociological Quarterly* 41: 125–50.

McAdam, Doug. 1996. "Conceptual Origins, Current Problems, Future Directions." In *Comparative Perspectives on Social Movements: Political Opportunities, Mobilizing Structures, and Cultural Framings*, ed. Doug McAdam, John D. McCarthy, and Mayer N. Zald, 23–40. New York: Cambridge University Press.

Melucci, Alberto. 1995. "The Process of Collective Identity." In *Social Movements and Culture*, ed. Hank Johnston and Bert Klandermans, 41–63. Minneapolis: University of Minnesota Press.

Metzger, Tom. 1997. Leader of White Aryan Resistance (WAR), interviewed February, 1997.

Murphy, Troy. 1997. Grand Wizard, Knights of the Ku Klux Klan (HQ North Salem, IN), interviewed May, 1997.

New Dawn. 1997. National Socialist, interviewed April, 1997.

New Kastle Kounty Knightriders. 1996. "Exalted Cyclops Opinion Page." http://members.gnn.com/termite34/ecpage.htm (accessed December 3, 1996).

Nix, Dennis. 1997. Head of Fenix Books, interviewed May, 1997.

Pendergraft, Rachel. 2005a. "Our Vision—the 6th Era—and Why You Should Support Pastor Robb and the Knights of the Ku Klux Klan!" http://www.kkk.bz/vision.htm (accessed June 6, 2005).

———. 2005b. "Welcome." http://www.kkk.bz/hello.htm (accessed June 6, 2005).

Robb, Thom. 1997. National Director, Knights of the Ku Klux Klan (HQ Harrison, Ark), interviewed February, 1997.

Schroer, Todd. 2001. "Issue and Identity Framing Within the White Racialist Movement: Internet Dynamics." *The Politics of Social Inequality* 9: 207–31.

Skinheadz. 2005a. "Gutz Skinhead Crew." http://www.skinheadz.com/boosters/crew.html (accessed June 29, 2005).

———.2005b. "Skinhead FAQ." http://www.skinheadz.com/docs/ideology/faq.html (accessed June 3, 2005).

Smith, W. 1997a. "Project hook-up." *NSNet* e-mail newsletter, April 10.

———. 1997b. "Winston on Tabloid TV?" *NSNet* e-mail newsletter, August 2.

Snow, David A., and Robert D. Benford. 1988. "Ideology, Frame Resonance and Participant Mobilization." In *International Social Movement Research*, ed. Bert Klandermans, Hanspeter Kriese, and Sidney Tarrow, 197–217. Greenwich, Conn.: JAI.

————. 1992. "Master Frames and Cycles of Protest." In *Frontiers in Social Movement Theory*, ed. Aldon D. Morris and Carol McClung Mueller, 133–55. New Haven, Conn.: Yale University Press.

Snow, David, et al. 1986. "Frame Alignment Processed, Micromobilization and Movement Participation." *American Sociological Review* 51: 464–81.

Stormfront.org. nd. "What World Famous Men Said About the Jews." http://stormfront.org/jewish/anti-Semite.html (accessed August 14, 2003).

Swidler, Ann. 1995. "Cultural Power and Social Movements." In *Social Movements and Culture*, ed. Hank Johnston and Bert Klandermans, 25–40. Minneapolis: University of Minnesota Press.

Tarrow, Sidney. 1992. "Mentalities, Political Cultures, and Collective Action Frames: Constructing Meanings through Action." In *Frontiers in Social Movement Theory*, ed. Aldon D. Morris and Carol McClung Mueller, 174–202. New Haven, Conn.: Yale University Press.

Taylor, Verta, and Nancy E. Whittier. 1992. "Collective Identity in Social Movement Communities: Lesbian Feminist Mobilization." In *Frontiers in Social Movement Theory*, ed. Aldon D. Morris and Carol McClung Mueller, 104–29. New Haven, Conn.: Yale University Press.

Turner, Ralph H., and Lewis M. Killian, 1987. *Collective Behavior*. 3rd ed. Englewood Cliffs, N.J.: Prentice-Hall.

Voelker, Tommy. 2002. Creator of M.R.M.E.T.A.L. Newsletter, interviewed October, 2002.

Walker, Shaun. 2005. "Racial Populism: Can This Save Our Race?" ADV-list, June 3.

WCOTC. 2001. "Library to Close Doors Day of Meeting." *Creativity* e-mail newsletter, December 18.

Weitz, Rose. 1990. "Living with the Stigma of AIDS." *Qualitative Sociology* 13: 23–38.

Notes

1. The term white racialist is used in this chapter as a blanket term to refer to individuals variously described as white supremacist, white power, white separatist, white nationalist, pan Aryan, *and* other related movements. The term white racialist is used since, in the experience of this author, it is the label most widely accepted by members of the movement when describing themselves. This use of the term white racialist is not meant to obscure the characteristics of members of this movement or present them in a more favorable light. The author in no way agrees with or condones the actions or beliefs of members of this movement.

2. All titles listed are those held at the time of the interview or publication and do not reflect subsequent changes in affiliation or rank.

3. Interviewees who did not want their identities to be revealed chose how they wished to be cited.

4

Drawing Identity Boundaries:
The Creation of Contemporary Feminism

Jo Reger

The demise of American feminism has been declared so many times that Jennifer Pozner (2003) labels these pronouncements a part of the "False Feminist Death Syndrome."[1] In response, scholars and activists argue that feminism faces a backlash (Faludi 1991), has submerged into institutions (Katzensten 1990; Spalter-Roth and Schreiber 1995), or now is in a third wave, different from earlier forms of activism (Baumgartner and Richards 2000; Heywood and Drake 1997; see also Bhavnani et al. 1998; Zita 1997). Studies of contemporary feminism document a range of feminist behaviors, ideologies, and activism, from the punk-based Riot Grrrl movement of the Northwest (Rosenberg and Garofalo 1998) and Internet-based activism (Alfonso and Trigilio 1997) to the mainstream work of young women in established feminist organizations (Beechey 2005). These studies illustrate how feminism has not disappeared in the twenty-first century, and that feminist activism varies greatly in form and content. In this chapter, I explore how movements, such as the U.S. women's movements, give rise to a variety of movement identities. In doing so, I pose questions that are both empirical (what is the state of contemporary feminism?) and theoretical (how are variations in movement identities created?). I argue that one reason for the frequent pronouncement of feminism's "death" is that there are various types of feminism that exist, both at the community and organizational level. I further argue that these variations are shaped, in part, by the construction of activist-antagonist boundaries. This chapter therefore contributes to the overall themes of this volume by demonstrating how the lines of difference that activists create between themselves and others helps construct their collective identity.

The diversity of movement identities is a relatively new and growing area of concern in the social movement literature. Scholars have documented that collective identities diverge within movements, organizations, and networks (Bernstein 1997; Gamson 1997; Reger 2002; Robnett 1997; Whittier 1995, 1997). For example, Nancy Whittier's work on the radical feminist community in Columbus, Ohio reveals how micro-cohorts alter a feminist identity (1995, 1997). Others have shown how gender and sex can shape the construction and deployment of collective identities in creation of leadership styles (Robnett 1997) and participant identities (Einwohner 1999), and that multiple collective identities can be fostered by organizational structure (Reger 2002). An important aspect of all these factors is the larger social structure—that is, the environment in which social movement actors are located. While political opportunity theorists have posited that movements emerge and respond to favorable openings in the social structure (Jenkins 1983; Kriesi 1995; McCarthy and Zald 1977; Tarrow 1989), I argue that the larger social structure and the barriers it presents to activists can shape the construction of a collective identity. In particular, I find that environmental receptivity to types of activism influences the form and content of the collective identity constructed.

These findings are based on two case studies of communities with college campuses, one in the Midwest and one on the East Coast. These case studies were selected to examine regional variations in feminist activism.[2] In each case site, my primary research goal was to identify young feminists and ascertain the form and focus of their collective identities. To do so, from 2002 to 2004, I interviewed thirty young women and men[3] (seventeen from the East Coast and thirteen from the Midwest) and gathered organizational documents, such as newsletters, minutes, flyers advertising events, and students' academic writing on feminism and related issues. The interviews focused on the respondents' definitions of and relationship to feminism, as well as the broader community's political and social climate and its influence on feminist activism. In addition, I conducted additional interviews with one professor from each school to gain further insight on the nature of the social and political climate in each community. Before discussing my findings, I first turn to the literature on boundary construction and environmental influences on activists' collective identity.

Interaction and Boundary Construction

Social movement scholars have emphasized the importance of boundaries in the construction of collective identity. Boundaries "mark the social territories of group relations by highlighting differences between activists and the web of others in the contested social world" (Taylor and Whittier 1992, 111). Boundaries help to forge the creation of an internal group consciousness that delineates who is and who is not a member of the group. This process entails a withdrawal from the dominant group or society and the creation of new group-affirming values, beliefs, and ideologies (Taylor and Whittier 1992). As Joshua Gamson states, "All social movements, and identity movements in particular, are in the business, at least sometimes, of exclusion" (1997, 179). Once boundaries are established, determining who is a member of a group, social movement actors create a consciousness "that imparts a larger significance to a collectivity," (Taylor and Whittier 1992, 114). This consciousness and the consequent collective identity is maintained, in part, through "some degree of boundary patrol" (Gamson 1997, 181).

While the construction of collective identities depends on the enactment and monitoring of boundaries, the particular lines of difference that are drawn depend on internal dynamics and external social forces (see Gamson 1997; Taylor and Whittier 1992). Activists work to identify boundaries that signify how they differ from others. One notable group of "others," the dominant group, controls the social and political environment and therefore influences the culture in which the challenging group dwells. Activists assess whether they are socially, psychologically, or physically different from the dominant group by generating an understanding of that group and then using it to mark boundaries. However, multicultural feminists observe that individuals rarely experience the world through a singular characteristic or social identity (i.e., gender, race, ethnicity, class, sexuality) but instead experience a matrix of domination and privilege (see Zinn and Dill 1996; Collins 1990; hooks 1981; King 1988). Therefore, in cases where the lines of difference between activists and the dominant group are unclear, activists might turn instead to the internal dynamics of their group (i.e., how the matrix of domination and privilege is experienced and individuals' corresponding attitudes, values, and beliefs) to construct identity boundaries. For example, heterosexual allies of gay, lesbian, and bisexual people might draw upon their *recognition* of their privilege as a way of identifying themselves as different from predominantly heterosexual society (see Chapter 7).

In sum, the ability to perceive and articulate the differences between activists and dominant society is crucial to the construction of collective identities. I now turn to a discussion of how activists survey the dominant society and construct the boundaries that foster a collective identity.

Environment and Boundary Construction

Collective identities are necessarily "situationally specific identities" (Hunt, Benford, and Snow 1994, 186) and are located within space and time. Social movement actors interact within their own groups to identify both internal and external boundaries, a process Scott A. Hunt, Robert D. Benford, and David A. Snow refer to as "boundary framing." To adequately frame identity boundaries, social movement actors must identify three groups: protagonists, antagonists, and an audience (Hunt, Benford, and Snow 1994). The community in which activists reside can provide all three; in it can be found the protagonists (i.e., members or potential members of the activist group), an audience (i.e., observers such as the bystander public or the media), and antagonists (i.e., those targeted as the enemy or the "other"). Of the three, antagonists are particularly crucial for the creation of an oppositional identity stance facilitating micromobilization, the identification of collective grievances, and member recruitment (Gamson 1997; Hunt, Benford, and Snow 1994; Taylor and Whittier 1992).

It is important to note that activists collectively create antagonists through their identity work by drawing on their intersubjective definitions of "reality" (Gamson 1997, 204). As Hunt, Benford, and Snow explain, "Antagonist identity fields are constellations of identity attributions about individuals and collectivities imputed to be opponents of movement causes" (1994, 197). For example, Verta Taylor (1989) argues that feminist groups with strong collective identities are able to create abeyance structures that allow organizations to survive in hostile climates. The creation of abeyance structures depends on the framing of the external community as antagonistic, using multiple framings to cast others as those from which the group must protect itself.

Given that boundaries are created through the identification of a target or oppositional group and depend on the interplay of internal activist dynamics and external social factors, to understand the creation of identity boundaries in contemporary feminism, it is necessary to identify the climate in which feminists operate as well as the ways in which they construct and understand the protagonists, antagonists, and audience in the communities in which they live. Understanding this process of boundary construction, therefore, will illuminate why movement identities vary from context to context. To explore these dynamics empirically, I now turn to a description of my case studies and then to my data.

The Case Studies

Woodview

The Midwest case study focuses on a regional public university I call Woodview and its surrounding community. Because the university is largely a commuter campus, it lacks the sense of community that is usually characteristic of more residential campuses. The university is also relatively conservative in its political and educational stances, mirroring the community around it. Politically and economically, the surrounding community is primarily Republican, with a relatively affluent base. Most residents are employed as professional managers and the average housing costs are $260,000. Racially, the population is predominately white (88 percent) with small percentages of Asians (7 percent), blacks (2 percent), and Hispanics (2 percent). One indicator of the community's conservatism is the 52 percent countywide vote in favor of an antigay marriage state constitutional amendment.

Because its student body draws on students from the local community and neighboring cities and towns, which are more working class, Woodview reflects the larger community educationally as well. A faculty member, who worked with others to bring women's studies to campus, noted that when faculty started offering classes with a gender focus in the 1980s, "We all felt like we were doing the right thing. We were trying to advance the consciousness of women who were very suburban, very Republican." She said that the harder the faculty pushed for women's studies, the more "nervous" was the administration's response. The lack of the enthusiasm for women's studies and feminism was not restricted to the administration; for instance when the first director of women's studies brought Inga Muscio, the author of *Cunt*, to campus, she had a difficult time advertising the event when some staff and faculty objected to the word "cunt" being used on flyers.

Feminist activism at Woodview stems mostly from the student organization Forum for Women (FFW), which was founded in 2001.[4] The group's establishment was spurred by the creation of a women's studies program, which itself was developed after existing for several years as a concentration of study. FFW provides a central meeting place for feminist activists by holding weekly meetings with anywhere between ten to twenty-five people attending (mostly white and mostly women). While the attendees do not all know each other, many are connected through friendship networks, networks that have grown over the past three years to incorporate more men and more students from other student groups such as the Gay-Straight Alliance, which emerged in the 2002–3 school year. In the years that FFW has been in existence, its presence on campus has spread and the group is one of the strongest student organizations on campus, visible through the production of the *Vagina Monologues*, the antiviolence Clothesline Project, a women's fair involving other campus and local progressive groups and several other initiatives. The group also advocated for and obtained (along with other student groups and the women's studies program) a Gender and Sexuality Center on campus to provide resources to women, gay, lesbian, bisexual, transgendered, and questioning students.

Evers

The East Coast case study focuses on an all-women's college, which I call Evers, and its surrounding community. Unlike Woodview, Evers' students and faculty are generally liberal in their politics and the school's women's studies department is well established. In addition, the majority of students come from East Coast areas and the school is a residential campus. Moreover, the community surrounding Evers is equally liberal, with a tradition of openness to gay and lesbian people and an active assortment of progressive organizations. In stark contrast to the conservative leanings of the community surrounding Woodview, only 7 percent of Evers' community members are registered Republicans. However, like Woodview, the majority of the community is white (88 percent) with small populations of blacks and Hispanics (2 percent and 5 percent). The median household income in the community is $42,000 (as of 2000) and the median house value is $145,000.

Evers is home to a variety of student organizations that address gender issues and other related forms of inequality; these include Feminist Alliance, Feminists Unite, The Lesbian, Bisexual, Transgendered Alliance, the Council for Students of Color, Native American Women, and the Women World Affairs Committee. Feminists Unite, the most overtly feminist group, held a few well-attended programs in 2003 that were related to reproductive rights and abortion. However, despite being in existence for several years the group has an uneven history and often goes for periods of time with no visible mobilization. In 2003, the group's visibility on campus was largely due to the result of one dynamic student activist. Another group, The Student Coalition, drew much more student involvement in 2003. That group was formed in 2002 to address several racist and homophobic events on the campus, including graffiti written on doors to student housing. The group, with a diverse membership including women of color, queer women, and transgender people, held several demonstrations, prepared a list of demands, and met with administrators to have these events addressed. The Student Coalition continued to meet and created a documentary of the events of the 2001–2 school year that members regularly show to incoming students.

Given the differences between the campus and community climates of Woodview and Evers, one might expect to find variations in the ways feminist activists define themselves and feminism as a whole. I turn now to my findings and a discussion of the ways in which activists drew on their understanding of their similarities with and differences from others in their community to construct their sense of feminist collective identity.

Formation of the Collective Self through the Collective Other

As noted earlier, one step in the construction of a collective identity is the identification of antagonists (Hunt, Benford, and Snow 1994), which is accomplished through creating an understanding of the community context. I find that due to their location in the midst of a conservative community, from which they felt isolated, the identification of antagonists by feminists at Woodview was accomplished relatively easily, contributing to a feminist identity that focused mainly on issues of gender inequality and violence against women. In contrast, at Evers, the general acceptance of feminism both on campus and in the surrounding community led to the construction of antagonist boundaries focused less on gender inequality and more on issues of race, ethnicity, sexuality, transgenderism, and "outdated" modes of feminism.

Isolation at Woodview

With its generally conservative climate, activists turned to the only visible feminist group on campus as a means of seeking community. One activist, Leslie, who worked with the group early in its inception, reflected on her experience with FFW, "It made me feel more tied to the university, tied to campus you know, like I'm a part of something here and that we could establish a liberal, feminist community. It just amazed me that first year." Before finding the group, Leslie said that she had sought out a community on campus with little success. A young woman who often dresses in "punk" fashion with short skirts, combat books, and her hair in pigtails, explained,

> Well, before that [finding FFW], I would watch people around the school and if I didn't have anybody to eat lunch with, I'd look around. . . . I would look out for people who looked, who were maybe sending out flags, you know, not dressing the way that everybody dresses which if, I don't know it could be a judgmental thing but it sends up a flag for me anyway if they dress more like I do. . . . I didn't see a lot of it. I would see like one or two people here or there and I would kind of keep track of them. . . . And [we] never interacted but we'd spot each other and just keep walking and so I

didn't feel there was a place for me here on campus [with] any group of people that I fit in with or could make friends with.

While a student like Leslie may have felt isolated at any politically conservative campus, another factor producing isolation at Woodview was the fact that the majority of students were commuters and the campus did not foster a sense of community. However, although some of the student activists' sense of isolation can reflect the fact that it can be difficult to connect with students in general on a commuter (as opposed to a residential campus), the conservative feel of the campus is both palpable and influential. According to a faculty member who has been at Woodview for more that thirty years, "in the last 10 years has there been creeping conservatism." She continued, "I think there has been a growing disconnect between the administration and the faculty. And the administration has grown increasingly conservative." She added that the "disconnect" began with the hiring of the current [university] president and "then that solidifies that we have a Republican governor for 12 years . . . and we have a Republican [university] president so the two of them work together and it changes the climate dramatically I think in the schools. So [Woodview's] not the place it was even 15 years ago."

For many of the student activists, Woodview's politically conservative climate was still more liberal than their home towns and high schools. Maura, a member of FFW for several years recalled coming to Woodview. She said,

There's a whole another [*sic*] world out there besides my little bubble in [her home town]. I think about that a lot, just like all the people I went to high school with and just this little bubble we live in and how I think that's how the rest of the world is. And even though this is 15 minutes away from my home, it's still different, a lot different than my high school, you know there's actually black people here.

Despite its differences from the students' more conservative (and white) hometowns, however, Woodview was not seen as a liberal or feminist haven by any stretch of the imagination. For instance, Maura described the campus as "incredibly conservative." She continued, "There's not a lot of feminists on campus. There's a lot of girls that are just, you know, they come to school so dressed up and so "hooched" out and . . . the guys too. It's just frustrating." Laura agreed that the campus was in general not supportive to feminist issues. She said that when she introduces herself as a leader in FFW the response is often, "Oh, you are a male bashing club. Oh, one of you."

Other FFW members reported even more overt hostility from their fellow students. For instance, one year the group produced flyers containing information on a variety of issues including sexual assault, pay equity, and sexual harassment. On one flyer the group noted that 85 percent of the female students reported they had been sexually harassed. Someone removed the flyers, added the line "That's because 85 percent of them dress and flaunt like sluts," and then made copies and posted it around campus. This was not the only incident members faced when doing public events. Jane, another FFW leader, remembered a confrontation at the Clothesline Project where the students had placed a "rape free zone" tape around the display of T-shirts bearing stories of rape and sexual violence. She said that a male student asked the group members, "Does that mean I can rape someone for free here?"

These activists' accounts of their experiences working in a setting that they found both isolating and hostile also illustrate the distinctions they drew between themselves and the other members of the campus community. As a result of the construction of these boundaries, the collective identity of the members of FFW focused on the creation of a safe feminist space where issues such as sexual violence could be discussed freely, without hostile responses. Several members active in the inception of the group noted that talking and working on issues around sexual assault was critical in forming a sense of the group. For example, Paulina said, "We bonded due to our common ground of sexual violence. . . . We initially started talking more due to that [and] we really began to unite after that on different fronts." Describing the group's identity, Jane also said,

> I think it's very empowering for all of the members. I think it's comfortable, I don't know if comfortable is the right word, but very . . . knowing that there are other people that you can go to—to talk to about certain issues that are, that feel the same kind of passion towards certain issues. . . . So I think for a lot of us it is kind of a support, you have other people to talk to and it's a bunch of people that share the same passion for the issues that are work[ing] together. I think you build a friendship too. I know I hang out with a lot of them [FFW members] outside of the group now too, we have great friendships and we can go out and do anything.

Emily also felt a sense of connection that was fostered within the group. She said, "I've had a really good experience here because there is definitely a group of people I can relate to and I feel like I have common interests with and that I have fun with and especially over the last few weeks when we were doing the *Vagina Monologues* that's when I felt like I really got to know a lot of people and it was really fun." For others, the group also provided an end to social isolation that they had felt earlier in their lives. For example, Maura said, "Yeah, camaraderie—it's nice to have girlfriends again. I haven't had friends that were girls since like eighth grade."

Despite these feelings of connection and camaraderie, divisions have also emerged within the group, especially surrounding the topic of sexuality. While the group has had several lesbian and bisexual members and openly talks about sexuality in its meetings, it has not taken on many lesbian, bisexual, or transgender specific issues or events besides cosponsoring events with the campus gay and allies group. For many FFW members the issue of sexuality came to a head at a cast party after the 2002 production of the *Vagina Monologues*. Many of the heterosexual women who felt a close bond during the performances were surprised at how quickly the group divided along the lines of straight versus lesbian women. Kyra recalled feeling hurt about how she was treated: "It's hard for me and when I was at the cast party it was like I'd feel left out and I'd feel . . . I'd almost feel left out because I'm not gay and I was like well . . . it's their own culture and I respect that but I got to know a lot of them on a personal level and it was cool but it seemed like when they got together it seemed very exclusionary and I was like that sucks because I got to know you as a person. . . . I mean that shouldn't be an issue." Internal dissension arose as well over the group's various social networks or cliques. Several members discussed how they believed the group was cliquish or centered on some friendship networks over others. According to Leslie,

> this has been kind of an issue within the group lately that [another member] brought up at a meeting the other day that she feels like we're starting to segregate and starting to, not discriminate, but we're starting to make people feel left out, that there's like an old versus new kind of a thing, that there's a gay versus not gay kind of a thing within the group and that people are feeling pushed out or feeling not included.

In addition, other social characteristics threaten to disrupt the organization's cohesiveness. Issues of race and ethnicity have also begun to surface somewhat in the largely white organization as members grapple, at times, with diversifying their group. According to Emily, "I guess that with our group I feel like there's quite a bit of diversity with sexuality which I think is really cool but other than that [diversity in race-ethnicity and class] there's not so much. I think that that's definitely something to consider." Paulina agreed and said, "There's [*sic*] a lot of like bars to break down within just this one group of feminists, you know."

In sum, the feminist identity of FFW was initially shaped by a community and campus environment that is hostile to feminism. Because of the sense of social, physical, and psychological isolation experienced by the student activists, the group formed a collective (and very social) identity initially focused on the importance of ending gender inequality and acknowledging sexual assault. FFW members often speak of the group as a haven of like-minded people. However, as the prominence of the group continues to grow, the initially strong boundaries it drew between itself and the campus community begin to weaken. Ironically, as the campus community becomes more open to feminist thought and activism, contentious issues begin to arise within the group, resulting in a shift in its collective identity.

The Evers "Bubble"

Activist members of the East Coast community experienced different dynamics than their counterparts at Woodview. Because of the general emphasis on feminism at Evers College, most of the women I interviewed found that feminism as a political ideology was both "invisible" and expected. That is, through the efforts of second-wave feminist activists (many of them, perhaps not surprisingly, parents of Evers students), feminism was embedded in these young women's lives. As *Manifesta* authors Jennifer Baumgardner and Amy Richards argue, "For our generation, feminism is like fluoride. We scarcely notice that we have it—it's simply in the water" (2000, 17).

At Evers, this diffusion of feminism throughout the campus climate was reflected in common references to the college as a "bubble" that was insulated from the gender inequality of the "real" world. In fact, Becca, a leader in the group Feminists Unite, noted that feminism was so "diffused" at Evers that it was hard to mobilize feminists on campus. She described the single sex school as "woman land and feminist land" and said, "We feel like we don't have to talk about this stuff." Stella, a biracial student active in organizations for women of color, added that she had not become active in the feminist group on campus because "being at a place like [Evers] . . . we're all women and it feels a lot different and it does feel like maybe this is one thing that I don't need to work on it all the time." Terri, a sophomore and member of a pagan group on campus, added, "I think it is easy to become lazy in your feminism here, which is a problem." According to one Evers professor, "It's a very kind of weird environment because it's universally feminist and yet apolitical at the same time." Moreover, it was not only the campus but also the surrounding community that fostered such a feminist environment that activism was, ironically, muted. According to a professor and local resident, the community "is a totally progressive town, pretty much. There is no target [for feminist activism] here, either."

The students I interviewed acknowledged that their campus and broader community environment were unique. For some non-East Coast students, returning home was an awakening. Lila reported that when she returned to her home in the Midwest (coincidentally, near Woodview University) her friends would often ask her "Where do you go to school? What planet are you living on?" She said that she often received "conservative packages" from friends and family with news clippings as a reminder of life outside of Evers. She recalled one week where she was called a "crazy conservative" at Evers and returned home to be called a "crazy pinko leftist radical" by her uncle. Terri had similar experiences, noting that "usually once I go home for a break or something I will be reintroduced to that whole world and I'll be like 'Oh, that's why I'm a feminist.'"

The lack of an antagonistic environment led Evers activists to draw boundaries differently than the Woodview activists. While Woodview students faced a conservative administration and student body, Evers students operated in a more liberal climate, which made it difficult to articulate a collective identity as feminists. As Lila said, "There's no one for us to work against on campus. I wish that. . . . I honestly wish that they would bring more conservative students to [Evers] so that we would have more of a perspective on things." While all the Evers women I interviewed identified as feminists, most did not see that as a central identity in their lives and many talked of rejecting the third wave, young feminist label. For example, Becca felt that the image of the "punked out" woman with a tight "Slut" T-shirt on was a media invention that did not reflect the reality of women's activism. In addition, some women questioned whether feminism *could* be an identity or the basis for community. For Deborah, one of the few interviewees who were also women's studies majors, third-wave feminism was not an identity but rather a "gestalt" that had been oversimplified in the media.

For many of the Evers students, feminism was a common ideology in their lives, one that they learned about from their parents or in their high school classes. Feminism therefore was not a revelation from women's studies classes as it was for many of the Woodview students. Drawing on the presence of feminism in their lives and on the lack of antagonists in the college or external community, young Evers feminists constructed their identity by drawing boundaries against second wave feminism. This more internally focused boundary construction was, according to an Evers professor, "the main way that students define themselves as feminists . . . that's their boundary." For Sandra, drawing that boundary was personal. She said, "I used [to] think my mom was a feminist until we discussed queer issues and I think that was one of my big [feminist] issues was understanding that she is still stuck in the '60s, '70s mentality of women [who] want equality from men under the system of heterosexual normativity." Becca also distanced herself from second-wave feminism. She said,

> I do see myself—I use the term feminist when I describe myself and it has always been a little problematic for me because I sort of, I understand that feminism is largely a movement that has left a lot of people that raised me behind because I come from a working class background and my mom, she's on public assistance, things like that, and I recognize that a lot of these women are basically ignored by feminism. So my whole purpose of calling myself a feminist is to say that we do have faith in this movement and it belongs to us too.

The boundary between contemporary and second-wave feminism was not limited to family, but extended to the women's studies program at Evers as well. Many of the Evers students interviewed were critical of the "conservative" nature of the women's studies department and had not taken any women's studies courses in college themselves. Because these students felt that the women's studies department focused more on academics than activism, they found it "out of step" with their ideas of feminism and blamed it for the lack of feminist activism on campus. Terri said, "But perhaps if the Women's Studies department was more pushing activism, there would be a stronger base of students who were interested [in Feminists Unite]."

Along with targeting women's studies as too "second wave," activists also constructed boundaries between themselves, other students, and the administration in terms of race and ethnicity. Whereas the Woodview women focused on gender inequality and sexual assault, many of the Evers women put race, ethnicity, class, and transgender issues at the forefront of their activism. Stella noted that her sense of community came through an organization aimed at supporting queer women of color and not from the feminist groups on campus. This boundary construction was fostered by the aforementioned incidents with the racist and homophobic graffiti that led to the formation of the Student Coalition. For many, the messages scrawled in public buildings felt like a direct attack and highlighted social identities revolving around race, ethnicity, and sexuality. As Stella said, "I think because of the structure and the power and privilege of a place like [Evers] I don't need to find a source of other women because I can find that, I could find that almost anywhere if I wanted it, but I do need to find a space with other queer people and other people of color because we are not a majority on this campus." As a result of the events that led to the rise of the Student Coalition, the campus environment was affected, which changed students' perception of Evers. Terri said,

I feel like there's a very, it's a very tense environment in terms of racial issues to some extent which surprised me. . . . It really felt like students were sort of reverting into their general classifications and sort of withdrawing from those who were different from them. There was the sort of atmosphere of distrust and it was kind of scary to me because I had no idea where it was coming from and a lot of it, it was difficult because certain events had happened and the campus didn't really, the college didn't really publicize them. Towards the end of the year they made an effort to let the students know what was going on, but there was this whole tense situation.

The response to the graffiti brought to the forefront students' understandings of race, ethnicity, and sexuality. Lila, who attended a multiracial private school in the Midwest, saw the situation as embedded in the understandings students had of race from their communities. She said,

I don't think a lot of people at [Evers] know about or come from a background like that. I think those people are from very white progressive towns on the East Coast . . . and I think their approach then to fighting racism or whatever is different from black students who grew in an all-black environment. . . . And then for me who just grew up in a diverse background that wasn't necessarily very progressive at all but I was certainly exposed to a lot of a lot of different cultures and a lot of different racial groups. So I think that . . . I think that there's an obvious sense of awkwardness when . . . wealthy white girls from the East Coast who are from very wealthy progressive communities trying to come here and fight racism.

In the case of the racist and homophobic incidents, the boundary constructed brought together students of color and white students who "got" racism in a particular way. The "enemies" became white students who did not acknowledge their privilege and the college administration that the students saw as slow to act. According to Sandra, who was active in the Student Coalition, the campus reaction was the result of "a long stemming tradition of the administration at this college ignoring the fact that it's an unhealthy environment for a lot of people."

Despite this focus on race, ethnicity, and sexuality, gender was not completely ignored. All the women interviewed talked about the importance of identifying and supporting transgender students and students exploring a transgendered identity. However, many of them saw feminism as distancing itself and not addressing transgender people. In fact, several of the women no longer viewed their mothers as "true" feminists (similar to Sandra and her mother's response to queer issues) because of their inability to understand transgender dynamics. For example, Skye said she preferred the identity of humanist or womanist to distance herself from the gender-focused feminist identity of her mother, who did not understand transgender. For Tadeo, a transgender student from the West Coast, there were divisions within the Evers administration and student body in general about transgender. She[5] said, "I think like three years ago it was more radical and the students on campus were able to push the administration further politically and open mindedly on social justice issues but now recently there's a lot more students who are a lot more traditional and there aren't that many out there that have their analysis of all sorts of oppressions."

The push for transgender acceptance created an internal boundary, the result of which labeled some feminist students themselves as antagonists. Lila, a campus leader, faced much hostility from transgender activists because of her resistance to changing the Evers constitution to include more gender neutral language. She explained,

> I hold I guess like I said a more conservative perspective on transgender here on campus which is not brought me much popularity. . . . But I don't . . . I'm sure you've heard about the constitution change? . . . And I'm whole-heartedly against that. . . . It's not a popularly expressed opinion because people are afraid of speaking up and saying that because it's not PC enough for this campus. So there's a lot of people actually who . . . because I've been I guess associated with those people who are working to repeal that constitution change. I've gotten a lot of people who have e-mailed me basically just speaking up saying "Oh I don't want you to publicize this but I really support you and if I can do anything to help please let me know and don't tell anyone."

In sum, Evers feminist student activists created a collective identity that was quite different from the identity of feminist activists from Woodview. The Evers identity tended to shift with the environment, focusing on race and homophobia after the "hate" graffiti appeared on campus and embracing transgender people as more such individuals began to identify on campus and the college's constitution became an issue. While this identity is grounded in an acceptance of feminism, it is distanced from other feminists, both third and second wave. However it is important to note that despite the boundaries drawn, Evers students still construct an essentially feminist identity with students accepting that label and identifying as feminists.

Conclusions

Discussions of social movement participation and mobilization need to take into account how the individual, the organization, and the larger environment interact. As outlined in Taylor and Whittier's (1992) work, identity construction depends on a series of processes that allow activists to define who they are, who they are not, and the significance of this difference. In the case studies of Woodview and Evers, community and campus environments shaped the types of feminist identities constructed. The identification of boundaries involves the recognition of protagonists, audience, and antagonists. While audience was less of a focus for the activists in the case studies, both Evers and Woodview provide evidence that the clarity and cohesiveness of the protagonist identity (in this case, feminist) depends on the strength of the antagonistic "other" and the particular community context.

These findings provide insight into the questions posed at the beginning of this chapter; what is the state of contemporary feminism and how are variations in movement identities created? To say that young women and men do (or do not) embrace feminism is to ignore the particularity of their situations. Although the feminists in both case studies are relatively similar to each other in terms of demographics (age and social class in particular) and their overall beliefs about gender equality (i.e., most defined feminism similarly, as the struggle for gender equality), they create forms of feminism that are in many ways quite different from each other. For example, at the time of the interviews, none of the Woodview feminists discussed transgender as an issue facing feminists[6] and issues of race-ethnicity were confined mostly to infrequent discussions of how to increase the participation of people of color. It is tempting to conclude that because Woodview focuses more on issues of gender inequality, they are the more "feminist" of the two groups. However, as U.S. feminism continues to shift and change, so do the issues addressed by feminists. I argue that Evers is no less feminist than Woodview. These findings illustrate the role of the community and campus context in which activists are situated in their creation of different ways of doing and understanding feminism. Social observers who limit their focus to previously identified types or styles of feminist activism or identity are bound to miss some of these meso-level variations, which can only lead to another premature (and incorrect) assessment of the state of contemporary feminism.

In addition to illustrating how identities, organizations and environments interact, this study also reconfirms what symbolic interactionists have long argued. That is, identities are not only shaped by the environment, the environment is shaped by the construction of identities (Blumer 1969).

This point is particularly clear in the shifting of Woodview's identity and the growing dissension around issues of social networks and sexuality. As FFW's presence grows on campus, the group influences the environment by reaching an audience sympathetic and interested in feminism.[7] Although most audience members might never become activists, their support of feminism decreases the sense of hostility on campus, changing some of the boundary markers and causing variations in the content and nature of the activists' collective identity. At Evers, the relationship between the environment and identity is also evident. As the activists raise issues around events that have occurred in their environment, for example, by addressing hate graffiti or the college constitution, they alter their interpretation of their surroundings and, consequently, change their feminist identity. What this means to scholars of social movements, and the women's movement in particular, is that to understand current rates of mobilization within movements, attention must be paid not only to how activists construct an understanding of who they are but also to the particular boundaries that are constructed in that process.

Collective identity and community are intertwined concepts in understanding both the internal functioning of a movement and its external processes such as the formulation of strategies, goals, and tactics. We need to continue to explore how external factors link to internal movement dynamics. In particular, this chapter suggests that the study of boundary construction has much to offer scholars interested in movement emergence, outcomes, and identity processes.

References

Alfonso, Rita, and Jo Trigilio. 1997. "Surfing the Third Wave: A Dialogue between Two Third Wave Feminists." *Hypatia* 12(3): 7–16.

Baumgardner, Jennifer, and Amy Richards. 2000. *Manifesta*. New York: Farrar, Straus and Giroux.

Beechey, Susanne. 2005. "When Feminism Is Your Job: Age and Power in Women's Policy Organizations." In *Different Wavelengths: Studies of the Contemporary Women's Movement*, ed. J. Reger, 117–36. New York/London: Routledge.

Benford, Robert D., and Scott A. Hunt. 1992. "Dramaturgy and Social Movements: The Social Construction and Communication of Power." *Sociological Inquiry* 62: 36–55.

Bernstein, Mary. 1997. "Celebration and Suppression: The Strategic Uses of Identity by the Lesbian and Gay Movement." *American Journal of Sociology* 103: 531–65.

Bhavnani, Kum-Kum, Kathryn R. Ken, and France Winddance Twine, ed. 1998. "Feminisms and Youth Culture." *Signs: A Journal of Women in Culture and Society*, 23 Spring: Special edition.

Blumer, Herbert G. 1969. *Symbolic Interactionism.* Englewood Cliffs, N.J.: Transaction.

Collins, Patricia Hill. 1990. *Black Feminist Thought: Knowledge, Consciousness, and the Politics of Empowerment.* Boston: Unwin Hyman.

Einwohner, Rachel. 1999. "Gender, Class and Social Movement Outcomes: Identity and Effectiveness in Two Animal Rights Campaigns." *Gender & Society* 13(1): 56–76.

Faludi, Susan, 1991. *Backlash.* New York: Anchor.

Gamson, Joshua. 1997. "Messages of Exclusion: Gender, Movements and Symbolic Boundaries." *Gender & Society* 11(2): 178–99.

Heywood, Leslie, and Jennifer Drake, ed. 1997. *Third Wave Agenda: Being Feminist, Doing Feminism.* Minneapolis: University of Minnesota Press.

hooks, bell, 1989. *Talking Back: Thinking Feminist, Thinking Black.* Boston: South End Press.

Hunt, Scott A., and Robert D. Benford. 2004. "Collective Identity, Solidarity and Commitment." In *Blackwell Companion to Social Movements*, ed. D. A. Snow, S. A. Soule, H. Kriesi, 433–57. Malden, Mass.: Blackwell Publishers.

Hunt, Scott A., Robert D. Benford, and David A. Snow. 1994, "Identity Fields: Framing Processes and the Social Construction of Movement Identities." In *New Social Movements: From Ideology to Identity*, ed. E. Laraña, H. Johnston, and J. R. Gusfield, 185–208. Philadelphia: Temple University Press.

Jenkins, J. Craig. 1983. "Resource Mobilization Theory and the Study of Social Movements." *Annual Review of Sociology* 9: 527–53.

Katzenstein, Mary F. 1990. "Feminism within American Institutions: Unobtrusive Mobilization in the 1980s." *Signs: A Journal of Women in Culture and Society* 16: 27–54.

King, Deborah. 1988. "Multiple Jeopardy: The Context of a Black Feminist Ideology." *Signs: A Journal of Women in Culture and Society* 14(1): 42–77.

Kriesi, Hanspeter. 1995. "The Political Opportunity Structure of New Social Movements: Its Impact on Their Mobilization." In *The Politics of Social Protest: Comparative Perspectives on States and Social Movements*, ed. J. C. Jenkins and B. Klandermans, 167–98. Minneapolis: University of Minnesota Press.

McCarthy, John D., and Mayer N. Zald. 1977. "Resource Mobilization and Social Movements: A Partial Theory." *American Journal of Sociology* 82: 1212–41.

Morris, Aldon. D. 1992. "Political Consciousness and Collective Action." In *Frontiers in Social Movement Theory*, ed. A. D. Morris and C. M. Mueller, 351–73. New Haven, Conn.: Yale University Press.

Pozner, Jennifer. 2003. "The 'Big Lie': False Feminist Death Syndrome, Profit, and the Media." In *Catching a Wave: Reclaiming Feminism for the 21st Century*, ed. R. Dicker and A. Piepmeier, 31–56. Boston: Northeastern University Press.

Reger, Jo. 2002. "Organizational Dynamics and Construction of Multiple Feminist Identities in the National Organization for Women." *Gender & Society* 16: 710–27.

Robnett, Belinda. 1997. *How Long? How Long? African American Women in the Struggle for Civil Rights*. New York: Oxford University Press.

Rosenberg, Jessica, and Gitana Garofalo. 1998. "Riot Grrrl: Revolutions from Within." *Signs: Journal of Women in Culture and Society* 23: (Summer): 811–41.

Spalter-Roth, Roberta, and Ronnee Schreiber. 1995. "Outsider Issues and Insider Tactics: Tensions in the Women's Policy Network during the 1980s." In *Feminist Organizations: Harvest of the New Women's Movement*, ed. M. M. Ferree and P. Y. Martin, 105–27. Philadelphia: Temple University Press.

Tarrow, Sidney. 1989. "Struggle, Politics, and Reform: Collective Action, Social Movements, and Cycles of Protest." Ithaca, N.Y.: Center for International Studies: Cornell University

Taylor, Verta. 1989. "Sources of Continuity in Social Movements: The Women's Movement in Abeyance." *American Sociological Review* 54: 761–75.

Taylor, Verta, and Nancy Whittier. 1992. "Collective Identity in Social Movement Communities: Lesbian Feminist Mobilization." In *Frontiers in Social Movement Theory*, ed. A. D. Morris and C. M. Mueller, 104–29. New Haven: Yale University Press.

Whittier, Nancy. 1997. "Political Generations, Micro-Cohorts, and the Transformation of Social Movements." *American Sociological Review* 67: 760–78.

———. 1995. *Feminist Generations: The Persistence of the Radical Women's Movement*. Philadelphia: Temple University Press.

Zinn, Maxine Baca, and Bonnie Thornton Dill. 1996. "Theorizing Difference from Multi-Racial Feminism," *Feminist Studies* 22(2): 321–31.

Zita, Jacqueline N. ed. 1997. "Third Wave Feminism," *Hypatia* 12, Special edition.

Notes

1. For a contemporary example see Neal Conan's introduction of feminism on *Talk of the Nation*, April 22, 2004, National Public Radio, where he claims fewer and fewer women are claiming the identity of feminist. Retrieved from Lexus Nexus May 28, 2004, http://web.lexis-nexis.com/universe/document?_m=3a78dc441d9d8cb0c763ba26291d910.

2. As noted by Hunt and Benford (2004), studies of collective identity often take the form of localized versus nationally focused studies allowing for a more in-depth examination of the variations and dynamics in identity construction.

3. The two groups are similar in terms of sex (Midwest, 92 percent female, East Coast 100 percent female) but diverge in terms of race-ethnicity (Midwest, 92 percent Caucasian; East Coast 59 percent Caucasian, 35 percent biracial, Latino, or

Chicana) and sexuality (Midwest, 46 percent lesbian, 23 percent heterosexual, 30 percent bisexual or queer; East Coast, 59 percent queer, 18 percent heterosexual, 18 percent bisexual or lesbian). Both groups had respondents that preferred not to identify race, ethnicity, or sexuality.

4. All student groups have been given pseudonyms to protect the anonymity of the interviewees.

5. Although Tadeo identifies as transgender (female to male), she prefers to use feminine pronouns when describing herself.

6. This could be changing as ideas about transgender spread across the nation. See Cline, Elizabeth. July 22, 2004, "Transmale Nation: Remaking manhood in the Genderqueer Generation," *Village Voice.* http://www.villagevoice.com/print/issues/0425/cline.php (accessed August 12, 2004).

7. For example, at the productions of the *Vagina Monologues* put on by FFW members, a significant portion of the audience came from the surrounding communities and had no affiliation with the university.

5

Passing as Strategic Identity Work in the Warsaw Ghetto Uprising[1]

Rachel L. Einwohner

Much of the extant literature on identity and social movements highlights the construction of identity during the course of collective action (Fantasia 1988; Melucci 1989; Reger 2002; Taylor and Whittier 1992, 1995; Whittier 1995). According to this research, the adoption of a new activist identity— or the affirmation of an existing one—is an important component of protest activity. Put another way, because many scholars argue that collective action is the enactment of identity (Calhoun 1994; Neuhouser 1998), people participate in protest partly because doing so matches with their sense of who and what they are (see also Loeb 1994). Members of social movements are therefore thought to "find themselves" through their activism.

In some movement settings, however, the opposite may be true as well. This chapter describes some of the processes at work when activists *hide* themselves during the course of protest activity. Specifically, I address the concept of "passing," or hiding one's true identity by publicly adopting and enacting a different one. Drawing on Erving Goffman's (1963) classic work on the management of stigmatized identities, I describe "passing" as a form of strategic identity work used by social movement activists, especially those engaged in the type of high-risk activism (McAdam 1986; Taylor and Raeburn 1995) in which the activists' identity puts them at risk for experiencing some kind of dangerous outcome.

Empirically, my discussion uses case data from the Warsaw Ghetto Uprising, an armed rebellion staged by Jews interned in the Warsaw Ghetto in 1943. Because plans for resistance required that the resistance fighters obtain weapons and other supplies from beyond the walled ghetto (a region referred to as the "Aryan side,"), the uprising depended upon the efforts of a number of Jewish activists whose abilities to pass as Gentiles allowed them to move in and out of the ghetto and facilitated their activist tasks, such as the transport of weapons. I focus on the strategies these activists used to hide their Jewish identity, which I conceptualize as a form of identity work.[2]

By describing these activists' experiences, this chapter contributes to the themes of this volume in three ways. First, it shows how activists draw on notions of sameness and difference when engaging in identity work. As I show below, passing required that activists understand and adhere to culturally dictated scripts for the performance of Jewish and non-Jewish identity. Second, by showing how the broader context of Nazi-occupied Europe determined the content of these activists' performance scripts, this chapter demonstrates the crucial role of the activist setting in identity work. Finally, it illustrates the "hard work" of identity performances. While this last point might seem obvious—clearly, nothing was "easy" about collective action in the context of genocide—it shows that activists' identity "workload" is variable, depending on the setting in which they work. As I note further in the chapter's conclusion, the level of difficulty associated with identity work may also have implications for other protest dynamics, such as commitment and sustained mobilization.

I begin with a discussion of "passing" as a form of identity work. Then, after a brief description of the Warsaw Ghetto and the emergence of armed resistance, I describe some of the identity work on which that collective action depended. I conclude with a discussion of the "politics of passing" or the advantages and disadvantages of choosing this type of strategic identity work in a variety of movement settings.

"Passing" as Identity Work

By "passing," I refer to those efforts made by individuals to hide or otherwise obscure some aspect of their identity by adopting a different identity, the presentation of which negates or refutes the individual's true self. As Brooke Kroeger explains, "it is passing when people effectively present themselves as other than who they understand themselves to be" (2003, 7). Such behavior has drawn the interest of scholars from a variety of academic disciplines, including social scientists as well as journalists (Kroeger 2003), novelists (Larsen 1997) and other literary analysts (see Ginsberg 1996). Well-known examples of passing that have been explored by such work include African Americans passing as whites, gays and lesbians passing as straight, and women passing as men (Ginsberg 1996; Johnson 2002; Kroeger 2003; Sanchez and Schlossberg 2001).

Many studies describe passing as a strategy for managing stigma. For instance, Goffman's classic study of stigma focuses centrally on passing, which he defines as "the management of undisclosed discrediting information about the self" (1963, 42). Passers therefore work actively to conceal information about themselves that can confirm their membership in a stigmatized group. Another example is found in Kristin Park's (2002) analysis of voluntarily childless women and men—who are stigmatized in a pronatalist context—which points to passing as an identity strategy used by relatively young childless people. When queried about their childlessness, instead of explaining their decision not to have children some of her respondents made remarks such as "I'll have a child someday," or "I'm just not ready yet," thereby passing as people who ostensibly want children (32). Similarly, Liebow (1993) describes passing among homeless women, another stigmatized group. Some of his subjects managed to avoid being labeled as homeless by maintaining the physical appearance of someone with a home (e.g., by always wearing clean, pressed clothes, paying careful attention to hair, makeup, and nails, etc.). Passing as a person with a home did not necessarily lead these women directly out of homelessness; however, this sort of strategic identity work helped some women find employment as well as fend off the depression and other emotional stresses of homeless life.

Passing, then, implies a *successful* attempt to hide a particular identity (Kroeger 2003, 7); if the identity in question is revealed, the individual is no longer passing. Further, as the above studies demonstrate, passing is an interactional achievement; to pass successfully, an individual must convince others with whom she interacts of the validity of her false identity. As Goffman notes (4), passing is achieved through the management of information, which can include details about one's body or physical state, character, or heritage. Importantly, though, passing depends on the actions of the passer as well as the interpretations and reactions of her audience. Goffman illustrates this point by drawing a distinction between "virtual social identity" and "actual social identity" (2); the latter refers to one's true identity or state, including the facts that may "discredit" the individual, while the former refers to the "unblemished" state that others presume we occupy. Stigma, which is a particular type of discrepancy between the virtual and actual identity, therefore occurs in the context of interaction; it refers to the assumptions that others make about the individual and the extent to which those assumptions are supported or refuted by the information that is revealed (or concealed) about the individual in question.

Other scholars have identified additional strategies used by members of marginalized or stigmatized groups to manage their identities. For instance, David A. Snow and Leon Anderson's (1987) study of verbal identity work (what they call "identity talk") among the homeless points to three strategies by which homeless people "create, present, and sustain personal identities that are congruent with and supportive of the self-concept" (1348): distancing, or drawing a distinction between themselves and other homeless people; embracement, an acceptance of and attachment to the homeless identity; and fictive storytelling, or describing one's life fictively, either through embellishment or fantasy. Thomas J. Gerschick and Adam Stephen Miller (1994) identify similar strategies by which disabled men reconcile their disability with their sense of masculinity, either by relying on hegemonic notions of masculinity, reformulating those ideas to incorporate their own abilities, or rejecting such images altogether. Passing is distinct from these other identity strategies, however; the goal is not to incorporate the stigmatized identity into one's sense of self or recast it more positively but to hide it completely.[3]

While the passer's goal is to hide a particular identity, it is important to note that one identity is concealed through the active display of another; in other words, to pass is to be *and* not to be. As the previous examples illustrate, the passer's task is to present him or herself in a way that is consistent with the interactionally desired identity and inconsistent with the identity to be hidden; thus, homeless women hide their stigma by avoiding the display of obvious markers of homelessness (such as shopping carts filled with belongings) and by presenting evidence that gives the appearance that they have homes. Passing is therefore an example of strategic identity work, used to manage others' impressions. Yet it is also understood differently than other forms of impression management. As Kroeger explains,

> Everyone puts on masks or adopts different personas from time to time, often short-term, to achieve a variety of reasonable aims. We are forever modulating our voices and adjusting our styles to manipulate outcomes, to get the best result. People are forever feigning interest in other people's lives in order to soften requests for help in unrelated ways. . . . These are ordinary performances, mundane practices, acceptable acts of deception. . . . But when we perform in this way, we are not assuming a false identity; generally speaking, we are choosing among aspects of an identity that we recognize as our own. It is not, then, an act of passing. What [the passer] describes is something different. It is passing because she does not recognize the persona she assumes as her own. She feels it is outside of herself.

Her experience is distinct from cases where the shifting back and forth feels natural, where the various aspects of self are reconciled. (2003, 78–79)

Some scholars go so far as to suggest that passing is not always intentional. That is, because passing is an interactional accomplishment, individuals might pass unwittingly if others attribute a false identity to them. For instance, at certain parts of their lives, two of Kroeger's (2003) respondents passed without realizing it; in both cases, others attributed identities to them that were either unknown or unproblematic. One, a gay man who was actually unaware of his homosexuality, allowed others to maintain their assumptions about his heterosexuality because he was making the same assumptions about himself; the other, an olive-skinned Caucasian woman who socialized primarily with African Americans, did not realize at first that other people assumed she was African American as well. Such examples would not qualify as identity work, as the term is used in this volume, since they do not involve active efforts to construct or deploy a particular identity. My focus in this chapter is, therefore, on intentional acts of passing.

Finally, while passing is an individual act, I argue that it can be used strategically in the course of collective action. In various movement contexts, activists can find it useful to pass as members of groups other than their own. Depending on the setting and the nature of the identity being concealed, activists can pass for a variety of reasons, such as performing clandestine operations or creating the illusion of mainstream support for their cause. In addition, when activists pass as members of a group that ostensibly will not benefit from movement activity, they can enhance their own credibility as movement advocates. More to the point of this inquiry, passing can be particularly useful, and even necessary, in settings in which it is dangerous for activists to reveal a certain aspect of themselves. Taylor and Raeburn's (1995) study of activism among gays and lesbians, which finds evidence of workplace discrimination leveled against gays and lesbians who make their identities known, is a case in point (see also Creed and Scully 2000). When activists pass, therefore, it can be understood as a social movement tactic, used strategically to establish credibility, minimize repression, and gain access to resources and advantages that would otherwise be denied to the activists if their true identities were revealed.

In what follows, I explore the strategic use of passing in a setting in which activists faced heavy costs for the display of their true identities: Nazi-occupied Warsaw. My analysis makes use of both primary and secondary sources that describe the Warsaw Ghetto and the armed resistance that happened there. Primary sources include twenty published diaries and memoirs written by residents of the Warsaw Ghetto, some of whom survived and others of whom perished yet were able to hide or safely transport their written records. I also draw on several published collections of excerpts from diaries and other documents from the Warsaw Ghetto. Due to space limitations, only a subset of these materials is quoted and cited here. I use these data to examine how activists hid their Jewishness in the course of their resistance activities. This chapter therefore provides one illustration of how identity work is done.

The Emergence of Collective Jewish Resistance in the Warsaw Ghetto

Like Jews living in many cities in Nazi-occupied Poland, Warsaw's Jews were ghettoized, or forced by Nazi edict to live in a particular section of the city (Corni 2002; Gutman 1982, 1994). With as many as five hundred thousand Jews confined to the Warsaw Ghetto—an enclosed area of less than 1.5 square miles, carved from the city's Jewish Quarter—food supplies were limited and cleanliness and sanitation were compromised. The resultant hunger and disease contributed to a mortality rate that climbed steadily from the creation of the ghetto in November 1940 through 1942 (Ainsztein 1979; Gutman 1982, 1994).

In general, Jews in the Warsaw Ghetto believed that their difficult situation was temporary; although some loss of life was expected, given the harsh conditions, they felt that their community as a whole would endure and ultimately survive the Nazi occupation. Such views actually forestalled the emergence of calls for resistance. Since many people believed that they would eventually be freed from the ghetto (e.g., by some liberating army, such as the Red Army), there was little need to resist (Gutman 1994; Katsh 1999). Moreover, many ghetto Jews did not feel that resistance would succeed. These views played out in an exchange between two men rounded up for deportation in August 1942, as described by ghetto survivor Wladyslaw Szpilman:

> [The dentist] was nervous and bitter. "It's a disgrace to us all!" he almost screamed. "We're letting them take us to our death like sheep to the slaughter!" . . . Father listened . . . and asked, "How can you be absolutely certain they're sending us to our death?" The dentist clasped his hands. "Well of course I don't know for certain. How could I? Are they about to tell us? But you can be ninety percent sure they plan to wipe us all out!" Father smiled again, as if he were even more sure of himself after this reply. "Look," he said, indicating the crowd at the Umschlagplatz [the square from which transport trains were loaded with deportees]. "We're

not heroes! We're perfectly ordinary people, which is why we prefer to risk hoping for that ten per cent chance of living." (1999, 101–2)

Once Warsaw's Jews realized that they were targeted for death, however, calls for resistance began to emerge (Gutman 1994). At first glance, it might seem surprising that the ghetto residents only resisted once they realized that they would all be put to death; instead, one might reasonably expect that support for resistance would be the greatest when Jews had some hope of survival. However, the opposite was true. As long as the community believed that they could survive the conditions in the ghetto, resistance was seen as unnecessarily costly. In contrast, the reality of the Nazis' "Final Solution" encouraged the will to resist among the Jews, as illustrated by this excerpt from the memoirs of ghetto resident Ed Klajman:

> Now that I knew the Germans' "master plan" to exterminate the Jews, I promised myself that I would never be taken alive; I vowed never to allow them to ship me to the gas chambers. Dying was acceptable, provided I died with a purpose. I just wanted revenge—a chance to be able to fight back some way. (2000, 52)

Such desires for revenge were part of a broader framing that equated resistance with honor and dignity (Ainsztein 1979; Borzykowski 1976; Cochavi 1995; Gutman 1982, 1994; Kurzman 1993; Lubetkin 1981). Again, these views stemmed from the realization that everyone in the ghetto would eventually be put to death. Since death was seen as certain, those calling for resistance felt that it was more honorable for Jews to die while fighting than to allow themselves to be murdered in the gas chambers (Einwohner 2003; Gutman 1994). Such beliefs were expressed by members of two different activist organizations, both of which advocated and planned for armed resistance: the Jewish Fighting Organization (*Żydowska Organizacja Bojowa*, or ŻOB) and the Jewish Military Union (*Żydowski Związek Wojskowy*, or ŻZW). Due to political differences between the two groups, each operated separately (Gutman 1982). By January 1943, each organization had amassed a small amount of weapons and homemade explosive devices, which they put to use in a four-day uprising against Nazi troops who entered the ghetto to deport the residents to Treblinka. Another episode of fighting erupted in April 1943 under similar circumstances and ended with the destruction of the ghetto several weeks later (Ainsztein 1979; Gutman 1982, 1994; Kurzman 1993).

This chapter examines the experiences of those members of the ŻOB[4] who slipped out of the ghetto to the "Aryan side" to make contact with the Polish Underground so as to obtain weapons and other supplies needed for the resistance effort. Because Nazi edict decreed that any Jew found on the Aryan side would be put to death (Gutman 1982), these individuals had to pass as non-Jews to be able to carry out their tasks.[5] Below, I describe how these activists performed this identity work.

Passing on the Aryan Side

Appearance and the Use of Symbols

Jewish activists working on the Aryan side used a number of strategies for concealing their identity. According to Goffman, one common interactional strategy for passing involves the use of symbols. As he explains, the display of situationally relevant "prestige symbols," such as a wedding ring or reading glasses, can in some contexts give the appearance of certain "normality" or prestige; similarly, other symbols can reveal stigma. When passing, individuals will therefore go to great lengths to display prestige symbols and, at the same time, conceal "stigma symbols" (the latter of which can include, in Goffman's examples, wrist scars indicating suicide attempts or arm tracks suggesting drug use). In the context of Nazi-occupied Europe, the Jewish star that Jews were forced to wear[6] was an obvious symbol of their stigmatized identity, yet was one that was also relatively easy to remove: when on the Aryan side, activists simply removed these symbols from their clothing (Meed 1979; Zuckerman 1993). Much more difficult to remove or conceal were facial features and other physical traits (e.g., hair and eye color) stereotypically associated with Eastern European Jews, which also functioned as stigma symbols in that context. Due to the high visibility of these symbols, Jewish activists had to have "good looks," or the looks of a Gentile, to work effectively on the Aryan side (Engelking 2001; Gutman 1982; Meed 1979; Rotem 1994; Szwajger 1990; Zuckerman 1993). Not surprisingly, ŻOB leaders selected activists for work on the Aryan side primarily on the basis of physical appearance (Meed 1979; Szwajger 1990). For instance, many memoirs and other writings from ghetto residents mention the particularly "good" looks of Arieh ("Jurek") Wilner, a ŻOB activist who was caught and tortured by the Gestapo and eventually died during the April uprising. About him, his sister Gustawa Wilner wrote, "When he came walking down the street, I was amazed at how wonderful he looked. Blond hair, blue eyes, slender, agile, wearing a sporty coat and a small felt hat" (quoted in Grynberg 2002, 473). ŻOB leader Marek Edelman also mentioned Wilner's appearance, noting that Wilner, who spent some time hiding in a convent in Lithuania, was "the favorite of the Mother Superior—blond hair, blue eyes, he reminded her of her own brother" (quoted in Krall 1986, 98–99). In fact, Wilner's appearance fooled even some of his fellow activists. Describing her first encounter with him, ŻOB courier Vladka Meed wrote in her memoirs,

> I was in our cellar at Gornoszlonska 3 when a young man in his twenties, well-dressed, with a ruddy complexion and a snub nose—obviously not Jewish, I thought—delivered several wooden crates [of nails]. . . . I was not at all surprised by the stranger's visit, but I found it odd that Michal should give him such a warm welcome and appear so pleased with the transaction. . . . Later I learned that the deliveryman was Aryeh[7] Wilner . . . and that the crates contained not nails but the first ten revolvers to be secured. (1979, 86)

All activists working on the Aryan side had to possess similar physical characteristics. In addition, because names and certain styles of dress also represented Jewishness and non-Jewishness in that setting, activists working on the Aryan side adopted Polish nicknames (such as Arieh Wilner's name, "Jurek") and paid particular attention to how they dressed. For example, due to the Nazis' routine confiscation of furs and other valuables from Jews, individuals not wearing fur could be suspected of being Jewish; ŻOB courier Adina Szwajger's memoirs thus note that she was given a fur collar to sew into her coat to conceal her identity as a Jew (1990, 77). Furthermore, because Yiddish was the first language of most Polish Jews, language and accent were also setting-specific symbols of Jewishness (Engelking 2001). Effective passing therefore required that activists speak fluent Polish without any traces of a Yiddish accent. In fact, the following excerpt from the memoirs of ŻOB leader Yitzhak ("Antek") Zuckerman, which describes the appearance of courier Tosia Altman, suggests that language may have been even more important than appearance: "She didn't have dark skin and hair; she had a 'neutral,' long face. She was a beautiful person and a devoted courier, who worked a long time. With a face like hers, she needed a lot of courage to be a courier and walk around where she did; but her Polish was fluent" (1993, 259).

Situational rules for the performance of Jewishness and non-Jewishness went beyond appearance and language skills to include behavioral symbols as well. Not surprisingly, Jews had to follow Roman Catholic religious rites and observances to maintain the pretense of being non-Jewish Poles (Engelking 2001). For instance, Vladka Meed's memoirs note that she once made the sign of the cross over a corpse in a hospital—an action that, as a Jew, she would not ordinarily perform—to protect her identity (1979, 80–81).

As these examples illustrate, passing on the Aryan side required that ŻOB activists pay careful attention to a wide variety of culturally and contextually specific indicators of difference (e.g., language and physical traits)

and draw on them to mask their differences from the non-Jewish community. In this regard, this case is similar to other cases in this volume, which
also illustrate the use of sameness and difference in activist identity work. At
the same time, this case highlights a dynamic that differs from the others.
Unlike other examples of activist identity work explored here, most of which
focus on the construction or negotiation of collective identity, the efforts
made by Jewish resistance fighters on the Aryan side of the Warsaw Ghetto
involved an adherence to contextual rules for the performance of a given
identity. Indeed, given the repressive anti-Semitic tactics of the Nazi regime as
well as broader cultural understandings that cast Jews as different from non-
Jews in this setting, there was no room for the negotiation of the activists'
Jewish identity at all. Whether or not identities can be negotiated is therefore a
context-dependent variable that affects the nature of identity work.

Fear, Sadness, and Emotional Management

In addition to clear rules for the performance of Jewish and non-Jewish identities, Nazi-occupied Warsaw dictated clear regions for these identity performances as well: all Jews were expected to be in the ghetto, and no Jews were
expected to be on the Aryan side. Thus, whereas Goffman (1963, 81) posits three different regions relevant to the stigmatized (the "out-of-bounds"
places, where persons with the stigma are forbidden to be; the "civil places,"
where the stigmatized are tolerated but not necessarily treated well; and the
"back places," where the stigmatized identify themselves freely and interact
with their own), in the Warsaw Ghetto there were effectively two regions,
with the ghetto being the "back place" and the Aryan side considered "out
of bounds." More important, there were very clear—and, obviously, very
harsh—penalties for Jewish existence in both places. As previously stated,
Jews in the ghetto suffered from hunger and disease; they were also subject
to various harsh treatments at the hands of Nazi soldiers, including beat-
ings, forced labor, and death (Ainsztein 1979; Gutman 1982, 1994). On
the Aryan side, Jews who successfully hid their identity were able to avoid
these treatments; however, they faced a death penalty if their identity was
revealed. Activists on the Aryan side therefore lived in a constant state of
fear (Engelking 2001; Meed 1979; Szwajger 1990). Not only did they have
a great deal to fear from German soldiers, they were also harassed by blackmailers (*shmaltsovniks*) or Polish civilians who waited outside the ghetto
gates for Jews who escaped to the Aryan side and then extorted money or
valuables from them, ostensibly in exchange for keeping the Jews' identity
secret (Engelking 2001; Meed 1979; Rotem 1994; Zuckerman 1993). For
instance, blackmailers are mentioned in the following excerpt from the

memoirs of ŻOB leader Yitzhak Zuckerman, whose Polish looks allowed him to move relatively freely on the Aryan side:

> There was danger from Polish blackmailers lurking on the other side who were as familiar as we were with all the comings and goings. The blackmailers . . . were one of the greatest dangers for a Jew seeking refuge on the Aryan side of Warsaw. Dozens of blackmailers were usually swarming around the exits and gates. They would rob the Jew by threatening to turn him over to the Germans; if they had a hope that this Jew had something left, they would follow him and extort everything from him, down to his last cent. After they extorted everything from him, they would turn him over to the Polish police or the Germans. Many Jews paid with their lives for an attempt to cross to the Aryan side. (1993, 276–77)

Moreover, because blackmailers were especially adept at detecting traces of accents and other indicators of an individual's Jewish identity (Engelking 2001; Zuckerman 1993), they possessed what Goffman calls an extremely high "decoding capacity" (1963, 51). The actions of these "specialists at uncovering identity" (50) therefore increased Jews' visibility on the Aryan side, making it that much more difficult to successfully perform the identity work on which their survival, and the resistance movement, depended.

Given the presence of blackmailers and other dangers, expressions of fear also became setting-specific indicators of Jewish identity. ŻOB activists were well aware of the damaging potential of emotional displays on the Aryan side; many activist memoirs note that any individual expressing fear in the presence of non-Jews could be suspected of being Jewish (Meed 1979; Rotem 1994; Szwajger 1990; Zuckerman 1993). Of course, this "fear rule" was not reserved simply for activists on the Aryan side but also applied to any Jew attempting to pass. One such individual, Franciszka Grünberg, described her efforts to control her fear on her first day after escaping from the ghetto:

> I was afraid to look anyone in the face; I felt that every glance would betray me. . . . I had covered nearly all of my face with the shawl, as if I had a toothache, and I kept wiping my nose with my handkerchief, so that I crossed the courtyard almost completely concealed, with my eyes downcast. I had the feeling that everyone was staring at me, that I looked peculiar, and that everyone recognized the fact that I was Jewish. . . . I was shaking with fear; I struggled to control myself and not break into a run. (quoted in Grynberg 2002, 317)

To pass successfully, this fear had to be managed; activists therefore performed "emotional labor" (Goodwin and Pfaff 2001; Hochschild 1979, 1983; Whittier 2001) in the context of their identity work. Sadness—especially, sadness expressed with regard to the fate of the Jewish people—was another emotion that could similarly reveal Jewishness and had to be managed as well. For instance, it was forbidden for members of the resistance to cry on the streets (Szwajger 1990). The memoirs of ŻOB fighter Simha ("Kazik") Rotem illustrate the work activists had to do to manage their sadness. After the end of the April uprising, he escaped to the Aryan side from where he could still see fires burning inside the ghetto; however, as a Jew he had to be careful not to display any sadness in public:

> I would walk through the streets of the city, and some invisible force drew me to the walls of the Ghetto, an inexplicable longing to see the Ghetto as the fire was still destroying parts of it. I felt free but helpless. . . . No one paid much attention to what was happening on the other side of the walls. I had to pretend so as not to be discovered. Since every careless wink was liable to give me away, I had to be careful not to express any sympathy or grief. It took me weeks to get used to the idea that the Ghetto no longer existed for me. (1994, 62)

Similarly, Szwajger's memoirs describe her efforts to conceal her identifying emotions. Witnessing the April uprising—including the destruction of her own home—from the Aryan side with a fellow activist, she wrote, "We stood in Krasinski square and told each other jokes to make ourselves laugh. . . . We stood holding our flowers listening to the explosions, while Swietojerska street burnt and we stood laughing. I saw my own house burning. And I kept laughing" (1990, 89).

As other research has demonstrated (Chapter 1; Einwohner 1999; Montini 1996; Whittier 2001), activists working in a variety of settings often manage their emotions to present themselves strategically to external audiences. The experiences of ŻOB activists on the Aryan side therefore provide an additional example of the explicit role of emotion and "feeling rules" (Hochschild 1983) in activists' identity work. More broadly, the necessity of emotion work for Jews on the Aryan side reiterates the role of sameness and difference in these activists' identity work. To pass as non-Jews, these activists had to interactionally negate their differences from the majority and, at the same time, establish their sameness. Doing so required that they "know the rules" for proper behavior in that setting (including the proper behavior of "normals" as well as the stigmatized). As Vladka Meed wrote in her memoirs (1979, 89), "It was not easy to maintain the pretense of being a Gentile. One had to be wary of each movement, each word, to avoid giving oneself away." More important, following these rules correctly required detailed knowledge about the setting-specific expectations for sameness and difference.

Conclusion: The Politics of Passing

This chapter has examined the experiences of Jewish resistance fighters in the Warsaw Ghetto to illustrate passing as a form of strategic identity work in social movements. Because armed resistance depended on weapons and other supplies from outside the ghetto, it was necessary for some Jewish activists to slip out of the ghetto to obtain these materials. However, since Nazi law stated that any Jew found outside the ghetto would be put to death, these activists had to follow a number of culturally and situationally determined scripts to pose as non-Jews and, therefore, mask their true identity while working on the "Aryan side." While their motives for passing as non-Jews were obvious, it is important to note that these activists' overall goal was not to hide their Jewishness. On the contrary, the Warsaw Ghetto Uprising itself is understood by many scholars to be an expression of collective identity, the result of the fighters' desires to affirm the dignity and honor of the Jewish people (Cochavi 1995; Einwohner 2003; Gutman 1994; Lubetkin 1981). Their identity work—in the form of passing as non-Jews—was therefore a means to an end, that is, a strategy made necessary by the setting in which these activists operated.

This case furthers our understanding of activist identity work in several ways. First, identity work in social movements is not necessarily confined to discussions about creating "we." Although such efforts clearly fall under the heading of identity work, this case illustrates another application of identity work, namely, passing. Nonetheless, sameness and difference are still central to this case. Successful passing required that these activists both recognize their differences from the majority and work interactionally to conceal those differences.

In the context of Nazi-occupied Warsaw, where the laws and practices of a genocidal regime clearly cast Jews as different from others, recognizing these differences was hardly difficult. Performing this identity work was another matter, however. The setting in which these activists operated made their identity work quite hard; in the language of this volume, these activists' identity workload was "heavy." An examination of passing is therefore useful because it brings the difficulties of identity work to light. In closing, I discuss some of the advantages and disadvantages of this kind of hard identity work.

Although passing as non-Jews on the Aryan side was necessary to the overall resistance effort, it was not without its costs. As the preceding discussion has shown, passing can have emotional consequences, which can be intensified in extremely repressive contexts (see also Adams 2003 and Yang 2000). Not surprisingly, it was quite difficult for ŻOB members to manage the fear and sadness they experienced in the course of their activist work. Interactionally denying their Jewishness was even more painful and difficult when activists had to witness harsh treatments of other Jews and could do nothing to help. As Goffman (1963, 87) notes, a passer can feel "torn between two attachments" and experience guilt when unable to fend off offensive remarks about the stigmatized. Such difficulties were definitely experienced by Jewish activists passing on the Aryan side, as Vladka Meed's memoirs suggest:

> The ghetto was a dreary place, but it was my own, real world where I could be myself. Here I had no need to maintain the forced smile I wore before my Polish neighbors. Here I did not have to listen to snide remarks from the Poles that the Jews had had it coming to them and that Hitler was purging Poland of the "Jewish plague." Here I did not have to live in constant fear of being unmasked as a Jewess. I was among my own. (1979, 105)

These activists' identity work was therefore hard on two different levels: it was difficult to perform successfully and also had emotionally painful consequences.

While passing can be disadvantageous for both individuals and groups, at the same time, the advantages of passing can be considerable. Clearly, in the case of the Warsaw Ghetto Uprising, the advantages of passing included aiding resistance efforts and, for some individuals, the chance to survive the war. More broadly, passing affords members of marginalized groups access to resources that would otherwise be denied to them. Beyond the individual level costs and benefits, there is a politics of passing as well. Depending on the situation, passing can be either politically expedient or dangerous. For instance, by concealing their true identities, passers can be said to be "selling out," or reaffirming the status quo by contributing to the marginalization of their group. Other disadvantageous consequences of passing might include being suspected of being a double agent or accused of acting out of self-interest rather than the good of the group. Given the strong ties among the members of the ŻOB (Rotem 1994; Zuckerman 1993), such suspicions were unlikely; however, for activists who are part of larger organizations or who work in less repressive situations, such suspicions might come to light and can be damaging for group solidarity and effectiveness (e.g., if the presence of passers leads to arguments about who is a "real" member of the group). (For more on the outcomes of identity work see also Chapter 6).

On the other hand, passing can also be seen as a form of resistance, and therefore politically "noble." While the activists described here used passing to facilitate broader resistance efforts, Shneidman (2002) argues that individual acts of passing among Jews during the Holocaust were themselves acts of resistance, since passing allowed Jews to survive and therefore thwart the Nazis' genocidal agenda. More generally, passing can be resistance in the sense that it provides the marginalized with power and social standing and therefore gives them the opportunity to work "from the inside" to achieve social change (Kroeger 2003).

Given the harsh penalties for being discovered on the Aryan side, Jewish activists working in that setting had no choice but to pass as non-Jews; however, activists in other, less repressive contexts might have more options for identity work and can therefore choose whether passing is an appropriate strategy. As previously suggested, such choices can have implications not only for the comfort of the passer but also for solidarity and harmony within the group. The setting in which activists operate therefore determines both the nature and the utility of their identity work as well as its potential consequences.

References

Adams, Jacqueline. 2003. "The Bitter End: Emotions at a Movement's Conclusion." *Sociological Inquiry* 73: 84–113.

Ainsztein, Reuben. 1979. *The Warsaw Ghetto Revolt*. New York: Holocaust Library.

Borzykowski, Tuvia. 1976. *Between Tumbling Walls*. Beit Lohamei Hagettaot and Hakibbutz Hameuchad Publishing House.

Calhoun, Craig. 1994. *Neither Gods nor Emperors: Students and the Struggle for Democracy in China*. Berkeley: University of California Press.

Cochavi, Yehoyakim. 1995. "The Motif of "Honor" in the Call to Rebellion in the Ghetto." In *Zionist Youth Movements during the Shoah*, ed. A. Cohen and Y. Cochavi and trans. T. Gorelick, 245–54. New York: Peter Lang.

Corni, Gustavo. 2002. *Hitler's Ghettos*. London: Arnold.

Creed, W. E. Douglas, and Maureen A. Scully. 2000. "Songs of Ourselves: Employees' Deployment of Social Identity in Workplace Encounters." *Journal of Management Inquiry* 9: 391–412.

Einwohner, Rachel L. 2003. "Opportunity, Honor, and Action in the Warsaw Ghetto Uprising of 1943." *American Journal of Sociology* 109: 650–75.

———. 1999. "Gender, Class, and Social Movement Outcomes: Identity and Effectiveness in Two Animal Rights Campaigns." *Gender & Society* 13: 56–76.

Engelking, Barbara. 2001. *Holocaust and Memory*. London: Leicester University Press.

Fantasia, Rick. 1988. *Cultures of Solidarity*. Berkeley: University of California Press.

Gerschick, Thomas J., and Adam Stephen Miller. 1994. "Gender Identities at the Crossroads of Masculinity and Physical Disability." *Masculinities* 2: 34–55.

Ginsberg, Elaine K., ed. 1996. *Passing and the Fictions of Identity*. Durham, N.C.: Duke University Press.

Goffman, Erving. 1963. *Stigma: Notes on the Management of Spoiled Identity*. Englewood Cliffs, N.J.: Prentice-Hall, Inc.

Goodwin, Jeff, and Steven Pfaff. 2001. "Emotion Work in High-Risk Social Movements: Managing Fear in the U.S. and East German Civil Rights Movements." In *Passionate Politics*, ed. J. Goodwin, J. M. Jasper, and F. Polletta, 282–302. Chicago: University of Chicago Press.

Grynberg, Michał, ed. 2002. *Words to Outlive Us: Voices from the Warsaw Ghetto*. New York: Henry Holt and Company.

Gutman, Israel. 1994. *Resistance: The Warsaw Ghetto Uprising*. Boston: Houghton Mifflin Company.

Gutman, Yisrael. 1982. *The Jews of Warsaw, 1939–1943*. Bloomington, Ind.: Indiana University Press.

Hilberg, Raul. 1979. *The Destruction of the European Jews*. New York: Harper Colophon Books.

Hochschild, Arlie Russell. 1983. *The Managed Heart*. Berkeley: University of California Press.

———. 1979. "Emotion Work, Feeling Rules, and Social Structure." *American Journal of Sociology* 85: 551–75.

Johnson, Carol. 2002. "Heteronormative Citizenship and the Politics of Passing." *Sexualities* 5: 317–36.

Katsh, Abraham I., trans. 1999. *Scroll of Agony: The Warsaw Diary of Chaim A. Kaplan*. Bloomington, Ind.: Indiana University Press.

Kermish, Joseph, ed. 1986. *To Live With Honor and Die With Honor: Selected Documents from the Warsaw Ghetto Underground Archives "O.S." [Oneg Shabbath]*. Jerusalem: Yad Vashem.

Klajman, Jack, with Ed Klajman. 2000. *Out of the Ghetto*. London: Vallentine Mitchell.

Krall, Hanna. 1986. *Shielding the Flame: An Intimate Conversation with Dr. Marek Edelman, the Last Surviving Leader of the Warsaw Ghetto Uprising*. New York: Henry Holt and Co.

Kroeger, Brooke. 2003. *Passing: When People Can't Be Who They Are*. New York: Public Affairs.

Kurzman, Dan. 1993. *The Bravest Battle: The Twenty-eight Days of the Warsaw Ghetto Uprising*. New York: Da Capo Press, Inc.

Larsen, Nella. 1997. *Passing*. New York: Penguin Books.

Liebow, Elliot. 1993. *Tell Them Who I Am*. New York: Penguin Books.

Loeb, Paul Rogat. 1994. *Generation at the Crossroads*. New Brunswick, N.J.: Rutgers University Press.

Lubetkin, Zivia. 1981. *In the Days of Destruction and Revolt*. Beit Lohamei Haghetaot (Ghetto Fighters' House).

McAdam, Doug. 1986. "Recruitment to High-Risk Activism: The Case of Freedom Summer." *American Journal of Sociology* 92: 64–90.

Meed, Vladka. 1979. *On Both Sides of the Wall: Memoirs from the Warsaw Ghetto*. New York: Holocaust Library.

Melucci, Alberto. 1989. *Nomads of the Present*. Philadelphia: Temple University Press.

Montini, Theresa. 1996. "Gender and Emotion in the Advocacy for Breast Cancer Informed Consent Legislation." *Gender & Society* 10: 9–23.

Neuhouser, Kevin. 1998. "'If I Had Abandoned My Children': Community Mobilization and Commitment to the Identity of Mother in Northeast Brazil." *Social Forces* 77: 331–58.

Park, Kristin. 2002. "Stigma Management among the Voluntarily Childless." *Sociological Perspectives* 45: 21–45.

Reger, Jo. 2002. "Organizational Dynamics and Construction of Multiple Feminist Identities in the National Organization for Women." *Gender & Society* 16: 710–27.

Rotem, Simha. 1994. *Memoirs of a Warsaw Ghetto Fighter: The Past within Me*. New Haven, Conn.: Yale University Press.

Sanchez, Maria Carla, and Linda Schlossberg, ed. 2001. *Passing: Identity and Interpretation in Sexuality, Race, and Religion*. New York: New York University Press.

Shneidman, N. N. 2002. *The Three Tragic Heroes of the Vilnius Ghetto*. Oakville, Ontario: Mosaic Press.

Snow, David A., and Leon Anderson. 1987. "Identity Work Among the Homeless: The Verbal Construction and Avowal of Personal Identities." *American Journal of Sociology* 92: 1336–71.

Szwajger, Adina Blady. 1990. *I Remember Nothing More: The Warsaw Children's Hospital and the Jewish Resistance*. New York: Pantheon Books.

Taylor, Verta, and Nicole C. Raeburn. 1995. "Identity Politics as High-Risk Activism: Career Consequences for Lesbian, Gay, and Bisexual Sociologists." *Social Problems* 42: 252–73.

Taylor, Verta, and Nancy E. Whittier. 1995. "Analytical Approaches to Social Movement Culture: The Culture of the Women's Movement." In *Social Movements and Culture*, ed. H. Johnston and B. Klandermans, 163–87. Minneapolis: University of Minnesota Press.

———. 1992. "Collective Identity in Social Movement Communities: Lesbian Feminist Mobilization." In *Frontiers in Social Movement Theory*, ed. A. D. Morris and C. M. Mueller, 104–29. New Haven, Conn.: Yale University Press.

Whittier, Nancy. 2001. "Emotional Strategies: The Collective Reconstruction and Display of Oppositional Emotions in the Movement against Child Sexual Abuse." In *Passionate Politics*, ed. J. Goodwin, J. M. Jasper, and F. Polletta, 233–50. Chicago: University of Chicago Press.

Whittier, Nancy. 1995. *Feminist Generations: The Persistence of the Radical Women's Movement*. Philadelphia: Temple University Press.

Yang, Guobin. 2000. "Achieving Emotions in Collective Action: Emotional Processes and Movement Mobilization in the 1989 Chinese Student Movement." *The Sociological Quarterly* 41: 593–614.

Zuckerman, Yitzhak. 1993. *A Surplus of Memory: Chronicle of the Warsaw Ghetto Uprising*. Berkeley: University of California Press.

Notes

1. I thank Dan Myers, Mary Bernstein, and an anonymous reviewer for their comments on previous drafts of this chapter. This research was supported by a Purdue Research Foundation Summer Faculty Grant, a College of Liberal Arts Dean's Incentive Grant, and a Library Scholar's Grant, all from Purdue University.

2. Passing as Gentiles was also a survival strategy used by non-activist Jews who were able to escape the ghetto (see Engelking 2001). However, my focus in this chapter is on the experience of activists who used this identity strategy in the course of their resistance work. Like nonactivist Jews on the Aryan side, these activists passed as Gentiles in order to survive, but personal survival was not their ultimate goal; instead, they hoped only to survive on the Aryan side long enough to carry out their activists tasks, after which they expected to return to the ghetto and die in battle (Meed 1979; Rotem 1994). For these individuals, then, passing was not simply a survival strategy but also a component of their resistance work overall.

3. Snow and Anderson (1987, 1339–40) note explicitly that passing is not a form of identity work available to the "street people" they studied, given the visibility of their status as homeless; the same may be true of Gerschick and Miller's respondents, all of whom had visible physical disabilities.

4. I limit my focus to the ŻOB because of a dearth of scholarly materials available on the ŻZW (Gutman 1982).

5. It is difficult to state how many ŻOB members worked on the Aryan side. Yisrael Gutman (1982, 348) estimates that the ŻOB had five hundred members as of April 1943. Given the language skills and physical attributes needed for passing,

only a relatively small portion of the membership was able to perform these tasks. Well-known and oft-referenced activists who worked on the Aryan side include Arieh Wilner, Yitzhak Zuckerman, Tosia Altman, Vladka Meed, Simha Rotem, and Frumka Plotnicka, but additional activists worked outside the ghetto as well.

6. In a slight variation on the gold stars Jews were obliged to wear in Germany, Jews in the Warsaw Ghetto were forced to wear white arm bands with blue Stars of David (Gutman 1982, 1994; Hilberg 1979). Since Warsaw Jews' identifying badges were worn on top of their clothes (as opposed to being sewn into their clothes), these symbols were relatively easy to remove.

7. The English spellings of Polish, Yiddish, and Hebrew names vary some-what. In this paper I use the most common English spellings of these names but do not change spellings when quoting directly from other texts.

6

I Am the Man and Woman in This House: Brazilian *Jeito* and the Strategic Framing of Motherhood in a Poor, Urban Community

Kevin Neuhouser

Collective identities are essential for successful mobilization, yet their creation, maintenance, and deployment are problematic. Among many potential difficulties, activists frequently struggle with whether to frame their collective identity as similar to or different from those of movement audiences, such as potential allies and decision makers (Bernstein 1997). An identity deployment strategy that works with one audience may jeopardize success with another. Activists, then, often juggle multiple strategies as they interact with various audiences (Gamson 2004). To complicate matters further, the identity choices available to activists are constrained by gender—their own and that of their audiences. This is especially so in cultures where female activism may be considered deviant, risking greater resistance.

A growing body of research has focused on how female activists negotiate and transform their identities in the context of collective action. Concepts such as "centerwomen" (Sacks 1988) and "activist mothering" (Naples 1998) have been used to describe the creative ways that women simultaneously employ and transform traditional gender identities to attain their political interests. Much of this research has focused on the constraints women face as they negotiate identities in the context of activism and the extent to which activism transforms traditional gender identities.

To explore these processes, I analyze the identity work of women activists in Caranguejo—a Brazilian *favela*[1]—by asking the following questions:

Why do some identities, rather than others, spur collective action? How do women negotiate multiple and potentially conflicting identities in relation to various movement audiences? Finally, what are the consequences of identity work for the transformation of individual and collective identities?

Beginning with the invasion in 1971 that founded the community, women activists in Caranguejo led and participated in a series of collective campaigns (Oliver 1989; Snow, Soule, and Kriesi 2004) that achieved significant material benefits for the community—housing, water, electricity, healthcare, and traffic lights. These campaigns were "feminine" in that women sought solutions to "practical" gender needs such as resources for the reproductive work of caring for their households (Molyneux 1986; Alvarez 1990; Craske 2003a, 21).[2] Although collective action was motivated by a traditional maternal identity (Neuhouser 1998), activism seemed to contradict the identity that motivated it, because it required women to engage in traditionally male behavior, that is, acting like men to get what they needed as mothers. Reflecting on decades in this *luta* (struggle), Edeleuza[3] concluded, "I am the man and the woman in this house." Drawing attention to this gender deviance, however, risked provoking a male backlash (Craske 2003b, 67–68), so women activists adopted a complex mix of framing strategies that, depending on the audience, hid or highlighted the gendered nature of their collective action.

To explore these dynamics of identity construction, management, and deployment, I briefly describe Caranguejo and six collective campaigns that occurred there between 1970 and 1995. Next, I explore the foundation of women's identity work in the community's gender norms for motherhood and fatherhood. To explain how women activists drew from this "cultural toolkit" (Swidler 1986; Porta and Diani 1999, 68) to accomplish their identity work, I introduce the Brazilian concept of *jeito*[4]—an ingenious subversion of the "laws, customs, and facts of life" (Levine 1997, 83) that avoids an overt confrontation, which would invite resistance. The *jeito's* paradoxical nature is captured in the Brazilian saying "to obey but not comply" (*obedecer mas não cumprir*). Caranguejo women proved masters of the *jeito*, presenting themselves as faithfully complying with traditional gender norms even as they circumvented them to access resources for their families. Thus, women alternated their collective identity frames as they addressed audiences of local men (potential allies) and male police officers and city officials (resource gatekeepers). Successfully utilizing the *jeito*, however, appeared to limit women's ability to redefine or transform traditional gender identities.

The Community

Caranguejo is one of approximately five hundred *favelas* in Recife, the poorest major Brazilian city.[5] Women are a slight majority (52 percent) of the approximately 3,300 inhabitants.[6] Severely handicapped in the labor market by lack of education (87 percent had not completed elementary school), 26 percent of residents were unemployed in 1996, and 57 percent for more than a year. Only 39 percent of the employed were in the formal economy (ETAPAS 1998). Because most residents were unable to access sufficient resources through individual income, most major improvements in the quality of community life required mobilization to press government for basic infrastructure. Thus, Caranguejo's history has been marked by periodic outbursts of collective action.

Having lived and worked as a community organizer in Caranguejo for three years (1980 to 1983), I knew of this history of struggle and also knew many of the participants. During the 1990s, I returned four times to collect data, conducting over seventy interviews with activists, participants, and witnesses of the collective campaigns.[7] In addition, between 2000 and 2007, I briefly visited Caranguejo four times, obtaining community updates. The following analysis, then, is based on interviews and over twenty-five years of participant observation in Caranguejo. Given this long-term relationship, to many residents, I appeared to be a "trustworthy outsider": someone both known and committed to the community and therefore "safe." Surprisingly, it was easier to interview women than men. While living in Caranguejo, I worked closely with women but had not fulfilled important local male behavioral norms (e.g., binge drinking and having multiple female partners). Thus, women tended to see me as a sympathetic audience to their often frustrating relationships with men, while men tended to view me more neutrally, as a nonthreatening anomaly.[8] Openness in interviews also was aided by the physical organization of the community, which ensures that privacy cannot even be imagined, so most residents adopt the attitude that it is better to share their side of any story than try to keep anything secret. This willingness to talk, even about potentially embarrassing details, constantly amazed me and I have tried to honor that trust by presenting what they shared in ways that cause them no harm or discomfort.

The Collective Campaigns

There have been six major campaigns in Caranguejo and women led, and were the majority of the participants in, all but one campaign.[9]

Invasion of the Canal

During the early 1970s, as part of the military government's emphasis on large infrastructure projects to spur economic growth, a system of drainage canals was built in Recife. During construction through a marsh along the Capibaribe River, dirt was thrown up on either side of the new canal. This unoccupied "land" caught the attention of poor women living nearby with their families in rented rooms. Lacking adequate, reliable income, they owed back rent and were threatened with eviction. So, one weekend in March of 1971, Niçinha began building a small shack. Other women soon followed and a line of shacks materialized along the canal. Police attempted to remove the residents, knocking down houses and throwing building materials into the canal, but each time the shacks were rebuilt. Although men helped with construction, it was primarily women who confronted the police and also filled city offices to contest the destruction of their homes with officials. After months of conflict, the city relented, allowing the shacks to remain.

Acquiring Public Utilities

With de facto possession of the land, women turned their attention to infrastructure. Over several years, they collected signatures to petition the city for water and electricity. They delivered the petitions by noisily invading downtown government offices. Aided by politicians seeking electoral support, the water and power lines eventually were extended into Caranguejo's main streets.

Forming Neighborhood Associations

During Brazil's democratic transition in the mid-1980s, city politicians initiated the formation of two competing neighborhood associations. The associations perpetuated the traditional patron–client model: politicians helped the associations access government resources in exchange for electoral support. As Arlindo, a long-time association president, admitted, "The government gives so it can later collect votes." Local men were recruited to lead the associations, although many women became members (to be eligible for government programs) and a few even became officers. Several years later, government funding disappeared, so the associations now exist primarily on paper and in the minds of a few men hoping to revive them by accessing new resources through political contacts.

Creation of a Health Post

In 1984, UNICEF invited twenty-one women from Caranguejo for training in basic health care skills (giving shots, making oral rehydration fluid, etc.). The women were paid during the training but afterward received no material or institutional support. The women, however, offered free services to their neighbors and even rented a house to serve as a health post. Eventually, over half the original health agents dropped out, but those who persisted succeeded in accessing resources (minimal salaries, attending doctors, equipment) from local and international organizations. They organized local fundraising campaigns to build a brick health post. Eventually, a foreign donor provided funds to complete the construction. This is the only women-led campaign that produced a formal organization.

Campaign for Legalization and Urbanization

Caranguejo residents' possession of their homes is tenuous. As the 1980s ended, rumored plans to expel the residents and use the land where they lived for anything from a shopping center to a viaduct spurred residents to seek legal title. It was hoped that the city, then, would "urbanize" the community by providing infrastructure, such as a much needed sewer system. Helped by two lawyers, the community held educational meetings and trained leaders (primarily women) in the bureaucratic processes of legalization and urbanization. Documents were drafted and residents marched to city offices. After many difficulties, the petition was granted only to have the documentation "lost" in the change of city administrations following an election. Although legal title has yet to be confirmed, the campaign effectively forestalled any plans to evict the residents.

Installation of Traffic Lights

Caranguejo's neighborhood school is located in a Catholic church on the far side of a very busy one-way street. Without traffic lights, children darted across whenever a gap appeared in the chaotic flow of traffic. Inevitably, some were hit by vehicles; most suffered broken bones but several were killed. Mothers repeatedly petitioned the city for traffic lights without success. In April 1994, a child was struck, breaking her leg. Several women (none of whom were the girl's mother) decided that it was time to force the city to respond. The women recruited neighbors door-to-door to shut down the street during the following Monday morning rush hour. To gain public support as well as some protection from police and irate drivers, they called local newspapers and radio and television stations to alert them of the upcoming "big" news story. Early Monday morning, residents piled old furniture, trash, and tree branches across the street. Children in their school uniforms lined the front of the barricade, creating a dramatic media photo opportunity. Traffic quickly backed up for several miles. Police ordered the blockade's removal, but the women retorted that although they could be forced to reopen the street, as soon as the police left they would return and would continue doing so until their demands were met. At that point, the police turned the problem over to the city transit department. After hours of tense negotiation, the city promised to provide police officers to stop traffic for children to cross until signals could be installed. Several weeks later, traffic lights were up and functioning and schoolchildren were safely crossing.

Maternal vs. Paternal Identities

Elsewhere, I have argued that women were more active in these campaigns because they were more committed to motherhood than men were to fatherhood (Neuhouser 1998). Differential commitment was produced by the interaction of culturally available identities with structural constraints on access to the material resources needed to perform those identities (Becker 1960; Calhoun 1991; Stryker 1968, 2000; Snow and McAdam 2000). Brazilian gender ideologies provided specific expectations for "motherhood" and "fatherhood," while the Brazilian economy constrained the fulfillment of those expectations. When men failed as fathers, they had other identity options; women did not, leaving them little choice but to collectively struggle to succeed at the only available positive identity (Neuhouser 1998).

To understand men's and women's differential participation in these campaigns, then, it is necessary first to understand the meanings associated with the identity of "mother" and "father." In Caranguejo, men understand the father's role as "provider." According to Reginaldo, who is a father of five, a "family father,"[10] "takes responsibility for the house, makes sure there is nothing lacking, puts his children in school, teaches them, provides for their health, food for the house, recreation, as much comfort as possible for the family." Women agree that this is men's understanding of fatherhood. According to Lení, a mother of two small children, the majority of men believe that "the man is only to work and provide food." Zefa elaborated:

> They think that they only have the responsibility of taking care of work and putting food in the house, the family's food and that's it. Then he thinks he's done everything. He doesn't think that he has the obligation to help his wife in the house with the children.

Women want a broader definition of fatherhood (Hunter de Bessa 2004), but men rarely fulfill even the basic economic provider role. Most men in Caranguejo experience frequent unemployment, so even when trying to be good fathers, they often fail to fulfill the minimal requirement of providing food for their families—an extremely painful experience, as Sergio explained:

> These family fathers that have two, three kids and are unemployed. They get home . . . and there is nothing to eat. There is no work. They look for it and there really isn't any. There are many that go out looking for work in the morning and don't find it. That hurts his conscience—his children hungry.

If fatherhood provides few opportunities for status and positive self-esteem, there are alternative identities that offer better chances of success. Reginaldo described two such identities.[11] One is the *valentão*—a man who is "not afraid of anything. Police, thugs, whatever comes, he'll take it on." Another is the *mulherengo*—a man "who has lots of women." Men who are physically coura- geous or successful with women are admired by other men, even if they fail as family fathers. Although men say that the family father is respected, they express ambivalence about the role because, as Sergio noted, such a man "lives from home to work, from work to home," thereby no longer hanging out with other men and potentially ridiculed for forfeiting his independence. Thus, when the cost of being family fathers rises, many men abandon their fami- lies, shifting identity commitments to those offering greater social rewards. Consequently, many women agree with Edeleuza that "the father is only to produce kids and abandon them—just that."

Mothers in Caranguejo, however, do not have positive alternative iden- tities. From birth, girls are socialized into motherhood. As I interviewed Nenê—who took great pride in so vigorously defending her shack during the invasion that police declared her "worse than a man"—she affection- ately called her toddler granddaughter *maeinha* (little mother), a common exchange between mothers and daughters. This socialization is reinforced as mothers teach daughters all the domestic skills (cooking, cleaning, childcare) necessary to be good mothers. As mothers go off to paid extensions of moth- erhood as maids, cooks, laundrywomen, and nannies, daughters stay home to "mother" younger siblings. Thus, females in Caranguejo move from being "little mothers" while their mothers work to paid "mothers" in the workforce and unpaid mothers to their own children.

Positive female identities are so limited that "adult woman" is virtu- ally synonymous with mother. In Caranguejo, there are three female life stages. At birth, she is a *menina* (girl) and remains so until her first menstrual period, after which her mother calls her a *moça*.[12] Others note this critical change and also adopt the term. Although a girl has no control over her transition to *moça*, to become a *mulher* (woman) she must do something (i.e., have sexual intercourse); if not, she never becomes a "woman," no matter her age or responsibilities (Gregg 2003). Socialized into motherhood and lacking alternative positive identities through education or work, many girls become sexually active quite young, hoping to become mothers (Goldstein 2003, 244). Reflecting on her experiences as a health agent and mother of a teenage daughter, Aparecida said,

> here when a *moça* is fourteen, she's already a *mulher*. . . . A girl twelve, thirteen years old isn't a virgin anymore. There are girls that are fourteen that are already mothers. There's no time to think about what she's going to be. She wants to be a mother and that's it. For her to be a mother is the most beautiful thing in the world.

The health clinic provides free birth control, but many girls ignore it because they want to become mothers. Thus, for many teenage girls, initiation of sexual activity (womanhood) is quickly followed by pregnancy (motherhood).

Caranguejo women, then, are highly committed to motherhood, despite significant economic obstacles to fulfilling their duties as mothers. Unlike men, however, women feel that they have no choice but to do whatever it takes—even collective action—to be good mothers. Women express this lack of alternatives by saying that they "lack the courage" to abandon their children as men do, but then claim they do have the courage to "take on anything" to be good mothers. Aparecida described this paradoxical mixture of having no choice but to *be* mothers but therefore capable of doing anything *as* mothers:

> The mother just has to be the mother. If she isn't, who is going to do it for her? If she doesn't take care of them [the children], doesn't obtain things, doesn't struggle for her children, who is going to take care of them. It's just got to be her. It's very difficult for a mother to abandon her children, but the father leaves whenever he wants.

Women describe this willingness to do anything to be good mothers as *se virar*, that is, to turn oneself around or to take on whatever comes from whatever direction while remaining fixed in place.[13]

For Caranguejo women, individual strategies such as paid labor were necessary but insufficient to ensure their children's survival, so they repeatedly engaged in collective action to access additional resources. Paradoxically, this required nonfeminine behavior to fulfill the feminine role of mother.

To complicate matters, women had to sustain this tension between traditional role and nontraditional behavior while maintaining relationships with men already strained by conflict over the meaning of fatherhood. Thus, Caranguejo women had to use all their creativity to mobilize successfully without alienating men.

The Brazilian *Jeito*

Caranguejo women activists used a strategy known in Brazil as *jeito* to negotiate the potential pitfalls of collective action. Roberto DaMatta (2001) argues that Brazilian society is divided between a public sphere of impersonal laws and a domestic sphere of personal relations. *Jeito* is a uniquely Brazilian attempt to reconcile these contradictory social worlds.[14] In the confrontation between the impersonal legal "no"[15] and the personal domestic "yes," public authorities have the power to win a direct confrontation. *Jeito*, therefore, doesn't reject the "no" but creatively brings the "no" and the "yes" together by finding a way (*jeito*) "that can reconcile everyone's interests. . . . Generally this occurs when . . . both [parties] discover a common connection" (DaMatta 2001, 100).

While DaMatta focuses on the public–private split, Levine (1997) emphasizes the economic divide between "haves" and "have-nots." Brazilian society is characterized by a high level of political and economic inequality, with a wealthy elite dominating the political sphere. The rich occasionally find the universal application of (their own) legal rules inconvenient and therefore resort to *jeitos*, but it is the poor for whom the public sphere is most problematic. Not only are the rules not designed to address their needs, but the poor more desperately require a favorable response because of their economic vulnerability.

For poor Brazilians, then, survival requires incredible creativity in the art of *jeito*. Successful use requires one to be quick thinking, spontaneous, witty, sympathetic, ingenious, and even devious but never "arrogant or authoritarian" (Barbosa 1995, 39). Caranguejo women displayed all these traits as they struggled to get past both the legal "no" of the public sphere and the cultural "no" of gender roles in the domestic sphere. To accomplish this, they did something absent from the literature on *jeito*: they employed it, not individually, but collectively. In their campaigns, women jointly framed their activism in complex ways, sometimes highlighting, sometimes hiding its gendered nature to establish a common bond with different audiences.

Husbands and Boyfriends

The first audience that women addressed in their identity work consisted of husbands and boyfriends, who were potential allies. Although women's participation was motivated by motherhood, framing the campaigns as "feminine" would reduce male involvement. Because men in the community define masculine and feminine as opposites (aggressive vs. passive, dominant vs. submissive), the greatest violation of gender norms for men is to act like women (Parker 2003; Lancaster 1992). Thus, to male partners, women framed the campaigns in gender neutral language (Craske 2003b, 69).

One indication that women succeeded in framing collective action as gender neutral is that when I lived in Caranguejo, I never once heard these campaigns described by either women or men in any way that connected them to women as a group. I so completely accepted this framing that my initial research proposal did not include gender issues. During the first round of interviews (1991), residents, both male and female, continued to use gender neutral terms; participants were referred to as "people" (*o povo*), "we" (*nós* or *gente*), "they" (*eles*—the masculine form used for male or mixed groups), or the "community" (*a comunidade*). I was alerted to gender issues only when I began asking for names of the most active participants and learned that women predominated.[16]

When asked, however, many women activists talked openly of maternal motivations, acknowledging women's principal leadership and participation. Aparecida, an activist in three campaigns, described a conversation with another woman about the creation of the health post, in which they concluded that it was "necessary to be real women" to accomplish what they had. In a later interview (Aug. 25, 1993), she added that "these days its rare for a man to struggle to achieve something like this." In interviews with men, however, there was never any hint of this gendered dimension. By using gender neutral language, women succeeded in hiding the gendered nature of the campaigns from community men.

Concealing women's gendered motivation removed one obstacle to male participation, but men still lacked an incentive to join in the campaigns. Women, therefore, attempted to frame the motivation for collective action as "parental" not maternal (i.e., "good parents" are activists to help their children), expanding men's definition of fatherhood from breadwinner to a broader (more maternal) definition of doing whatever was necessary to support the household.[17] The results were mixed. At times men participated but, because of their weaker commitment to fatherhood, dropped out when participation costs rose, leaving women to carry the burden (Neuhouser 1998).

Moça recalled that during the canal invasion, men helped build the shacks but left when police arrived. Aparecida's husband participated in the fund-raising campaigns to build the health post but later withdrew his support, burning her health agent training certificate and blaming her activism for her decreased attention to domestic responsibilities.

Aware that men's participation was tenuous, women carefully acknowledged the support the men did provide. After describing how she and Ceiça organized the street closure to get a traffic light, Lení quickly added that "a lot of men helped," too. Even so, women expressed scathing criticism of individual men who failed to act courageously. Thus, Lení sharply criticized a Residents' Association officer for passivity during the traffic light negotiations. Surprisingly, even very activist women occasionally justified men's lack of involvement. Aparecida, normally blunt in her assessment of men's short-comings, tried to convince me that fewer men than women participated in the legalization campaign because "men worked" and therefore were "too tired." Reminded that women worked, too, she countered "but men tire more quickly." Ironically, one outcome of women's framing strategies was that male participation appeared greater in retrospect than it had been in practice, while women's more crucial roles faded from community memory.

Concealing the campaigns' gendered nature was far easier than framing women's individual participation in political activities (Craske 2003a, 19). In Brazil "the husband doesn't discuss politics at home with the woman, because 'politics' don't interest women, it's a man thing" (Tabak 1983, 55). In a study of women's activism in a São Paulo *favela*, Teresa Pires de Rio Caldeira (1990, 61) points out "the ambiguity of women's participation, which in spite of being carried out in the name of their most traditional role [motherhood], involves going out and leaving precisely that sphere used as a means of legitimation." Thus, female participants framed individual motivation as nonpolitical. Consequently, women were least active in the creation of the neighborhood associations, the most overtly "political" of all the campaigns, involving politicians, political parties, and electioneering. Aparecida did serve one term as association president but was disillusioned after experiencing two major frustrations. The first was the political maneuvering the position required. The second was that everyone seemed motivated by self-interest—"no one would do anything without money." Unlike the other campaigns, where (mostly female) participants struggled for the good of their children and community, in the male-dominated associations power and self-interest predominated.

To protect their nonpolitical framing strategy, Caranguejo women attempted to keep their own activism separate from the "political" associations. Aparecida emphasized that the traffic light campaign had succeeded without the associations: "the mothers of the community don't have anything to do with the [association] leadership, understand?" Ceiça and Lení, the two primary organizers, confirmed Aparecida's statement and contrasted the motives and methods of the male association leaders with their own. They had gone door-to-door, struggling to overcome their neighbors' fears and convince a critical mass to participate in the street blockade, but despite needing as many protestors as possible, they intentionally excluded the male leaders of the associations. Lení explained, "I was very clear. I didn't want any of the community [organizations]. It was the mothers who were there. The heads of the community . . . no. Just the mothers." When asked why, she explained, "Because they have the *mania* [habit] of having us do the work and then later they say that it was they who did it. So I said to them that I didn't want them involved. They can come but only to watch." The male leadership was perceived as motivated by personal advancement and therefore a potentially disruptive presence.[18] In contrast, for Ceiça activism was not a steppingstone to political influence: "just the traffic lights and then I'm gone!"

In their campaigns, then, women avoided framing their activism as "political." In Brazil, politics are perceived as a corrupting power struggle for self-promotion and self-interest. According to Niçinha, who is the recognized community "founder" because she initiated the canal invasion, "the government [i.e., politicians] just wants for itself." This is contrary to women's understanding of their own motivation—sacrificial, long-suffering effort on behalf of others (Caldeira 1990). In fact, the word the women use most often to describe their activism is "suffering," which they contrast to self-seeking "politics." By framing their activism in this way, however, collective action was linked to a particularly "feminine" trait—the suffering that women endure as mothers. As Niçinha concluded in her interview, "That's all I have to say about my life—its been a lot of suffering." Or, as Edeleuza stated, "we women have to suffer anyway."

By slipping into a "feminine" frame, women once again risked losing men's active support. If collective action really was women's work, then men had no reason to participate. Community meetings, for example, appear to have become defined as women's work, as women complain that men will not attend them. Lení disapprovingly claimed that it is common for husbands to tell their wives, "woman, there is a meeting . . . you go." In my community organizing work in Caranguejo, although men would participate when there was physical work to be done, it was extremely difficult to persuade them to attend meetings. Men concluded that "the struggle" is women's work: as Leni said, "here the men don't struggle because they think that women are to do everything—to struggle, to speak . . . everything is for the woman to do."

In relation to their husbands and boyfriends, then, women juggled a contradictory set of framing tasks. The maternal motivation for action was hidden so that the campaigns would not be defined by men as women's movements. At the same time, the maternal motivation was highlighted so that men would not interpret women's activism as a violation of gender norms. Women tried to reconcile these contradictory frames by emphasizing that activism was required of good "parents." Ironically, women largely failed to convince men that "fatherhood" required participation but succeeded in framing the campaigns as nongendered. Men participated minimally but perceived themselves as being as active as women. Paradoxically, when men's lack of involvement was recognized, it was justified because activism was "women's work."

Police and City Officials

If women in Caranguejo were to access resources for their families, they needed to exert enough pressure to overcome the resistance of police and city officials but not so much pressure that it provoked a backlash (Piven and Cloward 1979; McAdam, McCarthy, and Zald 1996). To exert pressure they needed to act in "unfeminine" ways, such as confronting police, disobeying orders, and invading streets and public offices. To soften this "masculine" behavior, women framed it to the authorities as maternally motivated.

With no alternative than to do whatever it took to be good mothers, Caranguejo women did not hesitate to act aggressively toward authorities. Twenty-two years after the canal invasion, Nenê proudly recalled an exchange with city officials:

> We went to the municipal government building. They gave us twenty-four hours to leave. When they saw this multitude of women, they said: "where did you live before?" "In rented rooms." "Why did you invade other people's land? "Don't you know this doesn't have an owner?" "You're worse than men!"

Unintimidated by male officials, the women were acknowledged as less manageable than men. When I asked Nenê if the women weren't afraid, she dismissed my concern: "No, they weren't afraid of anything. Afraid of what?"

Lacking the courage to abandon their children, women fearlessly risked the wrath of male authorities. Nenê was so indifferent to the risks that she helped her daughter in a later invasion. This invasion was unsuccessful because, as Margarida recalled, the city sent "police, they sent machine guns." Violent expulsion, however, failed to deter women, as many participated in more invasions—some successful, some not—for themselves and their daughters. Nenê recalled her experiences fondly: "Invasion is beautiful. You dig a hole and put in a post and soon the police arrive and everyone runs and then you do it again."

Surprisingly, Brazilian gender ideologies offered some support to women who acted aggressively. Although such behavior was deviant for women, men honor courage and aggressiveness and recognize that even they who "naturally" have these traits have difficulty displaying them in confrontation with well-armed police. Thus, when women acted "worse than men," they deserved respect. A positive identity existed for such women—*mulher brava* (a fierce, brave, wild woman). Few men desired to live with such a nonsubmissive woman, but still they could admire her courage.

Women, then, were permitted some deviance from gender norms, especially if they framed activism as maternally motivated. During the canal invasion, women successfully combined courageous resistance with motherhood. When the police attempted to demolish the shacks, women locked their children inside and dared police to carry out their orders. Margarida described what happened:

> They were throwing the wood into the canal. When he started taking mine, I grabbed it out of his hand. He gave me a push. "Oh, Joe, what's that?" . . . [The policeman said] "I'm going to tear it down!" I put my kids inside. [I said,] "tear it down!" "I am going to tear it down!" "Don't do that, you'll kill the woman [observers]."

Edeleuza described a very similar interaction with police:

> "Now, I don't have anything in this life, so if you want to tear it down, go ahead. There is a child inside sleeping—three years old. If you want to tear it down on top of her, go ahead." He said, "*Whoa*, I'm not crazy."

Thus, women physically and symbolically placed their children between themselves and the police, softening their aggressiveness by acknowledging the police's power to tear down their houses but appealing to their respect for motherhood to show restraint.

Two decades later, when a younger generation of mothers shut down the busy street bordering the *favela*, they employed the same combination of forceful action and symbolic appeals for authorities to respect motherhood. The women knew that blocking rush hour traffic risked inciting violence from police and furious drivers. Ceiça, one of the organizers, described the chaotic scene as they constructed the barricade: "We closed the street, but the drivers got so angry, so angry. They wanted to go through. The busses wanted to go through. The police said, 'let them through.' And we not wanting anyone at all to get through." The other organizer, Lení, added that some drivers tried to pass right through the protesters; one threatened them with a revolver. The women were most insistent that the police not pass:

> The police came. They said, "we are going through." "You're the very ones who are not going through. You are not going through. There's no way you are going through. If you want to go through, you can. You will kill someone, but there are lots of people here to get your license number."

As the tension escalated, women made two symbolic appeals to respect their desire to safeguard their children. First, they lined up the children in school uniforms in front of the barricade. Second, as Lení explained, "they brought some children that had been run over to be with their mothers." If the children weren't sufficient to communicate maternal motivation, the women made the point explicitly as they argued with drivers and police. Ceiça described one exchange:

> "This is a crime [i.e., blocking the street]." "You're the one's committing the crime because its not your child that crosses here. It's not your child that is run over. The crime is a child that's killed here."

The strategy was sufficiently effective that one off-duty police officer caught in the traffic jam joined the protestors, although initially he had tried to remove the blockade.

Although the *jeito* of combining aggressive behavior with appeals to motherhood generally was effective, it could be challenged. When the police attempted to evict Margarida from her shack, she too put her kids inside and dared the police to tear it down on top of them. The police threatened to arrest her, which would have separated her from her children. Margarida appealed to the officer's respect for motherhood, arguing that her children would be abandoned if she were arrested: "I said, 'I'm not going. I don't have a husband.'" But the policeman shot back: "Then why do you have kids?" In other words, if she was such a good mother, why wasn't there a husband? Edeleuza also was challenged by the police: "Who told you to invade?" She responded by arguing that because her husband was unemployed they faced eviction and living on the street with small children. Thus, it was not her moral failure but the economic failure of her husband that had forced her into this situation.

Because of the double moral standard in Brazil in which men gain status from fathering children outside of marriage while women are sanctioned for the same behavior (Gregg 2003; Goldstein 2003, 238), the many unmarried mothers in Caranguejo faced a potential problem when they drew attention to their motherhood. If they were "good" mothers, why were they "single" mothers? To counter this challenge, women relied on the fact that motherhood was so fundamental to women's identity that virtually any infraction, including sexual improprieties, could be forgiven as long as they cared for their children. The worst thing a woman can do, even worse than sexual relations outside of marriage, according to two health agents,

> [is to] abandon her children. Everyone will talk. "She's irresponsible, *safada* [immoral, shameless]."[19] No one cares if she puts horns on her man [making a "cow" of him by betraying him with another man]. It happens so much that it's normal.

Even prostitution, if done to feed one's children, is better than abandoning them. In fact, the line between "honorable" marriage and sex for pay blurs as poor mothers in Recife *favelas* engage in a variety of sexual strategies to access resources for their children (Gregg 2003). Thus, women could be challenged as morally deficient and therefore unworthy of respect, but ultimately motherhood could deflect even these charges.

Implications for Identity Transformation

According to Hunt and Benford (2004, 449), "participation in social movements can lead to enduring changes in personal identities, transformations that persist after the movement." Although plausible, relatively little research has tested this claim (Giugni 2004, 490). The studies done, however, suggest that activism has the potential to transform the attitudes and behaviors of participants (e.g., Jennings 1987; McAdam 1986). Did women's activism in Caranguejo transform understandings of and commitment to their identities as mothers?

After decades of activism, Caranguejo women appeared no less committed to motherhood than they were in the beginning. Their most positive memories and emotions remained centered on children and grandchildren. As I interviewed Paraíba in the shack that she built during the invasion twenty years earlier, we were interrupted several times by arriving grandchildren. Each time, Paraíba prompted, "Where's the blessing?" To which they quickly responded, "Bless me, mother." Smiling broadly, Paraíba concluded the little ritual with "God bless you." Observing Paraíba's obvious joy in her grandchildren, I asked if it was good to live near extended family. She described how on Sundays they all get together to eat and watch television: "Isn't that good? Its wonderful!" After recounting her lifetime of struggles as the head of the family, Paraíba ended the interview, stating simply, "I am here. I raised my children." Despite great difficulties, she fulfilled her culture's gender role demands and enjoyed the fruits of her accomplishment.

Enduring commitment to motherhood does not mean that some women have not begun to redefine its content. Many women believe that they struggled unnecessarily because of the timing and number of their children. Consequently, many counsel their daughters to delay motherhood. Lení says that women should give their daughters the same advice she gave her own: use contraceptives "because they can't be nuns, but later they can have children." Aparecida says she became a mother too young (at fourteen years old) and counsels her daughter, who says, "don't worry, I don't want to have the life you have."

Asserting control over the timing and number of children, however, has implications for the power that men traditionally exercised over women's bodies. At the health post, Aparecida, provides birth control for women, despite men's interference.

> I arranged a tubal ligation for her [a neighbor], but he [her partner] didn't allow it. He says that a woman who ties her tubes gets sick, gets thin, and he doesn't want her to get thin. This is just an excuse. So I bring her contraceptives in secret.[20]

Disputes over control of women's bodies also involved health agents in the issue of domestic violence, as Aparecida explained,

> if a man wants to kill his wife because she works and doesn't want to make love to him anymore, I have to go there and talk . . . so he won't kill her and this occurred with me here. . . . I have to go talk to him. I have to counsel him.

The problem, according to her, is that Caranguejo men "want to be the owner of the wife, their property."

Women who challenged police and city officials and won are not easily intimidated by husbands or boyfriends. Lení described how when her partner "raised his hand to hit me, I said 'you don't need to bring it down because I'm already leaving.' So I took my son . . . rented a room to live in and took a job as a maid." When Paraíba's husband complained there were too many of her relatives living in their house, she responded, "If you're going to upset and abuse me—leave!" Ceiça, after shutting down traffic and forcing police and city officials to meet her demands, gathered the courage to take her children and leave a husband who, for years, had physically abused her.

The complex framing strategies women employed in their identity work, however, may have limited the transformative impact of activism. Recruiting men by concealing their gendered motivations meant that meetings and protests were never forums for the discussion of gender issues. Emphasizing their maternal motivations to authorities did not push women to question the centrality of their identities as mothers. Women also were ambivalent about claiming a "political" identity tainted with negative connotations. Thus, women were uncomfortable with both parts of the "female activist" identity. Consequently, many women did not experience a transformation of their understandings of their traditional gender identities.

The primary exceptions are the health agents who have worked together for two decades. These women not only struggled with birth control and domestic violence but also sought changes in the power relations with their own partners. Of the nine health agents still working, four are single mothers. Some had husbands who left because they would not accept a working wife who expected to share domestic responsibilities. Aparecida says the other five have "husbands who now accept" their wives' work and activism. Through their common experiences of struggle, they created a supportive community that facilitates a renegotiation of their identities as women and their relations with men. In Aparecida's words, "We fight, but afterwards it's all okay—we defend one another, we support one another. We struggled a lot together."

Conclusion: Female Activist Identities

Over the last several decades, there has been an explosion of research on female activism and gendered identities (e.g., Molyneux 1986; Alvarez 1990; Einwohner 1999; Moghadam 2005). One critical distinction that emerged early in the literature was between activism motivated by traditional gender roles (feminine or practical movements) and activism motivated to transform traditional gender roles (feminist or strategic movements). The recognition that traditional gender roles like motherhood could motivate activism lead research in two directions: (1) How does motherhood motivate activism? and (2) Can activism motivated by motherhood provoke a redefinition of that identity?

There is evidence from many different societies that maternal activism is pervasive and frequently sparks a redefinition of motherhood, from caring for family to caring for the community and even society as a whole. This redefinition has been described as "political motherhood" (Bouvard 1994), "female consciousness"[21] (Kaplan 1997), and "activist mothering"[22] (Naples 1998). In each case, to access resources to fulfill the responsibilities of motherhood, women move into the political sphere. This activism creates the potential for a new consciousness of the political dimensions of motherhood and a wider scope of maternal responsibility. Less clear is whether or not, or under what conditions, this "feminine" activism transforms into "feminist" activism that directly challenges the power relations embedded in traditional gender roles.

Women in Caranguejo generally fit this model of "activist mothering." They moved into the political sphere to access resources for their families that were unavailable in the domestic sphere. Frequently, this activism led women to a broader, more collective understanding of motherhood that included the entire community. Less common was the emergence of an overt feminist consciousness. The paths to these various new understandings or the persistence of traditional understandings were not linear but were the result of complex identity framing strategies (*jeitos*) that women employed to attain their interests. The fact that women never clearly or consistently framed their activism as female activism appears to have limited the degree to which motherhood was redefined, although it increased their access to resources they needed to care for their children.

To clarify the conditions in which activism transforms traditional gender identities, then, it is necessary to carefully analyze the strategic framing practices adopted by women as they pursue their goals. The foregoing analysis suggests that women activists do not simply adopt new definitions of motherhood, but that multiple identity frames are utilized in complex and even contradictory ways, producing unexpected identity outcomes. Thus, more research is needed to understand the variety of strategies women adopt, the conditions that shape the choice of strategies, and the impact of different strategies on the transformation of identities. This will require both a broad range of case studies that highlight the complexity of identity framing strategies in different economic, political, and cultural contexts and carefully chosen comparative studies that begin to identify underlying patterns of framing strategies and identity transformation.

Every facet of the campaigns in Caranguejo—motivation, interaction with movement audiences, goal achievement, and the impact of participation on the activists—was fundamentally shaped by identity framing processes. Caranguejo women, to be good mothers, were both "the man and the woman" in the context of collective action. This gender deviance, however, was skillfully finessed to avoid a male backlash that could undermine their efforts. For activists, there is no easy (or even hard won) correspondence between personal and collective identity. Caranguejo women used every *jeito* imaginable to juggle a variety of identity frames depending on audience and goals. In doing so they achieved their primary material goals of securing housing, water, electricity, healthcare, and traffic lights. Their identity work *jeitos*, however, limited the transformative potential of their activism on female identities. Yet, given their commitment to motherhood, this is a trade-off they almost certainly would make again.

References

Alvarez, Sonia E. 1990. *Engendering Democracy in Brazil: Women's Movement's in Transition Politics*. Princeton, N.J.: Princeton University Press.

Barbosa, Lívia Neves de H. 1995. "The Brazilian *Jeitinho*: An Exercise in National Identity." In *The Brazilian Puzzle*, ed. D. J. Hess and R. DaMatta, 35–48. New York: Columbia University Press.

Becker, Howard. 1960. "Notes on the Conception of Commitment." *American Journal of Sociology* 66: 32–40.

Bernstein, Mary. 1997. "Celebration and Suppression: The Strategic Uses of Identity by the Lesbian and Gay Movement." *American Journal of Sociology* 103: 531–65.

Bouvard, Marguerite Guzman. 1994. *Revolutionizing Motherhood: The Mothers of the Plaza de Mayo*. Wilmington, Del.: SR Books.

Bueno, Francisco da Silveira. 1992. *Minidicionário da Língua Portuguesa*. 6th ed. São Paulo: Editora Lisa S/A.

Caldeira, Teresa Pires de Rio. 1990. "Women, Daily Life and Politics." In *Women and Social Change in Latin America*, ed. E. Jelin, 47–78. London: Zed Books.

Calhoun, Craig. 1991. "The Problem of Identity in Collective Action." In *Macro-Micro Linkages in Sociology*, ed. J. Huber, 51–75. Newbury Park, Calif.: Sage.

Craske, Nikki. 2003a. "Gender, Politics, and Legislation." In *Gender in Latin America* by S. Chant with N. Craske, 19–45. New Brunswick, N.J.: Rutgers University Press.

———. 2003b. "Gender, Poverty, and Social Movements." In *Gender in Latin America* by Sylvia Chant with Nikki Craske, 46–70. New Brunswick, N.J.: Rutgers University Press.

Dalsgaard, Anne Line. 2004. *Matters of Life and Longing: Female Sterilization in Northeast Brazil*. Copenhagen: Museum Tusculanum Press.

DaMatta, Roberto. 2001. *O Que Faz o Brasil, Brasil?* 12th ed. Rio de Janeiro: Editora Rocco Ltda.

Einwohner, Rachel L. 1999. "Gender, Class, and Social Movement Outcomes: Identity and Effectiveness in Two Animal Rights Campaigns." *Gender & Society* 13: 56–76.

ETAPAS. 1991. *Relatório Preliminar Campo Tabaiares*. Recife, Brazil: ETAPAS.

ETAPAS. 1998. *Caranguejo e Tabaiares: Historia Lutas e Conquistas*. Recife, Brazil: ETAPAS.

Folha de Pernambuco. April 10, 1990. *"Comunidades Reivindicam Criaçao de Zeis."*

Gamson, William A. 2004. "Bystanders, Public Opinion, and the Media." In *The Blackwell Companion to Social Movements*, ed. D. A. Snow, S. A. Soule, and H. Kriesi, 242–61. Malden, Mass.: Blackwell Publishing.

Giugni, Marco G. 2004. Personal and Biographical Consequences. In *The Blackwell Companion to Social Movements*, ed. D. A. Snow, S. A. Soule, and H. Kriesi, 489–507. Malden, Mass.: Blackwell Publishing.

Goldstein, Donna M. 2003. *Laughter Out of Place: Race, Class, Violence, and Sexuality in a Rio Shantytown*. Berkeley: University of California Press.

Gregg, Jessica L. 2003. *Virtually Virgins: Sexual Strategies and Cervical Cancer in Recife, Brazil*. Stanford, Calif.: Stanford University Press.

Hunt, Scott A., and Robert D. Benford. 2004. "Collective Identity, Solidarity, and Commitment." In *The Blackwell Companion to Social Movements*, ed. D. A. Snow, S. A. Soule, and H. Kriesi, 433–57. Malden, Mass.: Blackwell Publishing.

Hunter de Bessa, Gina. 2004. "Between 'Modern Women' and 'Woman-Mothers'; Reproduction and Gender Identity among Low-Income Brazilian Women." Women and International Development Working Paper No. 283. East Lansing: Michigan State University

Jennings, M. Kent. 1987. "Residues of a Movement: The Aging of the American Protest Generation." *American Political Science Review* 81: 367–82.

Jornal do Commercio. April 10, 1990. *"Funcionário da Urb Joga Carro ContraFavelados."*

Kaplan, Tamara. 1997. *Crazy for Democracy: Women in Grassroots Movements*. New York: Routledge.

Kurtz, Sharon. 2002. *Workplace Justice: Organizing Multi-Identity Movements*. Minneapolis: University of Minneapolis Press.

Lancaster, Roger. 1992. *Life is Hard: Machismo, Danger, and the Intimacy of Power in Nicaragua*. Berkeley: University of California Press.

Levine. Robert M. 1997. *Brazilian Legacies*. Armonk, N.Y.: M. E. Sharpe.

McAdam, Doug. 1986. "Recruitment to High-Risk Activism: The Case of Freedom Summer." *American Sociological Review* 92: 64–90.

McAdam, Doug, John D. McCarthy, and Mayer N. Zald. 1996. "Introduction: Opportunities, Mobilizing Structures, and Framing Processes—Toward a Synthetic, Comparative Perspective on Social Movements." In *Comparative Perspectives on Social Movements*, ed. D. McAdam, J. D. McCarthy, and M. N. Zald, 1–20. Cambridge, UK: Cambridge University Press.

Moghadam, Valentine M. 2005. *Globalizing Women: Transnational Feminist Networks*. Baltimore: The Johns Hopkins University Press.

Molyneux, Maxine. 1986. "Mobilization without Emancipation? Women's Interests, State, and Revolution." In *Transition and Development: Problems of Third World Socialism*, ed. R. F. Fagen, C. D. Deere, and J. L. Coraggio, 280–302. New York: Monthly Review Press.

Naples, Nancy A. 1998. *Grassroots Warriors: Activist Mothering, Community Work, and the War on Poverty*. New York: Routledge.

Neuhouser, Kevin. 1995. "'Worse than Men': Gendered Mobilization in an Urban Brazilian Squatter Settlement, 1971–1991." *Gender & Society* 9: 38–59.

———. 1998. "'If I Had Abandoned My Children': Community Mobilization and Commitment to the Identity of Mother in Northeast Brazil." *Social Forces* 77: 331–58.

Oliver, Pamela. 1989. "Bringing the Crowd Back In: The Nonorganizational Elements of Social Movements." *Sociological Focus* 17: 259–73.

Parker, Richard. 2003. "Changing Sexualities: Masculinity and Male Homosexuality in Brazil." In *Changing Men and Masculinities in Latin America*, ed. M. C. Gutmann, 307–32. Durham, N.C.: Duke University Press.

Piven, Frances Fox, and Richard A. Cloward. 1979. *Poor People's Movements: Why They Succeed, How They Fail*. New York: Vintage Books.

Porta, Donatella Della, and Mario Diani. 1999. *Social Movements: An Introduction*. Malden, Mass.: Blackwell Publishing.

Sacks, Karen Bodkin. 1988. "Gender and Grassroots Leadership." In *Women and the Politics of Empowerment*, ed. A. Bookman and S. Morgen, 77–94. Philadelphia: Temple University Press.

Snow, David A., and Doug McAdam. 2000. "Identity Work Processes in the Context of Social Movements: Clarifying the Identity/Movement Nexus." In *Self, Identity, and Social Movements*, ed. S. Stryker, T. J. Owens, and R. W. White, 41–67. Minneapolis: University of Minnesota Press.

Snow, David A., Sarah A. Soule, and Hanspeter Kriesi. 2004. "Mapping the Terrain." In *The Blackwell Companion to Social Movements*, ed. D. A. Snow, S. A. Soule, and H. Kriesi, 3–16. Malden, Mass.: Blackwell Publishing.

Stryker, Sheldon. 1968. "Identity Salience and Role Performance: The Relevance of Symbolic Interaction Theory for Family Research." *Journal of Marriage and Family* 30: 558–64.

———. 2000. "Identity Competition: Key to Differential Social Movement Participation?" In *Self, Identity, and Social Movements*, ed. S. Stryker, T. J. Owens, and R. W. White, 21–40. Minneapolis: University of Minnesota Press.

Swidler, Ann. 1986. "Culture in Action: Symbols and Strategies." *American Sociological Review* 51: 273–86.

Tabak, Fanny. 1983. *Autoritarianismo e Participação Política da Mulher*. Rio de Janeiro: Ediçoes Graal.

Notes

1. Urban communities founded through invasion of unused land.

2. This is in contrast with "feminist" movements that challenge traditional gender roles.

3. In this type of research, there is a "sad dilemma" (Kurtz 2002, xxxii) in balancing the need to protect informants and the desire to acknowledge their courageous efforts. Over the years, my informants have expressed little fear of reprisal and great pleasure in having their activism publicized. Therefore, I use their first names or nicknames so they can recognize themselves in these pages without undue exposure to risk.

4. Literally, "manner," "method," or "way" of doing something (Bueno 1992, 380).

5. In 1989, 47.7 percent of Recife's approximately three million inhabitants were estimated to fall below the absolute poverty line (defined as less than 60 percent of the monthly minimum wage), the highest in Brazil (ETAPAS 1991, 22).

6. Demographic statistics for Caranguejo are from a 1996 survey conducted by ETAPAS (*Equipe Técnica de Assessoria, Pesquisa e Ação Social* [Technical Team for Support, Research, and Social Action]), a local Brazilian nonprofit that conducts research on Recife's poor communities and their popular movements in order to provide support to their residents and participants—a model of applied sociology.

7. For more on methodology, see Neuhouser 1998.

8. When I first moved into the community in 1980 as a young, foreign, single male, everyone assumed I was a priest and quickly became known as "*padre barbudo*" (the "bearded priest"), to distinguish me from the local (clean-shaven) priest. Even though the community eventually realized I was not a priest, the image of sexual neutrality lingered in peoples' minds.

9. For more in-depth description of the first five campaigns, see Neuhouser 1995.

10. Caranguejo residents differentiate between a "father"—the biological father of a child—and a "family father" (*pai de família*)—the man who takes responsibility for children. No such distinction exists for mothers; that the biological mother will fulfill her duties to her children literally goes without saying.

11. These two identities illustrate the availability of alternative positive male identities in Caranguejo; for others see Neuhouser 1998.

12. There is no English word with the precise meaning of *moça*.

13. Gina Hunter de Bessa (personal communication) points out that *se virar* also has the connotation of "managing alone," in this context without the help of a man.

14. Although "most if not all societies have similar mechanisms of social adjustment . . . what is peculiar about the *jeitinho* is the recognition of the social category as a native

category that clearly identifies the spaces between what is socially desirable and what actually happens in practice" (Barbosa 1995, 38).

15. "[W]e are a country where the law always signifies the 'you cannot!'" (DaMatta 2001, 98).

16. Local newspapers also described this activism in gender neutral language. On April 10, 1990, Caranguejo residents presented demands for legalization to the city government. Both the *Folha de Pernambuco* and the *Jornal do Commercio* described the protestors as *pessoas* (people), *moradores* (residents), and *favelados* (favela-ites), despite an accompanying photograph that showed large numbers of women and a female lawyer assisting the demonstrators, who, in a later interview, stated that women were the primary participants in this campaign.

17. This changing definition of male roles appears to be an example of what Gina Hunter de Bessa (2004, 20) describes as poor urban Brazilian women's acceptance of "discourses of modernity."

18. In the 1990 legalization campaign, the local newspaper, *Folha de Pernambuco*, reported that the presence of a local city councilman had agitated protestors from Caranguejo "despite having been invited by the President of the Residents' Association . . . the rest of those present did not want 'the finger' of politics in the meeting." Given the make up of the participants (see note 15), "the rest of those present" almost certainly were women attempting to maintain the nonpolitical framing of the campaign.

19. Significantly, the terms describing a mother who abandons her children are the same ones used to describe a woman guilty of sexual impropriety.

20. For an extensive analysis of the complicated gender dynamics of female sterilization in northeast Brazil, see Dalsgaard 2004.

21. Female consciousness is "the state of mind exhibited by these women who accept the division of labor by sex of their culture and historical period and sometimes demand privileges associated with fulfilling their responsibilities" (Kaplan 1997, 185).

22. "Activist mothers" include "political activism as a central component of mothering and community caretaking of those who are not part of one's defined household" (Naples 1998, 11).

Part II
Working through Identities

7

Ally Identity: The Politically Gay[1]

Daniel J. Myers

Social movement scholars have come a long way in their attempts to incorporate the social psychology of identities into theoretical understandings of activism. Work on collective identity, addressing the dynamics of collective identity construction and the processes that attach individuals to movements, has expanded over the past two decades (see for example, Stryker, Owens, and White 2000; Melucci 1985; Johnston, Laraña, and Gusfield 1994). In particular, concepts of boundary construction, recruitment, self-verification via activism, and movement framing have brought together social psychology with the social movement literature. In the present volume, the contributors further explore the roles of identities by focusing on the critical and complicated boundary issues involved in the collective identity process—who is the "us" and who are the "them," how are these groups defined, how do we recognize the two, and how do we portray the sameness and difference that we wish to use to define these two groups. In short, how do activists create and wield sameness and difference to establish and maintain these boundaries and membership?

In this chapter, I address these questions by focusing on the formation and dynamics of ally identity construction. Scholars typically concern themselves with what I call *beneficiary* identities, those identities held by the rank-and-file activists who hail from the population that would expect or wish to benefit from the movement's activities (for examples see papers by Dugan, Einwohner, and S. Roth, this volume). Beneficiary activists are not the only ones involved in movements, however. In addition to activists who work for the benefit of a group to which they claim membership, there are also activists working for the benefit of groups for which they are outsiders. These are activists that I will call movement *allies*. Allies are movement adherents who are not direct beneficiaries of the movements they support and do not have expectations of such benefits.

Existing definitions of collective identity are, in fact, broad enough to include allies (Klandermans and de Weerd 2000). For example, Verta Taylor and Nancy Whittier (1992, 105) define collective identity as "the shared definition of a group that derives from members' common interests and solidarity." But when the notion of collective identity is applied empirically, it is often couched in an imagery of sameness through group membership that does not acknowledge the "insider-outsider" position that allies occupy in movements. As insider-outsiders, allies might fight for an outcome that will have objective *costs* for themselves or their group. Given the apparent lack of self-interest that could contribute to the onset of an activist identity, ally activists might not traverse the same kinds of identity-building processes as beneficiary activists, such as boundary construction, negotiation, and the development of consciousness as identified by Taylor and Whittier (1992). When faced with boundary-type questions about sameness to other activists and difference from the enemy, for example, ally activists have a different terrain to negotiate. As movement participants, they are members of the activist community but not members of the beneficiary population that underlies the collective activist identity and in fact are, by definition, part of the enemy.

In this chapter, therefore, I explore some of the identity-related processes and negotiation faced both by the ally activists and the activist groups, who include allies among their members. I contend that important qualitative differences exist between beneficiary and ally identity experiences. I also argue that the inclusion of allies in an activist group produces distinct gains for the movement group and challenges its functioning—dynamics that are not present when the activist group is populated only by beneficiaries. In doing so, I providing an initial exploration of insider-outsider identity dynamics and propose a series of theoretical areas for future consideration.

This chapter focuses on the case of heterosexuals who are advocates for gay and lesbian civil rights. I draw on data collected for a larger project on heterosexual activism in gay and lesbian settings during the years of Bill Clinton's first run for the presidency and first term in office. One set of data consists of articles that address "straight–gay" activism published in three publications that focused on lesbian and gay movement issues and target different audiences (*The Advocate, Out/Look,* and *Outlines*). The second set consists of electronic (computer-mediated) forums that contain topical conversation streams and represent contributions from across the globe.[2] I first examine the process of defining and creating an ally identity and then explore challenges that come with the presence of allies as well as some theoretical considerations that follow from this examination.

What Is an Ally Identity?

What exactly is an ally activist identity and how does it differ from beneficiary activist identities? Allies obviously have much in common with their beneficiary partners. They are activists, share a political stance, and define problems and solutions similarly. That they can each place themselves on the same "right" side of a line regarding attitudes toward an issue indicates a common identity that binds them together. Furthermore, they engage in common everyday practices that express and reinforce their identities as activists for their cause and members of the collective pursuing change. When, for example, allies and beneficiaries link arms at a civil rights rally or dance together on a float in a gay pride parade, they experience a sense of "we-ness" that binds them together in a common activist identity.

But there are differences as well and these are not insignificant. Heterosexual people cannot, in a sense, ever be "gay activists" because they are not gay. Likewise there has been a long-standing debate in activist communities about whether men can appropriately be labeled "feminists" because of their profeminist orientations. These kinds of debates point out a fundamental identity difficulty that separates allies from beneficiary activists. That is, there is something different in the belongingness and the experience of being part of the beneficiary population that cannot be shared or claimed by those who are not part of that population. Of less focus, however, is that the ally identity is a uniquely positioned one that separates the allies both from the beneficiary activist and the nonactivist population.

What differentiates allies from beneficiary activists? First, they must go through a process of proving that they are aligned with the movement. Being a beneficiary of the movement does not necessary mean that one supports the movement, but the credibility hurdle is far smaller for a gay man to be accepted as having a progay activist orientation than it is for a straight man. Second, allies do not have the life experiences as a member of the population to inform their understandings of the injustices that define the movement agenda. Beneficiary activists often complain that allies lack the depth of understanding of the issues at hand and of the risks and costs of activism that the beneficiaries face (see Chapter 8). Third, lacking these fundamental defining experiences, allies have a commitment-based rather than an experience-based activist identity. Allies' *ideology* drives their activism, which is important, but beneficiaries' activism is driven by experience, potential benefits, *and* ideology. From the beneficiary point of view, the combination is a far stronger impetus to continued, committed action than ideology alone. Fourth, as they participate in the movement, allies can more easily eschew their activist identity when it is inconvenient or dangerous, thus their experiences *as activists* do not inform their activism and their activist identity in the same way that it does for those who cannot hide or deny their identity. This experience parallels some beneficiaries' experiences in movement situations, such as the phenomenon of "passing" or remaining closeted, but it is a fundamental part of the identity struggle for allies because they inevitably must battle this perception to be considered even a partial insider.

For allies, the struggle to become a full movement insider often cannot be realized. Allies are trapped between not fully belonging to the group they chose and not fully belonging to the mainstream group they left. Doug McAdam's (1986; 1988) account of the experiences of white Freedom Summer participants provides a key example. For a variety of reasons, the white students were seen as outsiders to the beneficiary populations; subsequently, the African Americans involved in the campaign were imbued with a legitimacy that the white participants could never claim. Furthermore, when the white students returned north after the summer, they found that their activist identity also made them outsiders in communities where they once felt at home. Ally identities, then, can leave activists in an uncomfortable middle ground—they neither fit in completely with the beneficiary population connected to their activism nor fit in with those who do not share their activist ideals.

As ally activists present themselves inside the movement and out, they must make decisions about what exactly to present. Should they reveal, in any environment or interaction, that they are aligned with, support, and are active in this movement? Again, this challenge is not unique to ally activists. Others who are not immediately identifiable as members of a movement's constituency face a similar dilemma about coming out. Whether it is more or less difficult to come out as an activist or a beneficiary member of a movement, the point is that it is *different* to come out as an ally. Those interacting with beneficiary activists carry an obvious, immediately applicable assumption about why the person is an activist or supports the movement. "Why are you wearing that progay T-shirt?" "I'm gay" provides a satisfying response. The ally's response will usually not be as satisfactory unless it is considerably more complicated.

The ally can also face a "presentation of self" issue *within* the movement—that is, whether or not to identify oneself as an ally rather than a beneficiary. Should, for example, the heterosexual ally make a point of her or his heterosexuality when others might assume he is gay or she is a lesbian? If the ally does not come out as straight, he or she may feel dishonest—as through he or she is stealthily invading private space and interaction, such as insider humor, not intended to be open to heterosexuals. But giving up this false face also spotlights heterosexuality inappropriately in the environment and can lead to questions about why the ally is so intent on not being labeled as gay. This identity work is often revealed in the ambiguity that heterosexuals sometimes introduce into discussions about their own sexuality. Take this heterosexual woman who, after making a clear statement about her sexuality, follows up immediately with the introduction of uncertainty: "I'm a feminist who enjoys intimate sexual relationships with men. . . . I'm a feminist who, though neither lesbian or bisexual—*but one never knows*—loves women."(emphasis added) (*Outlines*, October 1993, 7).

Similar repartee crops up in many interviews with "straight gay activists," this one with Cybill Shepherd: "Asked if she's ever done it with a woman Cybill Shepherd grins, her eyes lighting up. 'No,' she says, 'and I get teased because I haven't.' Would she? 'Well, I've fantasized about it. Hey! It's never too late'" (Kuehl, 1993, 43). It may be that heterosexuals who are connected with the gay and lesbian community have developed this style of talking about their sexuality as a result of trying to avoid flaunting their heterosexuality in spaces intend to be safe for lesbians and gay men. This dilemma not only presents a different kind of identity work for the ally but also reinforces the inability of the activist to be a full member of the collective—she or he must either be an imposter or an acknowledged outsider.

While ally identity processes differ from those of beneficiary activists in these important ways, not all activist environments differentiate so clearly between allies and beneficiaries. For example, in environmental movements activists can be construed as beneficiaries of their movement activities, but just as often the beneficiaries have a broader scope—making the world a better place for everyone, including future generations. Environmentalists (and those involved in many other activist causes) may be working solely as allies for the benefit of others who are not involved in the movement at all (future generations, poor people in other countries). For instance, the antisweatshop movement in U.S. colleges and universities has taken on the cause of worker exploitation overseas without beneficiary presence in most of the movement organizations. In these activist groups, therefore, everyone is an ally and no one is a beneficiary. Collective identity in such organization is based primarily on ideology and commitment rather than belonging to an aggrieved group. At the same time, participants in these ally-dominated movements face substantially different identity negotiations. The tensions between beneficiaries and allies do not exist in the same way within these organizations, thus negotiating a sense of collective unity is different as well.

How Does the Ally Identity Develop?

The first question typically asked about allies is, where do they come from? This question arises because we have long expected that individuals will pursue collective interests through collective action—as emphasized by a history of theoretic logic predating and reacting to Mancur Olson's (1971) free-rider problem. As problematic as that logical link can be, scholars still cling to a presupposition that interests are reflected in action and that identities imitate this logic. Thus, it is no surprise to us when workers collectively identify as "labor" and contribute to the labor movement. But because this interest-structure link does not exist for allies, we have to turn to other sources to explain ally activism. The orientations and past experiences of allies, in particular whites in the civil rights movement, are examined in the social movement literature (e.g., McAdam, 1986; 1988; Demerath, Marwell, and Aiken, 1971; Blumberg, 1980; Oppenheimer, 1985; Rothschild, 1979; Fendrich, 1977). Less has been said about other ally activists, such as heterosexuals' support of gay rights, but parallel issues are important across cases.

The two sources of ally activism that are well established in the literature are the intergenerational transmission of values and the role of personal contact with beneficiaries. Given the apparent other-oriented nature of ally activism, a case has been made that, like altruistic behavior, ally activism is strongly influenced by parental support and childrearing. For example, two works investigating white student activists who worked in civil rights campaigns (McAdam, 1988; Demerath, Marwell, and Aiken, 1971) found that intergenerational connections to activists of the 1930s were positively related to the decision to become active in the civil rights movement. Social psychologists studying altruism have also documented intergenerational transmission of the values and predispositions that led to helping and heroic behaviors similar to ally activism (Piliavin and Charng, 1990; Rosenhan, 1970; London, 1970). It is important to recognize that it is not the specific activist issue that is transmitted from parent to child but rather a more general set of values. Thus, it is not likely that the parents of this past decades' allies were involved in supporting lesbian and gay civil rights in their youth, but they were likely to have been involved in other civil rights struggles. Their involvement developed and reinforced values about equality, justice, and the importance of taking political action based on their beliefs, which they then taught to their children. As the children became adults they would extend these general beliefs to lesbians and gay issues and begin to fight against the injustices faced by the community. Indeed, allies often report modeling by parents saying things such as singer Taylor Dayne's comment, "My parents never judged anyone" (Mason, 1993, 59).

As important as values are in producing activism, the testimonies of ally activists about their identity development are heavily focused on the influence of intimate others who are members of the beneficiary group. In the case of allies to gay and lesbian causes, these important connections are to gay and lesbian friends and family. Consistent with the literature on altruism (Buck and Ginsburg, 1991; Dovidio et al. 1991), contact with gay men and lesbians increases empathy and altruistic action. The literature also suggests, however, that casual contact is not enough to reduce prejudice and increase understanding; thus it is the connection to *intimate* others that makes the difference. In many cases, the influence of this relationship requires a long-term engagement in which the heterosexual person gradually understands the lesbian and gay community and its concerns. The example of archconservative Barry Goldwater, who took a strong and surprising position on gay and lesbian participation in the military, is illustrative. Although he claims that he supported ending the ban on gay and lesbian military personnel simply because it is right, he also admits that "when you have two gays in your family, you don't go around knocking [homosexuality]" (Bull 1993, 35). Goldwater's gay grandson, Ty Ross, believes he influenced Goldwater over the long haul by bringing boyfriends to his grandfather's house. "I think it was then that he realized that there are normal people out there who are gay and it's just a regular occurrence" (Bull 1993, 34). Ross also introduced Goldwater to a gay Air Force Sergeant who eventually pulled Goldwater directly into the battle about the ban.

Other allies also report similar long-term connections with gay men and lesbians. William Weld, the Republican, progay former governor of Massachusetts, roomed with a gay man in college who later served as a high-level aide. Weld also worked with a gay law partner who remains a close friend. Celebrity advocates like Roseanne Arnold report the influence of a gay family and friends (in Roseanne's case a brother and sister). Many heterosexual AIDS activists became involved because they lost gay friends to the disease (*The Advocate* 1993; *Outlines* 1992).

Beyond developing the empathy and understanding that undergirds action, personal contact is important in the development of ally identities in other ways as well. Persons who develop an ally orientation or are steeped in other-oriented values have a choice to make about who to support with their activism. A heterosexual man, for example, could become an ally to women through profeminist activism or choose to ally himself with gay rights. Why allies make the movement selections they do has not yet been a focus of much inquiry and a partial answer might come from the personal contact and biographical coincidences of allies and activist causes. If intergenerational values-transmission and personal contact are the main influences on developing allies, they provide a potential model of how ally identity and activism might develop. As an individual steeped in egalitarian values encounters the injustices suffered by a particular population (such as the lesbian and gay population) and observes the effects of the these injustices close up, an empathic chord might be struck. This emotional reaction, coupled with the notion that injustices must be confronted with political action, might lead the individual to not only become an activist but also choose the gay and lesbian movement as the focus of their activism and take on an identity as a "politically gay" activist.

But that is not all there is to it; many allies have had significant contact with many different populations in need but do not contribute as activists to all of them. Furthermore, many people become allies when they could be contributing to a movement whose goals reflect their own interests. Women who work for racial equality could have instead made the choice to work for women's rights. The sources (in terms of biographical antecedents) and the processes (in terms of conscious cognitive processes and emotions) behind these choices remain open questions and are fertile ground for investigating the development of activist identities.

Not all allies are behaving altruistically, of course. Sometimes allies are being opportunistic rather than other-oriented. In these cases, the ally behavior can be driven by the desire for personal or political gain or by the expectation of reciprocation. As the gay and lesbian community has become a greater political force, for example, the temptation to offer support for opportunistic reasons has increased. Growing support for the movement from some conservative politicians and attempts by the Republican Party to recruit gay voters exemplifies this point. Weld's Republican candidacy for governor in the Democratic stronghold of Massachusetts exploited his opponent's staunchly antigay stance, because it provided an opportunity to court a traditionally Democratic voting block (Bull 1993). Republican mayoral candidates struggling in inner cities with strong Democratic majorities have recognized economic consistencies with many gay and lesbian voters and began advocating gay and lesbian positions on issues that have traditionally kept gay voters firmly connected to the democratic ticket (Gallagher 1993). This type of coalition building has proven to be a winning strategy for a number of candidates, as a result, more courting of gay audiences has occurred. As Republicans become more willing to endorse lesbian and gay issues, Democrats will have to step up their own allied stances to maintain a once taken-for-granted constituency.

Other movements also provide an important source of allies. Individuals involved in other movements with similarities in goals, ideology, and strategies are good targets for ally activism, because they likely already share important foundational values that can be used to frame the movement's issues and draw in supporters. And there is clear evidence in the social movement literature that the best source of productive activists are the pools of individuals who have been involved in other causes (McAdam, McCarthy, and Zald, 1988), both because of ideological orientation and the know-how that comes from experience. Easy alliances are not always easy, however, because contributions across movements and organizations entail obligations, and expectations of reciprocation can damage alliances and the ally identities that link two causes. For example, movement organizations often resist umbrella coalitions with allied movements for fear that the movement's goals will be lost among the "broadening laundry list" of demands and issues (Troubled Alliance 1993; Horowitz 1988). Rather than being squarely focused on lesbians and gay rights, the relevant demands to this population would be lost in a call for broad-based equality:

> Our rally was a nonstop call for women's rights; bisexual acceptance; lesbian demands to raise children; screams against sexism, racism, and ageism; and even cries for more breast cancer research. Important issues, to be sure. But just how divisive and diluted do you community leaders plan to make our movement? ("Letters," *The Advocate* 1993, 10).

Implicit is a fear that efforts put forth for the sake of an outside group will not be reciprocated. Consider the potential ally relationship between the gay and lesbian movement and the African-American community. Both groups have been criticized for failing to come through for the other under various circumstances. Some leaders of the gay and lesbian movement have recognized the reticence of the gay community to act in support of African-American civil rights issues: "There's a lot of legitimate criticism that comes from people of color who are gay rights supporters but say, 'Where are you when we need you?'" (Hite 1993, 26). A careful examination of this dispute reveals that appeals to other groups are couched in terms of altruism, while justifications made to the internal membership for tapping other groups often employ opportunistic explanations. Activists seem to expect others to respond altruistically or empathically to their own group's needs but want to be able to show a calculated benefit from throwing their own support to another cause. Activists might feel that they cannot afford to expend effort on peripheral causes without a guarantee that a commensurate effort will be returned. Because such guarantees are difficult to come by, coalition attempts and overarching identities often face insurmountable impediments.

Living with and Sustaining the Ally Identity

The challenges related to ally identities and activism do not stop when the identity is first formed. As with any other social identity, the ally identity is constantly renegotiated, renewed, and revised as the activist either participates in movements or withdraws from them. Identity work is therefore required to maintain the ally identity. As I discussed previously, there are a variety of challenges involved in establishing the ally identity in the first place. Allies cannot demonstrate that they are members of the beneficiary group in the first place and thus maintain a sense of difference throughout their involvement with the movement. Because allies cannot claim membership in this way, they must do it in some other way. Mainly, they can do this through demonstrating their commitment to the movement. Thus, allies might feel compelled to demonstrate their orientation via overtly espousing their ideals or taking action in a different way than expected of beneficiary activists—the litmus test for sameness and belonging is different because they can never be de facto members. And even if the ally successfully establishes an ally status within the movement, their commitment can be continually called into question. Convincing one person of genuineness does not convince all, of course, and as allies encounters new activists who do not know their history, they must reassert their identity and repeatedly prove themselves—renegotiating their fundamental sense of belonging in ways that are unfamiliar to and unnecessary for beneficiary activists.

It is also possible that allies will overidentify with the gay or lesbian culture and intrude into situations where they are unwelcome. Discovering appropriate roles for themselves and learning which lesbian and gay private places to stay out of can be a time-consuming and painful process that many allies and heterosexuals are not willing to endure (Washington and Evans, 1993; Turner and Killian, 1972). Sometimes allies enter into the gay community with little knowledge of it and even less about where a heterosexual may fit. Expecting to be welcomed simply because they are on the "right side," they are often disappointed to find themselves criticized for their inappropriate behavior or simply because they are heterosexual. In these situations, allies often feel like outsiders who cannot possibly fit into the gay culture despite their desire to be there. They also do not feel comfortable in the homophobic world of which they once were a part and, therefore, struggle with resulting feelings of isolation, discomfort, and the realization that they are not real members of either community.

Some of the criticism and distrust directed at allies might not be warranted. For instance, some gay leaders have criticized the community for overprotecting its space:

> Our movement has enormously expanded the "'safe space'" in society, yet we often seem wedded to a marginal, separate existence. Example: a heterosexual woman in North Carolina makes the issue of gay oppression a priority, but she encounters suspicion and hostility in gay organizations. Her presence at meetings "'spoils'" the party. We'd rather have our in-jokes, the comfort of not having "'them'" around, than welcome allies into our organizations as volunteers, hire them as staff, or invite them on to our boards." (Thoms, 1993, 5)

Here the source of the conflict is shared by the ally and the gay members of the organizations. While this criticism is aimed at the gay members, it is important to remember that it is not only the woman's heterosexuality that causes a lack of fit but also her unfamiliarity with the cultural elements that prevent her from being a part of the "in-jokes." Furthermore, it is easy to see why lesbians and gay men feel the need to protect their safe space. Often heterosexuals who enter these environments are insensitive to the gay atmosphere. "Progressive" heterosexual bar patrons who frequent gay establishments might feel enlightened for their actions and then violate norms of behavior by acting out their heterosexuality in ways that destroy safe space.

All these ongoing struggles can threaten the allies' continued participation in the movement and his or her identity as an ally of the movement. One of the key theoretical explanations that exists for activist identity is that individuals seek self-verification by participation (Gecas 2000; Pinel and Swann 2000). Individuals might have a sense of self (rooted in values) that suggests or even demands activism. Majority group members, for example, might carry a notion of "good person" in their heads that requires righting past wrongs and working to eliminate discrimination. Thus, ally activism is a natural means of verifying that one is indeed a "good" person. Sometimes, though, the challenges of being an ally prevent self-verification. If activists do not get the confirmation or appreciation from beneficiaries that they expect, they may exit the activist environment and find another site for self-verification. The same can result simply because allies grow weary of the ongoing self-presentation and identity maintenance tasks.

Movements and Allies

While allies face a great deal of identity work, their presence in a move-ment creates work for their beneficiary partners as well. As social movements attempt to move toward their goals, they must consider the importance of gaining adherents who are not direct beneficiaries. In most cases, gaining such adherents—ranging in their involvement from active participation to tacitly allowing the movement to proceed without providing any resistance—is criti-cal to success (McAdam, McCarthy and Zald 1988). The gay and lesbian movement, for example, has long been aware of the importance of gaining "conscious constituents" (Adam 1987; Duberman 1993). Even in the earliest stages of the homophile movement, leaders recognized the value of befriend-ing those with political power. Convincing local governmental officials to at least look the other way allowed gay communities the space to form and develop the political identity that eventually propelled the movement into and beyond the Stonewall riots.

But just as the entry of allies into a movement is not simple for the allies themselves, neither is it straightforward for the movement and its traditional beneficiary activists. While there are clear and demonstrable benefits that arise from recruiting a nonbeneficiary base, conflicts about ally activity, as well as with the allies themselves, also arise. Disagreements almost immedi-ately emerge about the appropriate roles for allies within the movement; the views range from believing that allies have no place in the movement at all to accepting allies into leadership positions. In addition, conflicts typically arise about efficacy, empowerment, and privilege. The following section addresses such conflicts.

Empowerment, Building Collective Identity, and Leadership

Many activists downplay the importance of ally activism and focus on the beneficiaries developing their own power bases. The notion here is that true liberation comes from liberating oneself. With respect to the gay and lesbian movement, the issue is particularly poignant because of the ability to hide in the closet. Many activists view the act of coming out as the central key to movement success—the greater the visibility of the community, the greater political power it will wield. Despite this widespread orientation, other activists call for more conscious inclusion of heterosexual allies. For instance, the 1987 march on Washington was criticized as being "too internally oriented" and blamed the lack of het-erosexual involvement in the movement on activists who did not try hard enough to get outsiders involved (Horowitz 1988).

This debate stems from the orientation of activists toward their immediate agenda. Is their primary purpose to build pride and political self-efficacy within the beneficiary community? Or is this identity-building task secondary to the policy aims that will benefit from the political power added by nonbeneficiaries? Parallel disputes exist in other identity-based movements, such as debates about separatism in the women's movement (Japenga 1990) and concerns about the amount of white support that black civil rights activists should solicit. Thus the debate is not so much about whether to include allies or not but rather what is to be the focus of the movement.

Among gay and lesbian activists, many view the act of including heterosexuals as a means to gain popular support, but there is also a fear that courting allies involves compromises that will deradicalize the movement (Denneny 1989; see Jenkins and Eckert 1986 for a more general statement of this notion). Placing too much time and effort on accomplishing movement goals through allies also builds a dependency on outsiders that ultimately prevents the empowerment of the members of the community (Grusec 1991). The goal of the gay and lesbian movement is not simply to push through laws and policy initiatives but also to develop gay and lesbian identities:

> If we look outside ourselves to accomplish what is integral to our well-being or success as a movement—there's something bankrupt about that, giving away both respect and power. I also think there is a certain kind of passion that comes with being part of a silent minority and working through layers of self-homophobia in order to gain one's own voice. The foundation of that passion is an integrity that comes from the healing part of the self. (Gilbert-Neiss, 1990, 55)

The transformation of individuals and their culture is just as important to the success of the movement as is changing a law (Epstein 1991).

The efficacy and identity issues become even more poignant when an ally attempts to perform and manage a leadership role (McAdam 1988). When asked about a heterosexual taking a leadership role in the movement, many gay and lesbian community members respond emphatically with "no," "Never!," "Are you kidding?," and "bizarre." (see also Gilbert-Neiss 1990). Heterosexuals taking leadership positions directly contradicts the empowerment notions of the movement. Furthermore, leadership positions often entail decisions about the activity and direction of movement activities. Given the lower risk that heterosexuals face for their involvement, it seems somewhat inappropriate for them to make decisions about activities that might jeopardize gay and lesbian people more than themselves. At the same time, some allies may attempt to step into leadership positions *because* of the risk issue. Public leadership positions entail more exposure and thus more risk of negative repercussions than nonleadership positions. Because heterosexuals can weather these risks more easily, they may be able to engage in activities that are too risky for others.

Privilege and Other Challenges

There are other costs and benefits to having allies involved in the movement as well. One benefit is expanded awareness about lesbian and gay issues and culture. Allies become more educated through involvement and then transmit their understanding to other heterosexuals. Many allies, for instance, report success spreading their attitudes to their family members (Gilbert-Neiss 1990). Often allies are more effective in delivering messages to the heterosexual community, because their own heterosexual identity helps avoid suspicion of self-interest that would be directed at gay voices (Eagly, Wood, and Chaiken 1978). Such was the case for Dorothy Haldys, mother of Allen Schindler, a man who was gay-bashed to death while serving in the United States Navy. She has emphasized her identity as a mother rather than a gay activist and has been able to deliver her message all the more powerfully (Schoofs, 1993).

If movement activists welcome allies, they all must ultimately face the issue of privilege. Implicit in much ally activism is a utilization of the very privilege the movement is working to overcome. McAdam (1988) discusses how black leaders were concerned about the implicit message that white lives were more important than blacks ones. A white person speaking for racial equality was listened to more closely than a black voice, therefore having white allies involved in the movement reinforced racist power positions by allowing more importance to be placed on white contributions. The same dilemma exists within the gay and lesbian movement as heterosexual audiences are more apt to give credence to appeals made by other heterosexuals.

Finally, heterosexuals have legal rights and other privileges that protect them as they become involved in the movement (Washington and Evans 1993). Here, again, different risks for allies and beneficiaries is an issue. While heterosexuals may incur some costs for becoming involved in the movement, they do not have to deal with the issues of coming out, fear housing or employment discrimination based on sexual identity, or suffer the many other forms of discrimination directed at lesbian and gay individuals. These privileges allow allies to behave in ways that are too risky for many gay activists. While this ability to take higher-risk action may benefit the movement, it also places more power in the hands of heterosexuals and a disproportionately high value on heterosexual contributions, even as these activist pay smaller costs for their actions.

Conclusion: Theoretical Agendas

The identity work engaged in by allies and those around them is important in an empirical sense for scholars and as a practical matter of concern for activists. Ally activism is, after all, widespread and an essential element leading to the success of many movements. Such identity work is important for theoretical reasons as well, as more work that documents and understands ally activism can help us with our understandings of activism, identity formation, and prosocial behavior on a more general level. I conclude this chapter with a discussion of the utility of studies of ally activism for future research in the areas of altruism, activism framing, and values.

Altruism and Activism

The link between social psychological understandings of altruistic and prosocial behaviors and activism has received only limited attention, and this link is perhaps best investigated through ally activism. Like other behaviors that require some cost to the actor, and for which she or he can expect little or no direct benefit (Aronfreed 1970; Bar-Tal 1985–86; Piliavin and Charng 1990), ally behavior can readily be classified as altruistic. The altruistic impulse and its roots have the potential to explain an entire host of activist behaviors and orientation, if they are in fact rooted in the same sources as altruism. If, for example, altruism is genetically encoded, as claimed by sociobiologists and their intellectual descendents (Buss and Kenrick 1998), then yet another solution to Olson's free-rider problem could be traced to the altruistic gene. At the same time, understanding the social development of ally activism (such as the importance of intimate social contact in producing ally behavior and the development of moral reasoning that leads to such altruistic behaviors, [Krebs and Van Hesteren 1992]) can help to qualify claims about the biological roots of prosocial behavior.

Framing and Recruiting

Better understandings of ally activism can also inform and be informed by recruitment logics and practices—and in particular framing attempts (Snow and Benford 1988; Snow et Al. 1986; Benford 1993). Because the logic driving ally identity and action is different than that producing beneficiary action, the frames used to draw in these two different kinds of activists must differ as well. For example, framing efforts typically involve drawing some "we-they" kinds of boundaries. But the ally is not likely to respond to a purely group-based definition of the "we" because these kinds of boundary relegate them to the "they." Rather, a more flexible and inclusive boundary mechanism will be necessary (such as one based on values), if ally recruitment is to succeed. The efforts of Student Nonviolent Coordinating Committee (SNCC) to recruit volunteers provides a vivid example in which each of the targeted groups was approached using a value-based pitch rather than one based on common collective membership or interests with southern blacks (McAdam 1986).

A link between understandings of altruism and framing is also apparent in attempts to recruit allies. In movement appeals that rely on a rhetoric of altruism, activism is not based on self-interest but simply because help is needed. Consonant with the processes that invoke empathic action, activist appeals use emotionally laden language and poignant descriptions of conditions. These descriptions are intended to evoke empathy and provide a means for relieving the empathic suffering by acting (Eisenberg and Fabes 1991; Dovidio et al. 1991). If the framing attempt was successful, the audience will be convinced to act even if the act eventually results in a personal cost.

Of course there are attempts to communicate with heterosexuals that do not use a frame of altruism but rather of threat and demand. Nevertheless, this particular type of framing is not directed so much at potential allies as it is intended to make a statement to enemies of the movement. In other words, "we're here, we're queer, get used to it" is not directed at potential allies who presumably are already used to it. Rather than attempting to get heterosexuals involved in the movement, this style of activism is more an affirmation and declaration of power targeted at those who would oppose the movement.

Values

Viktor Gecas (2000) points out that social movement scholars have not attended enough to values and value-based identities when trying to understand the motivation for activism. One of the key mechanisms for activist identities ties activism to self-affirmation processes (see the volume edited by Styker, Owens, and White 2000 for reviews and development of this concept). For many activists, this self-affirmation, verification, and enhancement process is rooted in values because living up to these values produced the self-affirmation: Good people have these kinds of attitudes and act on them; I have these attitudes and exhibit these behaviors; therefore, I am a good person.

Movement allies' motivations to act are likely to be heavily tied to these kinds of value based logic, given that they lack the direct instrumental motivations. If one holds the value of equality, it can be an important motivator to engage in protest. But, there is a substantial difference between standing for equality when greater equality will improve one's position than when it will damage one's position. Thus, the self-affirmation process that follows from the value-orientation differs for allies. The self-affirmation for a self-conscious ally is commonly connected to a sense of self-as-altruist. This does not mean, however, that allies are completely pure of heart and fundamentally selfless, but understanding the role of other-oriented values is probably more important to understanding ally activism than beneficiary activism.

When an ally develops a sense of self-as-altruist, the activist identity can become one that is fundamentally about caring for others and being willing to fight for the downtrodden. This orientation can lead to other conflicts in the movement. For example, allies seem more likely than others to be fundamentally offended and mystified when others will not engage in ally type activism—especially those who the ally is helping. When the beneficiaries of the ally's efforts refuse to help or cooperate with others, the ally can become disillusioned with their activist site. The allies' (at least manifest) motivation is a value, while beneficiaries have a different (self-oriented) payoff involved, one that does not immediately lead them to volunteer their efforts elsewhere. Given these fundamental differences in orientation, it is not surprising that conflicts erupt among beneficiaries and their allies.

In conclusion, many issues about ally activism, both theoretical and empirical, remain to be investigated. I have identified those that seem most important and most clearly connected to the existing literature on identities and activism. But there is more to be done. As Snow and McAdam (2000) point out, there is a tendency to ignore the relationship between group and personal identities as we examine activism. The ally case is particularly important, then, not just because ally activism is ubiquitous but also because it is such a challenging case for connecting the individual to the group. When allies join a movement or when movements try to recruit allies, there is an inherent mismatch or conflict between the group identity and the individuals. Resonance between the two is difficult, if not impossible to fully achieve. Understanding the attempts to do so will not just illuminate how we involve allies but also demonstrate a larger variety of identity work in which activists engage.

References

Adam, Barry D. 1987. *The Rise of a Gay and Lesbian Movement*. Boston: Twayne Publishers.

Aronfreed, Jostin. 1970. "The Socialization of Altruistic and Sympathetic Behavior: Some Theoretical and Experimental Analyses." In *Altruism and Helping Behavior*, ed. J. MacCaulay and L. Berkowitz, 103–26. New York: Academic Press.

Bar-Tal, Daniel. 1985–86. "Altruistic Motivation to Help: Definition, Utility and Operationalization." *Humboldt Journal of Social Relations* 13: 3–14.

Benford, Robert D. 1993. "Frame Dispute within the Nuclear Disarmament Movement." *Social Forces* 71(3): 677–701.

Blumberg, Rhonda L. 1980. "White Mothers in the American Civil Rights Movement." *Research in the Interweave of Social Roles* 1: 33–50.

Buck, Ross, and Benson. Ginsburg. 1991. "Spontaneous Communication and Altruism: The Communicative Gene Hypothesis." In *Prosocial Behavior*, ed. M. S. Clark, 149–75. Newbury Park, Calif.: Sage.

Bull, Chris. 1993. "Right Turn: Archconservative Barry Goldwater's Surprising Stance on Gay and Lesbian Rights." *The Advocate* 637: 32–38.

Buss, David, and Douglas T. Kenrick. 1998. "Evolutionary Social Psychology." In *Handbook of Social Psychology*, ed. D. T. Gilbert, S. T. Fiske, and G. Lindzey, 982–1026. Boston: McGraw-Hill.

Demerath, N. J., Gerald Marwell, and Michael Aiken. 1971. *Dynamics of Idealism: White Activists in a Black Movement*. San Francisco: Jossey-Bass.

Denneny, Michael. 1989. "Chasing the Crossover Audience and Other Self-defeating Strategies." *Out/Look* 1(4): 16–21.

Dovidio, John. F., Jane A. Piliavin, Samuel L. Gaertner, David A. Schroeder, and Russell D. Clark III. 1991. "The Arousal: Cost-Reward Model and Process of Intervention: A Review of the Evidence." In *Prosocial Behavior*, ed. M. S. Clark, 86–118. Newbury Park, Calif.: Sage.

Duberman, Martin. 1993. *Stonewall*. New York: Dutton.

Eagly, A. H., W. Wood, and S. Chaiken. 1978. "Causal Inference about Communicators and Their Effects on Attitude Change." *Journal of Personality and Social Psychology* 36: 424–35.

Eisenberg, Nancy, and Richard A. Fabes. 1991. "Prosocial Behavior and Empathy: A Multimethod Developmental Perspective." In *Prosocial Behavior*, ed. M. S. Clark, 34–61. Newbury Park, Calif.: Sage.

Epstein, Barbara. 1991. *Political Protest and Cultural Revolution: Non-violent Direct Action in the 1970s and 1980s*. Berkeley: University of California Press.

Fendrich, James M. 1977. "Keeping the Faith or Pursuing the Good Life: A Study of the Consequences of Participation in the Civil Rights Movements." *American Sociological Review* 42(1): 144–57.

Gallagher, John. 1993. "Trick or Treat? Republicans in the Nation's Two Biggest Cities Embrace Pro-gay Positions. Are They a New Breed or a Pack of Wolves in Sheep's Clothing?" *The Advocate* 642: 52–55.

———. 1993. "Troubled Alliance." *The Advocate* 639: 36–40.

Gecas, Viktor. 2000. "Value Identities, Self-Motives, and Social Movements." In *Self, Identity, and Social Movements*, ed. S. Stryker, T. J. Owens, and R. W. White, 93–109, Minneapolis: University of Minnesota Press.

Gilbert-Neiss, Connie. 1990. "Meet Heidi Jones: The Straight Gay Leader." *Out/Look* 8: 54–55.

Grusec, J. E. 1991. "The Socialization of Altruism." In *Prosocial Behavior*, ed. M. S. Clark, 9–33. Newbury Park, Calif.: Sage.

Hite, Earnest E. Jr. 1993. "Lift the Ban on Gay Men and Lesbians in the Black Community." *Outlines* 7(3): 26.

Horowitz, Paul. 1988. "Beyond the Gay Nation: Where are We Marching?" *Out/Look* 1(1): 7–21.

Japenga, Ann. 1990. "The Separatist Revival." *Out/Look* 8(1): 78–83.

Jenkins, J. Craig, and Craig M. Eckert. 1986. "Channeling Black Insurgency: Elite Patronage and Professional Social Movement Organizations in the Development of the Black Movement." *American Sociological Review* 51: 812–29.

Johnston, Hank, Enrique Laraña, and Joseph Gusfield, ed. 1994. *New Social Movements: From Ideology to Identity*. Philadelphia: Temple University Press.

Klandermans, Bert, and Marga de Weerd. 2000. "Group Identification and Political Protest." In *Self, Identity, and Social Movements*, ed. S. Stryker, T. J. Owens, and R. W. White, 68–91. Minneapolis: University of Minnesota Press.

Krebs, D. L., and F. Van Hesteren. 1992. "The Development of Altruistic Personality." In *Embracing the Other: Philosophical, Psychological, and Historical Perspectives on Altruism*, ed. P. M. Oliner, S. P. Oliner, L. Baron, L. A. Blum, D. L. Krebs, and M. Z. Smolenska, 142–69. New York: New York University Press.

Kuehl, Sheila James. 1993. "Why is Cybill Shepherd Your New Best Friend? The Birth of a Straight Gay Activist." *The Advocate* 640: 42–49.

"Letters." 1993. *The Advocate* 632: 10.

London, Perry. 1970. "The Rescuers: Motivational Hypotheses about Christians Who Saved Jews from the Nazis." In *Altruism and Helping Behavior*, ed. J. MacCaulay and L. Berkowitz, 241–50. New York: Academic Press.

Mason, Kiki. 1993. "Taylor Dayne." *The Advocate* 634: 58–99.

McAdam, Doug. 1986. "Recruitment to High-Risk Activism: The Case of Freedom Summer." *American Journal of Sociology* 92(1): 64–90.

McAdam, Doug. 1988. *Freedom Summer.* New York: Oxford University Press.

McAdam, Doug, John McCarthy, and Mayer Zald. 1988. "Social Movements." In *Handbook of Sociology*, ed. N. Smelser, 695–737. Newbury Park, Calif.: Sage.

Melucci, Alberto. 1985. "The Symbolic Challenge of Contemporary Movements." *Social Research* 52: 789–816.

Olson, Mancur. 1971. *The Logic of Collective Action. Public Goods and the Theory of Groups.* Cambridge, Mass.: Harvard University Press.

Oppenheimer, Martin. 1985. "The Movement: A 25-year Perspective." *Monthly Review* 36(9): 49–55.

Piliavin, J. A., and H. W. Charng. 1990. "Altruism: A Review of Recent Theory and Research." *Annual Review of Sociology* 6: 27–65.

Pinel, Elizabeth C., and William B. Swann, Jr. 2000. "Finding the Self through Others: Self-Verification and Social Movement Participation." In *Self, Identity, and Social Movements*, ed. S. Stryker, T. J. Owens, and R. W. White, 132–52, Minneapolis: University of Minnesota Press.

"Quotelines." *Outlines.* October 1993: 7.

Rosenhan, David. 1970. "The Natural Socialization of Altruistic Autonomy." In *Altruism and Helping Behavior*, ed. J. MacCaulay and L. Berkowitz, 251–68. New York: Academic Press.

Rothschild, Mary A. 1979. "White Women Volunteers in the Freedom Summers: Their Life and Work in a Movement for Social Change." *Feminist Studies* 5(3): 466–95.

Schoofs, Mark. "Life after Death." *The Advocate* 633: 32–38.

Snow, David A., and Robert D. Benford. 1988. "Ideology, Frame Resonance and Participant Mobilization." *International Social Movement Research* 1: 197–217.

Snow, David A., and Doug McAdam. 2000. "Identity Work Processes in the Context of Social Movements: Clarifying the Identity/Movement Nexus." In *Self, Identity, and Social Movements*, ed. S. Stryker, T. J. Owens, and R. W. White, 41–67, Minneapolis: University of Minnesota Press

Snow, David A., E. Burke Rochford, Jr., Steven K. Worders, and Robert D. Benford. 1986. "Frame Alignment Processes, Micromobilization and Movement Participation." *American Sociological Review* 51: 464–81.

"Special report: Hetero Heroes." 1993. *The Advocate* 642: 57–70.

Stryker, Sheldon, Timothy J. Owens, and Robert W. White, ed. 2000. *Self, Identity, and Social Movements*, Minneapolis: University of Minnesota Press.

Taylor, Verta, and Nancy Whittier. 1992. "Collective Identity in Social Movement Communities: Lesbian Feminist Mobilization." In *Frontiers in Social Movement Theory*, ed. A. D. Morris and C. Mueller, 104–29. New Haven, Conn.: Yale University Press.

Thomas, Don. 1993. "Liberty and Justice for All." *The Advocate* 639: 5.

Turner, Ralph, and Lewis Killian. 1972. *Collective Behavior.* 2nd ed. Englewood Cliffs: Prentice Hall.

Washington, Jamie, and Nancy J. Evans. 1993. "Becoming an Ally." In *Beyond Tolerance: Gays, Lesbians and Bisexuals on Campus*, ed. N. J. Evans and V. A. Wall, 195–204. American College Personnel Association.

Note

1. Many thanks to Jane Piliavin, Pam Oliver, Jim Howley, Rachel Einwohner, and Jo Reger for comments on earlier drafts.

8

Being "Sisters" to Salvadoran Peasants: Deep Identification and Its Limitations

Susan Munkres

We love each other, we love people across the continents who our govern-
ments are set against and despise. We don't have an answer; we have love,
community and respect. And we have each other. When we have an
earthquake, we don't have an answer. We have each other. This is not just
a cute project.

—Bill, executive director of the National
Network of U.S. El Salvador Sister Cities

The strong emotions and sense of solidarity expressed in the above quote
might come as a surprise to those who study movements of privileged people
who work on behalf of others far less advantaged. When scholars examine such alliance movements, they often emphasize a range of difficulties
they see as inherent in the relationship between privileged "outsiders" and
the disenfranchised people who typically make up the bulk of a liberation
movement. What's more, many believe that privileged people face a unique
set of problems *as privileged people* simply in building movements. With
neither a history of resistance nor their own collective identities, which are
generally the province of oppressed groups (see Taylor and Whittier 1992),
it can be challenging for the privileged to develop a true oppositional or
insurgent consciousness.[1]

Recently, Aldon Morris and Jane Mansbridge suggested that privileged
people *may* be able to develop oppositional consciousness if they are able to

identify "deeply" (2001, 26) with subjugated others. This chapter examines deep identification through fieldwork in a local committee of the El Salvador sister cities movement whose approach to solidarity work is guided by the ideals evinced in the epigraph of this chapter. How is it that the members of El Salvador sister cities develop oppositional consciousness? How do they come to see themselves as connected in such a way as to believe that they and their Salvadoran sisters "have each other," as Bill describes? Does this sense of connection qualify as deep identification, and does it build oppositional consciousness, or is it in fact some other kind of identity work? And what are the consequences—negative and positive—of their path of oppositional consciousness?

In this chapter, I explore how the members of what I call Prairietown-Las Cruces Sister City (PLCSC), a midwestern chapter of the National Network of U.S.–El Salvador Sister Cities, build a collective identity and develop oppositional consciousness. I find that their collective identity of "sistering" encourages a deep identification with their Salvadoran comrades as a kind of naturalized family and builds an emotional commitment to them as a result. However, while deep identification enables these activists to construct a sense of sameness with their Salvadoran "family," it also pulls them to construct boundaries of difference against other American activists. Ultimately, though, their success at deep identification backfires in that it facilitates avoidance of the very kind of critical self-examination that is required if dominant group members are to develop insurgent consciousness.

Identity Work by Privileged "Outsiders"

It should come as no surprise that movements involving privileged people working on behalf of subordinated others face significant barriers. Social movement scholars have identified three major areas of concern: collective identity, ongoing commitment, and the relationships between the privileged and the subordinated others they would support.

Many scholars believe that privileged people face almost insurmountable difficulties in building collective identities; indeed, collective identity is often defined in such a way as to presume it develops among the oppressed (Taylor and Whittier 1992). Privileged people lack a history of common oppression, a sense of community, and, often, the shared cultural resources that result from such connections. They must develop "almost from scratch collective identities, appropriate injustice frames, and an oppositional consciousness" (Morris and Braine 2001, 36–37). Further, the privileged group may not become truly radicalized without these cultural supports to motivate them (Morris and Braine 2000). In addition, they might have difficulty maintaining such an oppositional perspective, even if gained; privileged people are thought to be more reformist in orientation, to value accommodation, and to see compromise as expedient (see Connell 1998; Mansbridge 2001; Marx and Useem 1971).

Similarly, without a community history of oppression and resistance to draw upon in building collective identities, many believe that privileged people will not be able to commit permanently to the cause of others. Because the issues are thought to affect them from a distance rather than lie at the heart of their own experience of personal oppression, they are thought to be "fickle" (McCarthy and Zald 1987), always having the option to opt out or move on to another movement.

Finally, privileged people are often thought to behave inappropriately vis-à-vis the subordinated others. The tensions between whites and blacks in both the abolition and the civil rights movement are commonly cited cases where problems included paternalism, condescension, and white dominance of leadership roles (Marx and Useem 1971; McAdam 1988). Still others suggest that differences in style (Lichterman 1995, 1996), ideology (Rose 2000), or relative power (Bell and Delaney 2001; Dolgon 2001) may make working together problematic.

But the existence of significant alliance movements belies all these obstacles. Rather than simply identifying all the reasons such movements ought to fail, we ought to ask what enables privileged people at times to build collective identities, maintain ongoing commitments, and negotiate the social divisions between themselves and those they support. In more specific terms, we ought to be inquiring about the particular kinds of identity work in which privileged people are engaging. The literature suggests a few possibilities: moral outrage, shared religious identification, religious cultural resources, and deep identification. Moral outrage is seen by a few as powerful enough to motivate long-lasting and full-fledged radicalization among the privileged: Jasper (1997) suggests that it can promote *movement* identities among people otherwise lacking shared experiences of oppression, and scholars of Central America solidarity highlight its power in driving that movement (Nepstad 2004; Smith 1996). At the same time, Christian Smith (1996) emphasizes the shared religious identification of North American Christians with the liberation theology components of the Central American revolution. Similarly, Morris and Naomi Braine (2001) suggest that religious resources alone may be powerful enough to motivate commitment and radical consciousness. Without religious resources, they argue that dominant group members may only be able to develop oppositional consciousness when they "identify deeply" (2001, 26) with the subordinate group.

My interest in deep identification stems from a desire to understand how groups of privileged people *not* motivated by religion could mobilize on behalf of others. According to Morris and Braine, deep identification with the subordinate would provide motivation to engage in self-education and radicalization and would underlie ongoing commitment. But does it work? Are privileged people in fact radicalized by deeply identifying with subordinated others? Do they commit for the long term, develop full-fledged identities as supporters, and overcome differences in style, perception, or ideology through such identification? And if they do, are there any costs of so doing?

It was with these questions in mind that I set out to examine identity work and consciousness among privileged outsiders in a political—rather than religious—Central America solidarity organization. In this chapter, I present results based on two years of fieldwork in PLCSC, as well as informal interviews with Salvadoran leaders and U.S. staff for the National Network of El Salvador Sister Cities in San Salvador. The central work of the organization is building a relationship of sistering, which includes financial and material assistance, regular communication, fundraising, and organizing in the United States, as well as sending delegations to El Salvador and hosting tours of Salvadoran leaders. I draw upon my observations of these activities to explore the process through which members of privileged groups develop deep identification with less privileged others, as well as the implications of their deep identification for their success as allies.

Fieldwork was particularly useful for these types of questions. Participant observation in social movements yields rich, nuanced data on the taken-for-granted assumptions that guide activists' decision-making (Lichterman 1998). Extended listening to PLCSC members—the conflicts and agreements, tales of past mishaps, stories of accomplishments, and explanations of who they are and what they do—reveals how sistering is enacted in practice. Both the ideals that guide their work and the ways that those ideals are not necessarily realized become visible. The advantages of fieldwork were further enhanced by the research question itself, which involved not studying "down" the social ladder as is often typical in field research, but by studying "across." More attention tends to be paid to the fascinatingly revolutionary Salvadorans than the seemingly more mundane U.S. citizens who would support them. As I wanted to study the U.S. citizens themselves, the data collection process was less troubled by social barriers of class, language, and nation between researcher and subject. As not only a fellow U.S. citizen foremost but also a white, middle-class, educated person with some experience in progressive movement activity, I shared a number of identities with the members of PLCSC. However, I had little experience with

Central America and none with El Salvador, so I had few preconceptions about their activism.

This group was the most open of any I have studied. Introduced to the group by a fellow graduate student respected in Prairietown for his own activism in Central America, I quickly came to be seen as sharing the group's own values and commitments. Several members expressed respect for what they saw as my desire to enact progressive values through careful study of activist groups such as theirs. Their belief in the importance of alliance activism not only dovetailed with my own but also contributed to their eagerness to share what they had learned in almost twenty years of sistering.

Through fieldwork, I was able to see how the members of PLCSC engaged in deep identification, which I treat as a form of identity work. Their talk and actions revealed the fundamentals of sistering that comprise their oppositional consciousness: deep emotional commitment to their Salvadoran partners and boundaries of sameness and difference that define who they are as allies. The sistering relationship that is supported by deep identification is inspiring and surprisingly reciprocal; however, it also has limitations. The boundaries of sameness and difference that are drawn through deep identification function to obscure important elements of the sistering relationship. Therefore, I conclude with a discussion of the pitfalls of deep identification as a form of identity work by privileged people.

The Case: PLCSC and Sistering

PLCSC is a small group, consisting of about twenty-five members. The membership is diverse in terms of age, gender, and political background. For instance, Judy Saunders-Martinez,[2] PLCSC's one staff person, and David Rosenbaum, a founding member, are the two self-avowed "hard core" solidarity activists in the group. They crack jokes about their own "lefty" tendencies. At a PLCSC celebration, Judy teased David publicly about a last-minute newsletter article in which they wrote that "global networks being built by sister cities are like a stake driven through the heart of global capitalism." She admits that the National Network will not distribute that newsletter because of their hyperbole. After a few beers, David can be persuaded to tell stories of visiting Salvadoran military prisons and dodging checkpoints in the early years of the sister cities movement. He is also a member of Jews Against the Occupation, a Palestinian solidarity organization.

The eldest members of the group are Dick and Kay Elliot. A retired pastor, Dick came to PLCSC through liberation theology and Christian base community efforts in El Salvador. He still belongs to a religious solidarity organization as well, and his wife serves as PLCSC's treasurer. In contrast,

Beth Johnson is (in the words of her daughter, one of the National Network's staff in San Salvador) a "quintessential soccer mom" who had no prior political experience and became active only through her daughter's involvement. Beth is joined by several other members with neither additional movement memberships nor previous political experience. Thus, while some members (particularly the long-term ones) are firmly rooted in left-wing politics, and a few base their commitment on religious grounds, other members come to the group without either basis.

The sister cities movement is part of the broader Central America peace movement that emerged in the United States in the 1980s (Gosse 1988; Nepstad 1997, 2004; Smith 1996). The history of sistering in El Salvador is tied not to the business exchanges that typically make up formal sister city relationships in many municipalities in the United States but instead to a few members of Committee in Solidarity with the People of El Salvador (CISPES) who wanted to create an additional venue for American involvement with El Salvador. Recognizing that many Americans would be uncomfortable supporting the armed guerillas of the Farabundo Marti National Liberation Front (FMLN), these individuals initiated sister cities as an alternative means of supporting progressive civilian peasant groups.

Peasants in the village of Las Cruces supported the FMLN during the Salvadoran civil war but were themselves primarily civilians. Fleeing the war, these villagers lived in the mountains for two years. In 1985, they repopulated their village in defiance of the Salvadoran government, setting up cooperatives and distributing the land equally. After a massacre in the village church in which nine young men were murdered by government troops, activists from a branch of the FMLN connected Prairietown and Las Cruces in a sistering relationship. Within days, American citizens from Prairietown began placing ads in the San Salvador papers as a notice to the government that attention was being paid to this village (a common tactic at that time). Within a few months, the Prairietown city council officially recognized the relationship, and delegations bringing food and medicine began entering the war zone to reach the repopulated village.

In the two decades since Americans from Prairietown first became active supporters of the villagers of Las Cruces, members of the two communities have built an enduring relationship. While the early aid missions functioned as life support to a village facing the scorched-earth tactics of low-intensity warfare, Prairietown's activities have evolved to include providing assistance with rebuilding houses, establishing cooperative childcare, developing woodworking and sewing workshops, and building a health clinic.

In the sections that follow I examine the PLCSC members' oppositional consciousness, collective identity, and commitment to their Salvadoran sisters. I show how they construct the collective identity of "sisters" and how this results in a particular kind of relationship with the Salvadoran villagers with whom they work. In addition, I show how this identity work is based on both sameness and difference, as the members of PLCSC emphasize their similarities with Las Cruces villagers and differences from other activists involved in Central America.

Sisterhood and Collective Identity

As Whittier writes, a collective identity is an "*interpretation* of a group's collective experience: who members of the group are, what their attributes are, what they have in common, how they are different from other groups, and what the political significance of all this is" (2002, 302; emphasis in original). How, then, does PLCSC interpret itself?

In the absence of other defining characteristics, the members of PLCSC share chiefly a *movement* identity (Jasper 1997)—that is, an identity based on the ideals to which they aspire. While many share some sociocultural attributes—for instance, they are primarily white, middle-class, and middle-aged—none of these identities are fully shared among the members. More important, these identities are not the *basis* for their involvement in El Salvador. As a result, the most important thing that PLCSC members have in common is a shared idea of what sistering is supposed to be like.

PLCSC members understand themselves as "sisters" to the Salvadoran peasants in the village of Las Cruces, El Salvador. This identity is applied to all members of the group, even newcomers. Based both on observations and my own welcome into the group as a participant observer, it appears that the criteria for membership in the group—and, therefore, for who qualifies as a "sister"—are rather broad. Anyone who commits a certain amount of time and attends meetings regularly is accepted as a member of PLCSC. This "instant sisterhood" creates an expectation that members share, at least to some degree, a commitment to Las Cruces and to the explicit ideals and process of sistering. However, the collective identity also contains *implicit* assumptions about what being sisters entails, and these implicit assumptions apply immediately to all newcomers as well.

Explicit Ideals: Respect and Mutuality

Above all, sistering is *respectful*. By this, PLCSC members mean that they, as U.S. citizens, should follow the Salvadorans' lead rather than imposing their own agenda. The structure of sistering supports such a mode of relating: the National Network has established a "board-to-board" relationship with CRIPDES (the Salvadoran peasant organization that hosts these sistering relationships), alone among the international organizations with which CRIPDES works. Every five years or so, CRIPDES sponsors an "Encuentro" (a "listening" session), which members of the National Network (including some PLCSC leaders) attend. At these meetings and in the board-to-board exchanges, the Salvadorans offer their strategic vision to their American sisters. The role of the American sisters is to listen, develop plans in concert with CRIPDES, and then follow through on these plans and other Salvadoran requests. David Rosenbaum made this commitment clear when reminding PLCSC members to attend an anti-School of the Americas demonstration: "Remember about how when we had our last big meeting with the Salvadorans [the Encuentro] the top of their list was to close the SOA [School of the Americas]—and work on remilitarization in relationship to the war in Colombia. So go to the demonstration!" Conversations among the members of PLCSC regularly return to these listening sessions and to the agreements that National Network sister cities make. Accountability to the Salvadorans is an essential component of respect.

The language developed for sistering reflects this principle. In particular, the use of the term "accompaniment" illustrates how strongly sisters feel about the principle of respect. Although the literal origins of the word rest in particular tactic—of walking alongside the civilian Salvadoran brigades as they marched from the refugee camps or from hiding in the mountains to reclaim and repopulate their villages—it has been expanded to refer to the sistering relationship itself. Occasionally, accompaniment is used metaphorically to mean something like "walking beside us in spirit," as when Judy commented after the events of September 11th, 2001, that "we have a relationship with people who have suffered so much, and we're hurting now and we need to ask them for accompaniment." Others commonly refer to sistering as "advocacy and accompaniment."

Respect is further evidenced in the priority given to Salvadoran understandings of what the sistering relationship is over Americans' desires about what the relationship could be. The recent changes in the economic situation in El Salvador required a transformation of the U.S. sisters' efforts. Until recently, local economic redevelopment efforts such as a woodworking shop or sewing collective have been highest priority, but as the Salvadorans grappled with the economic collapse of their society, national and international organizing moved to the forefront. Now the U.S. sisters raise funds to support regional and national-level projects in El Salvador, such as youth organizing and the development of popular education. An even more recent project is supporting the Salvadorans' work with other international efforts, such as the landless peasants movement in Brazil. As Judy, the PLCSC staff member, explained,

> [sistering is] becoming a whole organizing thing, a much better network, but we're trying to figure out how to keep the local, personal. People go to Las Cruces still and see people, but we can't stay at that level, because the struggle . . . doesn't allow for that . . . there's bigger forces.

Even as Judy highlighted the evolution of their work, she invoked the importance of the relationship with Las Cruces. Salvadoran requests for assistance in globalizing their work notwithstanding, the "local and personal" connection is what motivates U.S. citizens.

As central as respect is to the ideal of sistering, mutuality is an equally essential component. I use *mutuality* to highlight the emphasis PLCSC members place on their own gains from the sistering relationship, particularly in the areas of shared learning and emotional support. PLCSC members repeatedly invoke the mutual learning of sistering, beginning with their mission statement, which reads, "we work . . . as organized groups of citizens acting across borders to provide mutual support and raise awareness of our common struggle for peace, justice and democracy." The hope is that as the organization deepens its commitment to its sisters in El Salvador, it will become more effective at organizing for social justice within the United States as well.

In meetings and discussions, PLCSC members repeatedly invoke the lessons that Salvadorans teach them. Highlighting these lessons is part of their emphasis on mutuality. That is, although the American activists bring school supplies, medicines, and salaries for teachers, the residents of Las Cruces are not the only beneficiaries of these activities. Reflections of the members of a PLCSC youth delegation exemplify some of what activists feel they have learned from the sistering experience. For example, in their official "report-back" reception, many of the youth delegates commented on the generosity shown to them by the poorest of El Salvador's residents. One young woman told incredulously how the bus driver gave her his breakfast when she could not eat what her homestay mother had cooked. Others noted how the experience shattered their stereotypes of the poor. For instance, in reflecting on a meeting with a group of former gang members, Cara said,

> It was really neat, [the leader said] he'd take people that if we'd seen on the street we would avoid, and here we were making friends with them and

talking with them . . . their ideals and intentions were much better than some of the middle-class Americans who were apathetic.

Another young woman spoke about her own changed perspective after traveling to Las Cruces:

I'm reconsidering what I really want to do with my life, and what's really important to me, after the trip, so in that respect, it was a really life changing experience, and what I learned about the Salvadoran culture, and how hard they work.

Sharing their "own reality" with their Salvadoran sisters is another important aspect of mutuality for PLCSC members. Members do this by recognizing the Salvadorans as equally interested in understanding the realities of life and the struggle for social justice in the United States. For example, one youth delegation, which included several PLCSC members, prepared a skit on economic injustice in the United States and performed it regularly in El Salvador.

Finally, shared emotional support is seen as an additional aspect of the sistering relationship that enhances its mutuality. PLCSC members send letters to Las Cruces fairly regularly, reporting on their activities and asking after events in the village. After September 11, 2001, the town council of Las Cruces wrote to PLCSC expressing condolences for the events and stating that they were "with all of the U.S. people, especially those who lost loved ones in the attacks." They asked for more communication, particularly about the development of war. Such communication requesting clarification of the experiences of their U.S. sisters indicates the expectations of mutual sharing on the Salvadoran side as well.

In these and many other ways, PLCSC members and leaders attempt to live up to the explicit ideals of sistering. Judy wove all these themes together in one unscripted explanation of PLCSC's activities:

Our relationship is a political coming together out of the need for people to accompany people. . . . We are learning about the reality in El Salvador and our own reality, too . . . reaching out across borders here in the U.S. as well. We no longer believe we can work with just Las Cruces, but that the struggle is on both sides of the border.

This quote touches on all the explicit aspects of the sistering identity: the emphasis on accompaniment at the origins of sistering, the shared learning between Salvadoran and U.S. citizens, and the changing nature of the work done by sisters. These ideals guide the development of oppositional consciousness among PLCSC members; they are strongly encouraged to follow the Salvadorans in adopting the priority placed on organizing as opposed to material aid, understanding organizing as a strategy in response to economic globalization, and seeing themselves as part of a movement whose ultimate goal is to transform society.

Implicit Identity: Welcome and Intimacy

This sense of being part of a new, transformed society-in-the-making is supported by the implicit aspects of the Americans' collective identity as sisters. On the Prairietown side of the relationship, being a sister means feeling wanted by the Salvadorans of Las Cruces, assuming a level of intimacy with them, and, as a result, understanding oneself to be a legitimate partner in solidarity work.

From the very beginning of their relationship with Las Cruces, PLCSC members understood themselves as needed by their Salvadoran sisters. With the murders in the village church and the bombings and attacks that followed as the Salvadoran government attempted to eliminate all civilian presence in the war zones, the material and political support of U.S. citizens was vital. Many testimonies from Salvadoran leaders over the years attest to the impact of sistering on the survival of Las Cruces in those years. For example, as a young leader from another sister city explained as the civil war drew to a close, "many of you [sister cities members] do not even realize how much your work helps prevent human rights violations against us."

But even as the relationship between the two communities has continued into times of relative peace, it is clear to the Prairietown members that sistering continues to be deeply desired by the Salvadorans. When delegations from PLCSC arrive in Las Cruces, they are received with great warmth. As Lori, a youth delegate recounted,

> Then we went to Las Cruces. There were lots of people waiting for us to welcome us, even though it was really late and dark. And they said that just us coming made them feel like we cared. Even just coming and not doing anything would have been a real help. And we split into groups to our families.

The role of sistering in the lives of Salvadorans is visually confirmed as delegates wander the village. On the walls of many of the village's houses small stenciled paintings either commemorate Oscar Romero, a priest murdered by the death squads, or indicate support of the FMLN. Alongside these stencils, there is often a picture of Ana-Elsy, a German nurse who worked in the villages and in the FMLN for years. The stencils read *"¡Compañera Ana-Elsy presente!"* (Our comrade Ana-Elsy, still with us). Furthermore, when delegates enter the church, they find the fourteen Stations of the Cross painted on the walls, reinterpreted to reflect the Salvadoran experience. The thirteenth Station is *Solidaridad Internacional* (International Solidarity), represented by the image of the planet surrounded by ribbons. Displays at the elementary school also show students' artistic renderings of the sistering relationship in honor of the current delegation. Finally, sistering delegates see not only that outside support visible and alive to residents of Las Cruces but also that their specific contributions are displayed prominently. For instance, the community store, funded by PLCSC, is called *Tienda Prairietown* (Prairietown Store), and the health clinic for which PLCSC secured outside funds is named the *Clinica Martin Luther King, Jr.*

At a more personal level, delegates not only feel wanted as solidarity partners but also feel personally connected, even intimate, with their Salvadoran hosts. Delegates from PLCSC always stay with families rather than in the hostel. Homes throughout the village contain small mementos of international delegates, some brought as house gifts, others sent down with later delegations. For instance, when I visited Las Cruces as part of a small delegation in 2002, I stayed in the home of Lilia, who regularly hosts delegates. Her sons spent most of an evening showing me a small picture book, containing photos of previous delegations. They carefully pointed out each person that stayed with them and named these visitors each time they appeared in *any* photograph. Lilia inquired about some members of PLCSC and asked me to snap photos of her family, with the clear implication that I would show them to PLCSC members, who would pore over them as well, upon my return. It is common for members of delegations to carry official correspondence as well as personal letters in both directions; on my trip to Las Cruces, I transported official greetings, baby clothes for Beth Johnson's former host family, and photos for Lilia's children and returned with verbal requests from the town council, handwritten notes for David and Beth, and photos for the whole group. In these personal exchanges, sistering is affirmed as an intimate and personal relationship; furthermore, along with the emphasis on staying in homes, the closeness is constructed as almost familial.

PLCSC's oppositional consciousness is supported and nurtured by the sense of wantedness that being a sister brings. This sense of closeness and intimacy is the first sign of the deep identification in which the members of PLCSC engage. As "sisters," they become radicalized not only by exposure to the history of U.S. culpability in the region but also by their exposure to— and, even more important, welcome by—the Salvadorans. The Salvadorans' generosity is striking to their U.S. sisters, their acceptance of outsider support is inspiring, and the importance that they place on the relationship clearly spurs ongoing commitment by PLCSC members. PLCSC members are told that they are *part of* the struggle; this becomes a portion of their oppositional consciousness.

Creating Emotional Commitment

As the preceding examples suggest, PLCSC members develop an emotional commitment to their Salvadoran partners in the sistering relationship. PLCSC leaders employ a number of tactics to build this emotional commitment in new sisters. First and foremost, they attempt to send any interested parties to El Salvador as soon as possible. This strategy is endorsed by the National Network and by CRIPDES: Elena, the Salvadoran staff member in charge of the sistering relationships, told me in an interview that, from their point of view, the goal of the delegation is to "make people fall in love with El Salvador." PLCSC invests a significant amount of time, effort, and money in sending even potential members to El Salvador. For example, during my fieldwork, several delegates "borrowed" money from PLCSC to travel, which was not always repaid. Delegations are not a foolish tactic, however, they are life-changing for some and deeply moving for almost all.

In addition to delegations, PLCSC sponsors Salvadorans from Las Cruces to come up "on tour" to Prairietown. Their public talks are intended to educate people living in and around Prairietown, but the relationships built as Prairietown activists house the very people who housed them in El Salvador help to maintain the mutuality of the sistering relationship. Letters, hand-written notes, and exchanges of photographs foster the sense of family far away. Furthermore, just as visual cues in Las Cruces remind Salvadoran villagers (as well as Prairietown visitors) of the important of the sistering relations, art displayed in Prairietown serve as virtual reminders as well. For example, prominently displayed in the PLCSC office is a painting in Salvadoran style representing the arrival of a delegation; in the painting, rainbows and doves fly above stylized red-tile roofs as Americans and Salvadorans embrace. Alongside the painting, Judy placed a needlepoint of pink and brown hands shaking, titled "solidaridad internacional," made by a thirteen-year-old orphan from the war. In another corner of the office is a six-inch tall "house" made of wood and bearing the phrase *hermanamiento* (sistering) over the door, and children's' drawings from the school in Las Cruces decorate the office walls. These pieces of folk art remind PLCSC members of their importance, their connection, and indeed their obligation, incurred by the building of the sistering relationship.

Building an emotional commitment to Las Cruces (and by extension El Salvador) is not as hard as it might seem. PLCSC welcomes members easily, and once in El Salvador, the warmth inherent in the culture—intensified by the legacy of sistering—easily astonishes the Americans. Further, the history of the relationship serves not as a barrier for new members but as a welcome. The founding story, told repeatedly, is constructed to emphasize the connections built across distances in a time of great need. Newcomers to the group know right away that their involvement is wanted and that they are included immediately in this special relationship.

The collective identity offers significant rewards in that members find a way to get involved, a role to take on, and a "family" to connect with far away. For those who are politically progressive already, the collective identity is even more rewarding; the reception they experience in letters and handcrafted gifts is a kind of salve to U.S. citizens who are aware of their own indirect complicity in the both historic and current situation of the Salvadorans. As Jess, a youth delegate to Las Cruces in the summer of 2001, wrote for her subsequent report to PLCSC,

> El Salvador especially influenced my response to the events of September 11th, knowing that the sister city project was begun in the heart of civil war, when the United States was giving 6 billion dollars in aid to the people who were destroying the towns, and yet the Salvadorans and Americans were building relationships. They might hate us, but they do not hate us, instead there is a deeper connection.

With a collective identity as part of a "political coming together," as Judy describes, U.S. citizens find emotional recompense for the harms inflicted by their own country. Rather than inviting new members into work based on a sense of guilt or duty, PLCSC can offer them an emotional connection to others, thereby enhancing their sense of identification with the Salvadorans.

Who Are We Not? Constructing Boundaries against Other Activists

Social movements establish and nourish a collective identity as much through defining who they are not as in explaining who they are (Taylor and Whittier 1992). In this regard, PLCSC is no different from any other social movement. When constructing their collective identity, these activists therefore draw on notions of difference to establish themselves as distinct from other groups of activists. These symbolic boundaries evolve as well. While the clearest boundaries are still against other, more "charitable," El Salvador organizations, a more recent boundary is drawn against those antiglobalization efforts that do not draw upon people-to-people relationships.

Critical to PLCSC's sense of self is their belief that they are "political" in contrast with other groups that engage only in "charity." This orientation toward structural problems is typical of solidarity groups (Lahusen 2001). In PLCSC, such an orientation results in a language of "root causes," which are depicted as the opposite of "band-aid solutions." In a typical example, Judy described their group at a joint El Salvador gathering—that is, in front of the very kind of El Salvador organizations from which they differentiate themselves—as "trying to promote north-south equality, and not just be do-gooders from the North." Despite the implicit critique, the sister parish, the house builders, and the religious companion community seemed to either not notice or to overlook the implicit slight.

In private, PLCSC members are just as forthright, commenting frequently on their differences from the sister parishes. Sister parishes, claim PLCSC members, do not understand organizing as PLCSC members have come to conceive of it; instead, they want to support projects. "Projects" are insignificant activities that might benefit a few people but that do little to impact the community as a whole or to alter the structural forces shaping the fate of Las Cruces. In contrast, PLCSC members take pride in their support of "organizing," including contributing to the salaries of youth organizers who are building a progressive network of politically involved youth around El Salvador and the salaries of the popular teachers who are developing new models for expanding education into the rural countryside. From PLCSC's point of view, organizing contributes to structural change, while "projects" do not.

This concern for structural change runs through all of PLCSC's efforts. While they may not always achieve their goals, they strive to examine all their work in this light. For example, during the two-year period that I studied the group, Las Cruces developed a new initiative for scholarships to help students complete high school. While the sister parish jumped on board, PLCSC was hesitant. How would scholarships for individual students benefit the entire village of Las Cruces? How would the students be chosen? What was the larger strategy behind this initiative? The following dialogue, from one of the many discussions of scholarships, illustrates these concerns:

EMILY: But is [the scholarship program] a band-aid approach? Are we addressing the root causes of the problems, really?

KAY: And how will this benefit them for more than a few years? So many people take off [for the United States] how will we know that they'll stick around? Is that what's going to happen? I want to raise real questions about this.

GARETH: I'd argue that it's building the infrastructure of the community back up. Keeping youth together. Building up a sense of loyalty.

JUDY: The situation is so dire; they're really trying to put their hope in the next generation.

KAY: The word "organizing" is key. "Scholarship" says to me it's to support individuals. How are you really supporting the community?

GARETH: This is now their long-term hope. They've given up on getting it for themselves, but they want it for their children. It's a big change for them.

In addition to this core boundary of political support versus charity by which PLCSC understands itself as being different from other Central America activists, PLCSC began to distinguish itself from other antiglobalization efforts. Here again, the notion of sistering as involving closeness and intimacy is central to PLCSC's collective identity; they understand themselves as different from other antiglobalization groups because of the relationships they have built with Salvadoran peasants. As Bill, the National Network director, explained,

> We can insert ourselves in the anti-corporate globalization/peace movement— because of our relationship with people on the ground, that we have a vision of—we are in a unique position in the larger movement to bring those perspectives in. There's a critique of the [anti-globalization] movement that it's all white middle-class people. We can facilitate voices from the south—poor Salvadoran peasants being heard. Even the organizations with contacts in the region do not have 15+ years of experience under the most difficult circumstances [as we do].

Highlighting the unique experience of sistering, Bill invoked his organization's knowledge and experience. Interestingly, however, many of the "rank and file" members of PLCSC and other sister chapters did not feel as comfortable making such claims; I heard this boundary voiced mainly by those with broader political experience, such as Judy and David, in addition to the National Network staff.

The boundaries drawn reflect the oppositional consciousness of PLCSC members as sisters: political rather than charitable, engaged in a legitimate and mutual relationship of solidarity with people who want them. These boundaries reinforce a sense that PLCSC members share more with their Salvadoran sisters than with other U.S. activists. Ironically, then, PLCSC members identify with their "sisters" across deep social divisions more than they do with those with whom they share a far greater number of identities.

The Limits of Deep Identification

This study examined the collective identity of members of Prairietown Las Cruces Sister Cities, a Central American solidarity organization that has been in existence for nearly twenty years. Specifically, I focused on the "deep identification" of the Prairietown activists with their Salvadoran "sisters" and argued that the creation of this kind of solidarity and emotional commitment is a form of identity work that can, in fact, result in the development of insurgent consciousness among activists representing privileged groups.

However, this emphasis on similarity and emotional commitment sometimes backfires. For example, some members become deeply committed to *individuals* in Las Cruces, keeping their ties specific rather than generalizing even to the village. Beth Johnson, the "soccer mom" mother of Anna, a San Salvador staff person, felt closely connected to particular families in Las Cruces. When I traveled, she prepared carefully wrapped presents of baby clothes and photographs for "her" families. Her daughter Anna rolled her eyes when I arrived so laden and then carefully figured out how we could distribute the parcels so as to avoid setting off resentments between various families. Other members become attached to Las Cruces as a community but do not then develop an understanding of the principle of respect, in the sense of following the Salvadorans' lead. In another case, Anna told me a story of a PLCSC member who, without consulting anyone, carefully gathered five hundred pairs of shoes, which she then sent to Las Cruces with a delegation. Anna snorted at the memory, which exemplified to her the kind of charity mindset Sister Cities attempts to avoid. Moreover, this particular donation was not needed at all; not only do most residents of Las Cruces have footwear, but they also live in a climate where shoes are not a true necessity and many wear flip-flops comfortably year-round.

These examples suggest that, while "deep identification" is useful, it has its limitations. In this concluding section I argue that a strategy of developing a local and personal emotional commitment to Las Cruces, a strategy of "deep identification," can actually hinder the very development of the insurgent consciousness it was intended to motivate. It does so in two ways. First, this strategy discourages PLCSC members from appreciating the careful, long-term work behind the sistering relationship. Second, it discourages PLCSC members from grappling with their own privileges and assumptions as U.S. citizens, and therefore does not help PLCSC overcome some of the problems common to dominant group members in social movements.

The Invisibility of Bridge Work

When PLCSC and the other sister cities pursue the strategy of deep identification, they construct the sistering relationship as a "natural" coming
together of deeply connected people. The founding story is a good example.
As it is told, it strips the citizens of both Las Cruces and Prairietown of organizational identity and social movement affiliation; instead, the former are
citizens who "put out a call" while the latter are citizens who "responded."
Unfortunately, it isn't that simple. Moreover, when the relationship is naturalized in this way, the "bridge work" undertaken by both Salvadoran and
U.S. staff is effectively rendered invisible.

PLCSC underestimates the importance and the complexity of the roles
played by Bill, the National Network director, and Anna and Liz, the U.S.
staff in San Salvador. As bridge workers, Anna and Liz work closely with all
the sistering communities on an ongoing basis. Like Belinda Robnett's (1997)
"mainstream bridge leaders"—white women in the civil rights movement
who helped to connect the movement to the larger white world—Anna and
Liz work in El Salvador to build connections between Salvadoran peasants
and U.S. citizens. They facilitate the sistering relationship by encouraging
sister city committees in the United States to write regularly, translating confused messages, explaining Salvadoran initiatives, and more. For example,
some tensions emerged in Las Cruces over a grant that funded the health
clinic, and while I was in El Salvador, Anna met with the new leadership in
Las Cruces and carefully (but subtly) told the history of the project in order
to deflect jealousy directed at the clinic worker. Without Anna's ongoing
attention to the situation, ill feelings and difficulties in PLCSC's sistering
relationship would likely begin to fester.

As important as these efforts are, the work Anna puts into sustaining
and building the relationship between Prairietown and Las Cruces goes
largely unrecognized by most members of PLCSC. For example, while in
Las Cruces, I saw Anna make contact with at least ten community leaders,
inquiring as to the work they were doing. She met with the newly elected
leader of the town council in part to discuss the scholarship program proposed to PLCSC but also to support and reinforce the importance of the
sistering relationship. Privately, she mentioned a problem that had come to
her attention after the departure of a youth delegation earlier that summer.
The town council had allowed the delegation to go hiking in the mountains
even after several assaults had occurred in the region in the previous month;
as a newly elected group, they did not yet understand that U.S. citizens
should not be permitted to go into dangerous situations, even if Salvadorans

endure them daily. Anna realized that she would need to meet with the new council to train them in the reception and treatment of delegations. It is the idea that sistering happens "naturally" that makes this work so difficult for PLCSC members to recognize.

The naturalization of sistering also renders invisible the work behind the concrete skills and the political understandings needed to make sistering flourish. For instance, Anna and Liz work closely with the CRIPDES leadership to develop the political aspect of sistering. They see their jobs as helping Salvadorans to "move the North American base" (in Anna's words) toward a more political vision. To this end, they send monthly bulletins to the U.S. sister city chapters with news and updates on conditions in El Salvador. They report on privatization efforts, the struggles and successes of the popular movement, and the effects of free trade policies. Because of these communications, they are a major force for the politicization of the members of the National Network. Thus, a source of Sister Cities' legitimacy as an alternative model of relationship between North and South is the work of Anna and Liz. Yet PLCSC members rarely read these monthly bulletins and instead inquire after Anna's health and events in Las Cruces.

The construction of sistering as organic or natural, that is, as a form of deep identification, encourages the members of PLCSC to believe that the relationship does not require "work" but rather happens effortlessly through a caring relationship. Deeply identifying with their "sisters" obscures the ways that PLCSC and other local committees benefit from the hard work of the National Network.

Obscured Privilege

In addition to obscuring the work needed to bridge differences of language, nation, and class, deep identification with their Salvadoran sisters discouraged the members of PLCSC from grappling with and discussing openly their own privilege vis-à-vis the Salvadorans. That is, they gloss over their own social location and instead construct similarity through a metaphorical familial connection between Prairietown and Las Cruces citizens. The obscuring of privilege that results deeply compromises their oppositional consciousness.

While the members of PLCSC do attempt to confront their privilege, their emphasis is on structural inequality and political solutions—both of which are removed from the realm of individual action. In so doing, they emphasize what Patricia Hill Collins has called the "structural domain of power" (2000, 277), and they neglect the "interpersonal domain of power" (287). Collins writes that many people fail to recognize the contradictions of oppression, and that no group is purely victim or purely oppressor but instead "derives varying amounts of penalty and privilege" through their particular location amid intersecting oppressions. When Judy described the sistering relationship as a "political coming together," she implied a union unburdened by power or inequality. The omissions in her description are created by a construction of equality between people whose socioeconomic contexts render them fundamentally unequal. When PLCSC leaders emphasize their founding story, they continue this assumption of equality. When the founding story is placed at the forefront, it serves to emphasize the mutuality of the relationship and the ways in which U.S. activists respond to Salvadoran strategic initiatives.

While this mutuality serves as a powerful context for shared action, PLCSC consistently makes the mistake of conflating the structural equality that mutuality implies with the interpersonal equality that "sistering" longs for. They fail, therefore, to take into account in their relations with Salvadorans their social power as U.S. citizens, whites, and middle-class people; in so doing, they mask the operation of privilege in the relationship. For example, Anna pointed out that few Salvadoran villages will refuse an offer of assistance, even if it does not respond to a particular priority of theirs. Others have suggested that Central American organizations shape their requests to please internationals who can offer or withhold funds (Bayard de Volo 2001). Many acknowledge that Salvadorans find it impolite to refuse something offered by a valued guest. Without concrete discussion of the power U.S. citizens wield by providing material aid, members of the sister city committees are vulnerable to imposing their own objectives on their Salvadoran sisters while still believing they uphold an ideal of respect. Yet having these discussions fits uneasily into a discourse that emphasizes natural and deep connections. Indeed, I heard no such conversations during my fieldwork.

The level of warmth and welcome that PLCSC members experience in the sistering relationship can further encourage them to believe they have solved any interpersonal issues of power. For instance, long-term members of the group tend to speak of Salvadorans as "my friends," a tendency Anna noticed among most in-country volunteers for Sister Cities. By constructing these relationships as friendships, volunteers and long-term members can avoid grappling with the fundamental distinctions between their lives and those of the Salvadorans they work with. With that as the model, newer members may feel that their goal is to develop friendships rather than explore fully and reflect deeply upon their relationships to their Salvadoran hosts and sisters, people divided from them by history, geography, often language, and by one of the largest gaps in income and standard of living possible.

The limitations of deep identification that I have shown here only serve to highlight the original problem with which I opened this chapter: the difficulty in building and maintaining a radical consciousness among privileged people who lack collective identities forged in conditions of oppression or long-standing communities of resistance. Morris and Braine suggested that religious cultural resources might be helpful for dominant group members; absent those, deep identification with those they wished to support might enable commitment and transformation. Identifying deeply presumably causes enough empathy on the part of the privileged person to spark ongoing commitment to the other and to motivate changed consciousness and a willingness to investigate one's own social location and the privileges—perhaps as well as penalties, as Hill Collins puts it—that come with it. How then do the sisters of PLCSC fare?

In constructing the collective identity of "sisters," the members of PLCSC build personal, close, and emotionally significant relationships with Salvadoran peasants—very much like what Morris and Braine might have in mind when they suggest the possibilities of deep identification. This identity clearly supports PLCSC members in developing permanent commitments to particular Salvadorans and to a particular village long after the attention of progressive activists has moved on to other areas of the world. Deeply identifying further seems to encourage the radicalization of PLCSC members: they are inspired toward the ideals of mutuality and respect and toward structural solutions to the problems facing their Salvadoran sisters. They try to learn from them about how to organize in a globalizing world. But they are not as successful at interrogating their own social location and its implications for their work and their relationships with their Salvadoran sisters. In emphasizing mutuality and "natural" connections, they neglect barriers that actually require significant cultural work to manage. The emotional bond created by deep identification seems to discourage the difficult work of challenging the workings of oppression in the relationship with sisters. Thus, a cost here of deep identification is that it undermines the sisters' insurgent consciousness by allowing them to construct boundaries of sameness and difference in ways that obscure the permanent inequalities between themselves and their sisters.

But the realities of organizing privileged people are such that, despite these limitations—even costs—deep identification may be a viable strategy among imperfect alternatives. On what basis, other than a deeply felt emotional connection, might one reasonably expect a number of comfortable Americans to care—and to act on that care year after year—about poor people half a world away? As I have shown here, emotional connections are vulnerable to an obscuring of difference. Yet, other instances of deep identification might function somewhat differently. Further research should examine deep identification in other social movements of privileged people: what forms it takes, its benefits, and its costs. We should find out if there are ways that deep identification can inspire rather than inhibit the careful examination of privilege. Perhaps in some movements, deep identification functions as a "way in," where the commitment inspired through this strategy encourages or requires dominant group members to examine their own social location, perhaps in response to expectations of the subordinate group that they do so. Conversely, we may find that deep identification only in some cases provides the benefits I have documented here. But this particular case suggests, I believe, that we would do well to examine actual movements by privileged people on behalf of others with an eye to the way they achieve whatever measure of success accrues to their efforts. Despite doubt and neglect by scholars, these movements have much to teach about the work of negotiating sameness and difference between activists.

References

Bayard de Volo, Lorraine. 2001. *Mothers of Heroes and Martyrs: Gender Identity Politics in Nicaragua, 1979–1999.* Baltimore: Johns Hopkins University Press.

Bell, Sandra, and Mary Delaney. 2001. "Collaborating across Difference: From Theory and Rhetoric to the Hard Reality of Building Coalitions." In *Forging Radical Alliances Across Difference: Coalition Politics for the New Millennium*, ed. J. Bystydzienski and S. Schacht, 63–76. Lanham, Md.: Rowman and Littlefield.

Collins, Patricia Hill. 2000. *Black Feminist Thought: Knowledge, Consciousness and the Politics of Empowerment.* 2nd ed. New York: Routledge.

Connell, R. W. 1998. "Gender Politics for Men." In *Feminism and Men: Reconstructing Gender Relations*, ed. S. Schacht and D. Ewing, 225–36. New York: New York University Press.

Dolgon, Corey. 2001. "Building Community amid the Ruins: Strategies for Struggle from the Coalition for Justice at Southampton College." In *Forging Radical Alliances Across Difference: Coalition Politics for the New Millennium*, ed. J. Bystydzienski and S. Schacht, 220–33. Lanham, Md.: Rowman and Littlefield.

Gosse, Van. 1988. "'The North American Front': Central American Solidarity in the Reagan Era." In *Reshaping the U.S. Left: Popular Struggles in the '80s*, ed. M. Davis and M. Sprinker, 11–50. London: Verso.

Lahusen, Christian. 2001. "Mobilizing for International Solidarity: Mega Events and Moral Crusades." In *Political Altruism? Solidarity Movements in International*

Perspective, ed. M. Giugni and F. Passy, 177–95. Lanham, Md.: Rowman and Littlefield.

Lichterman, Paul. 1995. "Piecing Together Multicultural Community: Cultural Differences in Community Building among Grass-Roots Environmentalists." *Social Problems* 42: 513–34.

———. 1996. *The Search for Political Community: American Activists Reinventing Commitment.* Cambridge: Cambridge University Press.

———. 1998. "What Do Movements Mean." *Qualitative Sociology* 21: 401–18.

Mansbridge, Jane. 2001a. "The Making of Oppositional Consciousness." In *Oppositional Consciousness: The Subjective Roots of Social Protest*, ed. J. Mansbridge and A. Morris, 1–19. Chicago: University of Chicago Press.

———. 2001b. "Complicating Oppositional Consciousness." In *Oppositional Consciousness: The Subjective Roots of Social Protest*, ed. J. Mansbridge and A. Morris, 238–64. Chicago: University of Chicago Press.

Marx, Gary, and Michael Useem. 1971. "Majority Involvement in Minority Movements: Civil Rights, Abolition and Untouchability." *Journal of Social Issues* 27: 81–104.

McAdam, Doug. 1988. *Freedom Summer.* New York: Oxford University Press.

McCarthy, John, and Mayer Zald. 1987. "Resource Mobilization and Social Movements: A Partial Theory." In *Social Movements in an Organizational Society*, ed. M. Zald and J. McCarthy, 15–49. New Brunswick, N.J.: Transaction Books.

Morris, Aldon, and Naomi Braine. 2001. "Social Movements and Oppositional Consciousness." In *Oppositional Consciousness: The Subjective Roots of Social Protest*, ed. J. Mansbridge and A. Morris, 20–37. Chicago: University of Chicago Press.

Nepstad, Sharon Erickson. 1997. "The Process of Cognitive Liberation: Cultural Synapses, Links and Frame Contradictions in the U.S.-Central America Peace Movement." *Sociological Inquiry* 67: 470–87.

———. 2004. *Convictions of the Soul: Religion, Culture and Agency in the Central America Solidarity Movement.* New York: Oxford University Press.

Robnett, Belinda. 1997. *How Long? How Long? African-American Women in the Struggle for Civil Rights.* New York: Oxford University Press.

Rose, Fred. 2000. *Coalitions across the Class Divide: Lessons from the Labor, Peace and Environmental Movements.* Ithaca, N.Y.: Cornell University Press.

Smith, Christian. 1996. *Resisting Reagan: The U.S. Central America Peace Movement.* Chicago: University of Chicago Press.

Taylor, Verta and Whittier, Nancy. 1992. "Collective Identity in Social Movement Communities: Lesbian Feminism Mobilization." In *New Frontiers in Social Movement Theory*, ed. A. Morris and C. Mueller, 104–29. New Haven, Conn.: Yale University Press.

Whittier, Nancy. 2002. "Meaning and Structure in Social Movements." In *Social Movements: Identity, Culture and the State*, ed. D. Meyer, N. Whittier and B. Robnett, 289–307. New York: Oxford University Press.

Notes

1. Privileged outsiders can be privileged in many dimensions: race, class, nation, gender, sexual orientation, and so forth. In this case, "sistering" crosses lines of race, nation, class, and education.

2. All names used are pseudonyms.

9

Dealing with Diversity: The Coalition of Labor Union Women[1]

Silke Roth

Mobilizing broad and diverse constituencies represents a challenge for social movements. In particular, the literature on the women's movement is full of accounts of the challenges that cross-class and cross-race alliances face (see the collections by Bookman and Morgen 1988; Naples 1998; Ryan 2001). As long as institutionalized antiracist practices are absent from women's movement organizations, there is a risk that a gap will develop between abstract moral commitment to inclusiveness and concrete actions to challenge racism and practice equality (Ferree and Hess 2000, 124). Thus, the pursuit of social justice requires effective coalitions across difference (Bystydzienski and Schacht 2001). While the opportunities that broad coalitions offer are recognized and the notion of the second wave of the women's movement as a solely white middle-class movement is now clearly rejected (Robnett 1997; Roth 2003; Roth 2004), the question remains, what is the best way to integrate diverse constituencies? This is a crucial question for all social movements but in particular for the labor movement, which sees a growing number of women and minorities among the new membership (Milkman 2000). This chapter addresses this question by examining how identity work can successfully promote the integration of a diverse group of women into a labor movement organization.

As the editors of this volume point out in their introduction, collective identity plays a crucial role in the analysis of social movements (see also Snow and McAdam 2000; Polletta and Jasper 2001). Identity is an outcome of collective action (Fantasia 1988) and is reflected in organizational structure (Clemens 1996; Gamson 1996; Reger 2002a, 2002b). Verta Taylor and Nancy Whittier (1992) describe three elements of identity work: the setting of boundaries, the development of consciousness, and negotiation. Boundaries emphasize the differences between members of a social movement and others. As Taylor and Whittier point out, this "often involves a kind of reverse affirmation of the characteristics attributed [to it] by the larger society" (110). Joshua Gamson (1995) discusses this problem with respect to the gay rights movement and addresses the paradox that identity movements might engage in essentializing for strategic reasons. While boundaries locate activists as members of social movements or social movement organizations, consciousness provides the interpretative frameworks that are crucial for assessing shared interests and opportunities as well as making decisions about goals and strategies (which are at the same time an expression of collective identity). The development of consciousness is an ongoing process that is interwoven in the political work as well as in everyday life. Emphasizing interaction, Rick Fantasia (1988) describes how consciousness arises in "cultures of solidarity." Thus, consciousness is grounded in experiences and their (re)evaluation. Finally, negotiation involves the implicit and explicit attempts at new ways of thinking and acting in private and public settings (Taylor and Whittier 1992, 118).

Whether activists' similarities or differences to the mainstream are emphasized depends on strategies and political opportunity structures (Bernstein 1997). Furthermore, race, class, and gender affect the ways in which protesters are received, regardless of whether the collective identities that activists construct for themselves are the same as those as their targets attribute to them (Einwohner 1999). Collective identity is a precondition as well as an outcome of social movement emergence and is constantly (re)constructed. This process can be a pleasure or hard work for the participants when it involves negotiating sameness and difference (see the Introduction).

In this chapter, I analyze the identity work of the Coalition of Labor Union Women (CLUW), which is a national organization of union members. CLUW was founded in 1974 and adopted four goals at its founding convention: organizing the unorganized, bringing more women into union leadership, getting women involved in the political process, and bringing women's issues on the labor agenda. The members come from all occupational sectors; they include about 30 percent women of color and 10 percent male members. Elsewhere, I have argued that CLUW is a bridging organization in that it seeks to connect the women's movement and the labor movement by bringing women's issues on the labor agenda and forming coalitions with women's organizations (Roth 2003). CLUW's membership is involved in labor, women's, and civil rights organizations, as well as community activism, churches, and political parties, and it exemplifies how related movements share personnel (Meyer 2002). CLUW broadens the labor agenda and builds bridges between the labor movement and the women's movement by framing "women's issues," such as pay equity, day care, sexual harassment, and reproductive rights as "labor issues" (Roth 2003). Depending on the context, CLUW is perceived as either a "labor" or a "women's organization." For example, in the context of the labor movement, CLUW is primarily seen as a "women's organization." In contrast, in a coalition of women's organizations, CLUW represents "labor." These different attributions are very important for CLUW's collective identity of labor feminism, which reconciles class and feminist consciousness and builds bridges between the women's and the labor movement. In this chapter I ask, how does CLUW "deal" with diversity? That is, what strategies do members use to construct a shared collective identity that is sufficiently broad as well as meaningful to a diverse constituency?

My case-study is based on qualitative and quantitative data. Between 1991 and 1995, I conducted semistructured interviews with sixty-eight formerly and presently active CLUW members. On average, the interviews lasted one-and-a-half hours and addressed the lives of the interviewees before they became activists, how they got involved in CLUW, and what participating in this organization means to them. In addition, fourteen experts on the women's and the labor movement were interviewed.[2] During an internship in the CLUW Center for Education and Research in Washington, D.C. in the summer of 1995, I compiled a CLUW leadership directory, which provided information about the two hundred members of CLUW's national executive board and conducted a membership survey (N= 534, response rate 30 percent). Finally, I engaged in participant observation at chapter meetings and national meetings.

I first discuss how the structure of the organization addresses identity and makes the inclusion of a diverse constituency possible. Then I show—employing Taylor and Whittier's (1992) notions of boundaries, consciousness, and negotiations—how CLUW constructed its collective identity. I label this collective identity "union feminism" (Roth 2003) and argue that it allows sameness and difference to coexist. The identity work of CLUW includes organizational processes, such as integrated leadership and separate groups, and coalition building. I also show how the identity work of CLUW seeks to reconcile race, class, and feminist consciousness by mainstreaming gender and race into the framework of the labor movement. The organizational structure of CLUW is clearly reminiscent of the labor movement while pursuing the interests of working women of color and building coalitions with the women's and the labor movement.

Organizational Structure as Expression of Collective Identity

Scholars argue that organizational structure is an expression of collective identity (Clemens 1996; Gamson 1996). The collective identity of CLUW is expressed by using the framework of the labor movement with respect to its organizational form (modeled after the American Federation of Labor-Congress of Industrial Organizations [AFL-CIO]) and its coalition strategies (with unions and the AFL-CIO as well as community, women's, civil rights, and antiwar organizations). The organizational structure assures that CLUW includes a wide range of unions; to receive a charter, chapters must have members from at least five different unions. Union delegates and chapter delegates participate in the national meetings. Notably, women of color are represented at all levels of the organization although there is no formal mechanism for achieving this representation; the leadership and membership of the organization is committed to include women of color at all levels of the organizations. Furthermore, it reflects these members' high levels of unionization and tendencies to hold leadership positions in their unions. For example, Addie Wyatt, an African American woman who was one of the founding members of CLUW, was a leader in her union and the civil rights movements and became the vice-president of CLUW. In addition, after having been the national treasurer from 1974 through 1993, Gloria Johnson, was the first African American woman to become CLUW's national president (1993–2004). During interviews some activists claimed that Johnson's presidency resulted in more African American women becoming active in the organization, while others pointed out that African American women belonged to the founding members and participated in CLUW from the very start. The latter view was supported in the membership survey, which showed no significant differences between white women and women of color regarding the time they joined CLUW.

Members of CLUW were proud of the high proportion of women of color. One white respondent, who was in an interracial relationship and was active in antiracist work, explained that she was attracted to CLUW precisely because it was an interracial group. She remembered the first time she went to a meeting of the national executive board (NEB). She said,

> When I walked into the general plenary session of the NEB as an observer and saw a mixed-race group, I was floored. To be honest with you, I hadn't seen a mixed-race group like that in the labor movement, in the women's movement, anywhere before, and I remember that moment very clearly. I felt there was hope. And it was something I had always been looking for.

In terms of identity work, the organization from the beginning was aware that a diverse constituency must be represented by a diverse leadership. To attract members from all unions, racial and ethnic backgrounds, and regions of the United States and also to gain the respect of the labor movement, the leadership proactively suggested an inclusive slate of candidates for elected offices.

At the same time, however, diversity was problematic. Notably, some members noticed that CLUW had fewer Hispanic and Asian members relative to African American members. Such differences cannot be explained by differential unionization rates; for instance, the unionization rate of Hispanic women is about the same as that of white women, which puts to rest the explanation that Hispanic families are more patriarchal than other American families and that these differences are reflected in a lower unionization rate for Hispanic women (Zavella 1988). Hispanic and Chinese CLUW members mentioned language barriers as a possible reason for their relative lack of representation and also noted that they and felt insufficiently integrated in the organization. As one Hispanic founding member who belonged to a textile workers union said,

> I don't feel that women who are in position are doing enough to reach to the sisters and bring them up. I don't think so. The blacks have made more progress in CLUW than the Hispanics, and blacks have been more pushing and more accepting this than the Hispanic women. And sometimes I feel that our women who are not so fluent in English cannot tolerate that because they [African American women] are rough and they are sometimes rude.

This statement, which can be perceived as racist, indicates that even in an organization that is devoted to diversity, tensions can result from cultural differences (see also Chapter 10). Some members thought not only that more Hispanic and Asian women should be involved but also that their specific needs should be addressed. One of the questionnaire respondents wrote,

> I strongly believe that CLUW should deal with more issues concerning the Hispanic women. Many of our Hispanic members need the help, information, and support from a group like CLUW. Some of the topics which should be offered: family planning, AIDS and the Hispanic family, housing.

Other Hispanic members, however, credited CLUW with educating the leaders of the unions with fewer minority members about the needs of minority workers. In the 1980s a Hispanic caucus was formed in the New York City chapter to better address the needs of Hispanic women. Later, a Chinese caucus was modeled after the Hispanic caucus. These caucuses allowed immigrant women to communicate in their language and pursue their cultural traditions. The caucuses organized fundraising and other social events and supported local labor and community events. The caucuses were well respected by the organization and their members and served as an example for the diversity of CLUW. The activities of the caucuses were covered in the national CLUW newsletter, furthermore the caucuses had booths at the national meetings and conventions to inform about their work. One of the Hispanic founding members pointed out that socializing and connecting to the culture of Hispanic women was a strategy to get this group involved in the labor movement and in the political process in general. She explained,

> In [the garment workers union] we have a lot of classes. We have workshops with children. Acting, performing, singing, we have knitting, embroidery, quilting making, things that they like to do and they are very active. . . . So we do that a lot because we always, every mother, every Hispanic mother, even the American likes to have a piñata party for the kids because it is fun. And they learn about the traditions of the Latin American.

Similarly, the merger between Chinese tradition and American feminism was exemplified by the symbol of the Chinese CLUW committee, which was developed by a Chinese artist and consisted of the Chinese symbols representing power and equality. The creation of the symbol stood both for continuity with respect to ethnic identity and for a transformation of this identity (Roth 2000). Thus, the caucuses allowed these members to develop union feminisms that encompassed rather than ignored their ethnic identity.

CLUW recognized early on that women of color "had more needs," and therefore the national-level minority committee was created. Thus, diversity was framed in terms of "needs" rather than contributions to the organization. The minority committee addressed issues of minorities or diversity at the workplace or in the union. In 1995, the minority committee and the affirmative action committee merged at a national executive board meeting due to the low overall attendance. I was told that the affirmative action committee was previously dominated by white women, while the minority committee had been dominated by African American women. This situation hints at the difficulties involved with creating an integrated organization if even committees that deal with race issues are segregated by race. However, this integration took place through the merger of the committees. More recently, a "mature workers" committee and a "young workers" committee were founded to address the concerns of the aging membership and to attract younger members.

Moving from the national to the local level, however, one finds that the chapters were less diverse and more homogeneous than the organization as a whole. In some chapters only white or only African American women participated, while in others the majority of the members belonged to one racial or ethnic group. Furthermore, in mixed chapters, the executive board seemed more homogeneous than the chapter.[3] The racial and ethnic composition of the chapters can be explained by the characteristics of the local work force, area, and labor movement.[4] However, personal networks also played a big role in the recruitment and maintenance of membership (Roth 2005). As a result, the chapters were often either predominantly white or African American. This separation was not intended by the organization—on the contrary, the organization strived for a diverse membership at all levels of the organization. However, the sum of unions, chapters, and caucuses made CLUW an inclusive organization, while the subentities were more homogenous. Though members felt that CLUW chapters could be more diverse and do more outreach to nonwhite communities, they also noted that the chapters were more inclusive than the regional labor movement or their unions, and that CLUW had a record for building bridges between the labor movement and communities of color.

Constructing Collective Identity across Sameness and Difference

Activists rarely participate in only one social movement and are often active on behalf of multiple causes, building bridges between social movements (Rose 2000; Roth 2003; Meyer and Whittier 1994; Meyer 2002; Whittier 2004). The union feminism of CLUW members encompassed multiple and interrelated systems of oppression. Because these activists are concerned with sexism, racism, and economic inequality, they seek to address all of these issues. As I have already noted, CLUW's membership is diverse and the organization builds bridges between various movements, in particular the women's movement and the labor movement but also the civil rights movement (Roth 2003). In the remainder of this chapter I offer an analysis of boundaries, consciousness, and negotiations in CLUW's identity work that shows what role the external environment (social movement field) and the internal environment (membership) play in the process of constructing and maintaining this collective identity. As I will demonstrate, CLUW's collective identity constructs members as "union women" or "union feminists," thereby reconciling class consciousness with feminist consciousness by fighting for the rights of working women. Members criticize the women's movement for overlooking economic issues and issues of social inequality and the labor movement with respect to overlooking women's issues. Furthermore, they demand from the women's movement and the labor movement that each addresses the needs of women of color and family issues. Their loyalty to the labor movement, which is expressed in their identity as "union women," allows them to criticize sexist companies and legislation; however, sexist practices within the labor movement are not openly expressed due to union solidarity. As a bridging organization CLUW forms coalitions with women's movement organizations and is involved in the labor movement. Thus, the union feminism of CLUW allows for negotiations among the members on issues of sameness as well as difference.

Boundaries

Boundaries distinguish members from nonmembers, contrasting "us" with "them." They indicate whom one owes (and from whom one can expect) loyalty and solidarity. The process of creating, maintaining, and opening boundaries—which describes who belongs and who does not—is therefore identity work. In the case of diverse constituencies, boundaries must allow for a wide variety of members while distinguishing them from other, non-members of the collective. This identity work of uniting and boundary setting is reflected in the name of the organization: Coalition of Labor Union Women. Coalitions often are based on the lowest common denominator, in this case union membership. While CLUW is diverse with respect to race, class, and gender, what unites the (regular) membership is that they are all union members. Union membership is therefore a basis for unity as well as a boundary for group membership. One of the founding members explained that she was a

> strong advocate of women's equality and women's rights, and I was a strong advocate of civil rights for our workers, strong voice for women, strong voice for the non-white community and I was a strong voice for coalition building of all these groups. . . . [B]ut it also was *through the union that we were able to unite* with other people, other workers, who had common concerns and common goals. (emphasis added)

She and other founding members were convinced that the labor movement was a civil rights movement that supports workers', women's and minority rights equally. The theme of the founding convention "We did not come here to swap recipes" expresses that these women unionists did not want to be seen as an auxiliary of the labor federation AFL-CIO. As loyal unionists they were disappointed that the unions did not live up to their ideals of organizing all workers regardless of gender or race. They demanded more involvement of women in the labor movement but were not interested in criticizing the male leadership for its sexism, at least not openly. Another founding member of CLUW, an African American woman and a leader in the civil rights movement as well as in the labor movement, stated,

> Our women felt they needed to get together. They felt [as long as they were working] separately in their unions, they were not able to make the strides they wanted to . . . it became a question of wouldn't it be smarter if women got together from all the unions to work out general programs. It became very much like the needs of the Blacks or the Hispanics to get together in their particular organizations. Like in the NAACP or the Urban League or the civil rights movement generally. (cf. Roth 2003, 114)

Another founding member of CLUW, also one of the first women in a union leadership position, recalled,

> Union women worked in different shops across the country, but we had nothing that brought us together. . . . We decided, you know we are talking about 1974, that there ought to be an organization where women can come together and discuss what concerns us as trade union women, to air out our grievances, to pool out resources, to be a voice for ourselves in our own unions. We were dedicated trade unionists and we certainly were concerned with building our unions, because we know that in spite of the conditions from which we worked within our unions we were still better off than non-union women. (cf Roth 2003, 28)

The decision to restrict the full membership to union members was (and continues to remain) contested during the founding of the organization. Because only a small proportion of women workers were organized, some argued that CLUW should allow membership of all working women. However, former CLUW president Joyce Miller characterized the membership question as "non-negotiable" in 1991. She explained, "It would change the whole nature of CLUW. Then you are like any other women's organizations, you are not different than any other group." Although later on a new membership category was introduced that allowed nonunion members to join the organizations, they could not fully participate in the decision-making processes and felt marginalized. One of the interviewees stated, "I would very much like to find a role for myself in CLUW, but without union membership feel tangential. Many other women are in my position and I'd like to see CLUW define itself as an organization for all working women, organized or not." However, the leadership insisted on admitting exclusively union women because they felt that this would be necessary in order to be taken seriously by the (male) leadership of the labor movement.

Besides signaling loyalty to the labor movement, being an organization of union women distinguished CLUW from other women's organizations that were founded at this time. The broader environment—notably, the presence of the labor movement and women's movement—thus played an important role in constructing union feminism. The union boundary created an integrated collective identity of this organization by uniting women across (at times competing) unions and distancing themselves from those parts of the women's movement that openly criticized the labor movement for being sexist. The union feminism of CLUW united blue-collar and pink-collar workers, as well as semiprofessionals and professionals, in different sectors of the labor market, whereas the women's movement pointed out the discriminatory effect of seniority rights, CLUW celebrated "women in nontraditional jobs" and supported pay equity.

Consciousness

As noted earlier, consciousness refers to the interpretative frameworks that activists, SMOs, and social movements employ in order to develop their goals and strategies. CLUW members were both prounion and profeminist. Some segments of the women's movement saw this as a contradiction, since at the time of CLUW's founding, the women's movement supported the Equal Rights Amendment while the labor movement initially did not. Some women in the labor movement were afraid that the ERA would undermine protective legislation. CLUW pointed out that equal rights could also be achieved by extending protective legislation to men and thus improving the working conditions of all workers. CLUW members themselves experienced sexism and discrimination in the labor movement but rather than criticizing the unions, they defended the ideal of unionism externally and tried to change it from within. They thus could reconcile feminist and union consciousness by creating union feminism.

CLUW members sought to integrate feminist, racial, ethnic, and class consciousness; they felt that CLUW's unionism was compatible with a range of personal identities. In addition to their belief that the labor movement would provide the best vehicle to achieve equality and fight against discrimination, they were active in a wide range of community, women's, civil rights, and other social movement organizations. Furthermore, due to differences in political socialization, members varied as to whether they stressed class, gender, or race as most important for their identity. Reflecting the overall segregation in the labor markets as well as cultural differences with respect to family life, the women of color differed somewhat from the white women in their occupational and family careers. Some went to college after they started to work and became active in the union. They were somewhat more reluctant to call themselves feminists and put a stronger emphasis on race and ethnicity than the white women. Women of color emphasized that minority women were often married and had children and felt alienated by the (white middle-class) women's movement. One Chinese American member found it problematic that the "white feminist movement" rejected marriage and family. "We didn't view women's rights as one, as being against all men, or rejecting the whole question of families and children. So we looked at issues like child care, you know, or health care and all those issues were very important. And I think at different stages the feminist movement in the U.S. tended to just kind of ignore that or that was not an essential thing to them." She applauded CLUW's approach of "pushing the family agenda into the labor movement" and making such issues the concerns of the entire labor movement. CLUW represented to her a version of feminism that took the needs of working mothers and immigrant women into account.

Similarly, one African American CLUW member stated that African American women still believed the women's movement was a white-middle-class movement and rarely would call themselves feminists.[5] She explained,

> I am not the norm of African American women. . . . I have a different perception of the women's movement, because I had dealings with the women's movement at [university]. And I was part of the women's movement. In 1978, as a matter of fact, I was here, marched for the ERA, dressed in white like everybody else was.

Yet, although she described herself as part of the women's movement and different in this regard from other African American women, she rejected the label feminist. She said,

> I am a trade unionist in my heart and a politician, but I am not a feminist. Like I said, a lot of things that the feminist community espoused, I do not necessarily agree with. And it puts me in a real awkward position because [they support] a lot of the causes and a lot of the things we fight for, as a coalition; but I don't consider myself as a feminist. . . . They are workers' issues for me, not feminist issues, but workers' issues.

While the feminist issue that she referred to concerned abortion rights, as I will discuss later in this chapter, her disagreement with the issue did not prevent her from supporting it. Instead, she reframed abortion rights as workers rights that need to be covered by the bargaining agreement. Given this interpretation, CLUW's union feminism addressed the needs of working women and their families. They fought for better working conditions as well as legislation addressing women's issues (for example, health care). Due to the wide range of different working and living conditions and worldviews, members at times differed with respect to the support of certain issues but supported the position that the organization took. However, these positions had to be negotiated.

Women of color did not necessarily identify participation of women in leadership positions as feminist. Regarding her participation in CLUW and Nine-to-Five,[6] another African American CLUW member remarked,

> And it's so funny, because I never thought of it as feminism in joining the Nine-to-Five or being a part of CLUW. I thought of it as women coming together for their rights. I never really put that label on. And I think there are among Southern black women a strong tradition of fighting and coming together for their rights, always having worked most of their lives.

The African American women thus saw themselves in a long tradition of strong women leaders who had little or nothing to do with the white feminist movement. The union feminism of CLUW offered them a space where they could merge their support for civil rights, worker's rights, and women's issues and develop a union women identity.

Finally, an examination of CLUW members' participation in other social movements helps illustrate their identity processes. CLUW members were involved in and supported the civil rights movement and belonged to organizations of and for African American union members like the A. Philip Randolph Institute (APRI, the AFL–CIO support group of African American Union members) and the Coalition of Black Trade Unionists (CBTU). However, the differences in feminist, racial, and ethnic identities between white women and women of color were reflected in their affiliation in various social movement organizations (see Table 9.1).

More African American than white, Latina, and Asian women belonged to the civil rights organizations NAACP, CBTU, and APRI, while more white (followed by Latina and Asian) than African American women belonged to the women's organization NOW. However, over 50 percent of the respondents surveyed indicated that they had been involved in the civil rights movement. Thirty percent of all CLUW members were members of NAACP, 14 percent were involved in CBTU, and 19 percent were involved in APRI (CLUW membership survey). In sum, multiple group membership is a crucial part of the identity work done by CLUW members.

Table 9.1. Membership in various social movement organizations by race (CLUW membership survey 1995)

(Female Respondents)	White	African American	Latina	Asian
NAACP (N = 131)	17%	72%	29%	20%*
CBTU (N = 51)	2%	41%	11%	—
APRI (N = 76)	13%	33%	19%	20%
NOW (N = 423)	41%	15%	33%	20%

Source: CLUW Membership Survey. *N = 1

Negotiations

Negotiation refers to the process by which social movements work to change social meanings, either in private or public settings (Taylor and Whittier 1992, 118). Within CLUW, members negotiated how a union and a feminist agenda that pays particular attention to the needs of women of color could be reconciled, for example, with respect to issues like support of the Equal Rights Amendment, pay equity, and reproductive rights. Once CLUW members agreed on a position, they engaged in explicit negotiations in public settings, such as union conventions or rallies of the women's movement, where they framed women's rights as workers rights or worker's rights as women's rights, thus broadening the agenda of both movements.

Because the union feminism of CLUW brought together activists who were concerned with integrating minority and gender perspectives into the labor agenda and class and race into the women's movement, they needed to negotiate how to reconcile these various agendas. This included reevaluating and reframing issues in an effort to achieve consistency with their notion of union feminism. The support of the ERA, reproductive rights, and pay equity provide examples for negotiations among CLUW's diverse membership. In each case mainstream feminist and union ideologies were at odds and women of color differed from white women in their support for issues. Thus, CLUW members had to negotiate *what CLUW stands for*, representing women and their interests in the labor movement.

An example from CLUW's history illustrates the conflicts between feminist and race consciousness in the organization. In the 1980s, CLUW and the National Women's Political Caucus called for a boycott of a NAACP convention in one of the states that had not endorsed the ERA. As a feminist organization, CLUW supported the ERA. However, since many CLUW members (in particular, African Americans) belonged to the NAACP, this boycott was problematic for the organization. CLUW's decision to endorse the boycott forced NAACP members to choose between their support for feminism and civil rights. Some African American members were critical of forcing members to make such a choice. They argued that through such a boycott CLUW would risk losing support for the ERA from the NAACP as well as lose CLUW members and union members belonging to the NAACP. Furthermore, because the nonratified states were also states with weak labor movements, the CLUW's boycott deprived workers of a valuable exchange between unionists and feminists in areas where it was most needed. However, other African American CLUW members supported putting pressure on the NAACP. In this case, CLUW's collective identity as a feminist organization was emphasized.

Reproductive rights presented another potentially contentious issue in the organization. CLUW endorsed a prochoice position, challenged fetal protection policies, and fought against forced sterilization. African American women who personally were against abortion nevertheless represented CLUW in coalitions of organizations of the women's, civil rights, and labor movements and supported a prochoice position. CLUW members who were involved in political campaigns sometimes were confronted with the choice between a prochoice and a prolabor candidate. One white CLUW member recalled how she switched her vote for a prochoice candidate although as a labor delegate to the Democratic convention she was expected to vote for the prolabor candidate:

> And I sat there and I held my vote with this, and I was in tears, I was sitting there and I was absolutely in tears, because I kept being pressured by both sides, you know, and I stayed there, I hung with, and she was gaining votes, he was gradually losing votes. So finally, when I came around, I was told, it got to 14 ballots I was switching my vote, which I did. But it was one of the hardest things, I think I have ever done through this all night session balloting. (cf. Roth 2003, 136)

In this case, a prochoice position and a labor position could not be reconciled and the CLUW members suffered significantly by being forced to prioritize one of her two commitments. This quote also illustrates the emotional difficulties associated with identity work (see also Chapter 5).

Another contested issue involved a resolution to request CLUW members "to urge their unions and labor councils not to endorse any candidate who does not support pay equity legislation." After a heated debate, this resolution was toned down; the new version made the support of pay equity an important but not decisive criterion for the endorsement of candidates. However, not everybody agreed with this decision. One delegate who was against the amendment stated, "I think it violates everything that CLUW was founded on. It's like being a little bit pregnant."

These examples show that union feminism did not prevent CLUW members from feeling torn between their loyalties to the labor movement, the civil rights movement, and the women's movement. These activists feel loyal to the labor movement but also demand that the interests of women and minorities are included in the labor agenda. Since the support for feminist, union, and civil rights issues are at times at odds with each other, members need to negotiate whether gender, labor, or race consciousness are emphasized and which are downplayed. Based on this outcome the organization then positions itself publicly.

Conclusions

The Coalition of Labor Union Women engaged in constructing an inclusive collective identity that provided a space for a diverse membership and is a good example of the fact that activists belong to multiple movements. The organization brought together women and men from all racial and ethnic groups as well as a wide range of unions and occupational backgrounds who sought to increase women's participation in the labor movement. CLUW "dealt" with diversity by forming coalitions with other movements and movement organizations; it also represented a coalition itself with a number of caucuses (union caucuses, Chinese and Hispanic caucus) and committees (affirmative action, minority issues, mature women, young women). The diversity of the membership was thus addressed in the organizational structure.

The collective identity of union feminism allowed members to reconcile feminist and labor identities while emphasizing race, class, and feminist consciousness depending on their personal background as well as on the situation. Compared to other organizations of the women's movement, CLUW was exceptional because of the high proportion of women of color, reflecting the higher unionization rate of African American women compared to white, Hispanic, and Asian women. In addition, from the beginning the leadership emphasized that the officers must represent women from different backgrounds.

CLUW's union feminism merges feminist, class, and race consciousness. However, sometimes there are conflicts between feminism and a labor agenda. Since CLUW is loyal to both labor and feminism, it seeks to influence the labor movement to take up a profeminist position. These efforts are ongoing; while the labor movement eventually supported the ERA, some unions are prochoice while others are not. CLUW's continual negotiation of union feminism—internally as well as externally—exemplifies that the identity work involved in the construction of collective identity is a constant and evolving process.

References

Bernstein, Mary. 1997. "Celebration and Suppression: The Strategic Uses of Identity by the Lesbian and Gay Movement." *American Journal of Sociology* 103: 531–65.

Bookman, Ann, and Sandra Morgen, ed. 1988. *Women and the Politics of Empowerment*. Philadelphia: Temple University Press.

Bystydzienski, Jill M., and Steven P. Schacht. 2001. "Introduction." In *Forging Radical Alliances across Difference: Coalition Politics for the New Millennium*, ed. J. M. Bystydzienski and S. P. Schacht, 1–17. London: Rowman and Littlefield.

Clemens, Elisabeth S. 1996. "Organizational Form as Frame: Collective Identity and Political Strategy in the American Labor Movement, 1880–1920." In *Comparative Perspectives on Social Movements*, ed. D. McAdam, J. D. McCarthy, and M. N. Zald, 205–26. Cambridge: Cambridge University Press.

Einwohner, Rachel L. 1999. "Gender, Class, and Social Movement Outcomes: Identity and Effectiveness in Two Animal Rights Campaigns." *Gender & Society* 13: 56–76.

Fantasia, Rick. 1988. *Cultures of Solidarity*. Berkeley: University of California Press.

Ferree, Myra Marx, and Beth B. Hess. 2000. *Controversy and Coalition. The New Feminist Movement Across Four Decades of Change*. 3rd ed. New York: Routledge.

Gamson, Joshua. 1996. "The Organizational Shaping of Collective Identity: The Case of Lesbian and Gay Film Festivals in New York." *Sociological Forum* 11: 231–61.

———. 1995. "Must Identity Movements Self-Destruct? A Queer Dilemma." *Social Problems* 42: 390–407.

Kornbluh, Joyce L., and Mary Frederickson, ed. 1984. *Sisterhood and Solidarity: Workers' Education for Women, 1914–1984*. Philadelphia: Temple University Press.

Leidner, Robin. 1993. "Constituency, Accountability, and Deliberation: Reshaping Democracy in the National Women's Studies Association." *NWSA Journal* 5: 4–27.

———. 2001. "On Whose Behalf? Feminist Ideology and Dilemmas of Constituency," In *Identity Politics in the Women's Movement*, ed. B. Ryan, 47–56. New York: New York University Press.

McAdam, Doug. 1994. "Culture and Social Movements." In *New Social Movements: From Ideology to Identity*, ed. E. Laraña, H. Johnston, and J. R. Gusfield, 36–57. Philadelphia: Temple University Press.

Meyer, David S. 2002. "Opportunities and Identities: Bridge-Building in the Study of Social Movements." In *Social Movements: Identity, Culture and the State*, ed. D. S. Meyer, N. Whittier, and B. Robnett, 3–21. New York: Oxford University Press.

Meyer, David, and Nancy Whittier. 1994. "Social Movement Spillover." *Social Problems* 41(2): 277–98.

Miethe, Ingrid. 2000. "Changes in Spaces of Political Activism: Transforming East Germany." In *Biographies and the Division of Europe*, ed. R. Breckner, D. Kalekin-Fishmann, and I. Miethe, 315–34. Opladen: Leske and Budrich.

Milkman, Ruth. 2000. "Introduction." In *Organizing Immigrants: The Challenge for Unions in Contemporary California*, ed. R. Milkman, 1–24. Ithaca, N.Y.: ILR.

Naples, Nancy A., ed. 1998. *Community Activism and Feminist Politics: Organizing Across Race, Class, and Gender*. New York: Routledge.

Polletta, Francesca, and James Jasper. 2001. "Collective Identity and Social Movements." *Annual Review of Sociology* 27: 283–305.

Reger, Jo. 2002a. "Organizational Dynamics and the Construction of Multiple Feminist Identities in the National Organization for Women." *Gender & Society* 16: 710–27.

———. 2002b. "More than One Feminism: Organizational Structure, Ideology and the Construction of Collective Identity." In *Social Movements: Identity, Culture and the State*, ed. D. S. Meyer, N. Whittier, and B. Robnett, 171–84. New York: Oxford University Press.

Robnett, Belinda. 1997. *How Long? How Long? African American Women in the Struggle for Civil Rights*. Oxford: Oxford University Press.

Rose, Fred. 2000. *Coalitions across the Class Divide: Lessons from the Labor, Peace, and Environmental Movements*. Ithaca, N.Y.: Cornell University Press.

Roth, Benita. 2004. *Race, Ethnicity and the Women's Movement in America: The Separate Roads of Black, Chicana, and White Feminism*. Cambridge, Mass.: Cambridge University Press.

Roth, Silke. 2000. "Developing Working Class Feminism: A Biographical Approach to Social Movement Participation." In *Self, Identity and Social Movements*, ed. S. Stryker, T. Owens, and R. W. White, 300–323. Minneapolis: University of Minnesota Press.

———. 2003. *Building Movement Bridges: The Coalition of Labor Union Women*. Westport, Conn.: Praeger.

———. 2005. "Sisterhood and Exclusionary Solidarity in a Labor Women's Organization." In *Emotions and Social Movements*, ed. H. Flam and D. King, 189–206. New York: Routledge.

Ryan, Barbara, ed. 2001. *Identity Politics in the Women's Movement*. New York: New York University Press.

Snow, David A., and Doug McAdam. 2000. "Identity Work Processes in the Context of Social Movements: Clarifying the Identity/Movement Nexus." In *Self, Identity, and Social Movements*, ed. S. Stryker, T. J. Owens, and R. W. White, 41–67. Minneapolis: University of Minnesota Press.

Taylor, Verta, and Nancy Whittier. 1992. "Collective Identity in Social Movement Communities: Lesbian Feminist Mobilization." In *Frontiers in Social Movement Theory*, ed. A. D. Morris and C. McClurg Mueller, 104–29. New Haven, Conn.: Yale University Press.

Whittier, Nancy. 2004. "The Consequences of Social Movements for Each Other." In *The Blackwell Companion to Social Movements*, ed. D. A. Snow, S. A. Soule, and H. Kriesi, 531–51. Oxford: Blackwell.

Zavella, Patricia. 1988. "The Politics of Race and Gender: Organizing Chicana Cannery Workers in Northern California." In *Women and the Politics of Empowerment*, ed. A. Bookman and S. Morgen, 202–24. Philadelphia: Temple University Press.

Notes

1. This chapter draws on material published in Roth 2000, 2003, and 2005 as indicated. I gratefully acknowledge helpful and encouraging comments of the editors, in particular Jo Reger and Rachel Einwohner.

2. If not otherwise indicated, when I refer to these interviews, I use pseudonyms.

3. This description is based on participant observation, interviews with chapter presidents at NEB meetings, and ten chapter questionnaires. Only five of the ten questionnaires provided information about the racial and ethnic composition of the chapter. The organization does not collect data about the racial and ethnic composition of the chapters.

4. The high proportion of women of color in CLUW reflects the high unionization rate of women of color, especially African American women. In 2001, their unionization rate (15 percent) was higher than those of white, Hispanic, and Asian (11 percent) women and as high as that of white men (15 percent) (Bureau of the Census 2001). Unionization rates also reflected the racial segregation of the labor market. A higher proportion of members of unions that organize professional women (teachers, office workers) were white (CLUW membership survey). Unions organizing women in the service sector and female-dominated sectors of the labor market (communications sector, textile industry) had a high proportion of white, Hispanic, and Asian American women. The participation of African American women was especially high in the public sector and in industrial unions (for example autoworkers). At national meetings and conventions, the public sector was usually represented by a large number of African American members. The autoworkers union and the postal workers union also had many African American members. Hispanic and Asian

CLUW members tended to be members of the textile and garment workers and the food and commercial workers unions.

5. White and Hispanic respondents were significantly more likely to belong to NOW than were African American and Asian American respondents (CLUW membership survey).

10

Diversity Discourse and Multi-identity Work in Lesbian and Gay Organizations

Jane Ward

Feminist intersectional theory focuses on the way the multiplicative nature of structural inequalities affects both individual and group knowledge and identities (Baca Zinn and Dill 1996; Collins 1996; Lugones 1990). Because feminist intersectional theory developed largely in response to sexism in the civil rights movement and racism in the feminist movement, a critique of "single-identity" social movements was also central to its approach (Combahee Collective 1983; hooks 1981; King 1988; Robnett 1996). Feminist intersectional theory argues that single-identity movements are inevitably ineffective because they exclude constituents and support what Patricia Hill Collins (1998) refers to as the "matrix of domination" by addressing only one form of inequality and then failing to recognize the complex mechanisms that produce and maintain it (Kurtz 2002).

A growing body of social movement research grounds feminist intersectional theory by examining *how* social movements engage in multi-identity work. Some scholars emphasize the ways in which activists engage their targets from a multi-issue perspective, or work to address the multiple and simultaneous injustices people experience at the hands of dominant institutions (Kurtz 2002). Other approaches examine how multi-identity politics play out inside movements, including the way activists build oppositional consciousness around multiple inequalities. For example, Brett Stockdill (2001) explores the strategies that AIDS activists use to link one form of oppositional consciousness to another, such as using racial oppositional consciousness within communities of color to promote pro-lesbian and gay oppositional consciousness.

Such research reflects a crucial step toward understanding intersectionality at the macro and micro levels, and this chapter builds upon this body of work by addressing organizational processes. Social movement organizations often serve as activists' primary point of contact with movements, and become mediators of collective identity at the micro level and of sociopolitical trends at the macro level (Ferree and Martin 1995; Poster 1995; Reger 2002; Staggenborg 2002). Organizational form, including recruitment strategies and leadership choices, expresses the collective identity of a movement to prospective and actual movement participants (Roth 2000). As movements institutionalize, social movement organizations become an important site of identity work that provides participants with tools to develop congruence between personal and collective identities (Snow and McAdam 2000). Because personal identities are complex and multiple, effective social movements also create congruence between participants' most salient identities, including those that may appear to be in conflict (Snow and McAdam 2000). Lesbian and gay organizations, for example, are often engaged in teaching movement participants that gay identity is congruent with individuals' other salient identities, including racial, religious, and gender identities. Yet building an intersectional *collective* identity is another matter, one that requires individuals to see themselves as part of a group that includes identities that are *not* personally salient and may not be part of one's personal identity at all. Organizations do this by engaging participants in "multi-identity work," such as diversity trainings and other programs designed to build multiple oppositional consciousness, as well as a multiple and complex collective identity.

While other studies demonstrate how organizational discourses and practices successfully build and sustain collective identity (Reger 2002, Staggenborg 2002), this chapter examines the failed efforts of two lesbian and gay organizations to build and sustain an intersectional collective identity. I identify two developments affecting multi-identity work in lesbian and gay organizations: the influx of corporate diversity management models and the increasing prevalence of funding-driven approaches to diversity and representation. I find that resulting forms of multi-identity work reinforce structural inequalities, leaving intact a white collective identity in one organization and a male collective identity in the other.

Data for this study are drawn from two case studies of lesbian and gay organizations in Los Angeles: the L. A. Gay & Lesbian Center, a large lesbian and gay community resource center, and Bienestar, an HIV/AIDS organization founded by Latina lesbians and Latino gay men. These organizations were chosen to represent different lesbian and gay projects and for their ability to represent similar organizations in other large, urban cities where community resource centers and HIV/AIDS organizations are common. From January 2000 to September 2002, I conducted twenty-five open-ended, tape-recorded, and transcribed interviews (one to two hours in length) and hundreds of hours of participant observation in the two organizations. In one organization I was a paid employee (the Center); in the other, I took on a more conventional participant observer role (Bienestar). I also analyzed organizational documents and relevant media. All research participants' names are pseudonyms. I used a "grounded theory" approach to analyze the data I collected, allowing my hypotheses to surface and transform throughout the research process (Glaser and Strauss 1967).

By examining these case studies, I contribute to this volume's theme of identity work by drawing our attention to the ways in which collective identities are linked to organizational structures and dynamics. Specifically, I show how members of diverse movement organizations face challenges in the construction of an intersectional collective identity, challenges that stem from each organization's history, goals, and support from mainstream institutions.

Diversity in the Lesbian and Gay Movement

Lesbian and gay movement scholars have described the LGBT movement as the "quintessential identity movement," distinguished from other movements by its emphasis on the diversity of gay identities as well as its focus on deconstructing identity categories altogether (Armstrong 2002; Gamson 1995). This emphasis on diversity is reinforced by the movement's strategic use of symbols that invoke the politics of sexual identity while promoting the values of inclusion, unity, and the celebration of differences more broadly. Rainbow flags, "Celebrate Diversity!" T-shirts, and "We Are Family" bumper stickers represent lesbian and gay pride for people "in the know," as well as the politics of racial inclusion and even Black popular culture.[1] Recent scholarship suggests that the movement's ideological commitment to multiple lesbian and gay identities allows for the proliferation of special interest projects and organizations, while maintaining a strong collective identity and mobilized constituency (Armstrong 2002, D'Emilio 2000). However, the rhetorical focus on diversity in the lesbian and gay movement also makes it difficult for excluded groups to identify and challenge inequality at the movement level and remains predicated on the enduring notion that at least some aspect of the gay experience is universal (Armstrong 2002; Takagi 1996; Vaid 1995). According to Keith Boykin, past executive director of the National Black Gay and Lesbian Leadership Forum:

The words "diversity" and "inclusion" have been so overused in the language of lesbian and gay politics that one might expect the "queer community" to shine as an exemplar in multicultural representation, effortlessly integrating communities of color and their causes and concerns into the larger liberation struggle. Unfortunately, the politically correct rhetoric differs greatly from the politically incorrect reality. In reality, Black lesbians and gays play no meaningful role in the lesbian and gay political movement. (2000, 79).

Most scholars and activists agree that the lesbian and gay movement is divided by differences and inequalities within it, however disagreements remain with respect to whether the movement is primarily a successful model of a diverse and unified identity movement or an example of a movement characterized by fragmentation, exclusion, and undermobilization (Armstrong 2002; Boykin 2000; D'Emilio 2000; Vaid 1995).

Research on diversity in the lesbian and gay movement has focused on the movement's "unique" characteristics and development. However, to identify the particular evolution of diversity ideas and symbols in lesbian and gay politics, we must also examine how diversity ideas, and the practices that accompany them, are part of broader cultural and institutional phenomena. Just as organizational practices influence collective identity construction, organizational form is also influenced by political opportunity structures, including political climate and ideas available in the external environment (Roth 2000). Therefore, this chapter's larger aim is to examine the way ideas about diversity in the external environment are manifested in organizational practice and the effects of diversity practices on collective identity.

The emphasis on building unity through the celebration of difference is not unique to the lesbian and gay movement, but is a central theme within U.S. political and corporate discourse and practice. According to critical race scholars, celebrating diversity or multiculturalism is a particular approach to multi-identity work that encourages the development of antioppression values without changing the accountability structures that produce oppressive outcomes (Bonilla Silva 2003; Collins 2004; Gordon 1995). The diversity management approach reinforces sameness by embracing the differences in all people and rejects racism and other forms of oppression while rewarding the systems that produce unequal outcomes, such as managerial hierarchy, competition, and meritocracy (Gordon 1995). It is also an approach that has found its way into lesbian and gay organizations and is often transported by movement leaders who are now increasingly recruited from the corporate sector and valued for their experience with diversity management (Vaid

1995). I now turn to the ways in which diversity discourses were utilized in both of the organizations.

Diversity Management and the Reproduction of Whiteness: The L. A. Gay and Lesbian Center

Social movement scholars use the term "institutionalization" to refer to a range of movement processes and outcomes, including bureaucratization and ideological "mainstreaming"or co-optation (Armstrong 2004). The corporatization of social movements is an example of both processes. I use the term "corporatization" to refer to the influx of corporate funding, logics, practices, and leaders into social movement organizations. Targeted marketing by "diversity savvy" corporations results in a new level of financial interdependence between social movement organizations and private funders, and leaders of large social movement organizations are often recruited from the private sector to ensure their sufficient experience in human resources and diversity management, technological innovation, and ability to spearhead financial growth (Vaid 1995). In this section, I examine the relationship between these meso-level dynamics and the construction and maintenance of a white collective identity in the L. A. Gay and Lesbian Center.

Gay and lesbian community centers are a common feature of large and midsize cities throughout the world. According to its 2001 Annual Report, the L. A. Gay and Lesbian Center (the Center) was the largest lesbian and gay social service organization in the world, with an annual budget of $33 million, five locations and 250 staff members. Situated in the heart of Hollywood, the Center's programs include a homeless youth shelter, primary care, mental health services, a same-gender domestic violence program, an immigration law clinic, HIV services, and employment assistance. While frontline staff work with some of Los Angeles' most underserved populations (e.g., homeless queer youth), the grassroots nature of these programs stands in sharp contrast with the corporate look and feel of the Center's "executive management team," top-floor boardroom, and administrative offices. Due to its size, the Center has followed the model of national lesbian and gay organizations (such as Human Rights Campaign [HRC] and Gay and Lesbian Alliance against Defamation [GLAAD]) with respect to recruitment and organizational culture. Similar to these organizations, the Center recruits directly from gay-friendly corporations for executive-level managers who are valued, in large part, for their experience with diversity management.

Also similar to other lesbian and gay organizations, the Center's recent history is characterized by attention to the project of increasing "diversity," that is, increasing the number of people of color on the management team and board and improving the organization's public image in communities of color. While the Center now maintains a majority of people of color on staff (57 percent in 1998, 52 percent in 2001), employees of color occupy the lowest paid positions at the Center and its reputation as a "white organization" persists. Beverly, a Black lesbian employee at the Center, says,

> I've always had a job in corporate white America. So I've always had to learn how to leave my Blackness at home and come to work. When I came to the Center, it was no different. It was predominantly a white run organization, the same as corporate. They fought harder for the civil rights of gays and lesbians, but not for people of color. So it is just the same as if I was in a corporate job, but this is the way that it has been all my life, so I am pretty much accustomed to it.

In response to perceptions about the white identity of the organization, the Center's white executive managers frequently express their commitment to racial diversity, and the organization's annual "Diversity Day" is one manifestation of this commitment. Diversity Day was instituted in the early 1990s and has generally taken the form of a day of workshops designed to encourage employees to talk about racial and cultural differences. Robin, one of Center's white executive managers, explains the purpose of Diversity Day:

> The reason that they started Diversity Day is because . . . when you have a diverse workforce that reflects your clients, you are better able to serve your clients. And coming from the corporate environment, that is the feeling there. . . . You could have all the reasons to do good that you want, and in reality, you have a better product, you provide a better service, if you better understand your customer. So I think one of the reasons we started Diversity Day, was so that we can really look . . . at some of the ways that we are all alike and some of the ways that we may be different. Only through attempting to do that can you better your communications and your ability to work together towards your goal.

Robin's discussion of the motivations behind Diversity Day reflects three themes central to the corporate diversity management approach. First, diversity results in better service to clients and is contingent upon the demographics of clients. A diverse workforce is necessary when an organization's client pool is similarly diverse. Second, serving the interests of the organization is the bottom line, the most legitimate justification for wanting diversity, and more important than other "reasons to do good." Third, diversity is as much, if not more, about the ways that people are the same than it is about the ways that people are different. According to Robin, Diversity Day allows Center employees to simultaneously witness the ways they are both different and the same, and this experience unifies employees in ways that strengthen their ability to work together.

While Robin suggests that Diversity Day is designed to improve service to clients and increase communication among a diverse staff, the staff response to Diversity Day suggested an opposite effect. At a Center staff meeting I attended in 2001, several employees groaned when the date for the 2001 Diversity Day was announced. Acknowledging this, the Center's executive director added at the staff meeting that Diversity Day would be improved this year and that employee feedback from advance surveys would be used to determine the format of the event. A slide show intended to encourage enthusiasm about the improved event also implied a collective understanding that Diversity Day was an undesirable obligation by self-mockingly including phrases like "Not another Diversity Day!" and by announcing that the event had been renamed "We Can All be Heroes Day." The concept of "hero" had just taken on a new currency after September 11, 2001, and the Center's executive director punctuated the relationship between diversity and the heroes of the 9/11 attacks by asking all of the employees at the meeting to join her in singing "This Land is Your Land, This Land is My Land."

Given a high rate of employee turnover at the Center, the internal discourse on Diversity Day is informed by the perceptions of longer-term employees, generally overrepresented at the management level. The discursive culture of the Center, what many employees refer to as rumors about previous Diversity Days that "went wrong," also functioned to constrain the enthusiasm of new social change minded employees by consistently representing Diversity Day as an ineffectual obligation that distracts from one's work but must nonetheless be carried out as a matter of tradition and political correctness (as demonstrated at the staff meeting). According to Robin, Diversity Day was not developed in response to racial conflict at the Center but as a result of the management philosophy, based on private sector experience, that a diversity event would improve service delivery. Yet when asked about how the Center addresses race and racism, managers referred to the event as an important opportunity for staff to confront these issues. Indeed, Diversity Day has traditionally been the only formal opportunity to discuss race and racism at the Center, an "opportunity" that employees perceive as obligatory, ineffective, and distracting.

Part of the culture of the Center was the presumption of a shared understanding that employees did not want to talk about race. My interviews suggested that this was, in fact, the case. White employees generally complained that the event was boring, did not lead to organizational change, or was poorly organized. Beth, a white lesbian employee, describes Diversity Day as "kind of painful." She explains,

> You can spend a lot of time investing in this day and sharing from your heart about how you feel, and then there is this sense that you don't know the before or after. Is it going to lead to anything? . . . At the same time, I don't object to having measurements, or the Diversity Day, as long as . . . it is not the be all, end all. This is just one little thing.

In contrast, employees of color questioned the value of having a Diversity Day at all. According to Beverly, a Black lesbian employee, the very notion of training in diversity was designed for white employees and not useful for people of color:

> I don't even know what the purpose of [Diversity Day] is. . . . Why do you need people of color there? They've had to learn how to live and struggle in the white community, so it just doesn't make any sense. I sit there and it's just a joke. The first one I went to, they had this guy come up and part of his talk was about Blacks and Latinos. And he said "usually if you see a Black person in a meeting with their eyes closed, they're listening, but they just like to listen with their eyes closed." And I thought, well all be damned, here I am, if my eyes are closed, I'm asleep!

Beverly points out that another common feature of diversity training is its emphasis on teaching whites how to better understand the behaviors of people of color. This approach reinforces that the standard for employees is a white standard, and that diversity refers to its contrast: people of color. Diversity Day is therefore an opportunity for whites to make sense of the previously incomprehensible behaviors of people of color, such as listening with one's eyes closed. Diversity management takes as given that the behaviors of people of color may appear strange, rude, or crazy to even the most reasonable white person. The logic of diversity management suggests that translating these behaviors into codes that whites can understand will reduce racial tension, increase unity, and promote a sense of sameness that allows employees to work together more efficiently. From the perspective of some employees of color, such as Beverly, Diversity Day provides them with information of little value and *increases* racial tension by requiring people of color to look on while whites are provided with inaccurate generalizations about coworkers of color.

In addition to maintaining an annual Diversity Day, the Center's executive team developed a five-year strategic plan that named "commitment to diversity" as a central focus. The "commitment to diversity" goal in the strategic plan read as follows:

> At the L.A. Gay & Lesbian Center . . . we represent a range of racial and ethnic groups and embrace the importance of a diverse workforce to the services we provide. Because we value the benefits of racial and ethnic diversity at every level of the organization—including senior management and the board—we want to increase our recruitment and retention efforts. Our commitment requires the cultivation of long-term relationships with people of color community leaders and opinion makers who will work with us to improve our outreach in communities of color. . . . We also will increase our involvement with people of color organizations and colleague organizations that provide services to people of color, and to speak out on policy and political issues of concern to communities of color. In the end, we hope that every community within our community will feel reflected and be represented in all aspects of the Gay & Lesbian Center, and that we will have expanded our collaborations with communities of color.

After developing the "commitment to diversity" goal, senior managers selected employees to sit on implementation teams and provide feedback during the strategic planning process. According to the stated "commitment to diversity" goal, the Center's diversity efforts were to be focused on increasing the number of people of color on the staff and board and improving relations with people of color organizations.

Employees who sat on the implementation team ultimately questioned the very terms of the diversity goal as it had been developed and articulated by the Center's managers. They challenged the "us–them" dichotomy implicit in the suggestion that the Center should improve relations with people of color organizations, arguing that the Center itself *is* a people of color organization. While the strategic plan focused on prospective employees of color and relations with people working in other organizations, the implementation team argued that a real commitment to diversity would have started with giving more power to current employees of color. Leticia, a Black lesbian employee, points to the contradiction between what is said and what is done at the Center, calling for its leaders to stop talking and "do it":

> What we need to do as an agency is . . . either say that we . . . support people of color and put them in power and do it, or . . . don't do it, and stand behind what we say. They wimp out and say shit that makes them look stupid, like there wasn't anybody qualified, which we know is not true.

The implementation team took issue with the strategic goal to "increase involvement with people of color organizations," not only because this external focus distracted from racial inequality within the organization, but also because it accepted and reinforced the Center's reputation as a white organization. According to Ben, a Black gay employee,

> At the Center, we [refer to] their community, the African American community, the Latino community, or the Asian community. What does it make us? Who are we? Are we all of those things? Evidently not, because it's an us and a they. And until the us and the they become we, we'll be stuck having the same conversation thirty years from now. Either you are going to change, or you're not. If you're not going to change, then stop talking about it and go about your business.

Ben's comments reflect the consensus on the implementation team that the strategic plan's language reinforced an us–them dichotomy that marginalized the Center's employees of color, thereby maintaining the Center's identity as a white organization. According to Sabrina, a Latina lesbian senior manager,

> I have some real, not good thoughts about the whole strategic plan anyway. The [diversity] portion of it I think is a continuation of lip service . . . to try to make us look more liberal than we are. Organizations of color, why don't they come here? Because this is known as a white organization. . . . We are known as takers, not as givers. We don't participate in other organizations, although we send invitations for them to come to our events and we wonder, why don't they come? And so there's no motivation for persons of color or other cultures to come here.

Like Sabrina, many employees of color sensed that the strategic plan was motivated by a desire to improve the organization's reputation in the eyes of organizations of color without changing its structural relationship to them.

Being asked to strategize about how best to increase the number of people of color in management and on the board also necessitated that the implementation team examine the Center's racialized recruitment and hiring practices. White employees interviewed for this study, regardless of their particular political bent, generally agreed that diversity-based hiring efforts at the Center had been poorly executed. As in most predominantly white workplaces in which affirmative action efforts have been instituted, the question of whether "unqualified" people of color were being hired at the Center in a rush to diversify the staff was a matter of particularly contentious debate.

Sam, a white gay male director, employs the "reverse racism" argument to explain that race-based hiring has had a negative impact on the Center:

> We have hired people of color to be people of color and they tend to be really not qualified. Then because they are the only people of color around, we're stuck with them. I am a strong advocate of affirmative action, but to hire for color is wrong. It's racist, with like wom[e]n of color, they've all stayed way too long. They do damage to the programs. We tend to run with a pretty white board, and white directors, and when you do get the people of color in there, they could shoot somebody in the parking lot and they wouldn't be let go. I think the Center does not do a good job in . . . saying "we need to find the right woman for the job." If it needs to be a woman of color, that's an important thing, but I think they make rash hires sometimes.

Using racist generalizations (i.e., "all women of color stay too long") and racist imagery (i.e., a parking lot shooting) that most white employees at the Center would find inappropriate, or would be unlikely to state so freely, Sam nonetheless expresses a common sentiment among white employees, namely that the Center has made rushed hiring decisions in its effort to diversify.

The suggestion that hiring had been "too rushed," reminiscent of white responses to desegregation efforts more broadly, prompted employees of color to articulate the importance of a "just do it" approach. According to Beverly, "counting" employees and engaging in a strategic planning process to achieve diversity are outdated measures designed by whites to convince other whites that diversity is valuable:

> It's kind of hard to fight for change in an organization that does a strategic plan to figure out how to diversify or whether they need to. That's kind of the Stone Age times. A strategic plan scares me, because that means they're looking at numbers. It's not something that the organization believes needs to happen because it just needs to happen. You get tired of trying to fight for something that you know is right with people who are trying to convince themselves through their numbers and their strategic plans. You just get tired of trying to prove why you should be at the table, why you exist, why you're here. [The alternative is] you just go do it. . . . You just start doing it.

Beverly, and other employees who spoke out at the implementation team meetings (primarily employees of color, although some whites as well), perceived the diversity goal of the strategic plan as a form of statistical or "scientific" justification for hiring people of color and a distraction from the organization's current multicultural reality. Some employees of color also expressed that the diversity initiative was an example of the kind of self-fulfilling prophecy that helps maintain the Center's white identity. Marcelino, a multiracial gay male employee, explains that as employees of color experience burn-out after investing in failed diversity projects, they leave the organization:

> Rather than being an activity to try to get by in, [the diversity initiative] really turned me off. . . . The reception [to our feedback] was like, "no way." I was on seven subcommittees, and I think they put me on a lot of these because I would bring the diversity component. . . . I do get sad because when . . . you are part of this wonderful process and everybody contributes and it doesn't amount to anything, why do you want to be part of it next time around? . . . We are not going to be able to keep people of color here.

While projects such as the diversity initiative deflected attention away from the Center's current employees of color, it also simultaneously produced the "evidence" that such projects were needed by leading to a high turnover of employees of color.

The case of the Center demonstrates that instituting programs designed to increase and celebrate diversity not only may be ineffective but also may reinforce structural inequalities in the lesbian and gay movement. Rather than challenge inequality, diversity projects at the Center repeatedly reinforced the white collective identity of the organization by framing racial identity work as an obligatory distraction from gay identity work, locating race and people of color outside of the organization and institutionalizing a "statistical" approach to diversity that stood in contrast with the "just do it" approach articulated by employees of color. Diversity Day highlighted the importance of good cross-cultural etiquette, or "diversity," in the lesbian and gay movement while simultaneously reinforcing a white standard for employees and the centrality of whiteness in organizational discourse. It is not only the content of Diversity Day that reproduced whiteness in the organization but also the discourse about the event that presumed a shared understanding that talking about race is a distasteful and obligatory distraction from the "real" (i.e., gay) work of the organization. Similarly, the Center's diversity initiative naturalized whiteness by making invisible the presence of current employees of color and locating racial diversity outside of the organization. This reflects a larger problem at the Center, namely that a strong sense of organizational belonging is fostered among white employees and not by employees of color. Lastly, the statistical approach to social justice is also a seemingly race-neutral mode of operation that reinforces the centrality of whiteness. Statistics—the basis of affirmative action approaches to social justice—reflect a "euro-masculinist" system of producing knowledge about, and making meaning of, the social world (Collins 1990). In contrast, employees of color favored the "just do it" approach to challenging inequality. This approach prioritizes common sense, personal experience, and direct action over data-gathering, deliberation, and documentation of how equality serves the interests of something else (such as service delivery or maximizing profit).

The case of the Center demonstrates that organizational efforts to build an intersectional collective identity may, in fact, have the opposite of their intended effect; in this case, the solidification of a white collective identity. The successful construction of an intersectional collective identity presumably would have required multi-identity work that engaged employees in an equitable manner, as well as critically engaged the "celebrate diversity" discourse prevalent in the lesbian and gay movement.

Diversity, Representation, and Fundable Populations: Gay Male Collective Identity at Bienestar

Ideas about diversity and representation are also embedded in funding structures. It is not uncommon for public and private funders of social movement organizations to specify "target" populations their grants are intended to serve (e.g., homeless women, HIV+ Latinos, queer youth, etc.). Large grants naming specific identity-groups as target populations may lead social movement organizations to (re)structure their programs to meet contract requirements and create new identity discourses that justify this restructuring. While the very aim of targeting specific identity groups is to eliminate structural inequalities by reaching the underserved, new hierarchies may result as organizations work to justify their emphasis on one or more groups at the exclusion of others. Similar to the diversity management model, instrumentalist approaches to representation and diversity imposed by funding agencies often achieve the opposite of their intended goals by requiring that organizations count, document, and improve their interactions with some populations and not others. In this section, I examine the struggle of employees at Bienestar, a lesbian and gay Latino organization, to represent the diversity of the queer Latino community while meeting HIV-focused funding requirements. I demonstrate that these efforts reinforced the already marginal position of lesbians in the organization and consolidated the organization's gay male identity.

Bienestar began in 1989 as a health subcommittee of the East Los Angeles-based political and social group Gay and Lesbian Latinos Unidos (GLLU). According to Martin, the current and founding executive director of Bienestar, it was the lesbian leadership in GLLU that "forced the discussion about HIV in the Latino community" as early as 1985, while many of the male GLLU members did not want to discuss it. Similar to lesbian activists in other communities throughout the country, GLLU women led early efforts to develop an organizational infrastructure to address the epidemic in East Los Angeles (Stoller 1997). Ana, a current Bienestar board member who had been involved with GLLU since 1985, agrees with Martin's account and adds that "the women ran GLLU. There were a few men that were strong, but the women always ran the organization." In 1995, Bienestar became independent from GLLU and a powerful agency in its own right, with an HIV-focused mission no longer connected to the goals of GLLU. Although Bienestar maintains a lesbian presence on its board of directors, it is no longer officially a lesbian and gay organization. With seven centers throughout Los Angeles, it is now an HIV/AIDS-focused "health" organization whose mission is to serve all Latino communities affected by AIDS in Los Angeles.

At the same time that Bienestar is not formally an LGBT organization, it is informally known for its LGBT programs and its leadership in the gay Latino community. Gay men make up the vast majority of the staff and leadership at Bienestar, producing a dominant gay male culture in the organization, but the agency also dedicates one of its East Los Angeles centers, La Casa, exclusively to LGBT youth programs, including a Latina lesbian program called LUNA (Latinas Understanding the Need for Action). Bienestar is a regular presence at LGBT community events as well and widely advertises its services in the Los Angeles gay and lesbian press, such as the popular Los Angeles publication *Lesbian News*. During the time of my data collection, lesbian staff produced four dance parties for queer women, a women's poetry night called Café con Leche, a queer women's day-long retreat, and several other social events designed to build a community of young, queer Latinas. Bienestar is widely known among Latina lesbians in Los Angeles as the only organization producing Latina lesbian events in Los Angeles, however it also has a reputation as an organization dominated by gay men. According to Elena, a lesbian employee, it is difficult to build Bienestar's lesbian program "because the [Latina] community will say, when you go out into the community, that the organization all along has really been known for sexism." Indeed, Bienestar is supported by state and federal grants for HIV/AIDS prevention and rarely has funding for lesbian programs. With no more than two employees and no funding, the lesbian component at Bienestar suffers by comparison to the gay men's component that offers more support groups, free weekend retreats, and sporting events and is staffed by approximately ten gay men across seven locations.

Yet despite these disparities and the organization's HIV/AIDS focus, Bienestar's small lesbian component provides an exclusively Latina environment that fosters "*jota* pride," community-building, and romantic relationships among Chicana and Latina lesbians. Martin, the executive director, argues that Bienestar is needed because staff in gay and lesbian organizations with predominantly white leadership will claim that they "open the door and welcome [Latinos]," but despite this ideological commitment, "the music, the food, the everything, is not really welcome to Latinos." Martin asserts that cultural sensitivity and an environment free of racism is often more important to Bienestar's lesbian clients than having a large and well-supported lesbian program. Yet he adds that the supportive presence of Latinas in an organization run predominantly by and for Latino men is also a reflection of a "comfortable" and "natural" gender division of labor in Latino culture. In response to my question about why lesbians would be interested in serving on the board of directors for an HIV/AIDS organization with such limited resources for lesbian programs, Martin said,

> I think that in all of our family units, it is our mothers, our sisters, that are primarily our caretakers, the ones who give us that support and even in an environment of machismo, it is always the women. And I think they feel comfortable, just keeping on that role in coming every month to the board meetings and doing the work because they are taking care of their brothers. Without really stopping and analyzing, I think it's just a very natural progression of our culture, why they are in that capacity.

In contrast with Martin's assessment, many of the women staff and clients at Bienestar were dissatisfied with the marginal role of the women's program, leading ultimately to an organized critique of sexism at Bienestar (see Ward 2004). When I asked one lesbian staff member why she didn't "just quit" after hearing her account of sexism in the organization, she explained, "Bienestar is sexist, but if I leave, I'm afraid I'll never get to work with my community again. . . . I may be *pocha* and all that, but here there are other Mexican women who need me and respect me. And that's not going to be easy to find for a butch Mexican woman."

Lesbian staff members explained that they had more or less expected to struggle with sexism at Bienestar based on the organization's reputation and their own understanding of sexism as an unavoidable structural problem, particularly in a gay male-dominated environment. Gender inequality at Bienestar was complicated, however, by the centrality of gay men to the organization's HIV-focused mission and the external legitimacy given to Bienestar's programmatic priorities given the urgency of the AIDS epidemic and the availability of funding for gay male programs. The AIDS epidemic had transformed the gay and lesbian collective identity at Bienestar to an HIV-focused collective identity that was supported not only by the structure of the organization but also by available ideas about HIV, Latino culture, and representation.

HIV prevention and education services at Bienestar are guided by the belief that psycho-cultural factors (*machismo, familismo,* and taboos about discussing sex) are barriers to safer sex practices. According to this model, HIV prevention must move beyond sharing facts about transmission and instead provide "culturally relevant" interventions that address the host of cofactors that contribute to unsafe sex (Diaz 1997). Based on this model, Bienestar receives HIV/AIDS funding to provide support groups and social events for gay men that enhance general self-esteem and encourage healthy communication about sex and relationships, with the understanding that it may not be necessary to mention HIV/AIDS or safer sex at all in order for a group meeting to be a successful part of the prevention effort. Therefore, it was this model that was also used to justify the presence of a lesbian program in an HIV/AIDS organization because its method deemphasizes HIV and instead emphasizes issues that *are* of interest to young Latina lesbians (e.g., family, communication, dating). In response to my question about whether a lesbian program is appropriate in an AIDS organization that is managed by gay men and has no funding for lesbians, David, the director of the queer youth program, responded,

> It's appropriate for the fact that it's not just about HIV and AIDS issues, it's about cultural sensitivity and cultural relevancy. And I have seen and heard stories from women that go to the agencies that do have lesbian-specific money, and because the women are only able to identify along a sexuality basis, they still have to deal with issues of racism at those agencies and may not feel comfortable. You know, it's amazing to me, even taking into consideration how small the women's program is here, the overwhelming response we get from the community is that it's needed at Bienestar.

Bienestar's male leaders argued that while there was no funding to build the lesbian program, the need for Latina lesbians to have a culturally sensitive space outweighed the need for structural resources. Such discourses allowed for the inclusion of lesbians at Bienestar without challenge to the organization's gay male identity.

Although the use of the psycho-cultural model validates the importance of non HIV-specific cofactors, such as culture, family, self-esteem, and other issues that might be important to young Latina lesbians, it is based on accountability to HIV/AIDS funders and not lesbian clients themselves or the Latina lesbian community. According to Elena, her ability to use the same theoretical justification for social programming that gay male staff used did not compensate for other gender-related tensions at Bienestar:

A lot of what was done at Bienestar was always under the guise of there [being] a multiplicity of factors of why people contract HIV. . . . It was in that vein that it was kind of addressed, you know, identity politics, sexuality, home, family, religion, for all the different populations. . . . We found creative ways of doing things, so I could always justify why I was doing a dance for queer women of color. I could justify [it], but it doesn't mean it was supported. . . . [Gay men] can justify it along the way and link it back to HIV and AIDS. But the women's programming, it wasn't necessarily more difficult to justify, it just wasn't received well because it was a lot of personal conflicts. . . . It was real, you know, head-to-head bunting [sic] because it was very cut along the lines of gender.

As Elena's comment about "personal conflicts" illustrates, Bienestar's identity as a (gay male) HIV organization provided a logical rationale for lesbian marginalization (i.e., "there just isn't funding for your program") that made it difficult for lesbian staff to determine whether lack of support for their programs and for themselves as employees stemmed from a funding obstacle that the male leadership could do nothing about or a more "personal" conflict between gay men and lesbians in the organization. Similarly, Monica, another lesbian employee, points to funding obstacles but also emphasizes that the lesbian program was threatening to gay male staff and not prioritized by Bienestar's leadership:

In an agency that employs ninety plus employees, at any given time, they are only employing three queer women. Part of that I believe is because, as they say, the federal government does not provide funding to educate women on prevention. And so all the women who are brought in are brought in on non-gender specific contracts. So, they have implemented a queer women's component, LUNA, . . . but every time I think that women try to push the program out there, they are stopped, because of funding, they're stopped because of the reality that these men feel that the women are taking over the space when they come in.

These comments highlight the awareness of lesbian staff that the difficulty finding funds to support lesbian youth programs is a "real" obstacle, most likely faced by organizations other than Bienestar. Yet the constant attention to HIV funding as a means to explain disparities between gay men and lesbians in the organization begged other questions for lesbian staff, questions that focused more directly on employees' identities and had little or nothing to do funding structures.

Lesbian staff argued that another seemingly gender-neutral philosophy adopted at Bienestar supported gender discrimination in hiring and promotions. Committed to the notion that staff members should represent the population they serve, Bienestar's leadership emphasized the importance of "peer-led" programs in which the identities of employees closely matched those of their clients. On one hand, the ability to represent a disadvantaged community was a point of pride at Bienestar, as staff judged the quality of their services according to their ability to relate to, and remember being in the position of, their clients. According to Elena,

> [David] was always proud to say that, "we are the population that we serve. We are the ones who have been here before, in a sense." I know [David] was really proud of that. He had his bisexual, his transgender, he had the gay man, he had the queen, he had the dyke, he had the *chingona* femme.

While this articulation of diversity was central to Bienestar's collective identity, Elena also points out that this same philosophy was used to justify the absence of lesbians in leadership positions and in the organization in general. Here she describes an argument she had with David about why so few women had been hired at Bienestar:

> And then he said, to put a stop to it [the conversation], "well, the staff here represents and reflects the number of AIDS cases in L. A." And that was supposed to justify everything in that statement, so that was really the mentality. The ten to two [staff] ratio reflected AIDS cases, or reported AIDS cases.

The "number of AIDS cases" and other "facts" about lesbians and HIV were used at Bienestar to not only justify but also *naturalize* the predominance of gay men in the leadership positions and the glass ceiling or "sticky floor" that lesbian staff experienced (Martin 1991). While the psycho-cultural model could be used to explain why a lesbian program was *appropriate* at Bienestar, the number of AIDS cases could be used to explain why developing the program and, concomitantly, hiring and promoting more lesbian staff was not *necessary*. Together these logics produced among lesbian staff the sense that their presence in a queer Latino organization was a privilege or luxury, a sense to be contrasted with the feeling of entitlement that they perceived in gay men. At Bienestar, the good news of being theoretically at low risk for HIV infection became bad news for lesbians who hoped for job advancement in an organization in which the staff was expected to reflect AIDS demographics.

In the case of Bienestar, which began as a subcommittee of a lesbian and gay organization (GLUU), the urgency of the AIDS epidemic led to the formation of a new gay male-focused collective identity. While early GLUU women struggled with sexism, they were nonetheless central to GLUU's early mission and functioning. As GLUU became Bienestar, it was the new emphasis on HIV, paired with logic about HIV risk and prevention methods, which institutionalized the marginal position of lesbian staff and lesbian programs in the organization. In Bienestar's current iteration, the project of representation is framed as a powerful act of resistance given a history of queer Latino underrepresentation and invisibility in Los Angeles. However, the very arguments about culture and representation that Bienestar's leaders used to secure funding for underrepresented groups (gay Latinos) and justify the inclusion of lesbians were also used to solidify the male identity of the organization. The emphasis of funding agencies on target groups and diversity measurements also encourages instrumentalist approaches to diversity in which identity discourses and practices stem not from ideological commitments to communities but from financial commitments to funders.

Conclusion

This chapter explores two developments in multi-identity discourse and practice that reinforce rather than challenge structural inequalities in social movement organizations. In the case of the Center, diversity projects reinforced the organization's white identity, even as employees were actively engaged in discussions about race. At Bienestar, the very arguments about culture and representation that Bienestar's leaders used to secure funding for gay Latinos were also used to justify gender inequality in the organization and reinforce the organization's male identity. While both organizations gave discursive attention to multiple forms of difference, such efforts did not accomplish the additional work of challenging the "matrix of domination" or recognizing that these differences produced interlocking inequalities that were operating within the organizations themselves (Collins 1998).

These findings illustrate the gap between diversity rhetoric and structural realities in the lesbian and gay movement and the limited influence of diversity practices on the creation of intersectional collective identities.

While race, class, and gender inequality and segregation are not new to the movement, the current era is witness to new institutional and ideological tools that hide or naturalize these outcomes and lead lesbian and gay activists to believe they have succeeded at creating an inclusive, multi-issue movement. "Celebrating diversity" and the ideas and practices it represents is one such tool; it is a smoke and mirrors trick that distracts us while "diverse" people and ideas leave the movement. Yet the problem is not simply the rhetoric about diversity but also the organizational practices that celebrate (some) differences while keeping traditional race, class, and gender hierarchies in tact. Even social movement organizations that focus on multiple injustices will be "at risk" in this regard unless recognition is given to the ways in which all oppressed groups occupy positions of penalty and privilege (Collins 1996).

Research on how social movements engage in multi-identity work has emphasized macro- and micro-level dynamics, such as the way movement groups produce multi-issue campaigns or how activists develop oppositional consciousness around multiple oppressions. Meso-level analyses, on the other hand, emphasize the ways in which ideas about intersectionality and diversity are transformed into institutional practices—diversity trainings, hiring structures, grant writing, board recruitment, and so on—yet have minimal influence on the way activists see themselves collectively. These practices give shape to lesbian and gay organizing, but they also compel activists to think and talk about sameness and difference in ways that support organizational survival rather than structural change. While this chapter examines the failure of diversity-oriented approaches to create an inclusive lesbian and gay movement, these failures are not unique to the lesbian and gay movement and are best understood in the context of a diversity-obsessed national culture in which racism and other inequalities remain alive and well. Social movement organizations do not develop diversity practices in a vacuum—these practices are imported via the previous institutional experiences of movement leaders, the requirements of funding agencies and other organizations with which social movement groups interact, as well as the ideas about diversity in the broader culture. The lesbian and gay movement is a useful example of this relationship, not only because it is subject to the influence of multiculturalism to the same degree as any other movement, but also because it has made a unique effort to frame diversity as a central movement goal by emphasizing the diversity of ways to express gay identity. To understand the formation of collective identity in the lesbian and gay movement requires, then, a synthesis of social movement theory and critical race theory so that we may be view multiculturalism and diversity not simply as "real" characteristics of the movement but also as ideological formations that simultaneously challenge and reinforce race, class, and gender inequality.

References

Armstrong, Elizabeth. 2004. "Institutionalization and Revitalization of Social Movement." Panel discussion. American Sociological Association Annual Meeting. San Francisco.

———. 2002. *Forging Gay Identities: Organizing Sexuality in San Francisco, 1950–1994.* Chicago: University of Chicago Press.

Baca Zinn, Maxine, and Bonnie Thorton Dill. 1996. "Theorizing Difference from Multiracial Feminism." *Feminist Studies* 22(2): 321–31.

Bonilla-Silva, Eduardo. 2003. *Racism without Racists: Color-blind Racism and the Persistence of Racial Inequality in the United States.* New York: Rowman and Littlefield.

Boykin, Keith. 2000. "Where Thetoric Meets Reality: The Role of Black Lesbians and Gays in "Queer" Politics. In *The Politics of Gay Rights*, ed. C. Rimmerman, K. Wald, and C. Wilcox, 79–96. Chicago: University of Chicago Press.

Collins, Patricia Hill. 2004. *Black Sexual Politics: African Americans, Gender, and the New Racism.* New York: Routledge.

———. 1998. *Fighting Words: Black Women and the Search for Justice.* Minneapolis: University of Minnesota Press.

———. 1996. "Toward a New Vision: Race, Class, and Gender as Categories of Analysis and Connection." In *Race, Sex, and Class* 1(1): 25–45.

Combahee River Collective. 1983. "The Combahee River Collective Statement." In *Home Girls: A Black Feminist Anthology*, ed. B. Smith, 264–74. New York: Kitchen Table Women of Color Press.

D'Emilio, John. 2000. "Cycles of Change, Questions of Strategy: The Gay and Lesbian Movement After Fifty Years." In *The Politics of Gay Rights*, ed. C. Rimmerman, K. Wald, and C. Wilcox, 31–53. Chicago: University of Chicago Press.

Diaz, Rafael Jorge. 1997. "Latino Gay Men and Psycho-cultural Barriers to AIDS Prevention." In *Changing Times: Gay Men and Lesbians Encounter HIV and AIDS*, ed. M. Levine, P. Nardi, and J. Gagnon, 221–44. Chicago: University of Chicago Press.

Ferree, Myra Marx, and Patricia Yancey Martin. 1995. *Feminist Organizations: Harvest of the New Women's Movement.* Philadelphia: Temple University Press.

Gamson, Joshua. 1995. "Must Identity Movements Self-destruct?: A Queer Dilemma. *Social Problems* 42(3): 390–407.

Glaser, Barney, and Strauss, Anselm. 1967. *The Discovery of Grounded Theory.* Chicago: Aldine de Gruyter.

Gordon, Avery. 1995. "The Work of Corporate Culture Diversity Management." *Social Text* 44.13(3): 3–30.

hooks, bell. 1981. *Ain't I a Woman: Black Women and Feminism*. Boston: South End Press.

King, Deborah.1988. "Multiple Jeopardy." *Signs* 14(11): 42–72.

Kurtz, Sharon. 2002. *Workplace Justice: Organizing Multi-identity Movements*. Minneapolis: University of Minnesota Press.

Kuumba, Bahati M. 2001. *Gender and Social Movements*. New York: Alta Mira Press.

Lugones, Maria. 1990. "Playfulness, 'World'-traveling, and Loving Perception." In *Making Face, Making Sul/Haciendo Caras: Creative and Critical Perspectives by Feminists of Color*, ed. G. Anzaldua, 390–415. San Francisco: Aunt Lute Books.

Martin, Lynn. 1991. *A Report on the Glass Ceiling Initiative*. Washington, D.C.: US Department of Labor.

Poster, Winifred. 1995. "The Challenges and Promises of Class and Racial Diversity in the Women's Movement: A Study of Two Organizations." *Gender & Society* 9: 659–79.

Reger, Jo. 2002. "Organizational Dynamics and the Construction of Multiple Feminist Identities in the National Organization for Women." *Gender & Society* 16 (5): 710–27.

Robnett, Belinda. 1996. "African-American Women in the Civil Rights Movement, 1954–1965: Gender, Leadership, and Micromobilization." *American Journal of Sociology* 101(6): 1628–60.

Roth, Silke. 2000. "Developing Working Class Feminism: A Biographical Approach to Social Movement Participation. In *Self, Identity, and Social Movements*, ed. S. Stryker, T. J. Owens, and R. W. White, 300–323. Minneapolis: University of Minnesota Press.

Snow David, and Doug McAdam. 2000. "Identity Work Processes in the Context of Social Movements: Clarifying the Identity/Movement Nexus." In *Self, Identity, and Social Movements*, ed. S. Stryker, T. J. Owens, and R. W. White, 41–67. Minneapolis: University of Minnesota Press.

Staggenborg, Suzanne. 2002. "The 'Meso' in Social Movement Research." In *Social Movements: Identity, Culture, and the State*, ed. D. S. Meyer, N. Whittier, and B. Robnett, 124–39. Oxford: Oxford University Press.

Stockdill, Brett. 2001. "Forging a Multidimensional Oppositional Consciousness: Lessons from Community-based AIDS Activism." In *Oppositional Consciousness: The Subjective Roots of Social Protest*, ed. J. Mansbridge and A. Morris, 204–37. Chicago: University of Chicago Press.

Stoller, Nancy. 1997. "From Feminism to Polymorphous Activism: Lesbians in AIDS Organizations." In *Changing Times: Gay Men and Lesbians Encounter HIV and AIDS*, ed. M. Levine, P. Nardi, and J. Gagnon, 171–90. Chicago: University of Chicago Press.

Takagi, Dana. 1996. "Maiden Voyage: Excursion into Sexuality and Identity Politics in Asian America." In *Asian American Sexualities: Dimensions of the Gay & Lesbian Experience*, ed. R. Leong. 21–36. New York: Routledge.

Vaid, Urvashi. 1995. *Virtual Equality: The Mainstreaming of Gay and Lesbian Liberation*. New York: Anchor Books.

Ward, Jane. 2004. "'Not All Differences are Created Equal': Multiple Jeopardy in a Gendered Organization." *Gender & Society* 18 (1): 82–102.

Note

1. The phrase "We Are Family" was popularized by the song with the same title, performed by the Black quartet Sister Sledge. The imagery of the rainbow has also been used in racial justice projects, such as Jesse Jackson's Rainbow Coalition.

11

The Reconstruction of Collective Identity in the Emergence of U.S. White Women's Liberation

Benita Roth

Introduction: Feminist (Re)Constructions of Collective Identity

Renewed feminist movements were part of the post–World War II cycle of protest in the United States and worldwide. In the United States, feminist movements had, broadly speaking, two social bases: (1) networks of professional women brought together by government and liberal institutions, which formed membership organizations such as the National Organization for Women (NOW); and (2) radical women who were situated in oppositional communities engaged in challenging racial inequalities and the Vietnam War (Buechler 1990; Carden 1974; Freeman 1973, 1975; Hole and Levine 1971; Marx Ferree and Hess 1985, 1994, 2000; Roth 2004). In the latter case, feminist activism erupted within left-wing movement organizations as assertions of difference where once commonality of political vision seemingly reigned.

In this chapter, I look at the specific case of U.S. white women's liberation's emergence from the New Left and the civil rights movements in the 1960s, and I consider how feminists' political identity as leftists was reconstructed to accommodate an emergent identity as feminists. Unlike their sisters in the National Organization for Women (NOW), who organized quickly and bureaucratically beginning in 1966, emerging feminists on the left debated questions about how to organize to redress gender oppression for a number of years, from 1964 to 1971 (and beyond). Their debate took place on the ground in small groups and found expression in left movement grassroots journals. I argue that this protracted process of debate and emergence—identity work that was, in fact, a debate about emergence—was one of feminists reconstructing collective identity to assert fundamental difference (that of gender) where once fundamental common-ality (that of being "left") was most salient. I do not argue that "feminist" supplanted "left" in a zero-sum way; white women's liberationists considered themselves to be both left and feminist. But I do argue that constructing a feminist identity was complicated by feminists' immersion in a competing leftist milieu, because being in an existing oppositional community created a mandate to fix gender relations in the left first. The internal focus of feminist efforts was an indication that assertions of difference wrestled with assertions (and realities) of shared political investments with men. I further argue that this internal focus shifted to an external focus over the course of the mid- to late 1960s for three key and simultaneously occurring reasons: (1) a debate among feminists about the meaning of the failure to accommodate differ-ence, as male leftists were unreceptive to the feminist challenge; (2) a shift in resources, as emerging feminists increasingly built organs of communication that allowed them to organize within networks outside of existing left organi-zations; and (3) a shift in audiences as emerging feminists reconceptualized the audience for their efforts from left-movement men to all women in general.

After consideration of how current social movement theory's focus on the drawing of boundaries between challengers and targets leaves open ques-tions about *internal* challenges in movements—that is, factionalization—I narrate white women's liberation's emergence, highlighting the dynamics of the debate over the denial of difference, resource shift, and audience shift pre-viously noted. In the conclusion, I briefly consider what the case of the emer-gence of white women's liberation may suggest to us vis-à-vis the reconstruction of collective identity by activists already situated in challenging organizations.

Reconstructing Collective Identity from within Oppositional Communities

Useful definitions of collective identity focus on its formation within con-crete settings and in relationship to concrete others. For example, Francesca Polletta and James M. Jasper define collective identity as an "individual's cog-nitive, moral, and emotional connection with a broader community, which may be imagined rather than experienced directly" (2001, 285). Although Polletta and Jasper see the *having* of collective identity as such as the property of the individual, they also understand the process of its acquisition as social and as occurring within concrete settings. In terms of concrete settings, William Gamson points out that new collective identities can be fashioned either out of "base communities," that is, from disadvantaged but relatively unorganized social groups, or out of "preexisting movement identity" (1991, 41). Gamson (1991, 40) further posits that layers of collective identities coexist for individuals; individuals possess distinct "embedded" layers of collective identity—the organizational (group, organization, or "carrier"), the movement (possibly although not necessarily larger than the organizational layer), and the solidary layer (broader still and based on social location). In practice, these embedded layers may converge, overlap, or shift in salience.

White women's liberationists' forming of a feminist collective identity was clearly a case of (re)building "preexisting movement identity." In fact, because women have overlapping positions with social hierarchies and shared political investments with men, a collective identity approach to the defining of feminist activism is exactly what Leila Rupp and Verta Taylor (1999) advocate. They emphasize the concrete context of collective identity formation, as well as the relational and contested nature of feminist collective identity formation:

> Because the meaning of feminism has changed over time and from place to place and is often disputed, it requires a framework that allows access not just to what women (or men) in a specific historical situation believe but to how they constructed, sometimes through conflict with one another, a sense of togetherness. (Rupp and Taylor 1999, 364)

Feminisms, therefore, are made within complex and crowded political milieus in which constructing collective identity rests on the reconstruction and redrawing of boundaries. The collective identity approach to understanding feminisms goes a long way toward understanding the differences in feminist agendas over time and space

Social movement theorists have long understood that challengers need to form boundaries to establish themselves as players in a political field. For example, Taylor and Nancy Whittier (1992, 111) argue that challenger groups must form boundaries between themselves and "mainstream" society in order to become visible in a political landscape. Boundary-making involves "mark[ing] the social territories of group relations by highlighting differences between activists and the web of others in the contested social world." This "web of others" includes not only political enemies but also groups who are in some ways similarly positioned or already existing and working on similar issues. Knowing how one's (emergent) group is different from similar groups is therefore a key part of understanding the nature of one's collective identity.

Boundaries are also a key concept in the "relational" approach recently taken by McAdam, Tarrow, and Tilly (2001) in *Dynamics of Contention*.

Although they scrupulously avoid the term "collective identity," they define what they call "identity mechanisms" in episodes of contention. They focus strongly on the role of boundaries in defining identity, for example, in their identity mechanism of *category formation*, a mechanism that "creates identities" (2001, 143). A category is defined as "a set of sites that share a boundary distinguishing all of them from and relating all of them to at least one set of sites visibly excluded by the boundary" (McAdam, Tarrow, and Tilly 2001, 143). Furthermore, category formation is envisioned by McAdam, Tarrow, and Tilly as occurring in three chief ways: (1) *invention*, where authorities create new divisions within societies; (2) *borrowing*, where contenders in given social settings import ways of relating across boundaries from other social settings; and (3) *encounter*, where "previously separate but internally connected networks come into contact with each other" (2001, 157). But one kind of category formation is missing from this list: the invention of difference *from within* challenging groups, that is, the category formation dynamics of internal challenge and factionalization.

In shifting to a consideration of internal challenges to collective identity, I do not mean to imply that challenging groups exist in a vacuum; the relational perspective on contention put forward by McAdam, Tarrow, and Tilly is salutary, as are theorists' perspectives that emphasize the overall importance of the social movement milieu, sector, or field (Curtis and Zurcher 1973; Marx, Ferree and Roth 1998; McCarthy and Zald 1977; Ray 1999; Roth 2004; Tarrow 1988). Ideas "spill over" and travel across movements and organizations as do tactics and people themselves (Meyer and Whittier 1994, 277). But dynamics of boundary-making at the macro or meso levels cannot simply be assumed to be the same ones at play in micro- or intragroup contexts. White women's liberation emerged as a movement because of many discussions within social movements that were decentralized and reticulate (see Gerlach and Hine 1970), consisting of many loosely coordinated groups who considered themselves to be of the left. Naming sexism and asserting gender difference within this oppositional milieu inevitably brought up questions of where loyalties and political investments lay, and new feminist organizing was associated with personal costs, psychological and otherwise, for already committed activists.[1] Personal investments were made all the more weighty by the fact that the New Left and the civil rights movements were in large parts "prefigurative" political communities, where the distance between the personal and the political collapsed (Breines 1982; Stoper 1989; Taylor and Whittier 1992). The ideology *and* practice of radical community in the civil rights movement and the New Left were seen as opposed to dominant American culture; thus emerging white feminists were situated in a movement that made claims on their time and identity in almost all spheres of their lives, such that "[b]eing radical was not just part of their definition of themselves as feminists; it was a fundamental aspect of their self-identity" (Ryan 1992, 63).

The historical record shows that white women's liberationists engaged in considerable thought and discussion precisely about how to draw boundaries between themselves and others; they thought about the dovetailing of a left- ist and a feminist identity. Radical women activists asked questions about who was receptive to them and who was not; about what resources were available to them and what would they need to find themselves; and about who con- stituted a potential audience for mobilization and who constituted a potential (or real) enemy. Through the asking and answering of these questions, through words and deeds, white women's liberationists came to reconstruct a collective identity as leftists to accommodate a collective identity as left-wing feminists.

We have a number of case studies of postwar American feminism that narrate and analyze the discussions that occurred among activist women in the 1960s regarding the existence of sexism (Buechler 1990; Carden 1974; Echols 1989; Evans 1979; Freeman 1973, 1975; Hole and Levine 1971; Marx Ferree and Hess 1985, 1994, 2000; Roth 2004). All show a period of emerging white women's liberationists attempting to reform the (male) left and deal internally with contradictions raised by gender inequality. Given the early internal focus of white women's liberationists, one logical possibil- ity was that men could have been receptive to feminist organizing and made accommodation for it. Another logical possibility was that feminists could have "backburnered" their demands and prioritized existing left organiza- tions (see Gluck et al. 1998 on Native American feminism). So why did the recognition of internal difference and internal inequality lead to organizing another, organizationally distinct movement?

In the following section, I highlight how white women's liberationists' debate over the meaning of the denial of gender difference took place *within* the left for a number of years. Following that section, I consider the way that emerging feminists transferred their energies into building new communica- tion structures, so that they shifted resources from existing left groups to new groups. I then consider the question of audience shift and how emerging white feminists oriented toward a new pool of potential recruits before concluding.[2]

Second-wave White Feminist Emergence: Debating the Meaning of Hostility

For many, feminism might seem to have "happened" once the naming of sexism in left organizations began. But naming sexism was only the start for the forma- tion of a feminist collective identity and, in any case, was insufficient for the reconstruction of a leftist identity into a feminist one. Debates about the meaning of gender oppression took place on the left for a number of years. As early as 1964, radical white women in the civil rights movement and New Left began to develop an emergent norm of sexism—the "collective redefinition of a condition once viewed as a *misfortune* into a state of *injustice*"—within the oppositional movements of civil rights and the New Left extending the idea of liberation to address gender oppression (Turner and Killian 1987, 287, emphasis in original). In 1964, two female white members, Casey Hayden and Mary King of the Student Non-violent Coordinating Committee (SNCC), circulated an anonymous paper on the inferior status of women in SNCC that was attributed to Ruby Doris Robinson, a Black founder of the organization (Carden 1974; Evans 1979; Polletta 1999). By 1966, Hayden and King's memo had been circulated to other civil rights organizations, Students for a Democratic Society (SDS), and *Liberation* magazine (Baxandall 2001). Hayden and King's memo drew direct parallels between the position of women and the position of Blacks in society, thus applying SNCC's ideals of liberation to their own status as women within progressive groups. The analogy of women's status to that of Blacks was used by Hayden and King to illustrate a contradiction within the civil rights movement—and later, the New Left—that was seen as problematic for gender relationships in movement communities.[3] In November of 1967, a group of women activists, self-described as mostly "of the movement," published a "Preliminary Statement of Principles" in *New Left Notes* (Evans 1979, 240–41). After 1967, there was an outpouring of analysis of white women's position within New Left organizations and, to a lesser degree, within the civil rights movement, since there were fewer white women in that movement after 1965 (Seese 1969). These discussions led to the formation of the first left women's movement newsletter, the *Voice of the Women's Liberation Movement*, in 1968; in that same year, a conference was held in Sandy Springs, Maryland to address the concerns of radical women activists working within the New Left (Echols 1989).

As these women came together to talk, as they wrote to each other, and as they published pieces in left journals they focused on themes that represented a roll call of difference from the positions and situations of movement men. Radical women argued that they were relegated to roles that largely consisted of movement "housewifery" (Davidica 1968; Piercy 1970; Robinson 1970); they charged that they were exploited by men, especially male leaders, as sexual objects (Dunbar 1969; Evans 1979; Piercy 1970; Rominski 1968; Webb 1968); and they were concerned about their inability to have men take them seriously as public movement leaders or, indeed, to take seriously any of their public participation (Allen 1968; Evans 1979; Goldfield, Munaker, and Weisstein c. 1968; Piercy 1970; Robinson 1970; Vanauken 1971; Webb 1968). Radical white women argued that these problems—these differences with men—represented the New Left and civil rights movements' failures to live up to its own ideals on the level of practical and personal politics.

The chronology of written discontent by emerging white women's liberationists is, prior to 1968, evidence of a largely internal critique of movement organizations that most women's liberationists did not want to abandon. As Pam Allen wrote "[o]ne of the major disputes within the movement has been whether women's liberation groups should constitute themselves as an independent movement. Reaction was very strong in 1967 and early 1968 against further segmenting an already divided movement" (1968, 9). Since both the civil rights movement and the New Left were organized in a decentralized reticulate fashion, with small groups predominating, activists had serious questions about the wisdom of forming new groups, especially feminist ones. New group formation was seen as potentially upsetting to the organizational economies of existing movement groups (Roth 2004; see also Chapter 5). Radical white women activists who critiqued the left's treatment of women were in fact split between "politicos" and "feminists": politicos wanted to work within the New Left's existing organizations, with feminists advocating forming separate feminist organizations (Echols 1989). However, the latter group, "the feminists," were still organizing within oppositional communities and, significantly, still in the process of creating their own organs of communication. The split between politicos and feminists itself indicates that there were at least initially a set of choices about feminist organizing, with considerable sentiment existing for reforming the left in mixed gender groups.

Male activists (and some female activists, as previously noted) reacted to these assertions of *remediable* difference with famous disdain, but there was nothing inevitable about the New Left's hostility to women's liberation and nothing inevitable in such hostility automatically producing a new women's movement. Left organizations such as SDS could have tried to co-opt emerging feminists by adopting their agenda outright; they could have coexisted with new feminist groups by forming or encouraging women's caucuses within existing radical organizations, which did happen from time to time. While the source of New Left hostility is difficult to pinpoint (see Echols 1992; Roth 2004), the specter of difference that feminism raised—over and beyond the culturally accepted difference of race—led to particularly virulent reactions against it by some; the objections were couched in language that asserted feminism's divisive and diversionary nature (Dunbar 1968; Goldfield,

Munaker, and Weisstein c. 1968; Koedt 1968; Lund 1970; McEldowney 1969; Morgan 1968).

There was little question that male hostility to a feminist agenda was widespread, but the point I wish to emphasize is that this hostility in and of itself was contested by emerging feminists, and its meaning was debated. The question of how and whether to be tied to the left was important to white women's liberationists because, as members of oppositional communities, they saw a boundary between themselves and other women—that is, the solidary collective identity of *women* was not initially well-developed. In 1968, for example, the word "feminist" itself was problematic in its associations, as least for some radical women, as Marilyn Webb noted: "We are not the gray-suited women of the twenties but colorful members of a turned on generation of women who are asserting themselves as females as well as intellectual-politicos" (1968, no page given). The other "colorful members of a turned on generation" were, of course, leftist men.

Responses by eventual women's liberationists to male left hostility were not uniform. Take, for example, a well-known, egregious dismissal and humiliation of feminists and feminist politics—that of male reactions to feminists attempting to speak at the "Counter-Inauguration" sponsored by the antiwar National Mobilization Committee in January of 1969. Two radical women attempted to speak about women's liberation and were booed, heckled, and greeted with shouts of "take her off the stage and fuck her" (see Carden 1974, 61; Gitlin 1987).[4] And yet, emerging feminists' responses to the Counter-Inauguration debacle a month later in the February 1969 issue of *Voice of the Women's Liberation Movement* were mixed. What emerged in articles by radical women activists who had been critical of New Left sexism was debate about loyalties to the left as constituted and about whether organizational separation from the New Left made sense politically. The meaning of the Counter-Inauguration incident for male–female solidarity on the left was precisely the matter at issue, as Marilyn Webb wrote:

> There seems to be three distinct views on organizing and ideology within our movement. The first is the view that by raising women's consciousness about their own oppression and by working only on women's liberation issues raised in this manner, women will be in the vanguard of a revolution. . . . The second view is that women are a constituency, like the working class, blacks, etc. [within the New Left]. . . . A third position is that women's liberation must be a separate part of a revolutionary movement. It must organize around its own consciousness and its own concerns. (1969a, 5)

Even in option number three, Webb described the radical women's movement as constituting a "separate *part*" of the Movement, and she concluded that radical women must "do a better job on the local level of explaining what we are about to both men and women." Note that Marilyn Webb was one of the women who had actually been booed off the stage. Her equanimity seems unimaginable unless we consider how strong a leftist collective identity was held by Webb and others like here.

The debate among radical women activists about reforming the left centered on questions of commonality and difference, questions that were frequently placed in a rhetoric of effectiveness: How effective would or could women be in the mixed gender left? What were the possibilities and consequences of organizing the left as a whole along feminist lines? (Echols 1989). Some radical women favored a two-headed approach; women working within mixed organizations would be strengthened by the existence of an independent women's movement, and vice versa (see Baker 1970; Cagan 1971; Fraser 1970; New University Conference, Women's Caucus c. 1970a, c. 1970b; the Thursday Night Group of Berkeley Women's Liberation 1969; Weinfeld 1970), doing so on the grounds that such an approach would save the left from weakening. Note that as long as the project remained that of reforming of male activists in mixed gender groups, a feminist collective identity—as opposed to a feminist politics—was not a strict necessity. Commonality rested on a vision of shared political investments with movement men on a chosen politics that incorporated feminism but that was, in the main, leftist.

Over time—and 1968–69 appears to be the time that represented a pivotal point in the balance of the debate about collective identity—assertions of political commonality with men were supplanted by a vision of structural difference and of the inequality inherent in being a woman (see, for example, Jones and Brown 1968). As radical white women participated in a period of debate over what course to take regarding autonomous organizing, feminist organizing continued within existing left organizations and groups. The balance between the two approaches—organizing in mixed gender groups and organizing new all-female groups—would shift toward greater separation and autonomy for feminist organizing on the American left as feminists began to create new resources for organizing.

New Resources and New Groups

Radical white women's efforts to reform the left continued for a number of years in the mid-1960s, as emerging feminists named sexism and debated the meaning of hostility to feminism. Seen from a later perspective, the reluctance on the part of many eventual feminists to give up the dream of a united left seems rather startling. Beyond the debate, however, male left hostility spurred feminists toward the creation of new organs of communication and new organizational efforts. Organizing by radical women increased dramatically in the years 1968–71. The first national conference of radical women's liberationists in November of 1968 in Chicago (Echols 1989) was quickly followed by what Webb called an "avalanche of regional meetings" (1969b, 3) In the South, Wells (1969) reported that by February of 1969, groups had formed not just at University of Florida in Gainesville but also at the University of Arkansas at Fayetteville and in a variety of southern locales. In Atlanta, a women's conference was cosponsored by the Southern Student Organizing Committee (SSOC), and SSOC hired a women's liberation coordinator to establish a southern newsletter and work with campus groups (Wells 1969). Feminist women marched against the war under their own banner in demonstrations in San Francisco by November of 1969 (*The Militant* 1969). In 1970, an estimated "tens of thousands" of participants were at the Women's Equality March in New York City (Marx Ferree and Hess 1985, 62).

Developing grassroots journals and other organs of communications were key elements of emerging white women's liberation's praxis in the decentralized, nonhierarchical world of left politics. In 1971, Judith Hole and Ellen Levine estimated that there were already one hundred women's liberation journals in circulation (1971). The informal quality and grassroots nature of left-wing organizations and journals made access possible for feminists (Echols 1989; Freeman 1975). As they were building their own grassroots media, emerging white feminists on the left attempted takeovers of New Left journals, some of which succeeded to the point of permanence, for example, that of the grassroots magazine *RAT* or the successful efforts to bring women workers into the offices of Liberation News Service (Kearns 1970; Liberation New Service 1970; *RAT* 1971). Although any listing of white women's liberation's journals in the latter 1960s and early 1970s, such as the estimate of one hundred, must be partial, it is clear that efforts to start new journals and other organs of communication meant the withdrawal of time and effort from old entities. Resources—women's energies—were thus withdrawn from existing mixed gender groups and shifted into the establishment of new communications networks. This observation of resource shift is one of Freeman's original "preconditions" for feminist movement emergence given in her touchstone book *The Politics of Women's Liberation* (1975). Although a strictly resource-focused approach tends to downplay the internal debate that led to an organizationally distinct feminist movement on the white left, there is no doubt that the resources of movement experience—such as time, expertise, mimeograph machines, and mailing lists—were easily oriented toward new aims and, most importantly, toward new audiences.

Eventually, New Left communications organs were made superfluous by the existence of a radical women's communications network, but the initial placement of emerging feminists' critiques in movement journals meant that their audience was a movement audience. Their formation of new groups and new organizations indicates both the potential for feminist organizing in the New Left and civil rights movements that might have been in the absence of hostility and the presence of hostility itself; since feminist radical women faced continuous difficulties in their attempts to use the New Left's communications network, they built their own. They stopped battling for access to the New Left's resources when a separate women's movement communications network was in place. By 1971, feminist radical women had, for the most part, dropped efforts to communicate within mixed gender left organizations, and had established an autonomous communications network. Through an independent network of grassroots journals and through friendship networks developed outside of the New Left, the radical women's movement continued a process of institutional separation of their movement from the New Left. By 1971, most white women's liberationists regarded their movement as a distinct creation, that is, a "fourth world" of white women's liberation (Burris 1971, 102). The relative value of the New Left's resources changed for white women's liberation activists as they themselves grew in strength.

Audience Shift: "Women" as the New Movement

As previously noted, the first audience for emerging feminism was other movement activists. This happened because emerging white women's liberationists were enmeshed in an oppositional community and using left-wing resources to communicate. In order for a shift in audience to take place, emerging feminists developed an increasingly autonomous feminist media. These media resources developed as emerging feminists were able to appropriate and move skills developed within left movements and create new grassroots journals. As noted, the threshold in terms of costs for these journals was extremely low—most were informal and "published" only in the technical sense of the word (mimeographed, collated, and handed out is a better way of seeing the production and distribution process). In and of themselves, the development of autonomous feminist media could have remained designed for a movement audience; many journals probably did not circulate widely outside of the left. But feminist underground newspapers and magazines increasingly became places where emerging white feminists called into question the assumed boundary between their oppositional communities on the left and mainstream "straight" America and where they increasingly redrew the lines of actual and potential community—*that is, of actual and potential audience.* This reconsideration cannot be seen as a discrete moment in time; instead it was part of the process of deciding *how* and with *whom* to organize.

The audience shift of emerging white women's liberationists was a reimagining—due to on-the-ground material circumstances and fractured relationships, to be sure—of a potential and *mobilizable* community. While regarding themselves as a vanguard of sorts, activists and theorists within emerging white women's liberation eventually began to directly broach the question of the proper audience for their activist efforts. A participant and analyst of the radical women's movement, Marlene Dixon (1970a, 10) in fact used the term "audience" to explain why the emergence of the radical women's movement was such a struggle and to explore the kinds of thinking hampering feminist radical women's efforts. A sociologist by training, Dixon wrote that during the first independently sponsored conference of feminist radical women in November of 1968 there were actually two significant audiences addressed by the women who participated: "other women or Movement men." She argued that the dual audience was a result of the fact that "the radical women had a prior history engraved upon their foreheads"; their involvement in the left required that energy be diverted back into the left, into "arguing-pleading-justifying their cause, i.e., to fight male chauvinism, male supremacy in the [male] movement."

Dixon's concept of a movement "audience"—that there were people and not just ideals that feminists needed to address, to live up to—illustrated how intrinsically linked personal and political lives were for the radical women activists and how central questions of commonality were for activists. The oppositional communities of the left demanded a certain amount of bridge-burning with former social ties; this was particularly true for active participants. Radical white women self-identified as leftists; this collective identity put them on one side of a barrier between left and mainstream America. Forging a new identity as feminist radical women required that these women reorient their political efforts and come to see movement men as just "men," with access to privilege based on their gender (see "Ann" in *It Ain't Me Babe,* 1970; Densmore 1971; Estellachild 1971; Gitlin 1987; Goldfield, Munaker and Weisstein c. 1968; Vanauken 1971). Radical women also had to rethink their relationship with nonmovement women; as specific loyalties to the oppositional community of the New Left waned, white feminists asserted that all women, everywhere, were the new target of their efforts and therefore their community. A universal and mobilizable sisterhood was asserted.

Elsewhere, I have written that this positing of a universal sisterhood of women as the target of feminist organizing was problematic for cross-racial and cross-ethnic organizing among feminists from different racial and ethnic communities (Roth 2004). But in the white left-wing milieu, where activism was about the liberation of large classes of oppressed people, the shift in white feminists' audience and their new vision of commonality—their assertion of a feminist collective identity predicated on a mission of global female liberation—was galvanizing. Organizing by radical women increased dramatically from 1968 to 1971, as previously noted. Through an independent network of grassroots journals and friendship networks developed outside of the New Left, the radical women's movement completed the institutional separation of their movement from the New Left and existing civil rights organizations.

Conclusion: Reconstructing Communal Boundaries

I have argued that reconstruction of collective identity within oppositional communities is a complex process involving a debate about the meaning of (bad) reactions to difference, the creation of new communication organs, and a shift in the conceptualization of potential audience by an internally challenging group. Making initial use of the networks and concepts of the civil rights movement and the New Left to come together, white women's liberationists challenged the contradictions for a collective leftist identity produced by inequalities in gender relations. Ensconced in left-wing oppositional communities, emerging white feminists tried to reform their brothers on the left, debating the meaning of hostility to feminism and attempting for a number of years to work within left organizations. Left hostility, which spurred the emergence of an autonomous communications network, weakened emerging feminists' identification with men on the left. Feminist radical women shifted their audience from movement men to all women in society, erasing the boundary between the oppositional community and the rest of America (and indeed the world).

Beyond this particular case, what does this narrative of naming difference, reaction, creation, and reconceptualization—a process of identity work—do for our understandings of collective identity formation in social movements? New activist communities are often built out of networks or other forms of existing social relationships on the margins; within existing social movement organizations, marginal members may choose to exit and regroup, leading to factionalization. It is therefore a question of some interest as to how it is that actors redraw boundaries and categories of commonality and difference from within. Internal challengers might assert difference for any number of reasons, but we would expect unequal social structural locations (such as gender) to be important, insofar as inequalities often lead to dynamics of marginalization within movement organizations. Societalwide inequalities, such as gender or race, cannot simply be asserted away; if such were the case, oppositional groups would have far fewer problems with dynamics of fracture and factionalization, and quite the opposite seems to be the case. On the other hand, it is clear that even the actual marginalization that structurally unequal groups experience in social movement organizations does not necessarily lead to the establishment of a new movement from an old one.

It is my suggestion—only a suggestion at this point, as getting answers will necessitate further comparative research—that a component part of the reconstruction of collective identity in oppositional groups is the reimagining of audience. Thinking back to Gamson's framework of layers of identity, it is the case that within oppositional communities, new identities emerge as participants move from one layer of collective identity to another. Layers of identity that Gamson posited—the organizational, the movement, and the solidary—may always be present but at varying levels of salience for activists; as activists reevaluate allegiances to imagined others, we would see new emphases in collective identity. In the case of radical women activists in the 1960s U.S. left, the solidary (gender) level of collective identity became primary, leading to changes within organizational and movement layers of collective identity. The new salience of the solidary layer of collective identity depended in part on a reimagining of who feminists' audience and community were.

I wish to stress that the solidary layer of collective identity, even if firmly based on social location, is not automatically activated in social movement politics. Though emerging white women's liberationists were women, their shift in audience from other leftists to all women in the reconstruction of their collective identity was not inevitable but predicated on specific social relationships and constrained by the material and ideological resources at hand. A comparison might be useful. In contrast to emerging feminists in the 1960s white left, Black and Chicanafeminists organizing in their oppositional groups did not see those oppositional groups as strongly demarcated from their racial and ethnic communities as a whole. Instead, as they organized, Black and Chicana feminists reiterated the existence of a primary boundary existing between themselves and white America (Roth 2004). Black and Chicana feminists saw themselves as demarcated from mainstream

America by virtue of the race line, a boundary that their community as a whole was seeking to breach. Like emerging white feminists, as they initially organized, Black and Latina feminists saw other male and female activists as their audience; unlike white women's liberationists, the shift in audience to a universalized sisterhood did not occur. In short, even as they built autonomous groups, Black and Chicana feminists never shifted from their (oppositional) communities in searching for a new audience to mobilize.

The contrasting case of 1960s feminists of color raises questions about the role that the conceptualization of potential recruits, that is, audience, has for the reconstruction of activists' identities. For example, did the "double jeopardy" of being of color and female make clear the question of audience for feminists of color in the 1960s and 1970s (Beal 1970)? Did emerging white feminists' reorientation of political effort toward a new audience result from their privileged position in the race, ethnicity, and class hierarchy? Is audience shift itself a marker of social privilege, of a special kind of latitude in collective identity formation? As we study how collective identity formation takes place in concrete settings and in relationship to concrete others, we would do well to also specify how "others" figure in the constructions of an activist "we."

References

Allen, Pam. 1968. "What Strategy for Movement Women?" *Guardian* (October 5): 9.

"Ann." 1970. "Women and Anti-war Work." *It Ain't Me Babe* 1: 8 (June 11–July 1).

Baker, Sue. 1970. "Venceremos Part 2." *off our backs*. (March).

Baxandall, Ros. 2001. "Re-visioning the Women's Liberation Movement's Narrative: Early Second Wave African American Feminists." *Feminist Studies* 21.1 (Spring): 225–45.

Beal, Francis. 1970. "Double Jeopardy: To Be Black and Female." In *The Black Woman: An Anthology*, ed. T. Cade (Bambara), 90–100. New York: New American Library.

Breines, Wini. 1982. *The Great Refusal: Community and Organization in the New Left: 1962–1968*. South Hadley, Mass.: Praeger Publishers.

Buechler, Steven M. 1990. *Women's Movements in the United States: Woman Suffrage, Equal Rights and Beyond*. New Brunswick, N.J.: Rutgers University Press.

Burris, Barbara. 1971. "The Fourth World Manifesto." *Notes from the Third Year*.

Cagan, Beth. 1971 "Why Should Women Join the NUC?" New University Conference Women's Caucus Newsletter. Schlesinger Library, Harvard University (March).

Carden, Maren Lockwood. 1974. *The New Feminist Movement*. New York: Russell Sage Foundation.

Davidica, Maureen. 1968. "Women and the Radical Movement." *No More Fun & Games*. Boston.

della Porta, Donatella, and Mario Diani. 1999. *Social Movements: An Introduction.* Oxford: Blackwell Publishers.

Densmore, Dana. 1971. "On Unity." *No More Fun & Games* 5 Reprint of speech delivered at the "Conference to Unite Women" in Washington D.C., October 1970.

Dixon, Marlene. 1970. "On Women's Liberation." *Radical America*, 26–29.

Dunbar, Roxanne.1968. "Slavery." *No More Fun & Games*: 1.

———. 1969 (November). "Sexual Liberation: More of the Same." *No More Fun & Games*: 3.

Echols, Alice. 1989. *Daring to Be Bad: Radical Feminism in America 1967–1975.* Minneapolis. University of Minnesota Press.

———. 1992. "We Gotta Get Out of This Place": Notes toward a remapping of the sixties." *Socialist Review* 22: 2 (April/June), 9–33

Estellachild, Vivian. 1971. "Hippie Communes." *Women: A Journal of Liberation* 2 (Winter): 2.

Evans, Sara. 1979. *Personal Politics: The Roots of Women's Liberation in the Civil Rights Movement and the New Left.* New York: Vintage Books

Fraser, Clara. 1970. "Which Road Towards Women's Liberation?" *Women: A Journal of Liberation* 2 (Fall): 1.

Freeman, Jo. 1973. "The Origins of the Women's Liberation Movement." *American Journal of Sociology* 78(4): 792–811.

———. 1975. *The Politics of Women's Liberation.* New York: Longman.

Gamson, William A. 1991. "Commitment and Agency in Social Movements." *Sociological Forum* 6.1 (March): 27–50.

Giddings, Paula. 1984. *When and Where I Enter: The Impact of Black Women on Race and Sex in America.* New York: Bantam Books.

Gitlin, Todd. 1987. *The Sixties: Years of Hope, Days of Rage.* Toronto: Bantam Books.

Gluck, Sherna, Maylei Blackwell, Sharon Cotrell, and Karen S. Harper. 1998. "Whose Feminism, Whose History? Reflections on Excavating the History of (the) US Women's Movement(s). In *Community Activism and Feminist Politics: Organizing Across Race, Class, and Gender*, ed. N. A. Naples, 31–56. Philadelphia: Temple University Press.

Goldfield, Evelyn, Sue Munaker, and Naomi Weisstein. c. 1968. "A Woman Is a Sometime Thing." Pamphlet published by Literature Committee, Toronto's Women's Liberation and the Hogtown Press. Women's Ephemera Files, Special Collections, Northwestern University.

Hole, Judith, and Ellen Levine. 1971. *Rebirth of Feminism*. New York: Quadrangle Books.

Jones, Beverly, and Judith Brown. 1968. "Toward a Female Liberation Movement." Pamphlet. Women's Ephemera Files, Special Collections, Northwestern University

Kearns, Karen. 1970. "Grove Press: Crimes against women." *off our backs*. (April).

Koedt, Anne. 1968. "Women and the Radical Movement." *Notes from the First Year*. New York: New York Radical Women.

Liberation News Service. 1970. Advertisement.

Lund, Caroline. 1970. "Female Liberation and Socialism" (Interview with Pat Galligan). *The Militant* (November 27) 9–12.

Ferree, Myra Marx, and Beth B. Hess. 1985. *Controversy & Coalition: The New Feminist Movement*. New York: Twayne Publishers.

———. 1994. *Controversy & Coalition: The New Feminist Movement Across Three Decades of Change*, rev. edition. New York: Twayne Publishers.

———. 2000. *Controversy & Coalition: The New Feminist Movement Across Four Decades of Change*, 3rd ed. New York: Routledge.

McAdam, Doug, Sidney Tarrow, and Charles Tilly. 2001. *Dynamics of Contention*. *New York: Cambridge University Press*.

McEldowney, Carol. 1969. Unpublished letter. Carol McEldowney Papers, State Historical Society, Madison, Wisc. (July).

Meyer, David S., and Nancy Whittier. 1994. "Social Movement Spillover." *Social Problems* 41.2 (May): 277–98.

The Militant. 1969. "Feminist Women March against the War." (November 7).

Morgan, Robin. 1968. "The Oldest Front: On Freedom for Women." *Liberation* 8.5 (October): 34–37.

New Left Notes. 1967. "Chicago Women Form Liberation Group" preliminary statement of principles (November 13).

New University Conference, Women's Caucus (NUC). c. 1970a. "History of the Women's Caucus." Unpublished, unsigned position paper. Sophia Smith Collection, Smith College.

———. c. 1970b. "Whither the Women's Caucus?" Unsigned, unpublished position paper. Sophia Smith Collection, Smith College.

Piercy, Marge. 1970. "The Grand Coolie Damn." In *Sisterhood Is Powerful*, ed. R. Morgan, 421–38. New York: Vintage Books.

Polletta, Francesa. 1999. "'Free Spaces' in Collective Action." *Theory & Society* 28: 1–38.

Polletta, Francesa, and James M. Jasper. 2001. "Collective Identity and Social Movements." *Annual Review of Sociology* 27: 283–305.

RAT. 1971. Unsigned. "A Year Ago . . . A Sister Remembers." (January).

Robinson, Jo Anne. c. 1970. "Sex Discrimination and the Beloved Community."
    Reprinted pamphlet from *Fellowship* magazine. Women's Ephemera Files, Spe-
    cial Collections, Northwestern University

Robnett, Belinda. 1997. *How Long? How Long?: African-American Women in the
    Struggle for Civil Rights.* Oxford: Oxford University Press.

Rominski, Fran. 1968. "Sexual Service System." *Voice of the Women's Liberation
    Movement.* (June)

Roth, Benita. 2004. *Separate Roads to Feminism: Black, Chicana, and White Feminist
    Movements in America's Second Wave.* New York: Cambridge University Press.

Rupp, Leila, and Verta Taylor, 1999. "Forging Feminist Identity in an International
    Movement: A Collective Identity Approach to Twentieth-century Feminism."
    Signs 24(2): 363–86.

Ryan, Barbara. 1992. *Feminism and the Women's Movement: Dynamics of Change in
    Social Movement, Ideology and Activism.* New York: Routledge.

Seese, Linda. 1969. "You've Come a Long Way, Baby—Women in the Movement."
    Motive XXIX: 6–7 (March–April).

Stoper, Emily. 1989. *The Student Nonviolent Coordinating Mommittee: The Growth of
    Radicalism in a Civil Rights Organization.* New York: Carlson.

Taylor, Verta, and Nancy Whittier. 1992. "Collective Identity in Social Movement
    Communities: Lesbian Feminist Mobilization." In *Frontiers in Social Movement
    Theory*, ed. A. D. Morris and C. M. Mueller, 104–29. New Haven, Conn.: Yale
    University Press.

Thursday Night Group (Leslie Hawkins, Sydney Halpern, Anna Kehela, and Randy
    Rappaport). 1969. "On Autonomy." Position paper, Berkeley Women's Libera-
    tion. (August)

Turner, Ralph H., and Lewis M. Killian. 1987. *Collective Behavior.* Englewood
    Cliffs, N.J.: Prentice Hall.

Vanauken. 1971. "A Primer for the Last Revolution." Pittsburgh: Know Inc. Wash-
    ington, Cynthia. 1979 "We Started from Different Ends of the Spectrum." In
    *Personal Politics: The Roots of Women's Liberation in the Civil Rights Movement
    and the New Left*, ed. Sara Evans, 238–40. New York: Vintage Books

Webb, Marilyn. 1968. "Towards a Radical Women's Movement." Reprinted by Chi-
    cago-Hyde Park Women's Group. Social Action Files, State Historical Society,
    Madison, Wisconsin. (February)

———. 1969a. "We are Victims." *Voice of the Women's Liberation Movement.* (February).

———. 1969b. "History of Women's Liberation." *Daily Gater.* (December 10).

Weinfeld, Marta. 1970. "Women's Liberation Advances the Movement." Unpub-
    lished position paper for Wednesday Night New Course Group, Berkeley
    Women's Liberation. Women's Ephemera Files, Special Collections, Northwest-
    ern University (December 15).

Wells, Lynn. 1969. "A Movement for Us." *the great speckled bird* (February 28).

Willis, Ellen. 1970. "Women and the Left." *Notes from the Second Year.* New York: Shulamith Firestone and Anne Koedt (self published).

Notes

1. On the question of personal investment in movements, see della Porta and Diani 1999; on the issue of the costs of abandoning such investments, see Turner and Killian 1987.

2. In this chapter, I have used documentary sources gathered during the research for a larger study on the emergence of racial/ ethnic feminisms in America's postwar cycle of protest (Roth 2004). While documentary evidence is necessarily partial as a means of reconstructing a movement's emergence, it is particularly well-suited for understanding the intellectual debate about organizing that took place among feminists in this era.

3. Scholars have debated the extent to which white women activists, whose numbers in SNCC grew in the wake of 1964's Freedom Summer, were actually stymied by gender roles within that organization. Robnett (1997; see also Chapter 7) noted that Hayden and King's paper was not so much an attack on SNCC's sexism as an attempt to bring up issues of hierarchy as the group wrestled with its overall structure and direction. Hayden and King both felt relatively well-treated within the organization. However, it seems true that white women performed different roles in SNCC, and that Black women and Black men held more important positions in the organization (Evans 1979; Giddings 1984; Washington 1979).

4. The topic of women's liberation was in fact left off the list of issues listed in the Guardian advertisement for the Counter-Inauguration event. At the actual demonstration, Dave Dellinger forgot to mention the issue of women's liberation and announced the presence of speakers on the subject only after being yelled at by radical women sharing the stage (Willis 1970).

Afterword

The Analytic Dimensions of Identity:
A Political Identity Framework[1]

Mary Bernstein

This edited collection builds on and provides exciting extensions of the political identity framework that I introduced in my article "Celebration and Suppression: The Strategic Uses of Identity by the Lesbian and Gay Movement" (Bernstein 1997). In "Celebration and Suppression" (Bernstein 1997), I argued that what social movement theorists termed "identity movements" were defined as much by the goals they seek and the strategies they use as by the fact that they are based on a shared characteristic, such as ethnicity or sex. Multiple use of the term identity movements led to substantial theoretical confusion. I challenged the commonplace characterization of social movements as *either* identity-oriented and expressive *or* political and instrumental. The view that instrumental strategies were irrelevant to cultural change, while expressions of identity could not be externally directed was represented by the bifurcation in the social movements literature between political process theory and resource mobilization theory, on the one hand, and social movement theory, on the other. I demonstrated that this *essentialist* characterization stemmed from the conflation of goals and strategies apparent in resource mobilization, political process, and new social movement theories. In order to clarify the use of the term "identity" in the social movement literature and to provide a way to understand the role of identity in *all* social movements, I developed a theoretical framework that I call a "political identity" model. This framework posits that the concept of "identity" has at least three distinct analytic levels that I term, "identity for empowerment," "identity deployment," and "identity as a goal." This framework has led to a more comprehensive understanding of social movements and a more useful way of thinking about the relationship between identity and social movements (e.g., Polletta and Jasper 2001; Bernstein 2005).

In this chapter, I present a more fully articulated theory of identity for empowerment and identity deployment. Then, I challenge conventional understandings of power prevalent in the social movement literature to develop a research agenda to examine identity as a goal, the least developed of the three analytic dimensions of identity. I introduce the concept of "feedback loops" to theorize the relationships between the different analytic dimensions of identity. I conclude by raising questions for future research.

A Political Identity Framework

Identity for Empowerment

A shared collective identity is necessary for the mobilization of *any* social movement (Morris 1992), whether it is the women's movement or the labor movement (Calhoun 1995). I define this first level of analysis as "identity for empowerment" to capture the creation of collective identity and the feeling that collective action is worth pursuing. In other words, some sort of identity is necessary to translate individual interests to group interests and goals and individual agency to collective action. All social movements require such "political consciousness" (Morris 1992) to create and mobilize a constituency (Taylor and Whittier 1992; Calhoun 1995). Jane Mansbridge and Aldon Morris (2001) refer to identity for empowerment as insurgent consciousness or oppositional consciousness. However, the terms "insurgent" and "oppositional" signify rebellion or opposition to dominant beliefs and thus fail to adequately represent the perspectives of conservative and reactionary social movements. The term "identity for empowerment" is a more sociologically useful term than insurgent or oppositional consciousness, because it can be applied across movements rather than being linked to movements with progressive ideologies. Identity for empowerment is also better able to capture the complexities of ideology and hegemony rather than framing these in simple, dichotomous terms as opposing or supporting the status quo.

The creation of a collective identity—that is, identity for empowerment—remains the most developed analytic dimension of identity in the social movement literature. Much research, including many of the chapters in this book continue to rely on Verta Taylor and Nancy Whittier's (1992) three pronged framework for understanding identity for empowerment. In their now classic article, Taylor and Whittier (1992) argue that social movements develop and maintain a collective identity that is characterized by maintaining boundaries between group members and nonmembers, developing a political consciousness that defines and analyzes interests, and negotiating everyday symbols and actions as strategies of personalized resistance (see Hunt and Benford 2004 for a recent review of this research). While still useful for social movement theory, Taylor and Whittier's framework does not account for the ways movements contend with the realities of individuals' multiple identities. An intersectional approach to identity for empowerment can help to explain in more detail how the content of a movement's collective identity is created. Here, I outline the "nuts and bolts" of how the collective "we" is created, above and beyond the issues outlined by Taylor and Whittier (1992). These include internal organizational factors, external factors related to the political context, and the relationship of activists to the political issues at stake. I also argue that activists' experience, ideology, and emotions inform the content of activists' collective identity.

Organizational structure affects the ways in which social movements negotiate (or fail to negotiate) internal issues of sameness and difference to foster identity for empowerment. Individuals' identities based on the intersections between, for example, race, class, gender, and sexual orientation provide sources of internal differences within movements. Collective identities are not simply free-floating cultural phenomena but also historically, materially, and organizationally located. Organizational structure can serve to exacerbate differences within social movement organizations or to foster a more cohesive empowering identity. For example, Jane Ward (Chapter 10) shows that the imposition of diversity training by a lesbian and gay movement organization took place from the perspective of whites and so had the effect of reifying racial divisions and promoting a "white" organizational identity rather than one that is truly multiracial. By contrast, Silke Roth (Chapter 9) illustrates that organizational structure can facilitate the negotiation of differences within organizations through caucuses organized around race in order to produce a viable multiracial class-based feminist identity, as in the fusion identity "union feminism." Paul Lichterman (1999) suggests that successfully fostering solidarity across identities depends on the ability to freely discuss the identities that activists claim. This "identity talk" in the public sphere is culturally constructed through interactional routines and can exacerbate or mitigate tensions between identity groups. Organizational ideologies may also affect the content of identity for empowerment. Organizational structure can either facilitate or impede the creation of an empowering identity that can adequately address issues of internal differences.

The external environment, including the political context, opposing movements, the activities of other social movements, and the targets of activism are also important in creating identity for empowerment. Benita Roth (Chapter 11) discusses how the collective identity "women" only emerged when activists shifted their emphasis from reforming white leftist men to focus on mobilizing all women. Jo Reger (Chapter 4) examines the importance of antagonists in constructing identity for empowerment. Feminists structure the content of their identities in relationship to the political context. Thus Reger finds that when feminist ideals are generally accepted in the local political environment, activists will adopt more radical identities than they will when feminist ideals are less accepted. Because a movement must assert some similarity or commonality among activists in contradistinction to antagonists and bystanders, other social movement organizations become important factors in creating identity for empowerment. For example, Susan Munkres (Chapter 8) shows that American activists who serve as "sisters" to Salvadoran communities defined themselves against organizations that they dismissed as simply charity organizations. Thus part of the process of creating an empowering identity is to define the ways in which one's group is different from similar groups.

The external environment also affects how debates over inclusion and exclusion—that is, to decide "who we are" and "who we are not"—are resolved. Joshua Gamson (1997) argues that both the communicative environment and the audience to be addressed influence who is considered a part of a collective "we." Movements must not only identify antagonists but also struggle over contested membership. For example, Kathleen Blee (2002) illustrates that the concept of "race traitor" helps racist activists set a symbolic boundary to distinguish themselves from whites not in the movement.

A movement's collective identity is also important because an actor can use her or his identity to gain "political standing" or to legitimate participation in a social movement. In some cases, the collective identity must help activists justify political participation in a movement in which she or he is not directly implicated, as in the case of women organized as mothers and wives of coal miners (Beckwith 1996) or adoptive "sister" to Salvadoran peasants (Munkres, Chapter 6). Munkres points out that the constructed identity "sister," which justifies the participation of American women as witnesses, allies, and resources for Salvadoran communities is also constraining. By fostering an appearance of familial equality between groups with astoundingly different levels of structural privilege, the identity of "sister" shelters American activists from contending with their own issues of privilege.

Constructing the "we" or an empowering identity is complicated by the diversity of the group members and is facilitated or hampered by both internal and external factors. A collective identity can be produced through experience, ideology, commitment, or emotion. Daniel J. Myers (Chapter 7) explores the challenges that movements face when integrating "allies" who are not direct beneficiaries of the movement's activism. In the absence of a sameness of identity based on experience, emotion (Chapter 6) or ideology (Chapter 7) can fill the gap.

In this section, I theorized several factors that help to explain how social movements negotiate internal differences in order to create identity for empowerment. Social movement organizations must contend with the diversity of membership stemming from multiple identities rooted in structural and status differences. I have argued that the ability to negotiate internal differences is affected by a variety of organizational factors, the political environment, other social movement organizations, and the opposition. An empowering identity may also be produced through experience, ideology, commitment, or emotion in a way that overcomes internal differences. Later, I show that the content of the collective identity produced influences a movement's ability to mobilize, its choice of strategies and goals, and the outcomes it produces.

Identity Deployment

Identity can be used as a strategy by social movements, a second analytic level of identity. In "Celebration and Suppression" (Bernstein 1997), I introduced the term "identity deployment" to mean expressing identity such that the terrain of conflict becomes the individual person so that the values, categories, and practices of individuals become subject to debate. I argued that expressions of identity can be deployed at the collective level as a political strategy, which can be aimed at cultural and/or instrumental political goals.[2] Identity deployment can be examined at both the individual and collective level along a continuum from education to critique. Activists either dress and act consistently with mainstream culture or behave in a critical way. "Identity for critique" confronts the values, categories, and practices of the dominant culture. "Identity for education" challenges the dominant culture's perception of the minority or is used strategically to gain legitimacy by playing on uncontroversial themes. In the case of the lesbian and gay movement, identity for education may challenge negative stereotypes about lesbians and gay men, such as having hundreds of sexual partners a year or uncontrollable sexual urges. Deploying identity for critique, for example, may challenge dominant cultural assumptions about the religious or biological "naturalness" of gender roles and the heterosexual nuclear family. Although the goals associated with either identity strategy can be moderate or radical, identity for education generally limits the scope of conflict by not problematizing the morality or norms of the dominant culture. Using four campaigns for lesbian and gay rights ordinances as case studies, I explored the political conditions that produce certain identity strategies. I argued that interactions between social movement organizations, state actors, and the opposition determine the types of identities deployed. Elsewhere (Bernstein 2002), I also stress that movements can avoid identity strategies altogether by, for example, appealing to abstract notions of justice and fairness rather than calling attention to the specificity of particular groups' identities.

In this section, I elaborate additional ways in which identity can be deployed, specify more fully the conditions that produce a mixed model of identity deployment, and explore identity deployment in a variety of institutional venues. I then specify the mechanisms that produce identity strategies and consider the relationship between emotions and identity deployment. I introduce the concept "identity contest" to help clarify how targets and other social movements deploy the identity of those they oppose.

In contrast to the characterization of social movements as expressive or instrumental, the goal of identity deployment can be to transform mainstream culture, its categories, values, and practices, as well as its policies and structures. Identity deployment can also transform participants or simply educate legislators or the public. Rachel L. Einwohner (Chapter 5) shows that identities can also be deployed strategically as a way to gain the resources needed for collective action.

Identity deployment can be understood dramaturgically (Goffman 1959) as the collective portrayal of the group's identity in the political realm, whether in city council hearings or at sit-ins in segregated restaurants (Bernstein 1997).[3] In addition to understanding identity deployment in performative terms (e.g., the deployment of Aryan identities by Jewish activists [Chapter 5], of maternalist identities by Brazilian female activists [Chapter 6], or of gay, lesbian, bisexual, transgender, and gender-bending identities by drag queens [Chapter 2]), identity deployment as a political strategy can take place in other nonperformative ways through written discourse and printed images. For example, Todd Schroer (Chapter 3) shows that the Internet has become a prime location for the strategic deployment of identity by self-proclaimed white "racialists." The venue of the Internet provides an ideal way for groups who lack access to the media and to the polity to deploy their identity as a means of either educating dominant groups about their beliefs, motives, and politics or critiquing the practices, categories, and values of dominant groups. Of course, in chat rooms and other interactive venues on the Internet, identity can also be deployed in more performative and interactive ways. Kimberly B. Dugan argues (Chapter 1) that identity strategies are rhetorical and discursive as well as performative. Although such strategies do not have the direct interactional components of performative forms of identity deployment, the interactional component is implicit. For example, in the case of white racialists, activists respond through written documents placed on the Internet to negative depictions of their movement in the media and elsewhere.

In "Celebration and Suppression," I specified the conditions under which a mixed model of identity deployment would occur in the political realm—that is, where activists deployed both identity for education and identity for critique. I argued that if a movement faces organized opposition from outside the political establishment, and if the movement is led by exclusive, narrowly focused groups uninterested in movement building, the movement may split, with some groups emphasizing differences and community building, while the exclusive groups continue to emphasize sameness and narrowly focused policy change. In such cases, critical identities may be deployed as much in reaction to movement leadership as to the opposition. In writing this, the local social movement itself (i.e., the groups and individuals interested in the particular issue) was my implicit unit of analysis. While some organizations in my study shifted their own deployment of identity over time between critical and educational forms, in cases where critical and educational identities were deployed simultaneously, those identities were mobilized by different social movement organizations or by different factions within the social movement.

Here, I outline other conditions that may lead to mixed models of identity deployment. I hypothesize that the extent to which activists can simultaneously deploy sameness and difference depends on the logic of the arena where the action takes place. For example, placing documents and newsletters on a Web site provides no immediate interactional feedback. In contrast, in a legislative hearing, interaction is immediate and swift, as legislators often interrupt and interrogate presenters. In such a venue, narrative fidelity and consistency will be more important as legislators may challenge the accounts of presenters. Thus in a legislative hearing, it would be more difficult for activists to simultaneously deploy similarities and differences. In cultural venues, the performer has license to perform identity in multiple ways and need not answer to an external authority. Thus the extent of interaction and who has power in the interaction are likely to affect to what extent activists can deploy similarities and differences simultaneously.

The venue and audience where identity deployment takes place also shape the likelihood that activists will pursue a mixed model of identity deployment. Dugan (Chapter 1), in her case study of the lesbian and gay movement in Cincinnati, suggests that the same organization may simultaneously stress similarities and differences, yet she does not clearly specify the conditions in which such a mixed model will occur. Dugan states that when lesbian and gay activists underscore differences from the majority, they do so by highlighting that gay, lesbian, bisexual, and transgender people could become victims of discrimination. Yet the difference was not stressed as being an inherent characteristic of the group and thus did not make the identities, practices, and categories of lesbians and gay men subject to debate and so was not a case of identity deployment. In her case study, the "simultaneous" emphasis of sameness and differences was linked to the specific audience and venue of the deployment (an individual's letter to the editor or a social movement organization's postcards mailed to potential voters). In other words, similarities and differences were not deployed simultaneously in the same venue by the same actor. In contrast, some white racialists underscore similarities to the majority and deploy identity for education on the Internet, while other racialist Internet sites emphasize differences rather than similarities (Chapter 3). In this case, as in my original formulation of a mixed model, different factions of the movement or different movement organizations employ competing identity strategies to produce a mixed model of identity deployment. Social movements may alternate the deployment of sameness and difference depending on the venue and audience. It is also less likely that the same actors or movement organizations will deploy both similarities and differences at the same time in the same venue. Enumerating the ways in which activists are both different from and similar to the majority in most venues would threaten a narrative consistency. Yet competing social movement organizations or factions within organizations may deploy competing identities in the same venue and movements may change their emphasis on similarities and differences over time.

The strategic deployment of identity through cultural performance, however, provides an important exception to the need for narrative consistency. Drag performances and other political performances such as neo-Burlesque (Peluso 2005) are also forms of identity deployment. In the venue of the 801 Cabaret, Elizabeth Kaminski and Verta Taylor show that drag queens deployed their identities on stage to educate the heterosexual public about "the experiences, sexual practices, and problems that gays and lesbians face" (Chapter 2). But certain performers also deployed identity for critique to challenge and criticize dominant ideologies and practices of femininity, masculinity, and heteronormativity. In these ways, similarities and differences may be stressed simultaneously by the same social movement, movement organization, or individuals in politicized performances. Exploiting such contradictions can further the artistic and political goals in a cultural performance setting. In certain venues such as the Internet or drag club, the same individuals may simultaneously deploy identity for education and critique. In cases such as legislative hearings, the same organization will likely take a more unified approach to identity deployment at a single point in time (Olsen 2006).

Another key issue that was more implicit than explicit in "Celebration and Suppression" was the precise mechanisms that produce sameness and difference. How is identity deployment coordinated? What work goes into identity deployment strategies? The chapters in this book lay out some of these mechanisms. For example, the practical work that goes into identity deployment includes the use of clothing, cultural, and behavioral symbols. Whether that means dressing in "republican drag" in a legislative hearing (Bernstein 1997) or sewing fur into one's clothes to pass as Aryan (Einwohner, Chapter 5), or not wearing Klan robes to show that one is not part of an extremist group (Schroer, Chapter 3), identity deployment requires work.

Music and ritual are another mechanism by which identities are strategically deployed. When drag queens perform to music in order to critique or educate audiences, they rely on ritual and the power of music and their performance to accomplish the tasks of identity deployment (Kaminski and Taylor, Chapter 2). Another aspect of identity deployment is drawing attention to the motivations of activists. When lesbian and gay activists highlight scientific research that unequivocally demonstrates that heterosexual men, not gay men, are most likely to be child molesters, they draw attention to their own pristine motivations to justify their claims for rights. Drawing attention to motivations as a mechanism of identity deployment is also apparent when Brazilian women activists underscore that their role as mothers (not agitators or troublemakers) provides the impetus for their activism (Neuhouser, Chapter 6), while white racialists emphasize that their motivations to promote the white race do not stem from a place of hatred (Schroer, Chapter 3). Even the choice of organizational forms can be related to identity deployment, as when racialist organizations professionalize in order to illustrate their "mainstream" identity (Schroer, Chapter 3). Finally, identity deployment may also involve reframing the identities of opponents.

Other questions about identity as a strategy deserve further research, such as how to link identity deployment more closely to organizational structure. In other words, are there certain types of organizational structures that make it more difficult than others to shift modes of identity deployment? Which organizational structures are conducive to identity strategies and which to nonidentity strategies or both types of strategies? How constraining are past performances of identity for future performances? How easily can organizations shift their deployment of identity for future performances? Finally, how do activists deal with the emotional component of identity strategies? What are the long-term ramifications of such emotion work for activists and social movements more generally? How do social movement organizations negotiate dilemmas where strategic considerations and personal understandings of identity conflict?

Identity as Goal

The last analytic level of analysis I named is "identity as a goal." In this case, identity can be a goal of social movement activism, as activists strive to either gain acceptance for a hitherto stigmatized identity (Calhoun 1994) or deconstruct categories of identities such as man, woman, gay, straight, (Gamson 1995), black, or white. Thus far, identity as a goal is the analytic dimension of identity that has received the least scholarly attention. In this book, only two chapters even briefly touch on the issue (see Chapter 2 and 3). In this section, I argue that common theoretical assumptions in the social movement literature preclude a comprehensive understanding of identity as a goal. I provide a theoretical model to overcome these problems and sketch a research agenda that is designed to help scholars more fully understand social movements that have identity as a goal. I introduce the term "deconstructive movement" and lay out some important research questions that need to be addressed. I conclude by outlining some possible ways in which scholars can measure identity outcomes.

Theoretically, to grasp the importance of studying identity as a goal, two conceptual shifts must take place: First, movements for recognition must no longer be viewed as being interested solely in cultural recognition in contradistinction to movements aimed at political and economic change (Bernstein 2005). Second, scholars must explicitly theorize power and avoid relying on narrow, state-centered views of power that permeate political process theory. Instead, theorists should adopt a multi-institutional politics model that views power as rooted in multiple and contradictory institutions, each of which is constituted by "classificatory systems and practices that concretize these systems" (Armstrong and Bernstein 2008; Friedland and Alford 1991).

In contrast to viewing recognition and redistribution as unrelated, I argue that a *lack of* recognition can be intimately related to issues of redistribution and citizenship more generally. Even those theorists, such as Nancy

Fraser (1997), who argue that recognition is related to issues of redistribution do not specify how movements pursue recognition as a goal. To understand why movements pursue the recognition of identity as a goal, I argue that one must understand theoretically that identities are integrally related to structure and interest.

To understand identity as a goal, one must also challenge a second assumption that is common in the social movement literature regarding the operation of power.[4] Social movement theory tends to view power as state-centered and rooted in the political and economic structures of societies. For example, Doug McAdam (1982, 37), one of the architects of political process theory, argues that power stems from the various locations that groups have in relation to political and economic structures. Thus elites and subordinate groups differ based on disparate levels of political and economic access. In this view, power stems from the state and domination makes sense only in terms of groups' relationship to state power.

Even in *Dynamics of Contention*, which was meant to overcome the shortcomings of the political process model, McAdam, Tarrow, and Tilly (2001, 5, 10–11) continue to define contentious politics only in relation to the state (see Armstrong and Bernstein 2008 for further analysis). Challenges to other types of authority thus do not make sense in terms of political process and contentious politics models.

In contrast to the view of the state and power present in political process theory, I argue that in order to understand social movements that seek to deconstruct categories of identity, one must take a more expansive view of power. Armstrong and Bernstein (2008) argue that "domination . . . is organized around multiple sources of power, each of which is simultaneously material and symbolic . . . culture is a powerful, constraining force, instead of secondary or epiphenomenal." What I term "deconstructive movements" may target the state, institutions, and more general cultural practices. These movements are motivated by activists' understandings of how categories are constituted and how those categories, codes, and ways of thinking serve as axes of regulation and domination (Melucci 1996; Rochon 1998; Crossley 2002; Eyerman and Jamison 1991).

Numerous social movements seek acceptance for their identities and these struggles are intertwined with concerns for rights and redistribution. For example, nationalist movements often seek some type of official recognition from governments. Language rights pursued by French-speaking Canadians are linked to the ability to participate fully in Canadian society. Indigenous movements, such as American Indian movements seek official recognition from the U.S. Bureau of Indian Affairs. Such recognition can be accompanied by financial benefits, rights to land, and other gains such as tax exemptions and gaming and fishing rights. In Latin America, indigenous movements may seek official recognition through constitutional change, which also provides political rights and other instrumental benefits. In countries with proportional voting schemes, recognition becomes critically important for gaining political power. While recognition of the women's movement in the U.S. is not "official" inasmuch as such recognition is not officially sanctioned by the state, the movement has garnered a place at the table in public debates and is a recognized political constituency.

What I term "deconstructive movements," by contrast, seek to challenge the categorical identities that define movements with recognition as a goal. The logic that underlies these challenges is that the cultural ways of "doing business" that create these categories position some groups as normal in contrast to deviant others (e.g., Foucault 1978; Butler 1990; Seidman 1993; Bower 1997). The existence of the categories themselves is seen as creating the foundation for inequality and discrimination. Thus challenging and ultimately eliminating these categories motivates activism. For example, "queer" movements view the categories straight, gay, lesbian, and bisexual as socially constructed. Therefore, exposing the social basis for these categories by deconstructing them undermines the cultural and political bases for oppression. Some feminists such as Judith Butler (1990) view the categories "male" and "female" as socially constructed, created by performances that perpetuate the myth that these categories reflect some real, inner core. Thus performances that "gender bend" become protests against cultural sources of power and against the power of the category to organize and regulate social life more generally. Relatedly, multiracial activists view racial categories as socially constructed. They point out that many individuals cannot be placed simply into one category or another. In this view, continued reliance on such categories serves to reify those categories and organize thinking in racial and racist terms. Thus some multiracial activists seek to push the government to stop collecting data based on racial categories, while others such as Hapa activists continue to see data gathering based on racial and ethnic categories as important but advocate that respondents should be able to "check all that apply" when providing information about their racial and ethnic backgrounds (Bernstein and De la Cruz 2007).

Some questions that arise when studying deconstructive movements include the following: How are deconstructive movements linked to movements of recognition? Can deconstructive movements emerge in the absence of movements for recognition? If so, under what conditions do such movements emerge? What is the relationship between groups whose goal is to deconstruct identities and those groups whose political demands rely on deploying stable identities? How do government actors respond to movements for recognition? What types of dilemmas do deconstructive movements face? For example, how do movements negotiate identity for empowerment when the identity around which the movement is organized is also the basis for grievances? Can a movement seek both to deconstruct old categories of identity, while seeking recognition for new categories of identity? Gamson (1995) contends that deconstructive strategies that loosen categories of identity are better suited for contesting cultural sources of oppression than institutional sources of oppression, whose logic requires the tightening of categories. Some suggest that challengers such as queer and multiracial movements that seek solely to deconstruct social categories may ultimately undermine their own existence, presenting an interesting organizational dilemma (Gamson 1995; Lorber 1999).

The third issue that I wish to raise as an important area of research on identity as a goal is how do we assess identity as an outcome of social movement activism? Examining the extent to which identity as a goal is achieved remains relatively unexplored theoretically and empirically. In part, this stems from the difficulty in operationalizing cultural change more generally (Bernstein 2003; Earl 2004). I suggest several ways to examine such outcomes.

For movements of recognition, several possibilities occur. Movements may receive official recognition by governments that comes with tangible benefits or changes in practices. Court decisions can also confer official recognition. Movements that seek to challenge the stigma associated with a given identity may change the practices of institutions or the knowledge that is produced by these institutions. For example, lesbian and gay activists in the 1970s effectively challenged the American Psychological Association's classification of homosexuality as a mental disorder, removing one important source of stigma associated with homosexuality. This recognition had long-term political implications and made it easier to grant legal rights and protections to lesbians and gay men (Bayer 1987; Bernstein 2003). Feminists often challenge the stigma that can be associated with the term "feminist" (as in the commonplace claim, "I'm not a feminist, but I believe in equality between men and women"). Whether or not such identity goals are achieved can be assessed by examining public discourse through media outlets or public opinion polls.

Public discourse analyzed through studies of the media, public opinion, or popular culture can also serve to assess the impact of deconstructive movements and the achievement of identity as a goal. In order to measure the impact of politicized performances of drag on deconstructing identities,

Rupp and Taylor (2003) study audience reactions. Their findings suggest that, at least in the short run, dominant understandings of masculinity, femininity, and heterosexuality are challenged. The white racialists examined by Schroer (Chapter 3) also seek to challenge the stigma associated with being a racist. However, it remains unclear how effective identity deployment on the Internet is for achieving that goal.

In this section, I outlined a preliminary research agenda that can assist scholars in studying identity as a goal of activism. I argued for the theoretical importance of linking identity with structural location and interest so that scholars can theorize the multiple ways in which recognition and redistribution are related. In order to understand movements that seek to deconstruct identity as a goal, one must have a broader understanding of power than what is traditionally found in American social movement theory. I then suggested some fruitful lines of inquiry and ways to assess the extent to which identity as a goal of social movements is achieved. In the next section, I link the three analytic dimensions of identity by developing the concept "feedback loop."

Feedback Loops

It is important to understand the three dimensions of identity because these concepts help to explain the goals that a movement pursues, the strategies employed, who is mobilized, and what types of outcomes are achieved. This section introduces the concept "feedback loop" as a way to theorize the relationships between identity for empowerment, identity as a strategy, and identity as a goal and the ways in which these relationships influence movement mobilization, strategic choices, and outcomes. Thus far, no one has attempted to theorize the relationships between the role of identity across these different levels of analysis (Polletta and Jasper 2001). In what follows, I provide examples to illustrate these relationships and the importance of understanding identity for empowerment, identity as strategy, and identity as goal for answering core questions within social movement theory.

Social movements based on status identities are often considered to be isolated from structural locations. Activism is portrayed as expressive, seeking recognition for new identities (e.g., Cohen 1985; Melucci 1989; Touraine 1981) rather than tangible instrumental goals, such as redistribution (Gitlin 1994, 1995; Rorty 1998; for a critique of this view see Bickford 1997; Fraser 1997; Bernstein 2005). In contrast, I suggest that to understand how collective identity affects strategies and goals, scholars must keep in mind the ways in which interest, identity, and structure intersect. However, I am not arguing that the relationship between identity for empowerment, the strategies a movement chooses, and the goals it pursues is always straightforward. Instead, this relationship depends on the interpretation of what goals and strategies are appropriate for the empowering identity. For example, Francesca Polletta (2002) illustrates that consensus decision-making alternately came to be defined first as a "black" and then as a "white" strategy in the 1960s civil rights movement. Similarly, what is defined as an appropriate issue for a "women's" movement is also variable, depending on a variety of cultural, structural, and historical factors (Chapter 4). Once these associations are made, they trigger the feedback loops described below. Opposing movements (Bernstein 1995), shifts in the political context, and critical events in the life of a social movement may all alter the relationship between collective identity and its association with particular strategies and goals.

Figure A.1 represents some of the primary ways in which the three analytic dimensions of identity are related to a movement's choice of strategies and goals, its outcomes, and its ability to mobilize. Figure A.1 is comprised of identity for empowerment; identity as a goal, which is subsumed under the more general category goal choice; and identity as strategy, which is subsumed under the more general category strategy choice. Figure A.1 also includes mobilization, which refers to who is mobilized and the extent of mobilization, as well as movement outcomes. In this section, I consider several prominent relationships and feedback loops between the analytic dimensions of identity and movement mobilization, choice of strategies and goals, and outcomes.

Missing from this model is organizational structure. Organizational structure (as I discussed earlier with regard to identity for empowerment [see also Bernstein 1997]), will affect each part of the model. For example, an organization's mission statement and its structure may constrain and channel its forms of identity deployment or pursuit of identity as a goal. But theorizing all of these complex relationships is beyond the scope of this chapter and must be left for another day.

The content of the identity for empowerment is critically important for social movements because it affects who is mobilized (Figure A.1, path 1A) and what issues are deemed valid and pursued (1B).[5] Which goals are pursued, in turn, attracts others to the movement who have similar interests and thus affects mobilization (path 3A), which feeds back on the content of a collective identity (path 2A). Thus status identities are linked to real structural and social locations that influence what goals are deemed important, which then feeds back on the collective identity through mobilization. For example, when women's movements organize on the basis of the category "women" or "sister," without explicit acknowledgment of differences among women based on, for example, race, class, sexual orientation, and (dis)ability, the concerns of the dominant group (i.e., white heterosexual, able-bodied Western women) tend to prevail (e.g., Alexander and Mohanty 1997; Narayan 1997; Grewal and Kaplan 1994; Ryan 1997; Chapter 11). Women from marginalized groups are likely to be deterred from activism when the movement's identity excludes them and thus the dominant collective identity is reinforced. A leftist identity that failed to recognize the often distinct interests of women affected what issues were targeted and thus hampered the mobilization of women and led to the splintering of leftist organizations (see Bernstein 2005 for a review). Similarly, in the "lesbian and gay" movement, a white male collective identity often prevails. As a result, the political concerns of lesbians, such as child custody in the 1970s, and of bisexual and transgendered individuals have often been ignored (Seidman 1993), having implications for who is mobilized. In the case of the L.A. Gay and Lesbian Center (Chapter 10), activists tried to create an empowering identity based on sameness, relying on the idea that everyone is different and, therefore, all the same. But the effect of an identity that attempted to embrace all differences as equal had the effect of flattening and erasing those differences. Thus this identity ultimately ignored the structural basis of difference and the divergent political interests among activists. Broad categories of identity can have the effect of erasing structural privilege. Rather than being inclusive, such broad categories can marginalize people with less privilege and lead to

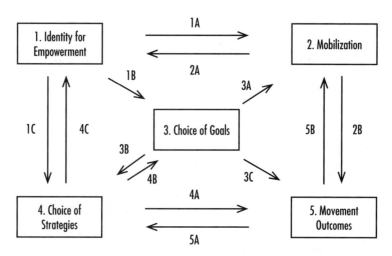

Figure A.1. Feedback loops between the analytic dimensions of identity.

neglecting the issues they face. Thus the group's understanding of the content of the collective identity affects both mobilization and goals pursued, which in turn affects the content of the collective identity. A movement's ability to mobilize will, of course, influence its ability to achieve its goals (path 2B).

A movement's identity for empowerment may lead activists to deploy that identity as a political strategy (see Figure A.1, path 1C). Often when a movement organization is based on a relational identity, such as parent, friend, or spouse, activists must employ some identity strategies in order to legitimate their political participation in a movement in which they are not directly implicated. Karen Beckwith (1996) refers to this justification as gaining "political standing." The method of gaining this political standing is, of course, identity deployment. Activists deploy their identity as part of their strategic repertoire and thus make the content of that identity, including motivations for action, subject to debate. For example, Beckwith (1996) describes how the mothers and wives of coal miners utilized their relational identities in order to justify their political claim making. Activists also sometimes use a relational collective identity in order to justify their participation in a movement in which they are directly implicated. For example, Naples' (1998) examination of what she calls "activist mothering" as an empowering identity justifies poor women's participation in community activism. Similarly, Neuhouser finds that Brazilian women activists also use their identities as mothers as a way to justify their political participation. The success of activists' ability to gain legitimacy for their identities and thus their claims will affect their ability to achieve their goals (path 4A).

Yet mobilizing based on a particular collective identity and then deploying that identity strategically as a form of collective action can constrain the choice of goals as well as the movement's ability to mobilize, creating feedback loops that may limit the likely scope and longevity of activism. For example, Naples (1998), Neuhouser (Chapter 6), and Beckwith (1996) all demonstrate that relational identities can limit the development a broader political consciousness and do not provide justification for other types of political participation, thus affecting which goals are targeted down the line (Figure A.1, path 4B). For example, the reliance on an identity of "mother" by the activists who Naples (1998) interviewed, hampered their ability to take their activism into more formal political positions.

If the content of the identity for empowerment affects which goals are pursued, then a movement's decision to pursue certain goals will in turn affect which strategies are employed (Figure A.1, path 3B). The goals and strategies will both influence whether or not goals are achieved (paths 4A and 3C), which will then feedback on mobilization (path 5B) and collective identity (path 2A). These relationships between collective identity, goals, and strategies are particularly evident in the case of AIDS activism. The differing economic positions of whites and people of color affect their general access to healthcare. As a result, many people of color who are AIDS activists prioritized gaining access to the health care system, whereas white AIDS activists were more interested in issues related to treatment (path 1B). In this case, the intersection of race and class directly affected the goal preferences of activists. Divisions between women and men centered on what to do about the exclusion of women from clinical drug trials. Women advocated noncooperation with medical authorities, while men opposed such a strategy, since their interests would not be achieved through noncooperation (path 3B) (Elbaz 1997; Stockdill 2001). In her study of black gay identities and AIDS, Cohen (1999) illustrates that the ways in which struggles over the content of collective identity are resolved and the resultant goals and strategies that are pursued have concrete impact on the achievement of goals (paths 4A and 3C), including material effects on how resources, legitimacy, and services are allocated within communities.

Deploying identity as a political strategy also invites what I term "identity contests," an important and often immediate feedback loop (Figure A.1, paths 4A and 5A). In these cases, opposing movements, dominant groups, or even bystander publics deploy the identity of other activist groups to draw attention to the other group's identity, to make the content of that group's identity subject to debate. Opposing movements (Bernstein 1995) may make claims about the identity of their opponents and thus deploy the opposition's identity in order to discredit that group. However, dominant groups may also employ identity strategies to either discredit or support a particular group, as in the case of welfare reform where the identities of welfare recipients are routinely deployed in multiple ways by a variety of groups in what becomes a vicious identity contest (e.g., Collins 1990). Poor women who deploy their identities as mothers to justify their political activism in Brazil (Chapter 6) have been challenged by opponents who underscore that many of these mothers are single mothers, thus undermining the legitimacy of their basis for activism. Whenever an activist group employs identity strategies, it invites an identity contest, since the group willingly makes its identity the subject of debate.

While relational identities may hamper the development of a broader political consciousness, they may increase the legitimacy of social movement actors whose motivations for action are deemed to be more pure, since they themselves will not directly benefit from the proposed changes. Along these lines, Myers (Chapter 7) suggests that the strategic deployment of identity by heterosexual proponents of lesbian and gay rights may make them more effective advocates since they are not acting on their own behalf. However, deploying a "straight" or mainstream identity may adversely affect mobilization efforts by lesbian and gay groups. For example, lesbians who are "butch" in appearance or gay men who are "effeminate" may feel excluded from the mainstream collective identity, which is rooted in traditional gender roles (e.g., Bernstein 1997).

In the case of drag performances, the feedback loop between identity as strategy and achieving identity as goal is interactional and immediate (Figure A.1, paths 4A and 5A). Identity is a goal of drag performers as they seek both to gain acceptance for stigmatized identities and to deconstruct hegemonic understandings of masculinity and femininity. By deploying identity for critique in their performances to challenge and criticize dominant ideologies and practices of femininity, masculinity, and heteronormativity, drag queens deconstruct the dominant categories of identity, thus achieving (temporarily at least) identity as a goal. When deploying identity for education by underscoring similarities to the majority, performers break down boundaries between heterosexuals and gay, lesbian, bisexual, and transgender people. Another way that boundaries between straight audience members and the performers are broken is through the blurring of heterosexual desire with same-sex desire that takes place when heterosexual men find themselves attracted to drag queens. In this way, a collective identity based on sameness, however fleeting, is produced. The performances also help foster a collective identity among lesbian, gay bisexual, and transgender audience members to the extent that drag is a part of gay culture (Figure A.1, path 4C). As a result, identity for empowerment is produced and challenged in the context of the drag club through identity deployment strategies. Thus deploying identity as strategy invites identity contests that have several possible feedback effects: activists can become more believable, they can be discredited, or the collective identity deployed can inhibit or facilitate the development of a broader political consciousness.

In this section, I have introduced the concept feedback loop as a way to theorize the relationship between the three analytic dimensions of identity and social movement mobilization, choice of strategies, choice of goals, and outcomes. Through a path diagram, I have outlined some of the most prominent feedback loops to illustrate these relationships. The feedback loops described here are not meant to be an exhaustive list. Instead, the feedback loops discussed present a starting point for a more thorough understanding of the multiple ways in which identities influence the careers of social movements.

Conclusion

This chapter has elaborated a political identity framework for understanding the three analytic dimensions of identity as they relate to social movements. To understand the first analytic dimension of identity, an intersectional approach is needed to understand how movements negotiate internal differences to produce identity for empowerment, which is necessary for mobilization. To achieve such an intersectional analysis, scholars must understand how organizations and movements negotiate the multiple identities that individuals bring to their activism. One must understand how identities are linked to structure and interest as well as how organizational, environmental, and political factors influence the construction and content of a movement's collective identity. The ways in which activists are linked to the constructed collective good pursued by a social movement positions them differently within the movement and can create challenges for social movements. The specific identity constructed will affect who is mobilized, what issues will be pursued, and how they will be pursued. Externally, the empowering identity may also be used to legitimate political action and will influence the extent to which activists develop a broader political analysis.

With regard to identity as strategy, I specified the mechanisms that produce identity deployment. The logic of the arena where the action takes place as well as the audience will affect the likelihood that similarities and differences will be simultaneously deployed. I introduced the concept "identity contest" to refer to the processes that take place when opposing movements or targets deploy not only their own identity but also the identities of those they oppose.

In my discussion of identity as a goal, I sketched out a research agenda with the hope of sparking more research interest in this neglected area of analysis. I linked the absence of research in this area to a narrow state-centered view of power that remains hegemonic in American social movement theory. I suggested that understanding power as both material and symbolic and as located in multiple institutions provides the theoretical framework needed to understand identity as a goal. I introduced the term "deconstructive movement" and provided examples of movements that seek recognition of identity as a goal and of movements that seek to deconstruct identity as a goal. I outlined some ways to assess the extent to which identity as a goal has been achieved.

In the last section, I introduced the concept "feedback loop" to understand how the three analytic dimensions of identity are linked to a movement's ability to mobilize to the strategies and goals it chooses and to the outcomes achieved. Thus I illustrate that the three analytic dimensions of identity are essential to answering core questions in social movement theory.

There are several other areas where research on the analytic dimensions of identity is needed. Still underexplored are the ways in which the three analytic dimensions of identity apply to nationalist movements. Therefore, I recommend research that compares movements based on nationalist identities with movements based on other status identities (see also Calhoun 1993). Such systematic and comparative studies of how identities become political might distinguish between identities based on how much such identities are a part of routine social interaction (see Tilly 2002). These studies might compare the implications of organizing based on identities that are experienced in daily life, often based on gender, shared language, ethnicity, religion, and culture, from "corporate identity forms," which are officially recognized by the state and its institutions and confer special rights and privileges.

Furthermore, identity for empowerment, identity as strategy, and identity as goal must be explored in the context of globalization. For example, how do transnational social movements develop an empowering identity from which to mobilize? How are identities deployed politically to challenge global governance institutions? How does globalization alter efforts to deconstruct status categories or efforts to gain rights based on those status categories? How does the content of a collective identity such as gay and lesbian spread across nation states?

In this chapter, I elaborated a more expansive political identity framework that can now be applied to other contexts, such as nationalist movements and globalization. I reviewed the key theoretical concepts developed in "Celebration and Suppression: The Strategic Uses of Identity by the Lesbian and Gay Movement" (Bernstein 1997), where I first introduced this political identity framework. In the next three sections, I developed the three analytic concepts of identity more fully and linked them to more general theoretical concerns centering on the relationship between identity, structure, and interest and on how movement analysts understand power. I then introduced and elaborated the concept "feedback loop" to understand how the three analytic dimensions of identity are linked to a movement's ability to mobilize, to the strategies and goals it chooses, and to the outcomes achieved.

References

Alexander M. J., and Chandra T. Mohanty, ed. 1997. *Feminist Genealogies, Colonial Legacies, Democratic Futures.* New York: Routledge

Armstrong, Elizabeth, and Mary Bernstein. 2008. "Culture, Power, and Institutions: A Multi-Institutional Politics Approach to Social Movements." *Sociological Theory 26(1): 74–99.*

Bayer, Ronald. 1987. *Homosexuality and American Psychiatry: The Politics of Diagnosis.* Princeton, N.J.: Princeton University Press.

Beckwith, Karen. 1996. "Lancashire Women against Pit Closures: Women's Standing in a Men's Movement." *Signs* 21(4): 1034–68.

Bernstein, Mary. 1995. "Countermovements and the Fate of Two Morality Policies: Consensual Sex Statutes and Lesbian and Gay Rights Ordinances." Paper presented at the 1995 Annual Meeting of the American Political Science Association, Chicago, Ill.

———. 1997. "Celebration and Suppression: The Strategic Uses of Identity by the Lesbian and Gay Movement." *American Journal of Sociology* 103(3): 531–65.

———. 2002. "Identities and Politics: Toward a Historical Understanding of the Lesbian and Gay Movement." *Social Science History* 26(3): 531–81.

———. 2003. "Nothing Ventured, Nothing Gained? Conceptualizing Social Movement 'Success' in the Lesbian and Gay Movement." *Sociological Perspectives* 46(3): 353–79.

———. 2005. "Identity Politics." *Annual Review of Sociology* 31: 47–74.

Bernstein, Mary, and Marcella De la Cruz. 2007. "The Hapa Movement: Understanding Identity as a Goal of Social Movement Activism." Paper Presented at the Workshop on Collective Behavior and Social Movements, Hofstra University

Bickford, Susan. 1997. "Anti-anti-identity Politics: Feminism, Democracy, and the Complexities of Citizenship." *Hypatia* 12(4): 111–31.

Blee, Kathleen M. 2002. *Inside Organized Racism: Women in the Hate Movement.* Berkeley: University of California Press.

Bower, Lisa. 1997. "Queer Problems/Straight Solutions: The Limits of 'Official Recognition.' In *Playing with Fire: Queer Politics, Queer Theories,* ed. Shane Phelan, 267–91. New York: Routledge.

Butler, Judith. 1990. *Gender Trouble: Feminism and the Subversion of Identity.* New York: Routledge.

Calhoun Craig. 1993. "Nationalism and Ethnicity." *Annual Review of Sociology* 12: 211–39.

———. 1994. "Social Theory and the Politics of Identity." In *Social Theory and the Politics of Identity,* ed. Craig Calhoun, 9–36. Cambridge, Mass.: Blackwell.

————. 1995. "'New Social Movements' of the Early Nineteenth Century." In *Repertoires & Cycles of Collective Action*, ed. Mark Traugott, 173–215. Durham, N.C.: Duke University Press.

Cohen, Cathy J. 1999. *The Boundaries of Blackness: AIDS and the Breakdown of Black Politics*. Chicago: University of Chicago Press.

Cohen, Jean. 1985. "Strategy or Identity: New Theoretical Paradigms and Contemporary Social Movements," *Social Research* 52: 663–716.

Collins, Patricia Hill. 1990. *Black Feminist Thought: Knowledge, Consciousness, and the Politics of Empowerment*. New York: Routledge.

Crossley, Nick. 2002. *Making Sense of Social Movements*. Philadelphia: Open University Press.

Earl, Jenn. 2004. "The Cultural Consequences of Social Movements." In *The Blackwell Companion to Social Movements*, ed. David A. Snow, Sarah A. Soule, and Hanspeter Kriesi, 508–30. Malden, Mass.: Blackwell.

Elbaz, Gilbert. 1997. "AIDS Activism, Communities and Disagreements." *Free Inquiry in Creative Sociology* 25(2): 145–54.

Eyerman, Ron, and Andrew Jamison. 1991. *Social Movements: A Cognitive Approach*. University Park: Pennsylvania State University Press.

Foucault, Michel. 1978. *The History of Sexuality: An Introduction*. Volume I. New York: Vintage Books.

Fraser Nancy. 1997. *Justice Interruptus: Critical Reflections on the "Postsocialist" Condition*. New York: Routledge.

Friedland, Roger, and Robert R. Alford. 1991. "Bringing Society Back In: Symbols, Practices, and Institutional Contradictions." In *The New Institutionalism in Organizational Analysis*, ed. Walter W. Powell and Paul J. DiMaggio, 232–63. Chicago: University of Chicago Press.

Gamson, Joshua. 1995. "Must Identity Movements Self-destruct? A Queer Dilemma," *Social Problems* 42(3): 390–407.

————. 1997. "Messages of Exclusion: Gender, Movements, and Symbolic Boundaries," *Gender & Society* 11: 178–99.

Gitlin, Todd. 1994. "From Universality to Difference: Notes on the Fragmentation of the Idea of the Left." In *Social Theory and the Politics of Identity*, ed. Craig Calhoun, 150–74. Cambridge, Mass.: Blackwell.

————. 1995. *The Twilight of Common Dreams: Why America Is Wracked by Culture Wars*. New York: Metropolitan Books.

Goffman, Erving. 1959. *The Presentation of Self in Everyday Life*. Garden City, N.Y.: Doubleday/Anchor.

Grewal Inderpal, and Caren Kaplan, ed. 1994. *Scattered Hegemonies: Postmodernity and Transnational Feminist Practices*. Minneapolis: University of Minnesota Press.

Hunt, Scott A., and Robert D. Benford. 2004. "Collective Identity, Solidarity, and Commitment." In *The Blackwell Companion to Social Movements*, ed. David A. Snow, Sarah A. Soule, and Hanspeter Kriesi, 433–57. Malden, Mass.: Blackwell.

Lichterman, Paul. 1999. "Talking Identity in the Public Sphere: Broad Visions and Small Spaces in Identity Politics." *Theory Soc.* 28(1): 101–41.

Lorber, Judith. 1999. "Crossing Borders and Erasing Boundaries: Paradoxes of Identity Politics." *Sociological Focus* 32(4): 355–70.

Mansbridge, Jane, and Aldon Morris. 2001. *Oppositional Consciousness: The Subjective Roots of Social Protest*. Chicago: University of Chicago Press.

Melucci, Alberto. 1989. *Nomads of the Present*. London: Hutchinson Radius.

———1996. *Challenging Codes: Collective Action in the Information Age*. Cambridge: Cambridge University Press.

Naples, Nancy. 1998. *Grassroots Warriors: Activist Mothering, Community Work, and the War on Poverty*. New York: Routledge.

Narayan, Uma. 1997. *Dislocating Cultures: Identities, Traditions and Third World Feminism*. New York: Routledge

McAdam, Doug. 1982. *Political Process and the Development of Black Insurgency 1930–1970*. Chicago: University of Chicago Press.

McAdam, Doug, Sidney Tarrow, and Charles Tilly. 2001. *Dynamics of Contention*. Cambridge: Cambridge University Press.

Morris, Aldon D. 1992. "Political Consciousness and Collective Action." In *Frontiers in Social Movement Theory*, ed. Aldon D. Morris and Carol McClurg, 351–73 Mueller. New Haven, Conn.: Yale University Press.

Olsen, Kristine. 2006. "Taking Sides Over Same-sex Marriage: Narrative as an Alternative to Frame in an Opposing Movement Scenario." M.A. Thesis. University of Connecticut.

Peluso, Natalie. 2005. "The New Bump 'n' Grind: Drag, Identity, and the Politics of Performance in the New Burlesque." M.A. Thesis. University of Connecticut.

Polletta, Francesca. 2002. *Freedom is an Endless Meeting*. Chicago: University of Chicago Press.

Polletta, Francesca, and James M. Jasper. 2001. "Collective Identity and Social Movements." *Annual Review of Sociology* 27: 283–305.

Rochon, Thomas R. 1998. *Culture Moves: Ideas, Activism, and Changing Values*. Princeton, N.J.: Princeton University Press.

Rorty Richard. 1998. *Achieving Our Country: Leftist Thought in Twentieth Century America*. Cambridge, Mass.: Harvard University Press.

Rupp, Leila J., and Verta Taylor. 2003. *Drag Queens at the 801 Cabaret*. Chicago: University of Chicago Press.

Ryan, Barbara. 1997. "How Much Can I Divide Thee, Let Me Count the Ways: Identity Politics in the Women's Movement." *Humanit. Soc.* 21(1): 67–83.

Seidman, Steven. 1993. "Identity and Politics in a 'Postmodern' Gay Culture: Some Historical and Conceptual Notes." In *Fear of a Queer Planet: Queer Politics and Social Theory*, ed. Michael Warner, 105–42. Minneapolis: University of Minnesota Press.

Stockdill, Brett C. 2001. "Forging a Multidimensional Oppositional Consciousness: Lessons from Community-based AIDS Activism." In *Oppositional Consciousness: The Subjective Roots of Social Protest*, ed. Jane Mansbridge and Aldon Morris, 204–37. Chicago: University of Chicago Press.

Taylor, Verta, and Nancy E. Whittier. 1992. "Collective Identity in Social Movement Communities; Lesbian Feminist Mobilization," In *Frontiers in Social Movement Theory*, ed. Aldon D. Morris and Carol McClurg Mueller, 104–29. New Haven, Conn.: Yale University Press.

Tilly, Charles. 2002. *Stories, Identities, and Political Change*. Lanham, Md.: Rowman and Littlefield.

Touraine, Alain. 1981. *The Voice and the Eye: An Analysis of Social Movements*. Cambridge: Cambridge University Press.

Notes

1. Special thanks to Nancy Naples and the editors of this volume for their helpful comments on earlier drafts of this chapter.

2. It should be noted that whether or not activism is defined as political is a *cultural* construct that changes over time. Activists sometimes challenge this divide between political and cultural realms, for example, when feminists claim political meaning for what is often viewed as cultural or personal behavior. Because these categories still inform activist thinking, I will continue to use the terms political and cultural for the sake of convenience (see Bernstein 2002 for a fuller discussion).

3. It should be noted that the strategic deployment of identity may differ from the group's (or individuals') private understanding of that identity.

4. The analysis in the next two paragraphs relies heavily on Armstrong and Bernstein (2008).

5. The paths labeled 1x originate from identity for empowerment. Paths labeled 2x stem from mobilization. Paths labeled 3x stem from choice of strategies. Paths labeled 4x stem from choice of strategies. Paths labeled 5x stem from movement outcomes. Any set of paths might be relevant in a particular case.

Contributors

MARY BERNSTEIN is associate professor of sociology at the University of Connecticut. Her scholarship seeks to understand the role of identity in social movements, how movement actors interact with the state and the law, and what factors influence sexual citizenship in social institutions. Her work has been published in *Annual Review of Sociology*, *Sexuality Research and Social Policy*, *Sociological Perspectives*, and *Social Science History*, and she is coeditor of *Queer Families, Queer Politics: Challenging Culture and the State*.

KIMBERLY B. DUGAN is associate professor of sociology at Eastern Connecticut State University. The focus of her research and writing is the gay rights movement and the Christian right, particularly on issues related to identities, framing, and opportunities for movement success. She is author of *The Struggle over Gay, Lesbian, and Bisexual Rights: Facing Off in Cincinnati*.

RACHEL L. EINWOHNER is associate professor of sociology at Purdue University. Her research focuses on protest and resistance, especially questions related to the emergence and outcomes of collective action. She has studied a diverse set of movements and acts of protest, including the U.S. animal rights movement, the college-based anti-sweatshop movement, and Jewish resistance during the Holocaust. Her work has been published in *American Journal of Sociology*, *American Sociological Review*, and *Social Problems*.

ELIZABETH KAMINSKI is assistant professor of sociology at Central Connecticut State University, where she teaches courses on social movements and the sociology of music. Her publications and research projects focus on collective identity, music as oppositional consciousness, and the formation and sustenance of social movement coalitions. Her current work examines depictions of domestic violence in American popular music.

DANIEL J. MYERS is professor of sociology, Director of Research and Faculty Development at the Joan B. Kroc Institute for International Peace Studies, and Director of the Center for the Study of Social Movements and Social Change at the University of Notre Dame. He is studying structural conditions, diffusion patterns, and media coverage related to U.S. racial rioting in the 1960s in a project funded by the National Science Foundation. He is editor of *Mobilization*, which is the leading journal of research on social movements and protest.

SUSAN MUNKRES is assistant professor of sociology at Furman University. Her research interests concern social movements, identity conflicts within them, and various forms of action on behalf of others. She is writing a book on alliance-making in social movements.

KEVIN NEUHOUSER is professor of sociology at Seattle Pacific University. He has studied how gendered identities shape collective action in poor, urban communities in Brazil and has written on the economic foundations of regime transitions in Latin America. He is author of *Modern Brazil*, and his articles have appeared in *American Sociological Review*, *Signs: Journal of Women and Society*, *Gender and Society*, *Social Forces*, and *Sociological Theory*.

JO REGER is associate professor of sociology and director of women's studies at Oakland University in Michigan. Her research examines the interplay between identity, organization, and community. Her work on the National Organization for Women and the U.S. women's movement has been published in *Gender & Society*, *Qualitative Sociology*, and *Sociological Perspectives*, and she is editor of *Different Wavelengths: Studies of the Contemporary Women's Movement*.

BENITA ROTH is associate professor of sociology and women's studies at the State University of New York, Binghamton. Her book *Separate Roads to Feminism: Black, Chicana, and White Feminist Movements in America's Second Wave* was awarded the Distinguished Book Award in 2006 from the Sex and Gender section of the American Sociological Association.

SILKE ROTH is senior lecturer in sociology in the Division of Sociology and Social Policy at the University of Southampton (UK). She is author of *Building Movement Bridges: The Coalition of Labour Union Women* (Praeger,

2003) and editor of *Gender Politics in the Expanding European Union. Mobilization, Inclusion, Exclusion* (Berghahn Books, 2008).

TODD J. SCHROER is associate professor of sociology at the University of Southern Indiana. He has studied the white racialist movement since the early 1990s and more recently has begun analyzing the pro-pedophilia movement. His publications and presentations have focused on the usage of the Internet and the importance of music to social movements as well as the creation, maintenance, and negotiation of deviant identities.

VERTA TAYLOR is professor of sociology and member of the affiliated faculty in women's studies at the University of California, Santa Barbara. She is coauthor of *Drag Queens at the 801 Cabaret* and *Survival in the Doldrums: The American Women's Rights Movement, 1945 to the 1960s*; author of *Rock-a-by Baby: Feminism, Self-Help, and Postpartum Depression*; and coeditor of eight editions of *Feminist Frontiers*. Her articles on women's movements, the gay and lesbian movement, and social movement theory have been published in *American Sociological Review, Signs, Social Problems, Mobilization, Gender and Society, Contexts, Qualitative Sociology, Journal of Women's History, Journal of Homosexuality*, and *Journal of Lesbian Studies*.

JANE WARD is assistant professor of women's studies at the University of California, Riverside. She is the author of *Respectably Queer: Diversity Culture in LGBT Activist Organizations* as well as several articles on queer politics and culture.

Index